WORKING
Today
and
Tomorrow™

Second Edition

Consultants

Marjorie Amado
Los Angeles Unified School District

Anita Barber
State Director of Career Education—
Business/Industry/Education Partnership
State of Alabama

Mary Gaskin
Special Assistant, Career and Occupational
Curriculum
Division of Curriculum and Instruction
New York City Board of Education

Mamie Hardy
Director, Professional Services
Changing Times Education Service

Daniel L. Martin
Cooperative Education Consultant
Indiana Department of Education
Division of Vocational Education

Howard E. McVicker
Professor of Industrial Technology
Purdue University

Barbara Anne Boggess Sikes
Vocational Teacher—Coordinator
Dallas Independent School District

Margaret Snell
Associate Professor
Vocational-Technical Education, Cook
College
Rutgers, The State University of New Jersey

Pat Tennison
Coordinator of Career Education
School District of Kansas City,
Missouri

WORKING
Today and Tomorrow™

Second Edition

Consulting Authors

Richard Campbell
Director, Cooperative Education/Youth Employment
Nebraska Department of Education

Mary J. Thompson
Consultant
Planning and Research
Division of Vocational Education
Florida Department of Education

Developed by
The Changing Times Education Service Division
EMC Publishing
St. Paul, Minnesota
and
Visual Education Corporation
Princeton, New Jersey

Program Editor:
Rosemary J. Barry
Project Editor:
Susan Joan Gordon
Editor:
Robert Weisser
Copy Editor:
Susan J. Garver
Writers:
Barbara Daniels, David Daniels, Margaret Robinson, Susan Sweet, Elizabeth Tener
Special thanks to:
Mark Epstein, Cindy Feldner, Paula Harris, Sharon Lucas, Katchen Stonehouse
Production Editor:
Anita Black
Text Designer:
Art Ritter
Picture Researcher:
Judith Burns
Cover Designer:
Cyril John Schlosser
Cover Photographer:
Christine Benkert

Library of Congress Cataloging in Publication Data

Campbell, Richard, 1946–
   Working today and tomorrow.

   Includes index.
   1. Career education—United States.   I. Thompson, Mary J.   II. Changing Times Educational Service.   III. Visual Education Corporation.   IV. Title.
LC1037.5.C36   1985   370.11'3   85-10161
ISBN 0-8219-0739-5

© 1991 by EMC Corporation

All rights reserved. No part of this publication may be adapted, reproduced, stored in a retrieval system or transmitted in any form or by any means, electronic, mechanical, photocopying, recording, or otherwise without permission from the publisher.
Published by EMC Publishing
300 York Avenue
St. Paul, Minnesota 55101

Printed in the United States of America
0 9 8 7 6 5 4 3 2

Preface

We are living in an age of almost unlimited choice in most areas of human existence, including careers. As choices multiply, the ability to make intelligent and informed decisions becomes increasingly important. That, essentially, is the goal of *Working: Today and Tomorrow*—to enable you to make choices that will bring you satisfaction as a worker, as a consumer, and as a citizen in our modern society.

One way to begin that process is through a comprehensive exploration of job possibilities. Such an exploration requires a broad-based approach that enables you to discover your own aptitudes, interests, values, and goals so you can best match them to an appropriate occupation.

To accomplish this goal, the text stresses the practical over the theoretical. Not only will *Working: Today and Tomorrow* help you decide which occupation is best for you, but it will also enable you to find a job and function knowledgeably in the workplace. To do this, the authors have focused on practical issues and situations that remain the same no matter what occupation you choose to train for. In addition, the text provides a wealth of information about consumer and financial affairs so that you can prepare to take your place in the economy. A simple and effective decision-making model is presented early in the text and then used throughout to give you practice in making thoughtful and systematic decisions as a worker and a consumer.

Working: Today and Tomorrow presents a carefully structured learning environment that makes use of a number of features to invite student involvement:

- A vignette at the beginning of each chapter dramatizes the various kinds of decision-making dilemmas that you will face in your different roles.
- The text constantly reinforces basic decision making by presenting material in ways to help you realize the rich array of options available in society.
- Important vocabulary terms are highlighted in several ways. Terms appear in boldface type and are defined in italic type to bring them to your attention. Completion sentences at the end of each chapter reinforce vocabulary by presenting terms in context. All terms are compiled in an easy-to-use glossary that follows the text.
- Frequent use of lists spotlights important information and makes it easy to locate for review. Review is also aided by end-of-chapter summaries of the main ideas presented in the text.
- Review questions follow each chapter to reinforce your learning of factual information. End-of-chapter activities encourage exploration of key concepts and strengthen your ability to make decisions.
- Full-color photographs, tables, and graphs spark your interest and provide visual reinforcement of key points in the text.

Intelligent decision making is crucial to analyzing and choosing among the vast array of job alternatives that exist today. The *Working: Today and Tomorrow* text is designed to help you master decision-making principles that can help you fulfill your various roles in the economy and in society.

Contents

PART ONE — MAKING DECISIONS ABOUT WORK

1 The Changing Nature of Work — 4
　Workers on the Move — 6
　Social Changes — 13
　Preparing for Change — 15

2 Finding Out More About Yourself — 21
　Discovering What Matters to You — 22
　Discovering Who You Are — 24
　Career Counseling and Aptitude Testing — 29
　Matching Personalities With Jobs — 33
　Compiling a Job List — 34

3 Exploring the World of Work — 37
　A Major Decision — 38
　Learning About the Jobs — 41
　Who Can Advise You? — 43
　Narrowing the Options — 47

4 Making Decisions About Work — 52
　Decisions, Decisions — 54
　Your Decision-Making Roles — 60
　Your Decisions and Other People — 62
　The Economy — 64

PART TWO — ENTERING THE WORK FORCE

5 How Business Works — 70
　What Business Does — 72
　How Businesses Earn Profits — 73
　Businesses Need Resources — 75
　Where People Fit In — 75
　How Businesses Are Organized — 78

6 Preparing for the Job You Want   **86**
    School or Work?   88
    Cooperative Education   88
    Working Part-Time   91
    On-the-Job Training   94
    The Armed Services   95
    Higher Education   96
    Cost and Financial Aid   100
    Take the First Step   102

7 Getting the Job You Want   **105**
    Getting Job Leads   106
    Preparing Your Resume   110
    Applying for Jobs   114
    Before, During, and After the Interview   118

8 Joining the Work Force   **124**
    Working With Others   126
    Rights and Duties in the Workplace   127
    Bargaining in the Workplace   129
    What Union Contracts Say   131
    Changes in Your Status   133
    Productive Workers Help Economic Growth   135

PART THREE   YOU AS A WORKER

9 Earning an Income   **142**
    Workers Earn Money in Different Ways   144
    Different Forms of Payment   147
    Income Taxes   148
    Disposable Income   151
    Where Do Your Taxes Go?   152
    Child Labor Laws   155

10 Working With Others   **160**
    The Importance of Attitude   162
    Stress and Conflict   165
    Getting Ahead in Your Job   168
    What It Takes to Be a Leader   171

11	**Health and Safety on the Job**	**178**
	How Great Is the Danger?	180
	Why Accidents Happen	180
	The Most Common Types of Accidents	187
	Costs of On-the-Job Accidents and Illnesses	187
	Preventing Accidents and Illnesses	188
	The Three-Way Partnership for Safety	192

PART FOUR YOU AND YOUR RESOURCES

12	**Planning to Use Your Resources**	**198**
	The Consumer Process	200
	The Benefits of Planning	201
	Your Time	202
	Your Skills	204
	Your Energy	205
	Your Money	205
	Your Budget and the Economy	210
13	**Becoming an Informed Consumer**	**215**
	The Value of Information	216
	How Influences Affect What You Buy	218
	Major Sources of Information	219
	Advertising	223
	Regulating Advertising	225
	Advertising: Good and Bad	226
14	**Shopping Around**	**231**
	Comparing Before You Buy	232
	Deciding Where to Buy	236
	The Most for Your Money	241
	Your Choices Affect Businesses	243
15	**Deciding About Saving, Spending, or Borrowing**	**247**
	Deciding How to Pay	248
	Solving and Borrowing Involve Interest	249
	Cash and Cash Substitutes	252
	Electronic Banking	257

PART FIVE — MAKING FINANCIAL DECISIONS

16 Getting Consumer Satisfaction — **266**
  It is a Contract — 268
  Satisfaction Guaranteed — 271
  Solving Consumer Problems — 273
  With Rights Come Responsibilities — 275

17 Purchasing Financial Services — **280**
  Shopping for a Financial Institution — 282
  Financial Services — 284
  Deciding Where to Put Your Money — 288
  A Final Decision — 289
  The Federal Reserve System — 290

18 Considering Credit — **293**
  Buy Now, Pay Later — 294
  A Credit Plan — 298
  Borrowing Ability — 299
  Finding Out About Credit — 301
  The Rights of Borrowers and Lenders — 304
  Comparing Credit Costs — 306
  Too Much Credit — 306

19 Buying Insurance — **310**
  How Insurance Works — 312
  Deciding What You Need — 313
  Protection on the Road — 314
  Protecting Your Property — 316
  Life Insurance — 317
  Paying Health Care Costs — 321
  Shopping for Insurance — 322
  Cutting Your Risks — 323

20 It Is Your Decision — **327**
  Decisions About Working — 328
  Learning About Yourself — 330
  Learning How to Make Decisions — 332
  The Value of Planning — 334
  Your Finances — 335
  How Your Decisions Affect Others — 336

Appendix: A Guide to Career Clusters — 341

Glossary — 379

Index — 391

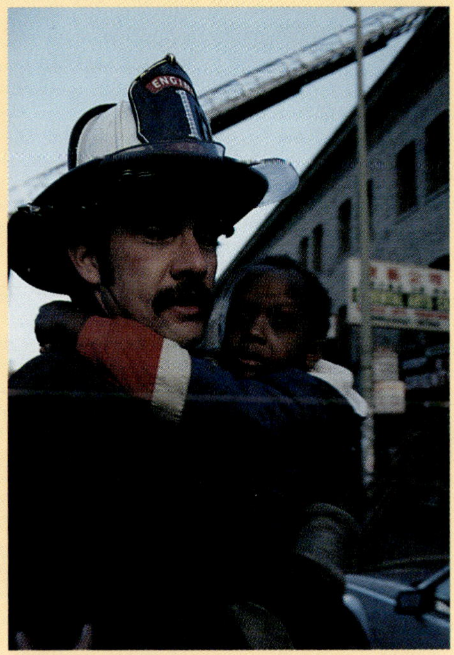

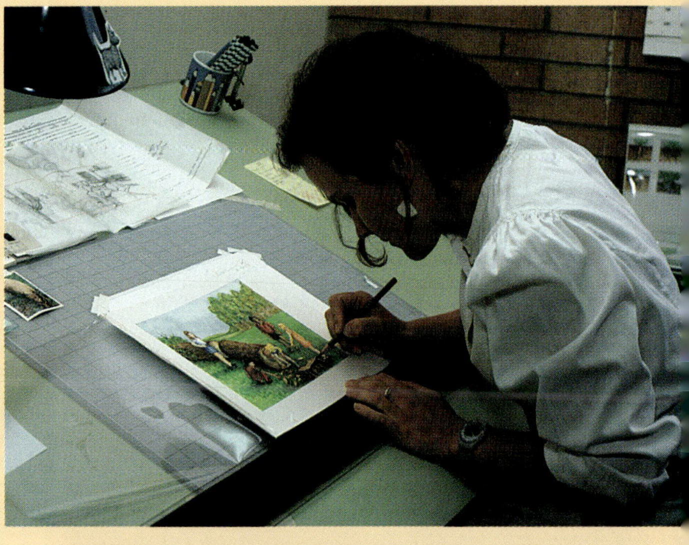

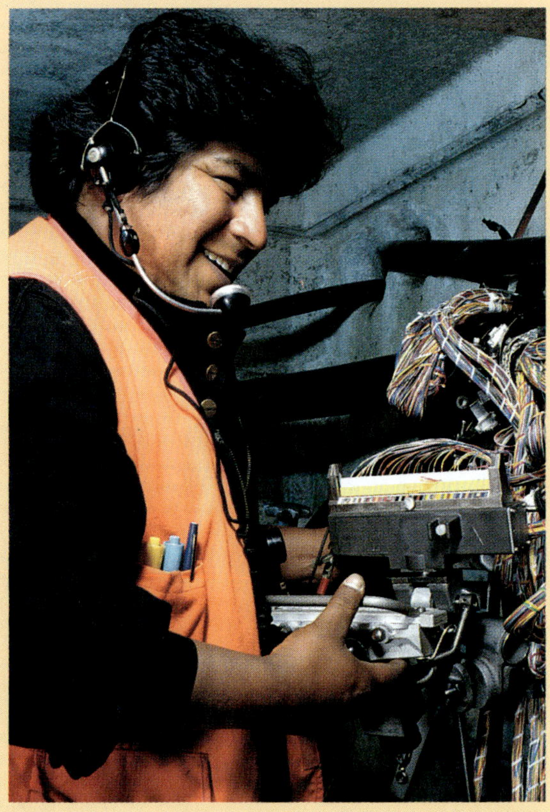

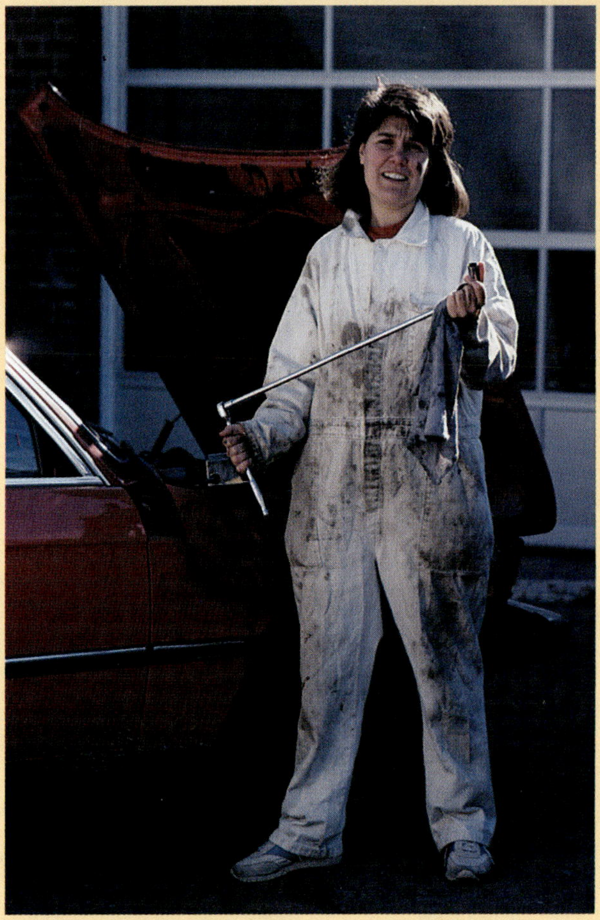

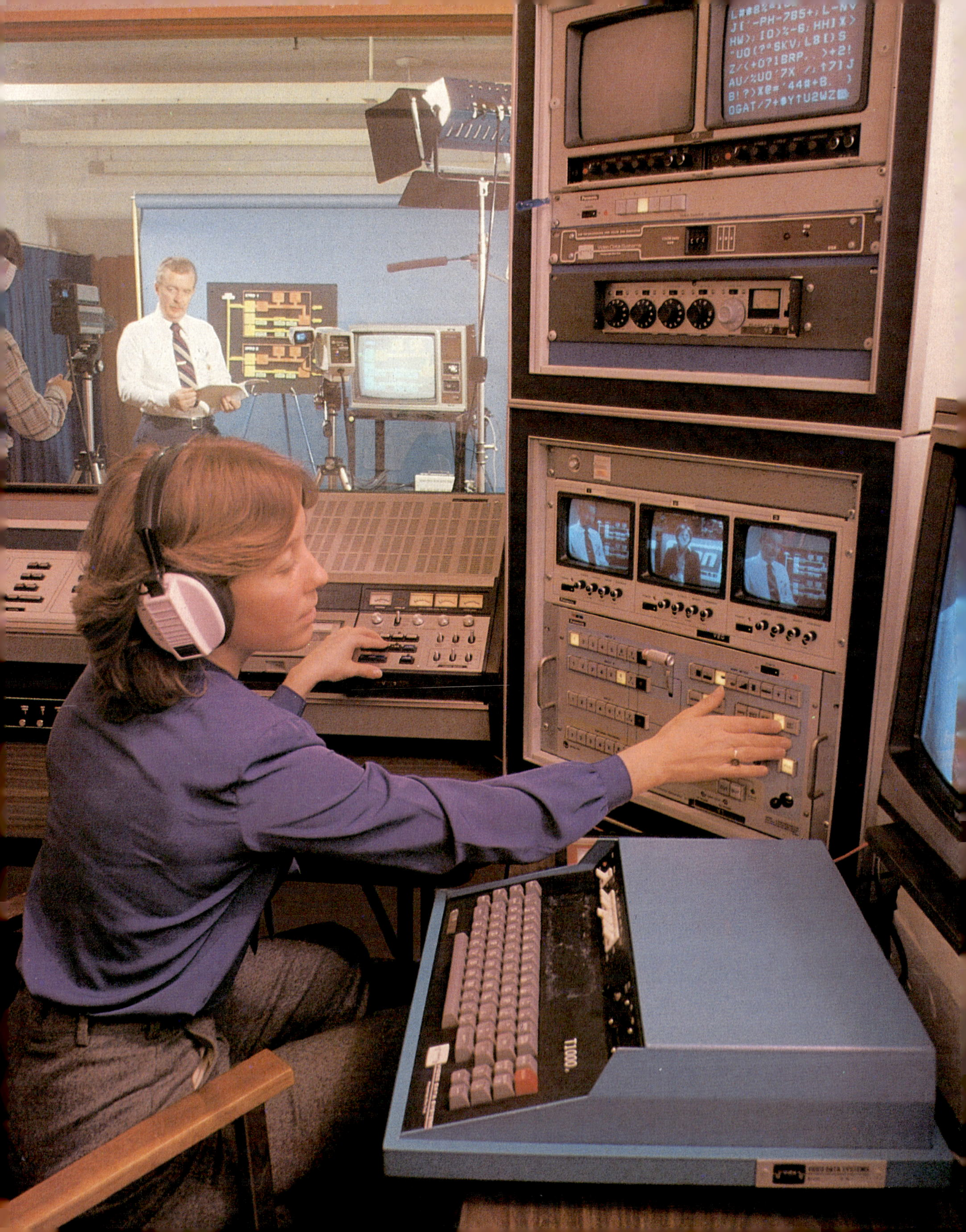
T1000.

PART ONE
Making Decisions About Work

In Part One, you will gather the kinds of knowledge you need for making an informed career choice. First, you will learn about the ways in which the world of work is changing—ways that can expand your job possibilities. Then, you will explore methods for finding out more about your aptitudes, values, and personality. You will also discover how to use your personal profile in your career search. Different sources of information and advice about careers are examined next, as well as techniques for making satisfying career decisions. In addition, you will consider the three important roles you play as worker, consumer, and citizen.

Chapter **1**

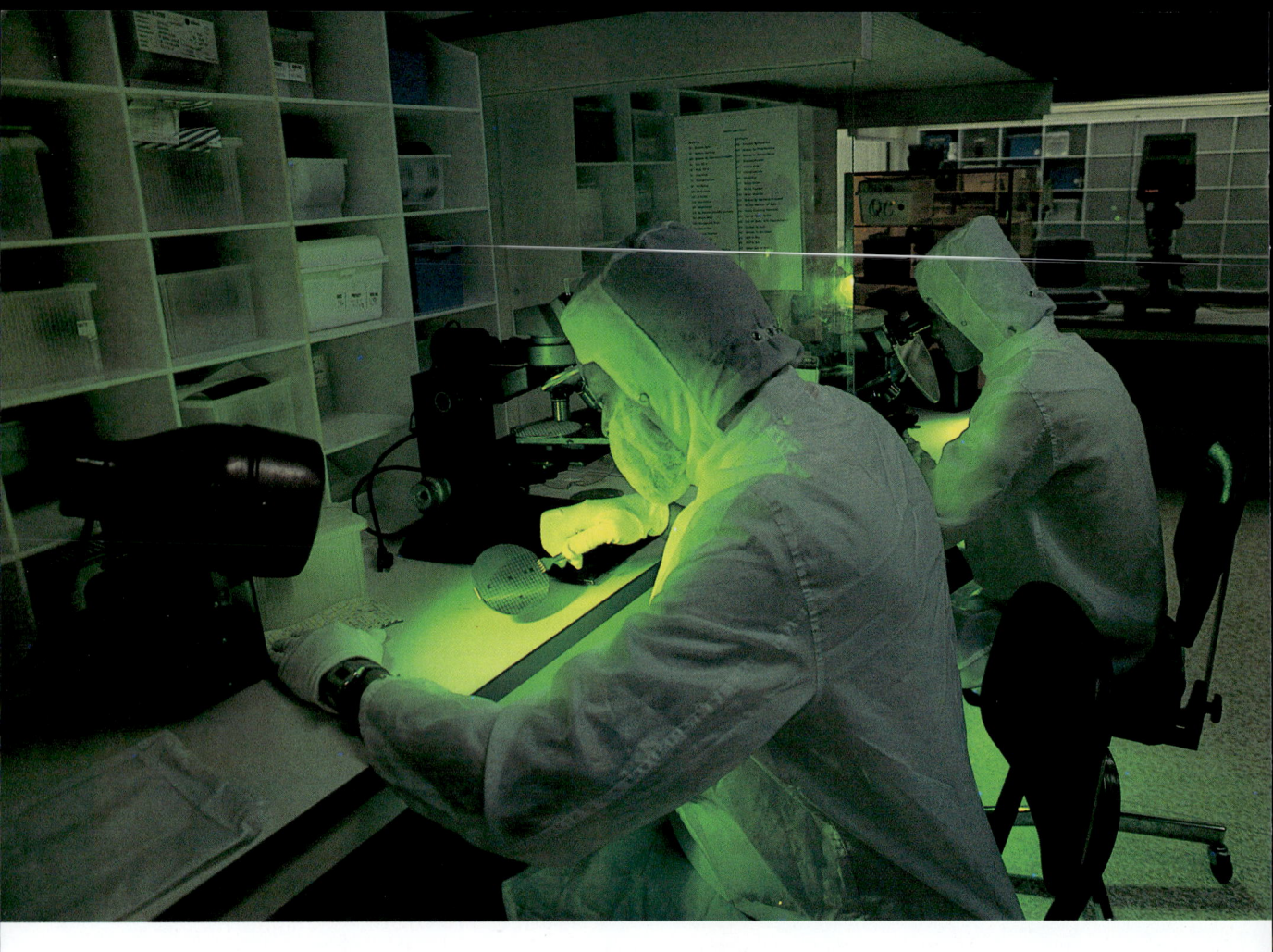

The Changing Nature of Work

OBJECTIVES

This chapter will enable you to:
- give reasons for various job trends and respond to future job trends.
- analyze the effect of high technology on the job market.
- identify new and emerging opportunities for women and men in the job market.
- describe how businesses have responded to social changes.
- deal effectively with stress.
- explain the importance of a broad general education, career education, and continuing education.

Pete

A few years ago, my mother worked at a truck assembly plant, painting the interiors of vans. It was messy work, and she had to wear special equipment to protect herself from the dangerous fumes.

Now a robot does that job, and my mother's job has been eliminated. My mother has changed careers altogether. When she found out that the company was planning to use robots, she decided it was time to use her abilities in another area.

She has always been good at working with her hands, so she knew she wanted to learn some sort of technical skill. She spent some time finding out where the jobs were going to be in the next few years, and she decided that the computer field offered the best opportunities. She also thought that working with computers would be safe and nonhazardous.

She started taking night courses at a technical school to become a computer repair technician. As it turned out, she really liked her courses and got good grades. She also liked the feeling that she was learning a new skill in an area where there would be plenty of jobs and opportunities for advancement. I pitched in by watching my brothers two nights a week and by helping out around the house.

Her schooling is just about over, and I am really proud of her. She is finishing her classes and is just about to start a job for a big computer company. My mother is proving that change can be good for you. It certainly seems good for her.

WORKERS ON THE MOVE

Pete's mother is part of a growing trend in this country. She is one of millions of workers who will change careers at some time during their working years. In fact, the Bureau of Labor Statistics reports that the average American today will have three different careers. In just one recent 12-month period, one-third of all American workers—except farm and household workers—changed careers.

Like Pete's mother, some people are forced to change careers when their jobs become outmoded. Others choose to change careers because they are in jobs that they find unsatisfying. The jobs they do not like are not necessarily low-level jobs that most people would find unsatisfying. There are cases of lawyers becoming teachers and doctors becoming artists. In both situations, these people had glamorous, high-paying careers, but their work did not make them happy. They had chosen careers that did not suit them.

How can you avoid losing your job to changing technology or entering a career field that does not satisfy you? There are several things you can do. You cannot entirely rule out the possibility of your job becoming outmoded, but you can develop abilities that you can transfer to other jobs. You can also find out—before you prepare for any career—what types of jobs will best suit your personality and abilities. Then, even if one job in a career area ceases to exist, you will be able to find another one that will satisfy your wants and needs. After all, you will probably spend about 40 years in the work force. It makes sense to do your best to make those years satisfying ones.

The Changing Picture

The job picture has changed greatly during this century. As some job areas grow, others decline. In 1940, for example, 1 out of every 5 Americans worked on a farm. That number is now down to 1 in 30. What caused this enormous change? Why are fewer people now

With farming methods such as the ones shown here, many workers were needed to produce food. Technology now enables one worker to feed more than 75 people.

needed on farms? One answer is that productivity has increased. **Productivity** is *the amount a person can produce per hour of work.* This change is due to better farming methods and the use of more sophisticated farm machinery and fertilizer. In 1950, the work of one farm worker could feed about 15 people. Now, one farm worker can feed more than 75 people.

A similar picture exists for manufacturing. Many of the workers who left the farms took jobs in factories. However, improved methods of manufacturing have reduced the need for factory workers. At the same time, the new methods have increased the productivity of each worker. The manufacturing output of the United States is now 2½ times greater than it was in 1950 and one-third greater than it was in 1970.

Where are the jobs today? Many people still farm and millions still work in factories. However, more than 70 percent of all workers are now employed in service industries. These people provide informational services, health care, financial services, and recreational services, to name a few.

Many are employed in the food service industry. The number of workers in service industries is growing; experts say that many more jobs will be created in the services by 1995. The current job trend is away from manufacturing and toward services and high technology. This shift may affect 10 to 15 million workers by 1995. As you can see from Figure 1.1, most of the new jobs will be in the services. A smaller but significant number of jobs will be involved with high technology.

High Technology

The world of high technology is an extremely important one—one that is having a great effect on the job picture. **High technology** is *the advanced scientific research that has led to new products in electronics, telecommunications, health care, and other fields.* High-tech industries have developed the personal computer,

More than 70 percent of today's workers provide services. A large number work in food service.

the car phone, and the artificial heart. Many high-tech industries are new companies, started by people who apply scientific discoveries and manufacturing techniques to make new or better products and who are willing to take risks on their own ideas. They are the creators of the computer age.

According to the Bureau of Labor Statistics, only 1 new job in 25 will actually involve high technology. However, the work done in this area will affect the jobs of millions. Pete's mother is an example of this; the robots designed and created by high-tech workers now perform the hazardous tasks she once did. She soon will repair the very same kinds of computers that helped create these robots. Pete's mother has moved into the high-tech area. High-tech has transformed the jobs of workers in many fields.

Certainly, technological advances have helped shape job trends. They have changed where the jobs are as well as what the jobs are. In some industries, computers and robots have eliminated jobs. In others, they have not. Some automation is aimed not at taking the place of workers' labor but at controlling quality and keeping track of inventory. Automation has replaced human labor mainly in jobs that involve semiskilled tasks.

Robots are used to perform hazardous jobs once done by humans.

Changing Directions

You may someday find yourself doing a job you did not expect to be doing because the kinds of jobs available are changing so rapidly. The possibility that you will make a change does not reduce the importance of making a wise career choice now. You should consider the long-term prospects for the careers you are considering. Is the demand for the jobs you would like to have increasing or decreasing? If demand is already decreasing, are there related jobs with better prospects? Putting time and effort into a career choice now will lessen your chances of making a mistake. If you do have to make a career change later, it could be costly. For example, if you have a family, taking time out to prepare for a new career can be difficult. Starting all over again in a new field could mean taking a pay cut. (On the other hand, many workers who retrain earn more money in the long run than they would have in their previous careers.)

Unfortunately, you cannot always predict the changes that will take place in the job market. Although one meaning of the word *career* is a person's life work, that may not always be a practical definition. For any number of reasons, you may find yourself switching careers sometime in the future. For instance, you may need to look for a new kind of job because you will be moving to another city or state. You may be moving because your spouse has found a job elsewhere. You may move because you want to see a new part of the country. When you reach your new location, you may find that there are not any jobs in your field.

Also, it is not always possible to make a decision for life while you are still in high school. As you mature, you may find that the career that once interested you has lost its appeal. You may want a different sort of challenge. If

Chapter 1 The Changing Nature of Work

Figure 1.1 Selected Jobs Expected to Increase Through 2000

Occupation	1986 Employment (est.)	Numerical Change in Employment, 1986-2000	Percent Change in Employment, 1986-2000
Computer Service Technicians	69,000	56,000	+80%
Medical Record Technicians	40,000	30,000	+75%
Computer Programmers	479,000	335,000	+70%
Computer and Peripheral Equipment Operators	309,000	148,000	+48%
Human Services Workers	88,000	34,000	+38%
Aircraft Mechanics and Engine Specialists	107,000	22,000	+20%
Electronic Home Entertainment Equipment Repairers	49,000	9,900	+20%
Surveyors	94,000	19,000	+20%

Figure 1.2 Selected Jobs Expected to Decrease Through 2000

Occupation	1986 Employment (est.)	Numerical Change in Employment, 1986-2000	Percent Change in Employment, 1986-2000
Telephone Installers and Repairers	58,000	−18,000	−32%
Stenographers	178,000	−50,000	−28%
Statistical Clerks	71,000	−19,000	−26%
Textile Machinery Operators	309,000	−67,000	−22%
Farm Operators and Managers	1,336,000	−285,000	−21%
Shoe and Leather Workers and Repairers	35,000	−5,900	−17%
Timber Cutting and Logging Occupations	103,000	−6,900	−7%
College and University Faculty	754,000	−32,000	−4%

Source: U.S. Bureau of Labor Statistics

this happens to you, you will find that career planning never really ends. As the years go by, you will need to think about what your goals and interests are and how they compare with what is actually going on in your life and in the world of work. If you keep your work in line with your goals, you will not wake up one day and realize you have been doing the wrong job for 15 years.

Jane, for example, faced a career change that she had not expected to make when she was younger. In high school, she had taken secretarial courses, and after high school, she worked as a secretary. Five years later, she left her job to have a baby. She decided to stay at home until her child started school.

During those years, she occasionally did work for companies that were setting up word processing systems. Jane gained a reputation for being good at selecting word processing systems and training employees. She enjoyed being in control of projects and sharing her expertise with others. She also liked working with many different people. When Jane was ready to go back to work full-time, her interests and skills had changed from the time she was a secretary. She wanted a new career.

Eventually, Jane became a salesperson for an office machine company. Each day, she visited a number of businesses to interest them in her company's systems.

Like Jane, you may find that you are attracted to jobs that match your changing interests and aptitudes. Understanding yourself will increase your chances of making good decisions. For example, if you like change, you might look for a job that involves travel. If you want to be independent, you might look into starting a business of your own.

The most satisfied workers are the ones whose jobs match their personalities. People who like to help others will probably enjoy jobs in the service industries. On the other hand, people who like to lead or influence others might prefer jobs in management. People who enjoy problem solving, will be best suited to other kinds of jobs, such as those involving science. Matching personalities to jobs is something that will not change. Whatever the jobs of the future might be, they should still match people's basic personality types. There will always be jobs, for example, that call for the ability to solve problems. (In Chapter 2, you will learn about the many tests to help you assess your interests and abilities.)

Anticipating Change

How can you tell what jobs will be available in the future? Nobody can predict the future. There are ways of anticipating changes, however. One way is to keep up with the news. Pete's mother chose her new career partly because she had heard and read about the increasing use of computers.

You can find out about a new field in the same way, by reading newspapers and magazines and by watching the news on television. The more you know about what is going on in the world around you, the better you will be able to predict trends.

Some news stories about jobs are based on predictions made by the Bureau of Labor Statistics. The Bureau bases some of its predictions on information about population changes. If, for example, the number of births goes down, it is likely that there will be less demand for elementary school teachers in the next few years. On the other hand, when the number of births increases, the job outlook for teachers should improve. When the population increases, demand for other services, such as police and electric power, also increases. Companies that make and sell toys, children's clothes, and appliances also have a brighter future.

The number of people in different age groups in the United States also influences job trends and can greatly affect the job market. As life expectancy increases, the number of people over the age of 65 is growing. This means more jobs in occupations that deal with the elderly, such as physical therapy.

Chapter 1 The Changing Nature of Work

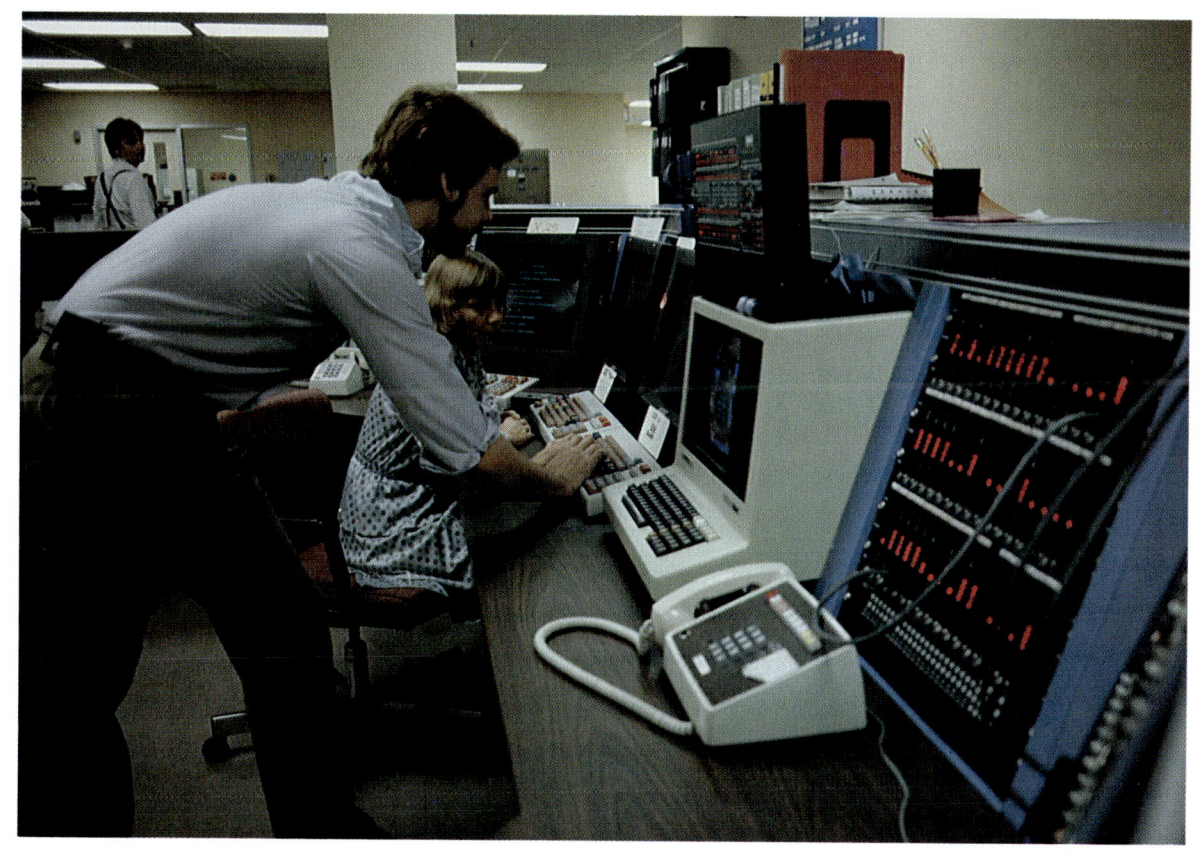

The more you know about what is happening in the world, the better you will be able to predict job changes.

Where you live can also make a difference in your career choice. The job situation in your area can differ from the national outlook. Aerospace technicians, for example, can find jobs only in certain cities.

To predict what jobs will be available, government workers also look at changes in the economy as a whole and in certain industries. If the economy is improving, there will be more jobs in general. If an industry is growing, people will have a better chance of finding a job in that field. One example is the food service industry. As more women take jobs outside the home, there are more two-career families. Such families cook less often, which translates into a greater need for restaurants. This trend creates new jobs not only for food service workers but also for construction workers who build new restaurants. Growth in one industry can create growth in related industries.

Understanding trends can help you guess more accurately what kinds of workers will be most in demand. For example, many experts predict that people will work fewer hours per day in the future and will have longer vacations. The extra leisure time will mean more jobs in certain fields. People will travel more, so there will be more jobs in the hotel and restaurant businesses. Jobs for travel agents will also probably increase, and people will have more time for sports and recreation. That means more jobs for people in those career

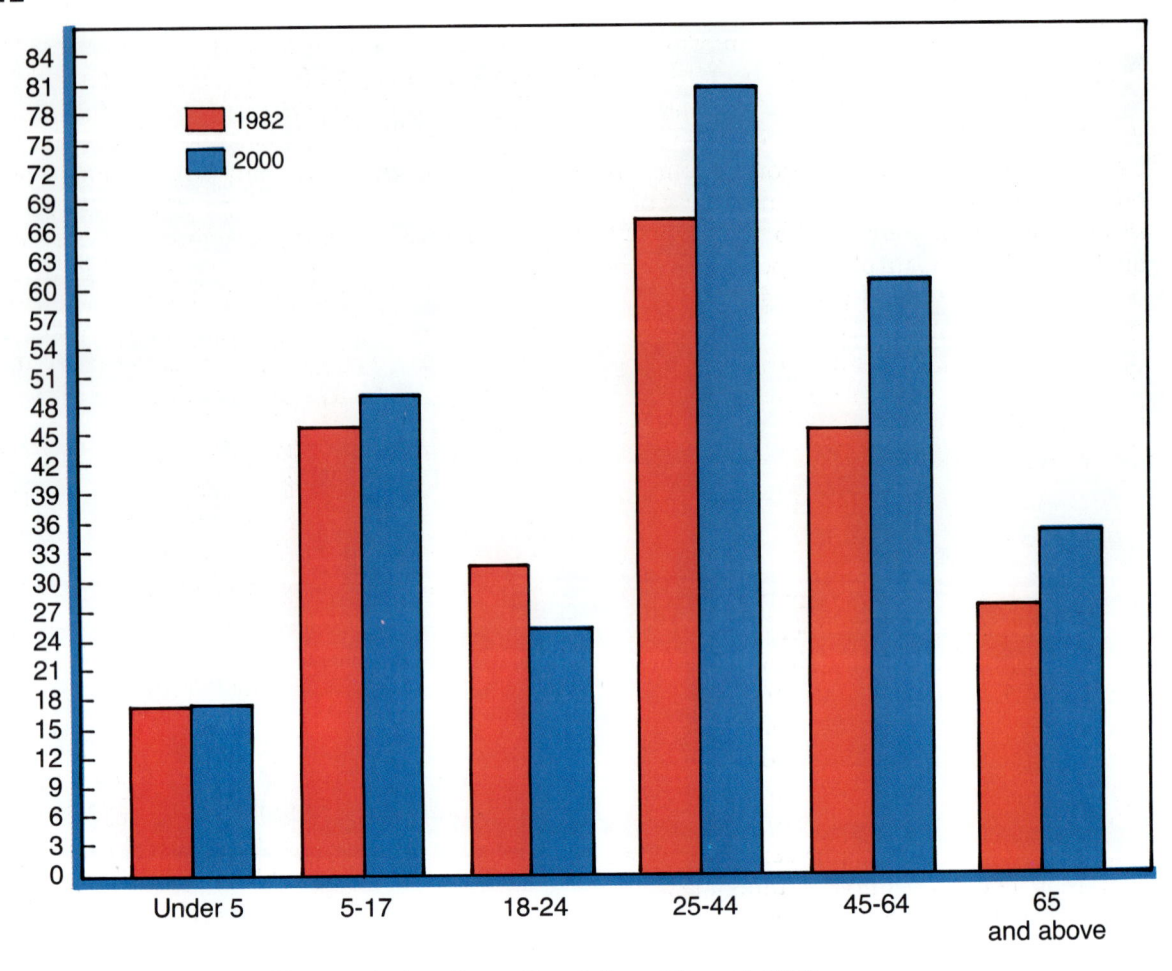

Figure 1.3 Projected Changes in Age-Group Populations Through 2000

areas, jobs ranging from manufacturing sports equipment to running summer camps to nursing people with sports injuries.

The trends that affected Pete's mother's job will probably affect other jobs as well. There may be fewer jobs on the assembly lines, but the increasing importance of technology in manufacturing, office work, and national defense will mean more jobs in the technology area. The outlook is especially good for technicians. Many new jobs will require technical training. However, scientists and engineers with advanced degrees will be critical to the success of high technology.

As you choose a career, one good source of information is the *Occupational Outlook Handbook*. Also called the *OOH*, this handbook is published every two years by the Bureau of Labor Statistics. In it, you can find a range of information about different jobs, such as salaries and working conditions. Most important, you can determine your prospects for finding jobs in the future. Information in the handbook is grouped by **career clusters**, which are *groups of occupations that require similar abilities and skills.*

Chapter 1 The Changing Nature of Work

Finding a career cluster that interests you can be helpful even after you begin to work full-time. If the job you have becomes outdated, perhaps because of new technology, you can look for another occupation in your cluster. In a related job, you could use many of the skills you used in your old job. You would be able to build on your past experiences rather than having to start all over again. Also, new types of jobs may open up in your career cluster. You will be better prepared to move into a new job than someone who has unrelated experience. (Chapter 3 contains more information about career clusters.)

SOCIAL CHANGES

Pete's mother is one of many women in the work force today. The number of women who work has increased greatly during the past 25 years. Today, many women with children hold paying jobs outside the home. Another change is that now more families are headed by single parents, most of them women. Still another change is the breakdown of the old stereotypes that women could do only certain jobs and that men could do only certain jobs. Businesses are finding ways to respond to these important changes.

Overcoming Stereotypes

Stereotypes are *fixed ideas about groups of people that are either too simple or completely false*. The idea that men do not deal well with small children and the belief that women are not good at math and science are two stereotypes. Stereotypes do not allow for individual differences; they assume that all people in a certain group are exactly alike. Stereotypes can lead to **sex discrimination**, *a form of prejudice directed against members of one sex*. Sex discrimination in the workplace has usually been directed against women. It is now illegal to deny a qualified applicant a job on the basis of sex.

At one time, women were restricted almost entirely to certain jobs. A woman could become a nurse but not a doctor, a nursery school teacher but not a truck driver. The reverse was true, too. Men could become doctors but not nurses, truck drivers but not nursery school teachers.

Many women today have jobs that were once thought to be only for men. Women are becoming plumbers, welders, chefs, and technicians, for example. Women are also business owners. In 1982, women owned 22 percent of the businesses in the United States, including more than 6,000 gas stations and almost 160,000 farms. Men are now entering fields once considered appropriate only for women. A growing number of men are becoming secretaries, nurses, and dental assistants.

Fighting stereotypes may take courage. When Juan, for example, decided he would like to become a licensed practical nurse, he took a lot of teasing from his friends. He stuck to his decision, though, and completed his training. Juan is very happy with his job because he likes to help people. His friends ended up admiring him for becoming what he wanted to be. They have also started to question their own ideas about who should do what kind of work.

The breakdown of stereotypes gives both women and men a greater range of job choices.

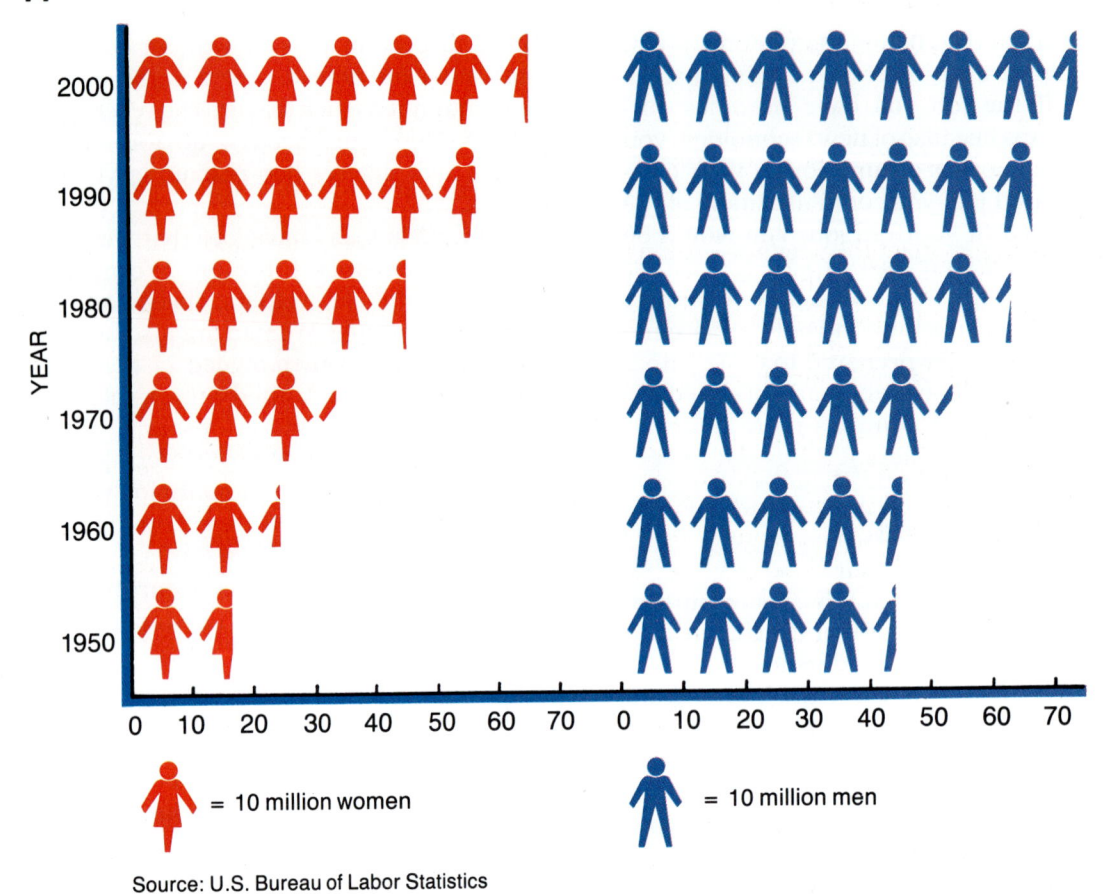

Figure 1.4 Increase in the Number of Women in the Labor Force

Source: U.S. Bureau of Labor Statistics

Family Changes

Like Jane, many women in the work force are married and the mothers of growing children. Often, these women are members of **dual-career families**. These are *families in which both the wife and husband hold jobs*. The spouses may share the tasks that need to be done in the home and the responsibility for raising their children.

In many families, both the husband and wife must work to meet expenses. In other families, however, the extra money earned is used to raise the standard of living. Often, both the wife and the husband are working at careers they enjoy. They gladly put up with extra demands on their time because their jobs are important to them.

Many other families consist of children with one parent. There are many more single-parent families headed by mothers than by fathers. Today, one out of every six families in this country is headed by a woman. Both kinds of single-parent families are growing more common.

Parents in dual-career families and single parents with small children face special difficulties. They have to work out special ways to take care of a child who is sick, for example. Meeting the needs of workers who are also par-

Chapter 1 The Changing Nature of Work

ents is one of the challenges facing businesses today.

How Businesses Have Responded

One way businesses meet the needs of working parents is by being more flexible about when people work. For example, in one company, people arrive at work any time between 8 A.M. and 10 A.M. They leave at different times, too, between 4 P.M. and 6 P.M. Each worker selects a particular time frame. Some work from 8 A.M. to 4 P.M., others from 8:30 A.M. to 4:30 P.M. This kind of work schedule is known as **flextime**, *a system that allows workers leeway in the times they begin and end their workdays.* Everyone works the required number of hours, but workers have flexible starting and ending times.

At some companies, the schedule is so flexible that people can work any time. Some people choose to do 35 hours or 40 hours of work in four days rather than five so that they have free days.

Flextime enables workers to arrange their schedules so that they are home when their children come home from school. When something special comes up, such as a dentist appointment, they may not need to take time off from work to go.

Flextime provides advantages for businesses as well. Satisfied workers are likely to be more productive and to miss fewer days of work. Also, a flexible schedule means that a company may be open more hours. This may increase the amount of business conducted.

Job sharing is another solution to some of the difficulties faced by working parents. In **job sharing**, *two people are hired part-time to do one full-time job.* A husband and wife might share one computer programming job, each working half a day. Two unrelated people might split one job as a bookkeeper. Workers split working time and salary. For the workers, job sharing provides more free time. The employer gains by having two satisfied, productive workers rather than one who might be distracted by too many responsibilities.

Some companies are also providing child care centers for children too young to go to school. Rather than having to find someone to care for their children, parents bring them to work. Trained staff care for the children in pleasant surroundings, and parents can visit their children during the workday. This means less worry and lost work time for the parents. Both the parents and their employers benefit.

PREPARING FOR CHANGE

You can prepare for the many changes you will face during your working life. One way to prepare is to understand what stress is and how to cope with it. Getting the best education you can will also help you adapt to changing situations that can create stress.

Change and Stress

Some people are afraid of change. Either they are comfortable with things as they are, or they think that any change will cause problems.

Change is a part of life. Whether you like it or not, the world changes and you must change with it. You can look at changes in your life as opportunities to grow. Then you can face even difficult changes with confidence and enthusiasm.

As a young person, you will go through many changes. You will leave school, start work, and perhaps get married. Even after you think your life is settled, you may still face equally dramatic and important changes in your personal and work life. In fact, you will continue to change as long as you live. The better you can adapt to the changes in your life, the happier you will be.

People respond to changes both mentally and physically. **Stress** is *the body's response to mental or physical change.* Stress is usually thought of as bad—the possible cause of heart attacks

More than 4,000 U.S. companies now help with child care for the children of their workers. Both families and companies benefit.

and ulcers. Certainly, too much stress can be a serious threat to health.

There is also a kind of stress that is good for people. When you reach the critical moment in a game you are playing, you can feel your heart beat faster. All your senses become more alert. These feelings of excitement can help you play better. In the same way, such feelings can help you do well when interviewing for a job or when explaining a new procedure to a group of co-workers.

When Pete's mother found out that she was about to lose her job, she felt terrible. She thought at first that she would not be able to find other work and that soon there would not be enough money to pay the rent or to buy groceries. After a while, however, she started looking into other jobs she thought she might like. The more she looked, the more it seemed she would be able to find new work that suited her. By the time she started her classes in computer repair, she was looking forward eagerly to her new career. She was feeling a different kind of stress, a kind that would help her do well in her classes and make the most of her new life.

Feeling stress when important changes are taking place is natural. However, you often can make these stressful feelings work for you rather than against you.

The Value of Transferable Skills

There are skills that you can use no matter what job changes you make. These are called **transferable skills**—*abilities that can be used in many different jobs*. Transferable skills include the abilities to organize your time, to work with people, and to express yourself well. Mechanical abilities and other skills are also transferable from one technical area to another. When you plan a career, it is wise to find out whether the skills you will be learning are transferable.

People with transferable skills have a great advantage when it comes to changing jobs. Sometimes workers need to learn specific new skills in order to keep the jobs they have or to move on to new ones. There can be several reasons for this.

Often, a firm may want to install new equipment to increase its productivity. The people who work there must then learn to run the new machines in order to keep their jobs. If Pete, for example, decides to become a machinist, the technical school he goes to will teach him to use computer-controlled machine tools. In ten years, however, these tools may become out-of-date. If so, Pete will need to learn how to run the new equipment that takes their place.

Learning the new equipment will be relatively easy for Pete because he already will be a skilled machinist. His years of experience will still be valuable to him. On the other hand, people who have been working in unrelated jobs may have to spend weeks or even months learning new skills.

Sometimes, workers learn new skills in order to prepare for a promotion. Suppose Pete is such a good worker that his employer decides to make him a supervisor. This new position requires skills in management and record keeping that Pete does not have. His company may pay him to take courses that will help him do his new job better.

Other people who learn new skills do so either because their jobs have been phased out or because they want to change careers. During your lifetime, there will be new careers that do not even exist yet. Other careers may become out-of-date. As technology changes, the job market changes, too. Many carriage makers, for example, lost their jobs soon after 1900 because cars became more popular than horse-drawn carriages. Some of the companies that made carriages began to make cars. Workers who knew how to paint carriages could then use their skills to paint cars. They used their past training in their new jobs.

Someday, you may have to face the same kind of change the carriage makers faced. Fortunately, today there is training available so workers can keep up with changing technology. In fact, people at all levels and with all different skills may need to train or retrain several times during their working lives. Those who can keep their current jobs may go to school in the evenings or on weekends. People who are unemployed may enter retraining programs sponsored by government or private industry.

Education today should be thought of as a lifelong process. Even something that does not seem job-related at one time can prove worthwhile at another time. An evening photography course you take just for fun may later help you make a photographic record of a project at work. It may even spark a whole new career interest.

What Employers Look For

It was once believed that the people who had the best chance to succeed in business or industry were those with highly specialized training. Now employers believe that a good general education is better preparation. As jobs change, you need to be flexible enough to change with them. The best preparation for this kind of change is a strong general background. Today, vocational training programs are changing their requirements. To be accepted, you will need a solid general education background.

Employers now hire new workers with the future in mind. They do not know exactly what changes will take place in their businesses over the next several years, but they do know that workers who are good at solving problems will always be valuable. People who can invent ways to do work better or faster will help their companies succeed regardless of how the job market changes.

People with good math skills will also be in demand. Most technology relies on math. You may think that a calculator or cash register can do math for you. That is true, but employers want people who understand the jobs they do. When your job changes, perhaps in ways you cannot guess today, good math skills will help you learn to adapt quickly to the changes.

Because more service jobs will be opening up in the future, dealing with people will become more important. People who can communicate well with others, either in groups or on a one-to-one basis, will be needed in many fields. Good writing skills, such as the ability to write clear and correct letters and reports, will also be required in many jobs.

Some people with specialized training have learned what to do on their jobs, but they do not always understand why they are doing it. Many vocational schools are now adding courses in the scientific principles on which technology is based. Students who work with machines, for example, are now learning how and why metals contract and expand. The better a person's background in the sciences, the better he or she will be able to learn new skills in the workplace. Employers now look for people who have this additional knowledge so that it will be easier to retrain them if retraining is needed.

Perhaps most important, employers are looking for people with good work habits. They want workers who are eager to do a good job. This means that employers look carefully at the employment backgrounds of applicants to see if they have been good, dependable workers. Employers want to hire people who come to work on time and do their work cheerfully and well. If you cooperate with the people you work with and are loyal to your employer, you will be a valued employee. Other qualities employers are looking for in workers include the ability to make decisions and the ability to adapt easily to new situations. (You will learn more about good work habits in Chapter 10.)

The workers who will do best in the future are the ones who have prepared themselves well today. You can reduce your chances of making an unwanted career change by learning more about yourself and about the workplace. A sound basic education will help greatly and will make any retraining you may need much easier for you. Continuing education, another possibility, may turn out to be fun as well as very useful in your career. The more you know about the kinds of skills and attitudes you need to be successful, the better your chances will be.

MAIN POINTS

- Many people change careers either because they grow tired of their jobs or because their jobs are lost through changes in technology.
- The job picture has changed in recent years and will continue to change. High technology has had an effect on many different kinds of jobs.
- When choosing a career, it is important to take into account possible changes in the job market. Keeping up with the news is one way to anticipate changes in society that will affect the job market.
- People are often attracted to jobs that call for interests and abilities they already have. Matching your personality to your job will help you find work that suits you.
- Social changes have influenced the

Chapter 1 The Changing Nature of Work

job market. More women are working outside the home now than ever before. Both women and men are working at a broader range of jobs than in the past. In many families today, both parents have jobs. Many other families are headed by single parents who work.
- Businesses have responded to social changes with flextime, job sharing, and company child care centers.
- Changes in life create stress. Some kinds of stress can help you perform better on the job.
- Transferable skills are those skills useful in a wide variety of jobs. Many workers will probably need additional training sometime in their lives. Education can be a lifelong process.
- Employers look for workers with a good general education who have problem-solving, math, science, and communication skills. Good work habits are also considered very important in any kind of job.
- Learning all you can about the career you choose can reduce your chances of having to change jobs after you enter the work force.

Terms to Know

Use the following terms to fill in the blanks of the sentences below.

career clusters
dual-career families
flextime
high technology
job sharing
productivity
sex discrimination
stereotypes
stress
transferable skills

1. Abilities that can be used in many different jobs are _____.
2. The body's reaction to mental or physical change is _____.
3. Refusing an applicant a job because she is a woman is an example of _____.
4. The amount a person can produce per hour of work is _____.
5. Workers on _____ can adjust their workday hours to fit their families' needs.
6. Fixed ideas about groups of people that are either too simple or completely false are _____.
7. The advanced scientific research that has led to new products in electronics, telecommunications, health care, and other fields is known as _____.
8. Families in which both the husband and the wife hold jobs are called _____.
9. Groups of occupations that require similar abilities and skills are known as _____.
10. When two workers share one full-time job, they have an arrangement called _____.

Chapter Review

1. What are some of the reasons why so many people change jobs each year?
2. For what kinds of jobs is the demand increasing?
3. How has high technology affected jobs?
4. How can people find out about job trends for the future?
5. How might population increases affect the demand for jobs?

6. What are career clusters?
7. What changes have taken place for women in the work force? For men?
8. What changes have businesses made in response to the growth of dual-career families and single-parent families?
9. How can stress be both positive and negative?
10. What kinds of skills do employers want in workers?

Activities

1. Make a family tree that goes back several generations. Next to each name write the person's occupation. Compare your tree with those of your classmates. What do the trees suggest about job trends?
2. How do you rate on the qualities employers say they want in workers? Give yourself a rating from 1 to 5 on each of the following items (5 is best): problem-solving skills, math skills, communication skills, understanding of scientific and technological basics, work habits. Summarize your results: Which of the areas is your strongest? What can you do to improve the areas that are not your best ones?
3. Visit several child care centers in your community. Rate them according to physical attractiveness, cleanliness, staff-child ratio, and the kinds of toys and activities they provide. Also, compare their rates. If you were a working parent with a preschool child, which center would you select? Why?

Chapter 2

Finding Out More About Yourself

OBJECTIVES

This chapter will enable you to:

- analyze your abilities, interests, and personality traits, and match them to possible career fields.
- discuss how your individual goals and values might affect your career choice.
- distinguish between needs and wants and give some examples of each.
- identify short-, medium-, and long-range goals for yourself and list some steps you can take to achieve them.
- use aptitude tests, interest tests, and career counselors to direct you toward the right job field.

Alex

I was sure all those aptitude and interest tests I took last week would be boring. Instead, they really opened my eyes. I learned a lot about myself that I never knew before. Then, my school counselor explained how all the information about my abilities and my personality could help me choose a career.

For example, I've always had some artistic ability. I especially enjoy designing sets for the school play and drawing cartoons for the school paper. My favorite class is photography. I used to daydream about working for myself as a cartoonist or commercial artist, but I never really believed I could make a living in the art field. I figured I'd have to choose a practical career and keep art as my hobby.

Well, the tests told me that my artistic interest and ability are very high. They also showed that I'm a very social person—that I like being around other people. My counselor pointed out that because I'm so outgoing, I might not like working on my own. She said I'd probably be happier working with others in an office than alone in a studio. She suggested several areas, including advertising and print design, where artists can work with other people and make a good living, too.

One important thing I learned is that a practical career is one in which you use your interests and abilities. Just because a special opportunity may be offered to you doesn't mean it's the right choice. For example, being an optician may sound like a good career for me because my uncle would take me into his eyeglass center. The tests showed that I wasn't interested in science, so I probably wouldn't be too happy working in that field. I'm sure glad I took those tests before I made any serious decisions about schooling or careers.

DISCOVERING WHAT MATTERS TO YOU

As Alex is learning, there is more to career planning than just looking through the classified ads. You will be much happier in your work and life if you plan a career path that gives you real satisfaction and a sense of achievement as well as an income. In order to find work that you will truly enjoy, you must do some **self-analysis,** which means *thinking hard and realistically about who you are and what matters to you.*

Your Wants and Needs

The first objective of working is to satisfy basic needs. **Needs** are *those things needed to sustain human life, such as food, clothing, and shelter.* We have many wants as well because we wish to live above the level of mere physical survival. **Wants** are *things we desire that we believe will make our lives more enjoyable or fulfilling.* Some wants are simple and easy to obtain, such as a new pair of jeans. Others, such as houses, cars, or luxury vacations, are expensive and take longer to acquire. Wants can also be complex and psychological, such as a desire to start a family or a yearning for adventure. Learning what you want out of life will help you determine the kind of job that best suits you.

Your Values

How do you discover what you want out of life? The first thing you should do is determine your values. Your **values** are *the standards by which you want to live your life and the things you consider important in life*. Being a good worker, becoming a parent, taking an active role in the democratic process—these are all values that are common in our society.

You learn values from your family, religion, school, and role models. You learn many of your values when you are very young. Although you may not even realize that you have values, they have a great influence on your life. Think of the times you have had arguments with your friends about a certain type of conduct. Did you say, "I would never do that" or "I wouldn't want my parents to be disappointed in me?" That is your value system at work.

Although our values are usually very strong, we hardly ever think about them unless we are faced with a major decision. Choosing a career is such a decision. Think about what you value in life. Rank your values according to their importance to you. By doing this, you will be able to match your career to your value system, and you will avoid conflicts between the two later in life.

As you rank your values, realize that some of them will change in importance as you get older. For example, now you may put a high value on getting to know as much as possible about the world. Thus, you may enjoy a job that requires you to travel a lot. If you later decide to marry and raise a family, you may find you prefer a different kind of work, one that permits you to stay closer to home. Here is a list of some other things people value:

- education
- independence
- security
- friendships
- religion
- political participation
- warm family life

Which of these values are important to you? If you think about your future, as Alex did, analyze your thoughts for hints about what you value. How well do your career plans fit into the kind of life you imagine for yourself?

Your Goals

In order to work toward the kind of life and career you want, you must set goals for yourself. To understand how important goals are, imagine you are walking along a road that stretches out to the horizon. There are no signs along the road. How do you know how far you have walked? How do you know where you are going?

Goals are the signposts of your life. Instead of reading Wrightstown—2 miles, they read Graduation—2 years, Promotion—6 months, or House—1 year after promotion. Notice that a goal has two parts—an end result and a time span. Once you know where you are going and when you want to get there, you will be able to figure out the best route to take.

You learn many of your values when you are very young. You learn some from your family, others in school.

Setting goals means you are committing yourself to a course of action. If your goal is to enter the high-jump competition in the state track meet, you will have to practice regularly. This means less time for other things, such as being with your friends or watching television. If the goal is important enough, achieving it will be worth all you give up for it. There are three types of goals: long-range, medium-range, and short-range.

Long-Range Goals. These goals are things you want to achieve in the next three to ten years. They can be career-related or personal. An example of a three-year goal might be getting accepted to a technical school for advanced training. A five-year goal might be getting married or moving to your own apartment. A ten-year goal might be starting your own word-processing service, buying a house, or becoming manager of a travel agency.

Medium-Range Goals. These goals are the stepping-stones to your long-range goals. Their time range is six months to three years, and you must first plan to achieve your medium-range goals if you are to reach your long-range goals. Some examples include the following: six months—doing 40 push-ups at a time; one year—having a B+ average; three years—saving enough money for a car.

Short-Range Goals. These goals range from one day to six months. They are goals you will set, achieve, and reset in order to reach the longer-range goals. A one-day goal might be writing a composition for English class. A three-month goal might be getting four new customers for baby-sitting. A six-month goal could be raising your grade average.

How does goal-setting work? Here is an example. Danielle wanted to get into a nursing program at her community college. She would need a B+ grade average upon graduation from high school, but she had only a C average at the end of ninth grade. She set her long-range goal: B+ average at graduation. Her medium-range goals were a B+ average in tenth grade and an A average in eleventh and twelfth grades. Her short-range goals included doing all her homework every day, studying for tests, and handing her papers in on time. She followed her plan, reached her goals in the next two years, and was accepted into the nursing program. Danielle then began her goal-setting all over again, now aiming for her registered nurse degree and her first paying job.

Getting Started on Your Plan. Setting realistic goals for yourself is not difficult. If you know what your needs, wants, and values are, you should have no trouble defining your goals.

Reread this chapter to this point. Then, make up lists of your needs, wants, and values. Start with needs—food, clothing, and shelter. Develop your needs into a list of wants—what kind of clothing, what sort of shelter, and so on. List as many wants as you can. Do not forget to include nonmaterial wants such as leisure time. Then, use your list of wants to help figure out your value system—what is most important to you.

Once you know what is most important, you can make a list of your goals. What would you like to achieve this year? In three years? In ten years? What short-range goals will be your signposts on the way to your long-range goals? What specific actions can you take right now to attain these goals? As you start on your way toward your goals, keep track of the steps you have taken. Check off goals you have reached. Learning how to set goals and reach them will help you in school, in work, and in your personal life.

DISCOVERING WHO YOU ARE

It is very important that you like the work you do because you will be working at a full-time job for at least eight hours a day. A good way to discover the career that would suit you best

Chapter 2 Finding Out More About Yourself

is to look at your personality traits and your aptitudes.

What Do You Enjoy?

The kinds of activities, hobbies, and interests you have can give you valuable clues about how you would like to spend your work time. Here are a few questions to get you thinking:

- Do you enjoy helping others? Have you been a nurse's aide, teacher's aide, child care center volunteer, or tutor? If you have worked as a baby-sitter, were you happy and creative with the children? You might find special satisfaction in a job that helps people.
- Do you enjoy getting others to do their best? Many people have a natural ability to organize groups and get them working smoothly. Are you comfortable being team captain, class officer, or bake sale organizer? You may enjoy a position involving leadership, such as supervisor in a machine shop or sales manager in a department store.
- Do you enjoy doing a project by yourself? Some people can spend hours alone—drawing, practicing an instrument, sewing, or making handicrafts. They are independent enough to complete a task with little supervision. If you are like this, there are many jobs that involve creativity or planning and that require thinking and working alone.
- Do you enjoy physical activity? Some people like to move around, to use their bodies. They would probably be much happier teaching a sport or working on a farm than spending time in an office.
- Do you enjoy talking? Can you make a point or explain a process quickly and effectively? There are many good career areas for people who can communicate well. A few examples are secretarial training, customer relations, and office-machine service hotlines.

If you enjoy using your body, you may be well suited for a job that requires physical activity.

- Do you like to explore subjects deeply, discover facts, and ask questions? Many fields need people who can dig out certain facts from mountains of information. Librarians, legal clerks, and detectives all do this sort of work.

You may find that you can combine several of your interests in one career field. For example, being a telephone repairer involves meeting the public, using mechanical skills, and solving problems. You might balance a fast-paced customer relations position with a quiet home life. There are many ways you can be satisfied in your career.

What Do You Do Well?

Another way to find out what you enjoy is to consider your **aptitudes**, *those mental and physical talents that are most natural to you.* Here is a list of some aptitudes. How many apply to you?

- Working with numbers. If you have an aptitude for numbers, you probably get high math grades, can do mental arithmetic quickly, and like working with columns of figures.

- Working accurately and systematically. You may enjoy being precise with numbers or words. You may also work slowly and carefully on tasks and finish them perfectly. This aptitude also makes you willing to concentrate on a lengthy task until it is completely finished.

- Working with your hands. If you have this aptitude, you have a knack for building, assembling, or fixing things. you may excel at handicrafts, model building, assembling computers, carpentry, sewing, or auto repair.

- Working with words. This aptitude means you enjoy writing, speaking, or acting. You may answer classroom questions and discuss issues with skill and ease.

- Working with children. Do you enjoy caring for babies and children? Are you good at teaching them beginning tasks? Are you a patient person? If so, you probably have an aptitude for this type of work.

- Working with animals. Have you enjoyed caring for and training pets? Are you interested in their life cycles and habits? This aptitude could lead to a highly satisfying career.

If you have a knack for working with your hands, you may be able to transfer this skill into the work place. This teen is working on a macrame project. In the future, she may decide to assemble computers or repair cars.

- Studying scientific subjects. Do you have a deep curiosity and an organized mind capable of doing experiments that show how the natural world works? With such an interest in the world around you, you may have an aptitude for science.
- Thinking logically. You may be good at the logical, step-by-step thinking that computer programming requires.
- Listening to others. If you easily retain information taught in class, you may have special listening skills. The ability to listen carefully and sensitively to others is necessary for a number of different career areas, such as nursing.
- Being creative. If you find yourself thinking up original solutions to problems, you are probably creative. You probably can use words, music, or artistic materials in unusual and beautiful ways.

A summer job can help you discover your dislikes as well as your likes. You may not like one job in a career field, but you may like another.

What Do You Dislike?

No job is perfect. In one job, your pay may be great, but there may be too much traveling involved. In another, you may enjoy working with the public, but complaints from customers may begin to get you down. It is important to know what you do not like to do so you can avoid positions that you will eventually dislike, no matter how good they may seem at first.

You can get clues about what you like and do not like to do by working after school, during the summer, or in cooperative education programs. Dorrie got a summer job working at the front desk of a resort hotel, but she found that her shyness made the job difficult. Bill worked as a waiter after school, but the noisy, busy restaurant was not for him. He realized that he preferred a quiet environment.

You should be careful, however, that your dislike for a particular job in a career field does not carry over to the whole field. Dorrie and Bill did not like their jobs, but they were still interested in those career areas. Dorrie discovered that she did not like working face-to-face with the public. On the other hand, she did well when dealing with people on the telephone. The next summer, she took a job at the hotel telephoning groups that might be interested in using the hotel as a convention site. Bill requested, and got, a cooperative education assignment working in the office of a caterer, where he helped plan banquets and order supplies. You can do the same thing—turn your bad experience into a good one. Think hard about the career field. What was its original attraction for you? You may simply have started in the wrong position.

What Are Your Weaknesses?

Some careers will not work out for you, however, no matter how often you rethink your approach to them. You may like everything about a career field but still be unable to find a position that suits you. In that case, you should examine the skills or areas that you do not like or for which you have no aptitude. This is the starting point from which to solve your problem.

For example, if long columns of numbers make your mind go blank, you may not be a good candidate for most of the jobs in the supermarket business. You may be very interested in the food business and may like to handle money. Supermarkets usually deal with thou-

A disability may keep you from doing certain kinds of jobs, but it will not prevent you from performing others.

sands of units in many different categories. A typical starting position as a cashier would require you to use a calculator, remember prices, perform mental math, and account for all receipts to the penny. This may just be more than you can or want to handle.

If you run into this type of situation, look at your list of goals again. Do you really want to work in a supermarket, or do you want to work somewhere in the food industry? If you are not too concerned with what part of the food industry you work in, you can probably find another position where your mathematical limitations will not hinder you. If you really want to work in a supermarket, you may have to turn your math weakness into a strength. Doing this will require long, repetitive practice to improve your math, but remember that achieving your goal will make that practice worthwhile.

There are other weaknesses that are much harder to overcome. A **disability**—*a mental or physical handicap*—may close off certain types of jobs to you. For instance, if you have a reading disability that causes you to see words or letters backward, word processing would be a difficult field for you, no matter how good you are with keyboards and computers. If you need a wheelchair to move around, a position requiring heavy lifting or getting into tight places may be out of the question.

However, there are ways to handle disabilities, too. Maybe you cannot read well, but you love the sound of words. You may want to look into a career as a recording engineer. Being restricted to a wheelchair may stop you from becoming an auto mechanic, but you could use your mechanical ability to operate robots in a factory or a research center. Put your mind to work, and see what you can come up with.

A Personality Profile

As with your goals, you need to put your likes and dislikes and aptitudes and limitations on paper for your self-analysis to be effective. Divide a large piece of paper into four columns, and label the columns "What I Like to Do," "What I Do Well," "What I Don't Like to Do," and "What I Have Difficulty Doing." Then, take some time to give yourself a thorough self-evaluation. List every activity that you can think of which is related to work, leisure, school, or home. You will end up with a basic personality profile.

You will find this profile very helpful as you research possible career fields. Because you will have much more information about yourself, you will be able to ask better questions about possible fields. It will help you answer the most important question, "Will I be happy in this career?"

How Do Others See You?

Get a second opinion on what you wrote down before you use your personality profile to start looking for a career. Ask family members, friends, teachers, or other people who know you well to discuss seriously what you listed. They may point out, for example, that what you see as a weakness is actually a normal ability. They may give you some good ideas on how to pursue an interest, develop a skill, or improve a weakness.

Chapter 2 Finding Out More About Yourself

For example, Jim always thought he was overly shy because he felt tongue-tied answering questions in class. His older brother Frank did not agree with Jim's self-evaluation. Frank knew that Jim was persuasive, talkative, and a good storyteller when he was with his family. After talking with Frank, Jim began to see that a little self-confidence would help him express himself better in class. He went to the library and checked out a book on public speaking. He also talked to one of his teachers about his problem. Encouraged by his teacher to talk more often in class, Jim overcame his shyness.

CAREER COUNSELING AND APTITUDE TESTING

Setting your goals and creating your personality profile are things you can do at home. Finding out what careers match your goals and profile, however, will require you to do some outside work. You will have to check reference books, such as the *Occupational Outlook Handbook*. You may also choose to get advice from **career counselors**, *people whose job it is to provide information about careers.*

Career Counselors

Career counselors can help you assess your interests, aptitudes, and skills. They can also help you do research on different occupations and learn techniques for getting and holding a job. There are several different kinds of counselors who can help direct you toward the right career.

School Guidance Counselors. These are probably the best career resource people for high school students. Guidance counselors generally have college degrees in education, educational psychology, or counseling. They have usually had teaching experience as well. You can use their knowledge to help you select the right classes. Guidance counselors are also trained to help you learn more about your talents and interests. They can inform you about possible career fields and advise you about further education. They can also alert you to cooperative education programs and part-time and full-time jobs in your community.

Job Counseling Services. People employed at professional career counseling centers can help you get to know yourself and decide on a career that interests you. A good career counseling service can be very useful, but it is often very expensive. You should investigate other sources of information before visiting a professional counselor. Your school guidance counselor can offer many of the same services.

Private employment counselors work not only with young people but also with adults who are changing careers or entering the job market later in life. These counselors often have degrees in psychology and experience in the business world. They usually offer a series of individual or group sessions for a fee.

If you do choose to go to a professional career service, ask these questions before you sign anything or pay any money:

- What is the nature of your program?
- What is the fee? When is it payable? What does it include?
- What is your success rate in finding jobs for your clients?
- Who will be my counselor? What is his or her background?
- Where do you get your job leads?

Ask for a list of references—letters from people who have used the service and are satisfied. Then, get a copy of the contract you will have to sign and take all the information home. Read it over carefully with your parents or adviser. Call the Better Business Bureau to see if any complaints have been made against the company. *Do not sign any contract or pay any fee until you have done this homework.*

Before hiring the services of a professional career counselor, check the reputation of the company with the Better Business Bureau.

Remember that with professional career counselors, you are buying a service. It is a good idea to comparison-shop and check out two or three services. Try to get recommendations about which service to use. Make sure you feel comfortable with the counselor. Beware of counselors who charge very high fees or whose promises sound too good to be true.

What Career Counselors Can Do

You can expect your career counselor to provide you with career information or to tell you how to research specific careers. In doing so, she or he may:

- direct you to certain books in the library.
- teach you how to use resources such as the *Occupational Outlook Handbook* or the *Dictionary of Occupational Titles* (mentioned in Chapter 3).
- give you pamphlets and brochures on careers.
- suggest groups you can write to for more information.
- recommend knowledgeable people to talk to about various career fields.

Your counselor can also give you advice about specific career areas. Counselors have a clear idea of what people actually do every day in various careers. They also know how much and what kind of education is required for a job. Counselors generally are well informed about job trends, such as how many welders or nurses will be needed in the years to come

Chapter 2   Finding Out More About Yourself

They can explain what entry-level jobs you should take in order to become a musical instrument repairer or a refrigeration specialist.

A counselor can direct you to people who will help you learn how to write a good letter of application or make a good impression during an interview. Counselors can also tell you about resume services. A **resume** is a *written summary of your education, job experience, skills, and accomplishments.* A well-prepared resume will emphasize your strengths and help convince an employer that you are right for the job he or she is offering.

Counselors are also trained to administer aptitude and interest tests, explain test results, and help you understand the meaning of your scores.

Aptitude and Interest Tests

In order to better understand your natural talents and skills, you might ask your school counselor to give you an aptitude test or an interest test. Aptitude tests measure your strengths and weaknesses in a number of different areas. Some tests even match your aptitudes to specific occupations.

One well-known test is the General Aptitude Test Battery (GATB). It is actually a series of tests that measure the following nine aptitudes.

- general learning ability
- verbal aptitude
- numerical aptitude
- spatial aptitude
- form perception
- clerical perception
- motor coordination
- finger dexterity
- manual dexterity

A widely used interest test is the Kuder Vocational Preference Record. Each item on the test describes three activities. You are asked to mark which activity you like best and which you like least. The test measures your interest levels in the following fields:

- science
- music
- clerical work
- social service
- outdoor activities
- literary activities
- mathematics
- art

You can also take the Armed Services Vocational Aptitude Battery (ASVAB) in order to discover your vocational strengths. The ASVAB is given free of charge and does not commit you in any way to military service. The test covers ten different areas:

- general science
- arithmetic reasoning
- word knowledge
- paragraph comprehension
- numerical operations
- coding speed
- auto and shop information
- mathematics knowledge
- mechanical comprehension
- electronics information

In Figure 2.1, you can see some sample questions from the ASVAB.

There are many other aptitude and interest tests that you can take. Ask your school guidance counselor which ones would be good for you, and find out where and when you would be able to take them. Your counselor may give you brochures on the tests and tell you what the tests measure and what you can expect to learn from taking them. Request a follow-up meeting with your counselor to have your scores explained. Your counselor can then help you choose the right job fields to explore. Keep in mind that your scores on aptitude and interest tests are not designed to give you a complete picture of yourself. They are only one factor in choosing a career.

Mechanical Comprehension

29. Which post holds up the greater part of the load?

    29-A post A
    29-B post B
    29-C both equal
    20-D not clear

30. In this arrangement of pulleys, which pulley turns fastest?

    30-A A
    30-B B
    30-C C
    30-D D

Electronics Information

31. Which of the following has the least resistance?

    31-A wood
    31-B iron
    31-C rubber
    31-D silver

32. In the schematic vacuum tube illustrated, the cathode is element

    32-A A
    32-B B
    32-C C
    32-D D

Auto & Shop Information

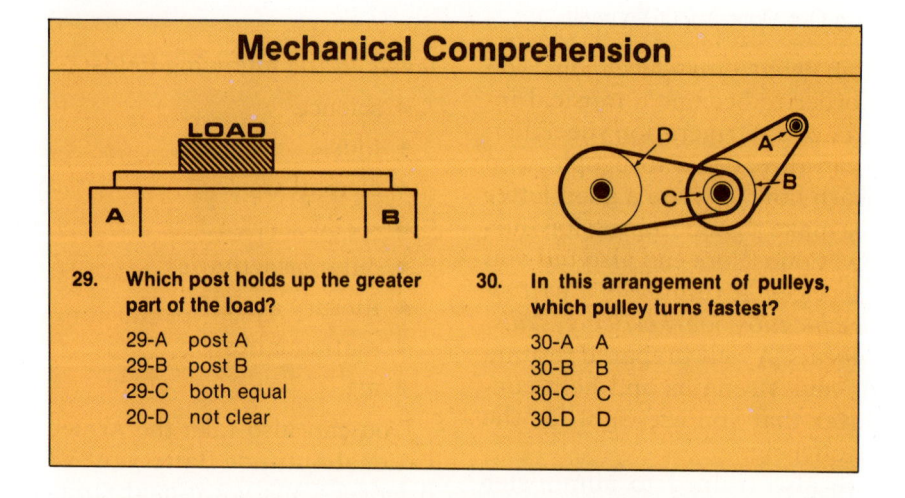

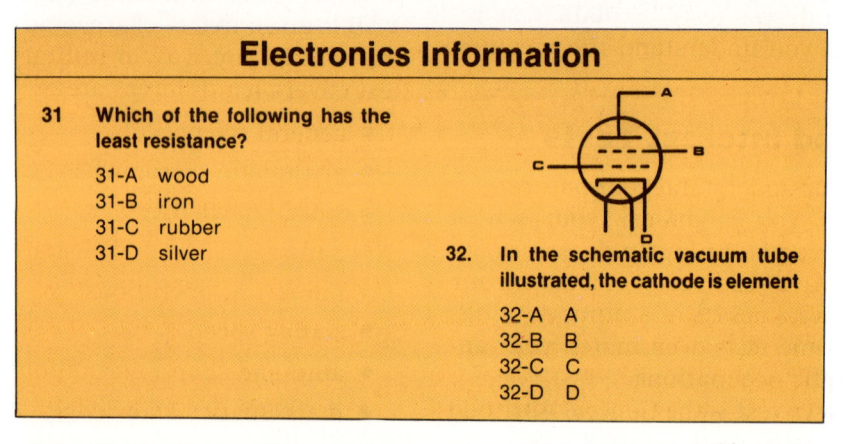

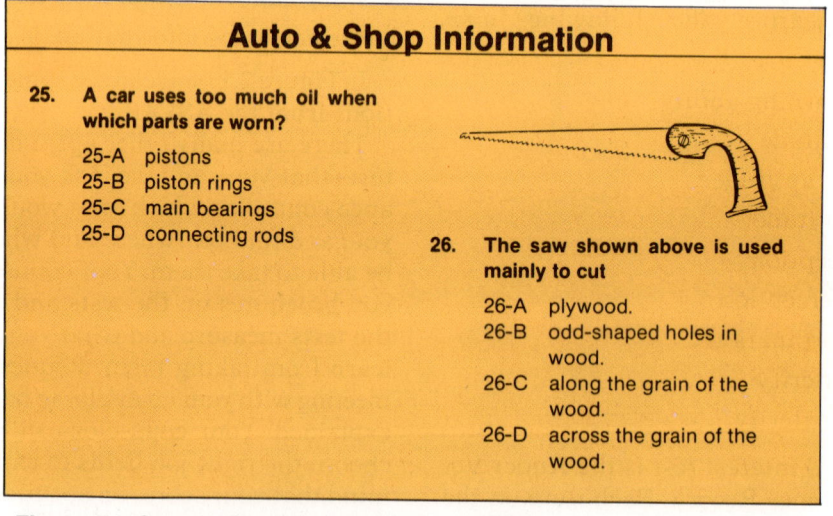

25. A car uses too much oil when which parts are worn?

    25-A pistons
    25-B piston rings
    25-C main bearings
    25-D connecting rods

26. The saw shown above is used mainly to cut

    26-A plywood.
    26-B odd-shaped holes in wood.
    26-C along the grain of the wood.
    26-D across the grain of the wood.

Figure 2.1 Sample Questions From the ASVAB

MATCHING PERSONALITIES WITH JOBS

Each one of us is a complex mixture of aptitudes and interests, fantasies and hopes, desires and needs. For this reason, matching jobs to personalities is a complicated process that often takes a long time. It used to be that once you chose a career, you would stay in that field for as long as you were employed. Today, however, people of all ages find new and challenging jobs in fields that are entirely different from those they started out in when they were 20. Do not be upset if you cannot get a clear picture right away of the kind of job you want. Choosing a career is like doing a jigsaw puzzle—you put the picture together gradually, one piece at a time.

Wendy, for example, went to her guidance counselor for advice. She was having difficulty making up her mind about her career interests. She already had plenty of information. In fact, she seemed to have too much information.

She had taken aptitude tests and had spoken with friends and teachers. Wendy also had learned a great deal about herself from a summer job as a junior camp counselor. She had always been athletic and excelled in several sports. She also discovered in her camp job that she enjoyed helping people. A senior camp counselor told Wendy that her patience in helping slow learners was especially impressive. The counselor noticed that Wendy did not mind demonstrating skills over and over for kids who could not pick them up right away. Wendy found that she loved working with one child at a time, but not with many children together.

Wendy's aptitude tests showed a high degree of independence. Her interest tests showed that she desired an active, outdoor life. Wendy wanted to get married, too, but not for several years. She also felt that higher education was not for her; she was ready to work. Yet she wanted to travel. All these conflicting desires were making her doubt whether she could make a decision. Her indecision was affecting other parts of her life.

The guidance counselor told Wendy to list her goals, ranking them in order of importance. This was a tough assignment for Wendy. There were many things she wanted to achieve, but she had trouble deciding which came first, second, or third. Working closely with her counselor, she finally came up with the following list. The items are numbered according to the order in which she wants to achieve them.

1. Travel around the country.
2. Coach individuals in gymnastics.
3. Work in the Special Olympics for disabled children.
4. Marry and start a family.
5. Start a preschoolers' gymnastics class.

Wendy and her guidance counselor then drew up the following list of possible careers:

- recreation coordinator for town parks
- airline flight attendant
- travel agent
- assistant in county office for handicapped people
- assistant in child care center
- aerobics dance instructor

Listing your goals and ranking them are important steps in matching yourself to a career.

None of these careers would let Wendy achieve all of her goals in her preferred order. Becoming a flight attendant would let her see the country, but she would have to work mainly with groups. Teaching aerobics would let her use her athletic skills, but she would be working mostly with adults. Getting to be recreation coordinator would probably take several years and might require further education.

Wendy learned that she had to **compromise** or *give up some of her goals in order to reach others.* She found, however, that this sort of compromise did not have to be bad. It made her career search more focused, so she was able to recognize new possibilities in the careers she was considering. Wendy realized that choosing a single area has other benefits. First, she would be more likely to advance in her career if she concentrated on that area. Second, as she advanced in her career, she might find ways to reach those goals she thought she would have to give up entirely.

COMPILING A JOB LIST

With the help of your parents, teachers, and counselor, put together your own list of possible jobs. Do your homework first by reading books and brochures on careers that interest you.

Matthew loved to work in the print shop at school. So he looked at various positions that involved printing. He found the following jobs:

- typesetter
- platemaker
- press operator
- proofreader
- bookbinder

Matthew first checked his personality profile. He did not type well and did not care to learn that skill. He did not want to sit for long periods checking spelling (proofreading), and he did not want to be at the end of the printing process (binding). Operating the presses was what he most wanted to do. He began to concentrate on getting information on that career.

Matthew still had a lot to think about. What kind of salary could he get? What kind of people work in printing plants? Were there any chances for promotion? What hours would he be required to work?

Fortunately for Matthew, he had a good start on his career search. He had done his personal research. By discovering his goals, creating a personality profile, and matching careers to his aptitudes and interests, he became more certain in his search. He was able to answer that question that stumps so many people: "What am I going to do?" You can answer this question, too, by using the pattern outlined in this chapter.

MAIN POINTS

- Employment provides for basic needs—food, clothing, and shelter. Wants are the things you desire that are beyond your basic needs.
- Your values are the things you consider important in life. You learn values from your family, religion, school, and role models. Common values include education, security, and a good family life. You need to discover your values before committing yourself to a career.
- Setting goals is one of the most important steps in a career search. If you have goals, you know where you are going and how far along the way you have already traveled. Long-range goals are those that take three to ten years to reach. Medium-range goals take six months to three years, and short-range goals take from one day to six months.
- Understanding your likes and dislikes and your aptitudes and limi-

tations will tell you what kinds of positions to look for.
- Family, friends, and career counselors can help you assess your personality and aptitudes. Guidance counselors can give you a variety of aptitude and interest tests. You can use the results to explore job clusters that match your aptitudes and interests.

Terms to Know

Use the following terms to fill in the blanks of the sentences below.

aptitude   disability   self-analysis
career counselor   need   values
compromise   resume   want

1. Ellen got some very good ideas about part-time jobs in her community from her school's _____.
2. Peter felt that working with his hands was a natural _____.
3. Betsy made lists of her values, goals, and aptitudes in order to do a(n) _____.
4. A flight attendant with a tendency for motion sickness has a real _____.
5. Food to nourish us each day is a human _____.
6. A candlelight dinner in an elegant restaurant would be classified as a(n) _____.
7. Choosing a career that satisfies some of your goals but not others is called a(n) _____.
8. The standards by which you want to live your life and the things you consider important in life are your _____.
9. When Mark went on a job interview, he brought with him a copy of his _____.

Chapter Review

1. Explain the difference between wants and needs.
2. Why are values important when a person is deciding on a career?
3. Why is it important to set goals and to work to achieve them?
4. List five common aptitudes people may have, and match each to a job that would utilize that aptitude.
5. Name five personality traits that you should take into account when job-hunting. For each trait, name one job in which that characteristic would be an asset and one job in which it would be a liability.
6. What are some kinds of information a career counselor can give you that might help you find the right job?
7. List the questions you should ask a private career counselor before hiring him or her.
8. Why are there no right or wrong answers on aptitude and interest tests?
9. Why does it take so long to match our personalities to careers?
10. List the steps you would take to make a personality profile and match it with a career.

Activities

1. Share your lists of values, goals, interests, and abilities with two other class members. Brainstorm with them about possible jobs for yourselves. List information resources you can use, people to talk to, and other ways you might learn more about suitable career fields.
2. Invite your guidance counselor to explain to your class what resources the guidance department has to help you learn about career fields. Ask her or him to bring samples of brochures and aptitude tests to the class. You also might want to ask a private career counselor to speak to your class.
3. Make up a scrapbook representing yourself, including interests, hobbies, sports, goals, wishes, and dreams for the future. Display each scrapbook—without names attached—and have class members guess which scrapbooks belong to whom. Discuss the three scrapbooks that most accurately illustrate their creators' personalities.
4. Ask your guidance department to give your whole class an aptitude or interest test. Discuss your scores as a group. How many were surprised by the test results? How many people already had a good idea of their aptitudes and interests?

Chapter **3**

Exploring the World of Work

OBJECTIVES

This chapter will enable you to:

- explain the importance of making a thoughtful career choice.
- describe the concept of a career ladder and how summer or part-time work can be part of such a ladder.
- make use of people, places, and other sources of career information.
- explain the career cluster system.

Julia

When I first started thinking about what I wanted to be, I had no idea that there were so many kinds of careers. Then, last week, my guidance counselor suggested I check out the career center for different kinds of jobs, just to get an idea of what was available. I went there and found dozens of books and pamphlets. One book lists 20,000 jobs! How was I going to know where to start?

When my brother Dan got home from work that day I told him he was lucky he got his job so easily. What planning did he have to do? His cooperative work-experience program got him work as a gas station attendant, and now he's an auto mechanic.

Dan said, "What do you mean? Things worked out for me because I *planned* them. I spent a lot of time finding out about careers that matched my interests and abilities."

Then I remembered how Dan had always been good with tools. He always wanted to know how things worked. Through his cooperative education program, he found out about jobs that used mechanical skills. He decided to become an auto mechanic. Now he enjoys his work, and he has a pretty secure future, too. People are keeping their cars longer, which means more work for mechanics.

Dan's been working for two years. Recently, he realized he likes working with people as well as with engines. Now he's aiming to become service manager at a car dealership. He figures that in another few years, he'll have the knowledge and skills to move up.

I'm beginning to feel better now. I guess I have to give my career choice a lot of thought. Then, I'll go have a *real* talk with my guidance counselor.

A MAJOR DECISION

Julia realizes how important her career decision will be. It will help determine her adult **life-style**—*the way she chooses to live and spend her time*. Her career decision will affect how much money she makes, the way she lives, her friendships, and how she feels about herself.

Career and Life-Style

The career you choose will affect how much money you make. Your **income**—*the amount of money you make*—in turn affects how you live. The more money you earn, the more you will be able to buy or do. Your take-home pay is not the only important aspect of a job. You will spend up to half of each workday either on the job or traveling to and from work. Therefore, satisfaction in your career is also important.

The demands of your job will affect your leisure time. Sometimes, you have to give up some free time when you take a job with more responsibilities and higher pay. A position such as manager of a busy printing plant requires a lot of overtime. That means much less time to enjoy the higher salary. This is offset somewhat by the people with whom you work. If you are in a career that matches your interests, it is a good bet that the people you work with have some of the same interests. Having good friendships on the job is important for career satisfaction.

Your job also affects your **self-esteem**, *your sense of personal worth*. Dan's career as a mechanic provides him with high self-esteem. He has pride in himself, his skills, and his earning ability. If you are proud of your work, you are more likely to do well on the job. A satisfying job can also give you the confidence to do well in other areas of your life.

Job or Career?

Are you thinking about getting a job, or do you want a career? What is the difference? You might say that you have a baby-sitting job or that you are looking for a summer job. A job can be short-term employment, work that you do because you need the money or because it is available. A career is more than that. It is your life's work.

If you are in a cooperative education program, you have already made some career decisions.

What Is a Career?

A **career** is *an occupation that you plan for, train for, and intend to keep for a long time.* You may move from job to job in your career. Thus, you hear people say, "I have a career in data processing," but "I have a job as a computer operator." Your career can lead you to many related **jobs**, *positions at which you work to earn a living.*

Take Julia's brother Dan, for example. He has a career in the automotive field. He has had two jobs in that field and is planning to move up to a third. He is climbing a **career ladder**—*a sequence of jobs in which each builds on the experience of the preceding ones.* Dan is using the skills he has learned at one job to advance to another job, one with more responsibility and higher pay.

If you are in a cooperative education program, you already have made some career decisions. Whether or not you have had a job in your chosen field yet, you have begun to learn the skills you will need. You have taken the first steps toward planning a career.

The No-Plan Trap

Dan planned his career to suit his interests and abilities. Not everyone does. Some people wait for graduation, read the want ads, and wait for something to turn up.

Some of these people find themselves in occupations that suit them, and they make a career for themselves. Others find themselves in jobs they dislike and for which they are not well suited. They may try to make the best of it and spend years working at something they hate, or they may bounce from job to job looking for something better. You can keep that from happening to you by thinking, planning, and getting experience now.

Work Experience

While you are still in high school, a work-experience program can be your introduction to the world of work. Many employers welcome applicants from work-experience programs. You may have a better chance of getting work in the field you want through such a program than if you simply applied as part-time help. If such a program is not available, a part-time or summer job could be the first step toward the career you want.

When Bill finished his junior year in high school, he started looking for a summer job. His friend Sean was a waiter in an ice-cream shop, one to which his friends always went. Bill thought he could get a job there. Bill's other work possibility was a job as a landscaper's helper. His neighbor owned a nursery and needed summer help. Both jobs paid the minimum wage.

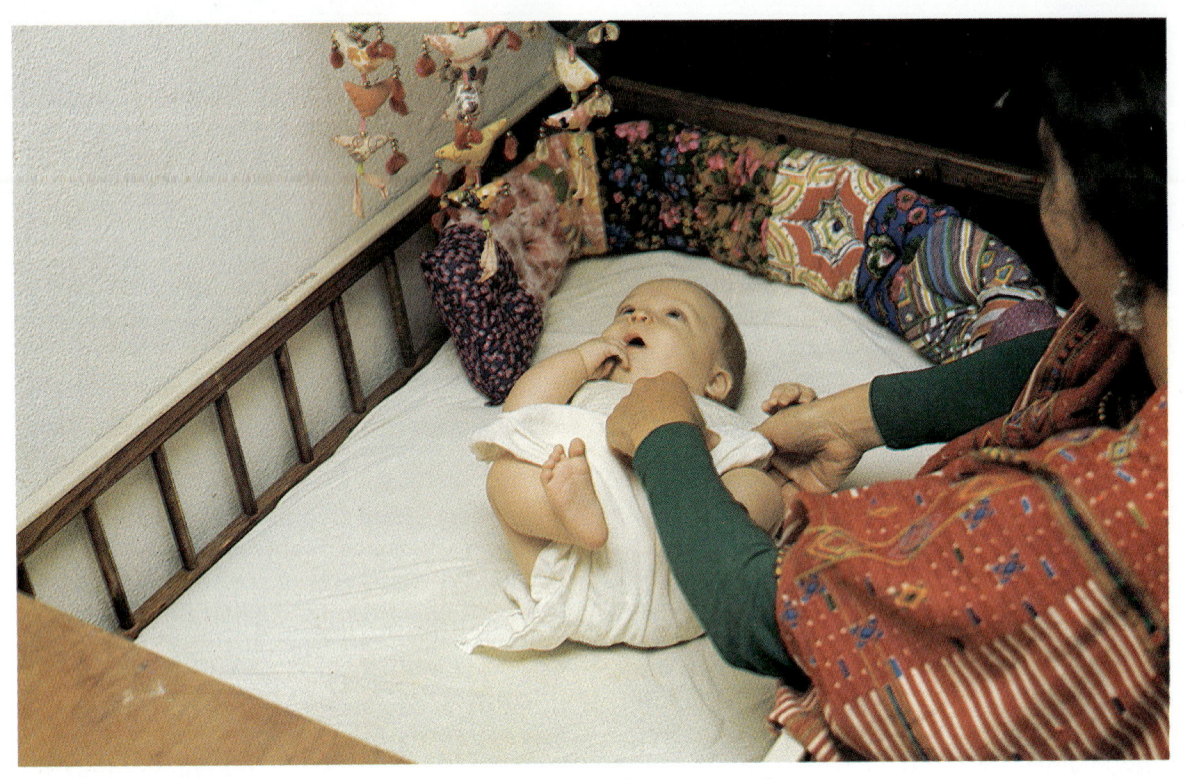

All jobs can be learning experiences. Working as a baby-sitter can teach you dependability.

Bill accepted the landscaping job because he saw it as the first step on his career ladder. He was interested in horticulture—growing plants—and in seeing how a small business operated. He thought that the job would let him explore both. A horticulture program at the community college appealed to him, and this job could help him make a decision about the field.

Bill also liked the idea of being his own boss someday. He wanted to see if owning a business was worth the extra responsibility. He also was looking forward to finding out more about business from his neighbor.

Bill's job was just about ideal for him, but part-time and summer jobs are sometimes hard to come by. You may be loading trucks in a milk plant when you would rather be in the front office. You are earning some money, but are you gaining any other benefits?

You can gain many benefits. What you get out of a job depends on your attitude. All jobs can be learning experiences. As a baby-sitter, you will learn dependability and whether you like working with children. In a restaurant, you will learn to work with others and discover if you can deal with the public all day. In almost any job, you will learn the basics about paychecks, fringe benefits, and social security.

Volunteer Work

Sometimes, there are no paying part-time jobs in the field you are considering. If you are seriously interested in finding out more about a field, you may be able to do volunteer work.

Many communities have central offices that list groups needing volunteer help. Tell the people at the volunteer office about your special interests and skills. They will do their best to find you appropriate work.

You may also be able to find volunteer work by inquiring at a business that interests you. Even if your tasks are simple, you will be in the work environment that interests you. You just might pave the way for a full-time position with that company when you finish school.

LEARNING ABOUT THE JOBS

There are more than 20,000 different kinds of jobs in the world of work. You may know exactly which one you want. More likely, though, you are just beginning to think about a career. Do not limit yourself by thinking one field is too difficult, too low-paying, or not challenging. Find out all you can about the field. You may discover an unexpected career that excites you. Make this phase of your career exploration an adventure.

There are certain questions to be answered as you explore any career. A book such as the *Occupational Outlook Handbook*, or *OOH*, describes the various aspects of jobs that are important to people exploring careers.

Nature of the Work. Exactly what does the work involve? What specific tasks can you expect to do on the job? It is not enough to have just a general impression of a job. You need to know exactly what a job requires. Finding this out can make a job that you thought you would like a lot seem much less attractive. It can also make a job you were not considering look more attractive. Larry, for example, was interested in repairing office machines. When he found out the job involved frequent contact with the public, he decided to reconsider. He knew that his shyness would make such a job difficult for him. He looked for another job in the same field, one that did not require him to deal frequently with customers.

When you find out about the nature of the work, note whether workers are closely supervised or expected to work independently. Is team work important? What about problem-solving skills? When Julia's brother Dan learned about the work of auto mechanics, he realized that the ability to solve problems was just as necessary as the ability to manipulate tools skillfully. A good auto mechanic has to be able to diagnose what is wrong with a car, because one problem can have many causes.

Qualifications. Employers try to get the best people for their companies. They look for applicants with the right **qualifications**—*skills, knowledge, and experience that fit people for a job.* Employers usually will not consider applicants who do not have the minimum requirements. A job might call for a certain kind of job experience or training. Sometimes, knowledge of a second language is necessary.

There are other kinds of qualifications as well. A job as a bricklayer would require lifting heavy weights and standing for long periods. A major qualification for this type of job is physical stamina. Other jobs, such as tool-

When you consider a job, you need to know exactly what it requires before you make a decision.

maker, require good finger coordination and the ability to work precisely.

Training. For some careers, you receive your training on the job. Many construction workers, for example, have learned their skills through on-the-job apprentice programs. Supermarket cashiers learn from more experienced cashiers. You may also receive training through a cooperative education program, or you may attend a community college. For some kinds of jobs, there are several avenues you can take for training. Once you know what they are, you can determine which one is best for you.

Salary. What is the starting pay? How does it compare to the pay in other careers? What income might you be making in ten years? Will your salary change if you become a supervisor? Will you be paid more for overtime? Salaries for the same job can differ from area to area. If you see that one area has a very high hourly wage compared with others, do not make immediate plans to move there. That area also may have a very high cost of living that would offset the high salary.

Working Conditions. The working conditions of a job include the number of hours you are expected to work each week. Working con-

Many workers learn their skills through on-the-job apprenticeship programs. For some jobs, there are several alternatives for training.

ditions also include physical and emotional demands. You may have to stand all day, or travel frequently. *The actual surroundings in which you work* are called the **work environment**. The environment may be outdoors or indoors, noisy or quiet. It can greatly affect how you feel about a job. There is a big difference, for example, between a job in an office and one in a warehouse. Some jobs involve hazardous working conditions. Boilermakers, for example, use torches and other equipment that can cause injuries. Because they often work at great heights, these workers are in danger of falling. The safety equipment some workers must wear, such as safety harnesses and helmets, is also part of the working conditions. When you consider different jobs in a field, look carefully at the working conditions.

Prospects for Advancement. When you consider a job, find out if there is **upward mobility**, which means *chances for advancement*. A secretary in an engineering firm can move up to executive secretary or office manager. A salesclerk in a shoe store chain can become the manager of a number of stores. Perhaps he or she can open an independent shoe store someday. Large companies usually offer continuing training and education programs for their employees. They may also offer more opportunities for advancement than smaller firms.

Job Availability. Government documents such as the *Occupational Outlook Handbook*, trade magazines, books on career areas, and the knowledge you gather on your own can tell you how many jobs are available in your chosen field. The number of jobs in a field is important. Someone who wants to be a professional dancer, for example, should take that into account. It is true that employment in the dance field is expected to grow faster than that of the average career field, but there were only 7,700 people employed as dancers in 1982. Finding out that a field will have few openings in the future should not rule it out completely.

It simply means that there will be more competition for jobs. If you really want to go into that career, you will probably need outstanding qualifications.

Long-Range Outlook. There may be jobs in a certain career field now, but what does the future hold? Will there be more or less demand for workers in that field? Consider whether the use of computers or machines may phase out a career you have in mind. Technology may also change the nature of a job.

When you look at the long-range outlook, be sure you know what the outlook descriptions mean. Figure 3.1 explains the meanings of the different statements in the *OOH* that describe job prospects.

WHO CAN ADVISE YOU?

Julia was lucky to have Dan to talk to. She had never thought of him as a career counselor. She does not realize it, but she knows other people who can help her focus her career interests.

Family and Friends

Your family and friends can be good sounding boards for your career ideas. After all, they are familiar with your strengths and weaknesses. They can help you decide whether a particular career would really suit you.

Julia, for example, confided in her family that she was interested in teaching recreation and fitness to the elderly. Her parents supported her wholeheartedly, explaining that her patience and enthusiasm would help her. They also felt Julia was wise to choose a career in a field that was expected to grow.

Your family and friends can also tell you about their own careers. You may know, for example, that your uncle is a bank teller or that your neighbor is a dental assistant. Do you know exactly what they do in their jobs? One way to find out is to make up a

Figure 3.1 The Meanings of Key Terms in the *Occupational Outlook Handbook*

Changing Employment Between 1982 and 1995

If the statement reads ...	Employment is projected to:
Much faster than average growth	Increase 50 percent or more
Faster than average growth	Increase 30 to 49 percent
Growth about as fast as average	Increase 20 to 29 percent
Growth more slowly than average	Increase 6 to 19 percent
Little change	Increase or decrease 5 percent
Decline	Decrease 6 percent or more

Opportunities and Competition for Jobs

If the statement reads ...	The demand for workers may be:
Excellent opportunities	Much greater than the supply
Very good opportunities	Greater than the supply
Good or favorable opportunities	About the same as the supply
May face competition	Less than the supply
Keen competition	Much less than the supply

Your family and friends can be good sounding boards for your career ideas.

questionnaire. A questionnaire can help you collect useful information about careers that will be helpful in your own career search.

Guidance Counselors and Teachers

Guidance counselors can help you explore the job market. They have had years of training and experience in helping students, and they know which books and pamphlets will help you. They also keep up with new trends in the

Chapter 3 Exploring the World of Work

Teachers can help you find careers that match your strengths. They may also put you in touch with graduates in those career areas.

job market. Counselors are not there to push you into a particular job or school but to assist you in making your own decisions.

Your teachers can also help. Most of them know you fairly well and may be able to help you think of careers that match your strengths. For example, a drafting teacher may recognize a student's interest in architecture. He or she can suggest careers that are well-suited to the student because the teacher is familiar with the work done by people who design buildings. Both teachers and guidance counselors may be able to put you in touch with graduates who have entered the career fields in which you are interested.

Other Advisers

Do not stop at talking with family, friends, and people at school. There are many other people who can give you career information.

Working People. If you already know people who are working in a field that interests you, that is great. Ask them questions. Find out what they like about their work and what they would change. Ask them to describe what they do during a typical workday. It is a good idea to talk to several people who have the same position. Each person may describe different aspects of the job. What one person may consider a negative characteristic, another may consider a positive one. That can give you further clues about the relationship between your interests, attitudes, personalities, and job satisfaction.

Job Shadows. An even better way to learn about a job is to be a job shadow. A job shadow accompanies a worker on the job for a day. By following a worker around, you will learn a great deal more than you can during an interview. You will see exactly what the worker does. You will see the work environment and perhaps have the chance to meet other workers. As different situations arise, you will see how the worker handles them. To arrange a day as a job shadow, talk to your school counselor or someone you know in the career field.

Librarians. If Julia had talked to the librarian who ran the career center, she would have been less confused. The librarian would have pointed out some books and magazine articles to help her direct her career exploration. Then, when Julia was ready, the librarian would have helped her find books, films, filmstrips, brochures, and articles about specific careers. Films and filmstrips that show workers on the job can be especially helpful. They can enable you to get a clear picture of the nature of the work in specific career areas.

Trade and Professional Associations. Many trades and professions have national organizations that promote and set standards for the people who belong to them. These organizations can give you information about

Figure 3.2 Trade and Professional Magazine Titles

Air Conditioning, Heating, and Refrigeration News	Industry Week
American Journal of Nursing	Marine Fisheries Review
American Machinist	Merchandising
Automotive News	Nursing Outlook
Beverage Industry	Parks and Recreation
Data Management	Plating and Surface Finishing
Factory Management	Print
Food Processing	Progressive Grocer
Graphic Arts Monthly	Quick Frozen Foods
Handling and Shipping	Radio and Electronic Engineering
Horticulture	Textile World
Hotel and Motel Management	

careers nationwide. They also do studies of new trends in their trades or professions. Career libraries often carry magazines published for these trades and professions. You can find out about news in your field of interest by reading these magazines or writing to the associations. (Figure 3.2 lists the names of some of the many trade and professional magazines published in the United States.)

Personnel Officers. Large companies have **personnel officers**, *employees who handle the first phase of hiring new workers*. If you know of a nearby company in an interesting field, call its personnel office. The staff will be able to tell you the qualifications needed for different types of jobs in the company. They can also tell you what benefits the company offers and what chances there are for advancement. They may even help you arrange meetings with employees so you can find out more information.

Military Recruiters. Recruiting offices for the Army, Navy, Air Force, Marines, and Coast Guard are located in most cities. They are staffed by military personnel who can give you information about each branch of service. The armed services offer training in a wide variety of careers for people who enlist. You can learn about electronics, engine repair, computer programming, flying, and many other fields. This training can be the foundation of a good civilian career. In order to determine your abilities, the military will administer its own aptitude test, the Armed Services Vocational Aptitude Battery (ASVAB). (In Chapter 6 you will find out more about career opportunities in the military.)

NARROWING THE OPTIONS

Julia discovered that there are so many jobs that no one could research every one of them before making a career choice. You do not need to if you analyze your interests, values, goals, and the job market. If you have done that, you will be able to narrow your options to a more reasonable number of careers. Those are the ones for careful study. To make your career exploration easier, the United States Department of Labor has classified jobs into groupings called career clusters.

Career Clusters

A **career cluster** is *a group of occupations that are similar in nature*. Each cluster may include hundreds of occupations. The cluster system can help you identify jobs that match your aptitudes and interests. The *Occupational Outlook Handbook (OOH)*, published by the government, discusses about 300 jobs. It divides them into the following 20 clusters. Some examples of jobs are given in parentheses.

- administrative and managerial occupations (accountants, hotel managers, purchasing agents)
- engineers, surveyors, and architects (civil engineers, architects, mining engineers)
- natural scientists and mathematicians (computer systems analysts, chemists, biologists)
- social scientists, social workers, religious workers, and lawyers
- teachers, librarians, and counselors (elementary through college teachers)
- health diagnosing and treating practitioners (physicians, veterinarians)
- registered nurses, pharmacists, dietitians, therapists, and physician assistants
- health technologists and technicians (dental hygienists, practical nurses, surgical technicians)
- writers, artists, and entertainers (commercial artists, photographers, musicians)
- technologists and technicians, except health (air traffic controllers, drafters, computer programmers)

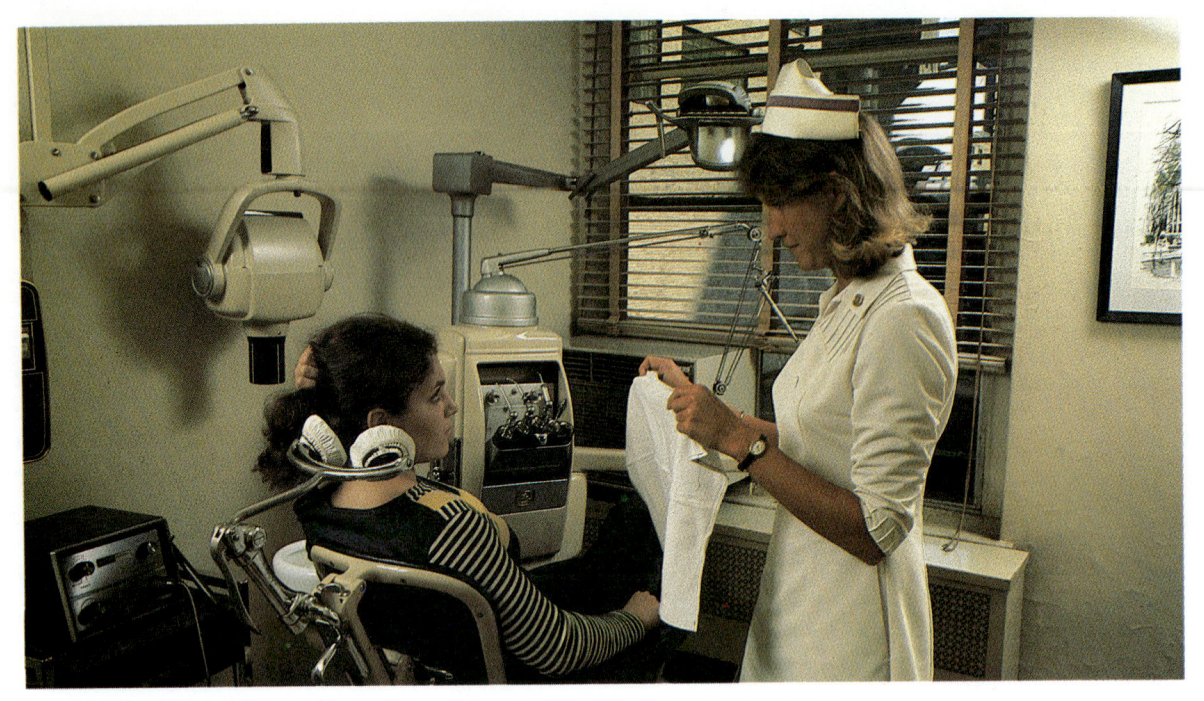

Dental hygienists work in one of the many occupations described in the health technologists and technicians cluster of the *OOH*.

- marketing and sales occupations (cashiers, insurance agents, retail sales workers)
- administrative support occupations, including clerical (bank tellers, bookkeepers, secretaries)
- service occupations (detectives, barbers, servers)
- agricultural and forestry occupations (farm operators, research technicians, forestry technicians)
- mechanics and repairers (automobile mechanics, appliance repairers, computer service technicians)
- construction and extractive occupations (bricklayers, ironworkers, glaziers)
- production occupations (dental laboratory technicians, tool-and-die makers, dispensing opticians)
- transportation and material moving occupations (airplane pilots, bus drivers, truck drivers)
- helpers, handlers, equipment cleaners, and laborers (fuel pump attendants, shipping packers, grocery baggers)
- armed forces

See the appendix on pages 341-378 for further information on career clusters.

Under each job description in the *OOH*, you will find information on the nature of the work, working conditions, number of jobs in the field, training, qualifications, advancement, job outlook, earnings, related occupations, and sources of further information.

Another book that uses a cluster system is the *Guide for Occupational Exploration*, published by the United States Department of Labor. This guide clusters occupations by worker

Chapter 3 Exploring the World of Work

interest. The clusters are broader than in the *OOH*. Examples are Artistic, Scientific, and Plants and Animals. There is a description of each field, which is followed by a list of some types of jobs in the fields.

Still another good source of career information is the *Dictionary of Occupational Titles (DOT)*. This book lists more than 20,000 different kinds of jobs. The *DOT* is published by the United States Department of Labor and is probably available in your library or career center. The jobs are arranged according to the 15 categories below. (Again, some examples of jobs in each category are given in parentheses.)

- agriculture (farmers, beekeepers, animal trainers)
- arts, humanities, and sciences (musicians, taxidermists, editors)
- business and office (personnel managers, stock clerks, computer programmers)
- communications and media (telephone line installers, radio operators, television announcers)
- construction (carpenters, roofers, electricians)
- health (nurses, medical technicians, laboratory aides)
- home economics (child care workers, clothing designers, interior decorators)
- hospitality and recreation (hotel managers, flight attendants, restaurant workers)
- manufacturing (bindery workers, machinists, product inspectors)
- marine science (fish farmers, marine engineers, divers)
- marketing and distribution (salesclerks, custodians, real estate brokers)
- natural resources and environment (foresters, miners, petroleum engineers)
- personal services (hairstylists, funeral directors, housekeepers)
- public service (fire fighters, police officers, prison guards)
- transportation (pilots, sailors, bus drivers)

Related jobs are grouped together in the *DOT*. Under each job listing is a brief description of the work involved in the job.

Values and Drawbacks of the Cluster System

By looking at jobs within a cluster, you can learn more about how jobs in a field relate to one another. You can check the qualifications required for each, and compare jobs easily.

However, the cluster system is not perfect. A job can differ greatly according to the field in which it is involved. People who are secretaries, for example, can work in many areas. You may also be limiting yourself by considering only one cluster. If you have a transferable skill, you may find a good career in a variety of career clusters.

Therefore, when you read about career clusters, know that your situation is different from the next person's. In the end, your career development depends on yourself, not on an outline from a book or from a personnel department. Think of the positives and negatives of each cluster as *you* see them. If you know yourself, your evaluation of a cluster will be much more worthwhile.

It is Your Responsibility

Once you have explored your career options, you are the one who must decide which career is right for you. Your parents and friends may know you well and give you advice, but you will be the person on the job each day.

This chapter has included many suggestions for ways to explore careers. Quite a few will take time and effort. Remember, looking for the right career is an adventure as well as a responsibility. During the search, you will learn much about yourself and the world of work.

MAIN POINTS

- Your career decision is one of the most important decisions you will make. It affects your life-style, friendships, and self-esteem.
- A cooperative education job or a part-time or summer job can be the first step on the ladder leading toward a meaningful career.
- When researching a job, you need to find answers to questions about the nature of the work, qualifications, training, salary, working conditions, prospects for advancement, and long-range employment outlook.
- It is a good idea to discuss your career plans with friends, family, teachers, and guidance counselors. You should also talk to librarians and people who work in the field.
- Careers can be grouped in clusters according to characteristics that they share.
- You can get information and advice from many sources, but in the end, your choice of career must be your decision.

Terms to Know

Use the following terms to fill in the blanks of the sentences below.

career	job	self-esteem
career cluster	life-style	upward mobility
career ladder	personnel officer	work environment
income	qualifications	

1. The way you choose to live and spend your time is your _____.
2. Being congratulated by her boss raised Rachel's _____.
3. The occupation that you plan for, train for, and intend to keep for many years is called a(n) _____.
4. The skills, knowledge, and experience that fit people for a job are known as _____.
5. A group of related jobs is a(n) _____.
6. The position you take to earn a living is called a(n) _____.
7. Jason learned about jobs in the company from the company's _____.
8. Salesclerk, assistant manager, and manager are jobs on the same _____.
9. Location, noise level, lighting, and furniture are all part of the _____ of a job.
10. A job with chances for advancement has _____.
11. The choice of career affects the amount of your _____.

Chapter Review

1. How does your career affect your life-style?
2. What is the difference between a job and a career?
3. Give an example of a career ladder.
4. What are the advantages of a cooperative education, a part-time, or summer job?
5. List three books that can help you explore career possibilities.
6. When you are considering a ca-

reer, why is it important to think about the long-range outlook of jobs in that career?
7. How can friends and family help your career exploration?
8. What is a job shadow? Why is it useful to be a job shadow?
9. List five career clusters from the *OOH* that you find attractive.
10. What are some of the advantages of the cluster system? What are some disadvantages?

Activities

1. Do some research into career ladders by finding an entry-level job for an interesting career and then seeing where the job can lead. Make a chart, putting the entry-level job in a box at the bottom. Above it, describe the next job you might have. Between the boxes, list any special training necessary to climb one step. Remember that several different ladders can start with the same entry-level job. You can show those ladders as well. Continue the ladder up to the level you would like to reach.
2. Interview someone in a career in which you are interested. Prepare questions to find out the nature of the work and the work environment.
3. Use the *OOH* to research a career cluster that interests you. Which careers in the cluster require a high school education? Which call for more technical training or a college degree? Find the career that seems best suited to you. Write a summary of the nature of the work, the qualifications, the salary, the chances for advancement, and the future outlook.

Chapter **4**

Making Decisions About Work

OBJECTIVES

This chapter will enable you to:

- measure the importance of your career decisions.
- explain why career decisions are major decisions.
- list the seven steps of the decision-making process.
- explain the roles personal values and goals play in making decisions.
- analyze your options when making a decision.
- describe three ways to reduce the risk involved in decision making.
- outline the benefits of using a system for making decisions.
- explain the differences and relationships between worker, citizen, and consumer decisions.

Jill

I never thought I'd have two summer jobs to choose between, but that's just what I have to do now. Last month, I applied to work as a candy striper at the hospital.

My cousin worked as one last year, and she really liked it, so I applied. It's a volunteer job. As the woman who interviewed me explained, "Your payment will be in smiles rather than in dollars." I never expected to be accepted into the program.

While I was waiting to hear from the hospital, I found out about an opening at the fast-food place downtown. I applied there, too. There must have been 20 other kids who also applied. There's a lot of competition for summer jobs around here—there are never enough to go around. Well, yesterday I got two phone calls. Both jobs came through.

I don't know what to do. I think it would be very satisfying to help make life more pleasant for people who have to be in the hospital. Maybe I'll get an idea of what it would be like to be a nurse. That's a job I sometimes think I might like. I would be working in the daytime during the week. That would leave me lots of free time to go out with my friends and enjoy the summer.

I'd have to work evenings and weekends at the fast-food place. I don't like those hours much. The pay is good, and I sure could use the money. I'm going to need it for school. I'll probably get to meet a lot of people, too. Who knows? Maybe I'll really like working in a restaurant. I have to let both places know as soon as possible. Maybe I should just toss a coin and make my decision that way. I'll think it over while I make myself a grilled cheese sandwich.

DECISIONS, DECISIONS

Jill has a difficult decision to make. She has to choose between two jobs. Each has definite advantages and disadvantages. Right now, the pros and cons of each job make them both seem equally attractive to Jill. She is going to have to consider the problem carefully.

Jill had no trouble, however, deciding that she was going into the kitchen to make a grilled cheese sandwich. That was a simple choice, one she could decide quickly. In fact, she was hardly aware of thinking about it.

Shortcuts

Jill's decision about food is one of many simple decisions she makes all through the day. From morning to night, in fact, she is involved in decision making. She decides when to get up, what to wear, what radio station to listen to, what to make for breakfast, what route to take to school, and so on. Spending a lot of time on such decisions would make it hard to get very much done.

Like Jill's daily decisions, most of yours are routine choices. You make them quickly and easily because you have developed a number of shortcuts:

- Experience. Experience guides you in many of your decisions. You choose breakfast cereal A over cereal B because you have tasted both and know that A tastes better than B.
- Habit. Many of your decisions are a matter of habit. You do not consciously decide to brush your teeth each morning; you do it automatically because you have done it thousands of times before.
- Example. You also make decisions based on other people's decisions. If your friend selects a particular brand of sneakers, you may follow his or her lead and buy the same brand. You may go out for the same team at school that your sister is on.
- Impulse. Then there are those decisions that are the result of impulse. An **impulse** is *a sudden desire to act*. You may be listening to a record and follow an impulse to get up and dance. When Jill opens the refrigerator to get the cheese for her sandwich, she may have the impulse to eat a piece of chicken for lunch instead.

Your Resources

In all decisions, both large and small, people make choices about how to use their **personal resources**—their *time, energy, skills, and money*. They decide how to use them in order to reach their goals.

No one has an unlimited amount of personal resources. Because these resources are limited, your time, energy, skills, and money are precious.

What you want to do, then, is to manage your resources so that you get the most out of them. You do not, for instance, want to buy something and then discover that you could have spent less on the item if you had bought it elsewhere. Nor do you want to spend more time and energy than you have to on chores that you find unpleasant.

To use your resources efficiently, you need to make decisions in a careful, logical manner.

How Important Is Your Decision?

One way to decide whether a decision is a small one, a major one, or somewhere in between is to look at the results, or consequences. The more important the decision, the longer lasting the consequences are likely to be, and the greater the cost in resources. If Jill realizes she is not really in the mood for a grilled cheese sandwich after she bites into it, she will not be affected by her decision for very long. Tomorrow she can have something different for lunch. The cost in resources is minimal.

If she buys a white winter jacket and then, after she gets home, decides that white is not

Looking at the consequences of a decision can help you decide its importance. Your career decisions have a high cost in time, energy, money, and skills.

a practical color, she can go back to the store and return or exchange the jacket. She has to pay for her wrong decision with the amount of time and energy it takes for her to travel to the store, make a new selection, and go home again. Still, the cost in resources is not very large, and the mistake is rather easily set right.

Major decisions have much higher costs. And they are usually harder to correct. If Jill makes the wrong choice about which summer job to accept, the results can be longer lasting and harder to undo. Let us say Jill takes the job at the fast-food restaurant. After a few weeks, she may be very unhappy in the position. She can, of course, quit the job. By that time, the candy-striper position most likely will be filled. Jill would have no summer job at all. Jill's decision about her summer job, then, is a fairly important one.

Your Career Decisions

The decisions you make about your career are even more important. The cost in terms of time, energy, money, and skills can be high. Many careers require specialized training. You may have to go to school for a few months to a few years. Tuition costs can run to thousands of dollars.

If you decide while in a training program that you would rather prepare for a different career, you will already have spent time, energy, and money preparing for a career that does not suit your abilities or personality. It is true that education never goes to waste. Still, it is more satisfying to be studying something that you will enjoy and put to a definite use.

At one time, people did not give much thought to their occupations. Boys and girls tended to follow in the footsteps of their parents. A boy became a farmer or a carpenter—whatever his father before him had done. A girl usually became a homemaker.

Now, however, young people have a wide variety of choices. There are literally thousands of occupations from which to choose. Because there are so many choices, your decision is an important one. You owe it to yourself to make your career decisions as carefully as you can. That means using a logical, step-by-step process that can help you select a career that suits you. It is a process you need to start using now, as Jill is learning to do.

The Decision-Making Process

None of the four shortcuts used to make simple decisions—experience, habit, example, and impulse—will help Jill decide which summer job to take. In order to make that difficult choice, she should learn to use a decision-making process. The one below is a seven-step process for identifying options and choosing between them. It is the process Jill will follow to increase her chances of selecting the summer job that will satisfy her the most.

Step 1: Define the Problem. This step may seem unnecessary, but it is not. Sometimes, there may be more than one problem involved. Other times, the problem may be broader than it seems at first glance.

On the surface, Jill's problem seems to be which summer job to take. She does need to decide that. She also needs to think in terms of summer jobs that can help her make a career choice. Her choice of a summer job, then, should be looked at within that larger framework.

Step 2: Identify and Rank Your Goals. Now, Jill needs to decide what her goals are and which goals are most important. **Goals** are *aims, or the ends that you try to reach*. The results you want from your decisions, for example, are goals. Whatever your goals are, they give meaning to your actions.

Jill has a number of goals. She wants to keep busy on her summer vacation. She wants to help people. She also wants to earn money so that she can continue her education after high school. In addition, she wants to have time to enjoy the summer with her friends.

Ideally, Jill would like to reach all her goals. Because she will probably not be able to fulfill all her goals, she needs to rank them according to how important they are to her. That way, she will be able to concentrate first on those goals that are at the top of her list.

Identifying your goals can be difficult because often you first have to determine your values. Jill must ask herself whether she values helping people more than earning money. She should also ask herself if she values earning money more than she values leisure time.

At one time, young people followed in the career footsteps of their parents. Now, however, there are many choices.

Brainstorming with a friend may help you find more ways to solve a problem than you could think of on your own.

Her choices are further complicated by the fact that earning money is a means to an end: training for a job. Earning money would also help reduce the financial burden on her parents when she enters training. However, it is the job that does not pay a high salary that can help Jill decide whether she might like nursing.

Two people may rank the same set of goals in entirely different orders, if their values are different. For example, you and a friend may both be looking for a winter jacket. One of you may search for the warmest jacket available; the other may be far more concerned with the style of the jacket.

Step 3: Determine the options. Now, it is time to consider all the possible ways to solve the problem. You may want to brainstorm this stage with someone else who may see options you missed. An **option** is *a choice*. On the surface, Jill has two options: to work at the hospital or to work at the fast-food restaurant.

Yet, there is a third option: to stay at home. Jill's sister came up with a fourth option: to work part-time at the hospital and part-time at the restaurant.

Not every way of solving a problem turns out to be an option. To be an option, a solution must help achieve a goal. It also must be possible. Otherwise, it is not a realistic option. Not all Jill's ideas about what to do this summer may be possible. Her parents may tell her that her staying at home is unacceptable to them because they think it is to her benefit to have a summer job. Working part-time at each job may also be unrealistic. Both the hospital and the fast-food place may require employees to work a minimum number of hours each week.

When you consider your options, you may have to spend time and energy gathering information. Talking to friends and family members is one way to do that. Jill also may be able to talk to people who have worked in the places she is considering. She could also visit the library if she wants information on job prospects in nursing or the food service field.

57

Figure 4.1 Jill Compares Her Options

Options	Help people	Decide on career	Make money	Enjoy the summer
Candy striper	✓	✓		✓
Fast-food worker			✓	
Part-time at each	✓	✓	✓	✓
Stay home				✓

(Goals)

Step 4: Analyze the Advantages and Disadvantages of Each Option. This step helps you figure out how well each option meets your goals. It is best accomplished by writing down each option and making a list of its advantages and disadvantages. This is what Jill did, as shown in Figure 4.1.

If Jill takes the job at the restaurant, she will be able to save money for school, an important goal. However, she will have to sacrifice her weekends. If she takes the job at the hospital, she can have her weekends free. She will also be able to help people. In addition, she will have a better idea of whether nursing would be a good career choice for her. If she takes no job at all, she would have plenty of time for swimming and hiking, two of her favorite summer activities.

Working part-time at each job would allow Jill to reach the greatest number of goals. However, the possibility of that option depends on whether her employers would agree to her plan.

Step 5: Choose the Best Option. The fifth step is to select the option that offers the most advantages and the fewest disadvantages. When Jill finished her chart, it was clear that the candy-striper position met more of her goals than the restaurant job. Working both jobs part-time would enable her to reach all her goals. That, then, would be the option that Jill will rank first. Not taking any job ranks last.

When you choose the best option, you often have to make a **trade-off**—*give up one thing in order to get something you want more*. For Jill, one trade-off she might have to make would be between the money she would earn at the fast-food place and the nursing experience she would gain as a candy striper.

Step 6: Act on Your Decision. Making decisions becomes just a mental exercise if you do not act on them. Once Jill decides what to do, she should act as soon as possible. If she waits too long, the situation may change. The hospital director and the restaurant manager may hire other workers if Jill does not give them her decision quickly.

Step 7: Evaluate Your Decision. The last step in the decision-making process is to evaluate the decision. When you **evaluate** something, you *judge the worth of it*. This step can cut down on the risk of making a decision that is not satisfactory. No one can ever know for sure what the result of a decision will be. Every decision involves a **risk factor,** *the chance that the choice you make will have more disadvantages and fewer advantages than expected.*

There are two reasons for this risk factor. One is that it is impossible to know all the possible advantages and disadvantages of an alternative. The second is that a new circumstance can turn up to change the situation. Because no one can predict the future, risk is involved in every decision.

You can, however, reduce the risks involved in decision making by following three guidelines. First, gather as much information as you can about each option. Your research may turn up some important facts about an option that can help you figure out its advantages and disadvantages. If Jill, for example, speaks to the hospital director and the restaurant manager one more time after she determines her options, she may discover some new and important aspects about each job. Maybe there is a special scholarship fund for candy stripers. Maybe the restaurant offers flexible hours. The more you know about an option, the better you can estimate its advantages and disadvantages.

Second, be flexible when you evaluate the results of each decision. What will you do if your decision does not work out the way you had expected? A decision may, of course, work out better than you had planned, with more advantages and fewer disadvantages. The opposite can happen, too. The decision may turn out to have more disadvantages and fewer advantages than you thought it would.

When you step back to take stock of a decision, remember that few decisions are per-

You have a good chance of using your resources effectively if you plan your career carefully.

manent. If one option does not work out the way you thought it would, you may be able to try a different option.

If your decision is not satisfactory, you should follow the third guideline: Evaluate the way you reached the decision. Did you skip a step or not carry it through thoroughly? Did you consider every option? Did you determine all your goals and rank them accurately? Looking at the process itself can help you improve your decision-making ability as time goes on.

The Benefits

The decision-making process has a certain cost. You must spend time and energy putting it to work. For important decisions, though—such as what career to pursue—the process offers five benefits that more than repay its costs.

1. Wise use of resources. The planning involved in the decision-making process gives you a good chance of using all your resources effectively. If you are planning to enter the commercial art field, it is wise to find out which career areas have the best employment outlook. Taking the time to look at different books and magazine articles that give job forecasts will give you a better chance of preparing for a career area in which you will be able to find a job.
2. Independence. The steps involved in the decision-making process can help you rely on yourself instead of on others. It is natural to be influenced by the opinions of other people. If you make your own decisions, you will be making career choices that match your personal goals. Learning to make your own decisions can also give you confidence.
3. New options. Studying the career situation carefully gives you a chance to discover new options. As the number of options grows, so do your chances of finding a career that allows you to meet your goals.
4. Easier decision making. The ranking system in the decision-making process lets you see the relative importance of your goals. The system also shows you how well various career options can help you meet your goals. That can simplify the task of selecting a career.
5. Fewer problems. Thinking about the results of each option allows you to become aware of possible difficulties. Evaluating your decisions serves a similar purpose. If you see a problem, you sometimes can do something to prevent it from growing or continuing.

The decision-making process, then, can give you greater control over your life and the work you will do. Using the process can help you find a career area that will bring you great satisfaction.

YOUR DECISION-MAKING ROLES

A career decision is just one out of many decisions you make each day, each month, each year. As noted before, some decisions are simple and routine, whereas others are large or complicated. Whatever the size of the decision, though, it involves one or more of the roles you play in our society. You, like the other members of society, act as worker, citizen, and consumer. These roles can be intertwined, as they often are in career decisions.

Your Worker Role

In your **worker role**, *you make decisions about how you will use your time, energy, and skills to earn money.* You do not have to actually be working in order to be involved in this role. You are in the worker role when you choose a career and decide how to train for it. Decisions about where to work and the way you will do your job also fit into this category.

The amount of money you earn at your job will help determine your consumer role.

Your Citizen Role

In your **citizen role**, *you make decisions about how to use and contribute to public resources.* **Public resources** are *the services local, state, and federal governments provide.* Many hospitals and parks fit into that category. When Jill considers the job as a candy striper, she is acting in both her worker role and her citizen role. She will be using the job to help her decide on a career. The position, though, is a volunteer one: Jill would receive no money for working in the hospital. She would, however, be working for the public good, while receiving training at the same time.

There are many decisions you will make as a citizen. Deciding on which candidate to vote for in an election is one such choice. The person elected will help decide how tax dollars will be spent on public resources and how citizens will be served by public resources. Elected officials also help decide policy regarding police and fire protection. They may direct services such as snow removal and trash pickup. Elected officials also administer public resources such as parks and libraries.

Deciding to do volunteer work and to vote are just two of a number of decisions that would place you in your citizen role. Giving a contribution to the political party of your choice or writing a letter to the local newspaper about a community issue would also place you in this role. Many of your daily decisions also involve you as a citizen. You are acting as a responsible citizen, for example, whenever you avoid littering and treat public property with care.

In a sense, you are also working for the public good when you do your job as well as you can. The work Jill might do in the fast-food restaurant, for example, can help protect the health and safety of the people who eat there.

Your Consumer Role

You act as a consumer in many of your daily decisions. In your **consumer role**, *you decide how to use your resources to obtain and use the goods and services you want.* Jill is a consumer when she makes plans to save money for advanced schooling. Later, she will use her money to purchase an education, which falls into the category of services.

You make dozens of consumer decisions each week. For example, you are a consumer when you buy lunch or a new record or when you pay a hairdresser to give you a haircut. You are also making a consumer decision when you decide to save money by doing a project yourself. For instance, you may prefer to change the oil in your car yourself instead of paying a garage attendant to do it. Then, you have to pay only for the oil. Even when no money changes hands, you are being a consumer. You can trade goods and services with someone else. For example, instead of buying a new record, you might decide to trade records with a friend.

Your job helps determine your consumer role. The amount of money you have to spend on goods and services will depend on what you do for a living. Your job will also affect the goods and services you want and need. Jill, for example, will need to buy comfortable shoes for either summer job, because she will be on her feet all day.

YOUR DECISIONS AND OTHER PEOPLE

Many of your decisions act like a pebble dropped into a pool of water. The ripples from the dropped pebble widen and widen, spreading outward from the center. The impact of your decisions, too, can create an ever-widening effect that touches others as well as yourself.

You belong to a number of groups, as shown in Figure 4.2. You are a member of a family. You are a student. You are also a resident of the town or city in which you live. In addition, you are a citizen of a nation. Your membership in these groups is automatic. You may also belong to groups that you have joined as a matter of choice. Maybe you are in the school chorus or the Future Business Leaders of America (FBLA). If you work, you are part of a group of employees.

You often make decisions that touch the lives of the other members of your family. Their wants and needs are affected by your choices. For example, if Jill earns some money for her education, she will reduce the financial burden on her parents. As time goes on and you shoulder more responsibility, you will be making even more decisions that affect the lives of others. Whenever you make an important decision, you will need to consider the values and goals of others along with your own.

Your Decisions as a Citizen

On a larger scale, your decisions affect society. The manner in which you choose to do your job will affect the people with whom you work. If you do your job well, your efforts may make their work easier. If you do your job poorly, you may be placing an extra burden on those around you. Consumers can also be affected by workers' on-the-job decisions and performance. These can determine whether a product is made well or a service is performed well.

Your decisions as a citizen can make a difference in the lives of other citizens. If the candidates you support are elected to office, they will make policy decisions that will affect all citizens, not just those who voted for them. In your citizen role, you can help change the lives of people on local, state, national, and worldwide levels.

Chapter 4 Making Decisions About Work

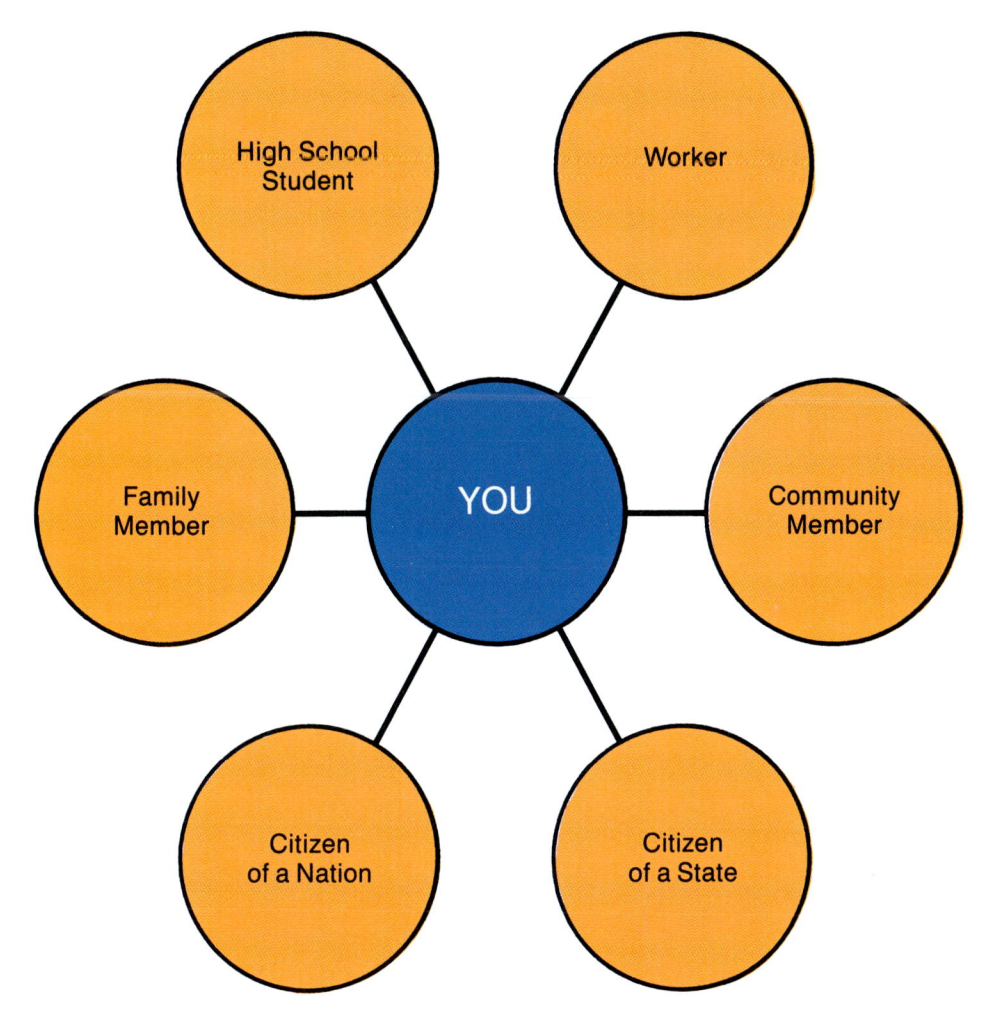

Figure 4.2 You Are a Member of Many Groups

Your Consumer Decisions

Whenever you make a consumer choice, you are also influencing the lives of others. You choose one brand of shoes over another, one gas station out of many, and so on. Each time you do so, you are acting as a consumer voter in the marketplace. With your dollars, you are electing to buy one good or service instead of another. Businesses that attract the dollars of a large enough group of consumers will succeed. Those that do not, will not.

Your reactions to products that you buy also involve consumer decisions. If something you buy does not work properly, your complaint to the company may help improve the product. The results can bring satisfaction to many consumers. When you decide to recommend a particular product to another consumer, you are also helping a company's chances for success. When businesses are successful, this creates jobs for workers. When businesses fail, workers lose their jobs. Ultimately, then, your consumer choices affect people's jobs, for better

The decisions made by others in their worker roles affect your life, too. The quality of the goods you purchase depends on the kind of job various workers decide to do.

or for worse. Your own job may be among those affected.

THE ECONOMY

Not only do your decisions affect the lives of others, but the reverse is true as well. Decisions made by others in their roles as workers, citizens, and consumers affect your life. Your clothing, your housing, and your food depend in part upon the kind of job various workers decide to do. The courses you study and the textbooks you use depend in large part upon the choices made by people acting in their citizen roles as members of the local school board. The choices people make in the marketplace as consumers help determine the products that are offered.

All in all, the personal decisions made by millions of people have a great impact on the way our economy works. An **economy** is *a system of producing, distributing, and consuming goods and services*. The resulting prices and the number and types of jobs available can affect your career decisions. Learning about your role in the economy, then, is one part of making a satisfactory career choice.

Your Role in the Economy

All the kinds of decisions you just read about are economic in nature. **Economics** is *the study of the way people and governments use their resources to reach their goals*. According to that definition, your career decisions are basically economic choices. You will be using your resources to achieve your job goals. As a worker, you will be involved in the American economy. Whether you decide to be a nurse, a computer programmer, a welder, or a salesperson, you will be involved in some aspect of that system.

You as a Resource

Earlier, you read about your personal resources—the time, energy, skills, and money at your command. When you are a worker, you

As a worker, this man is a human resource. He is using his time, skills, and energy to produce goods.

will be acting as a human resource. **Human resources** are *workers who use their time, skills, and energy to produce goods and services.* In other words, workers provide labor. In return for their labor, they receive money.

Workers make it possible for the economy to function. Once you enter a career, you will be taking your place in the economic system of this country. Your career decision, then, is one that can have an effect upon many people.

MAIN POINTS

- Most of our decisions involve how we use our time, energy, skills, and money. These personal resources are limited.
- The more important a decision is, the longer lasting its consequences are likely to be. Major decisions, such as choice of a career, also use up more of our personal resources.
- There is a logical process for making major decisions. The seven steps of this process are: define the problem; identify and rank your goals; determine the options; analyze the advantages and disadvantages of each option; choose the best option; act on your decision; and evaluate your decision.
- The decision-making process can help you use your resources wisely, be independent, discover new options, make decisions more easily, and encounter fewer problems.
- You play several roles when you make decisions. You act as a worker when you decide how to use your time, energy, and skills to earn money. You are a citizen when you decide how to use and contribute to public resources. You are a consumer when you decide how to obtain goods and services. In these three different roles, you affect many other people through your decisions.
- As a worker, you will be involved in the American economy. Workers act

as human resources by using their time, energy, and skills to produce goods and services. In return for their labor, they receive money.

Terms to Know

Use the following terms to fill in the blanks of the sentences below.

citizen role
consumer role
economics
economy
evaluate
goal
human resources
impulse
option
personal resources
public resource
risk factor
trade-off
worker role

1. When you follow a sudden desire to act, you are obeying a(n) _____.
2. Your time, money, energy, and skills are your _____.
3. A result that you want from a decision is an example of a(n) _____.
4. Another term for choice is _____.
5. When you judge the worth of something, you _____ it.
6. The chance that a choice will have more disadvantages than you expected is called the _____.
7. Your community library is an example of a(n) _____.
8. Deciding how you will use your resources to earn money places you in your _____.
9. Whenever you buy something, you are acting in your _____.
10. The workers in an economy are its _____.
11. When you give up one thing in order to get something you want more, you are making a(n) _____.
12. The study of the way people and governments use their resources is called _____.
13. Working for the public good places you in your _____.
14. A system of producing, distributing, and consuming goods and services is a(n) _____.

Chapter Review

1. List the four shortcuts we often use when making simple decisions.
2. How can you decide the level of importance of a decision?
3. Explain why your choice of a career is a major decision.
4. List the seven steps in the decision-making process.
5. What are three ways to reduce the risk factor of a decision?
6. Describe the five benefits of using the decision-making process.
7. Explain the three different roles you play in the economy.
8. Briefly describe the different ways in which your decisions can affect others.
9. In what ways can the decisions made by other people affect you?
10. How do workers act as human resources?

Activities

1. Make a chart with four columns. In the first column, list five decisions you recently made on the basis of experience. In the second column, list five decisions you made from habit. In the third column, list five decisions you made by following someone else's example. In the fourth column, place five decisions that were based on impulse. Which of these 20 decisions do you think could have turned out better if you had used the decision-making process? Why?

2. Working in teams, explore the different opportunities for part-time and summer work in your community. Assign different teams to interview school counselors, youth employment services, local merchants, the chamber of commerce, and so on. (The information librarian in your local library may give you additional advice about where to go and whom to see.) Each team should then write a brief description of each job the team learns about. Post the descriptions on a bulletin board in the classroom. Which jobs do you consider most attractive? Why? What does that suggest to you about your values and career interests?

3. Interview a friend or relative about a major decision she or he recently made. Ask questions based on each of the seven steps of the decision-making process. Would the person have chosen the same option today? Why or why not?

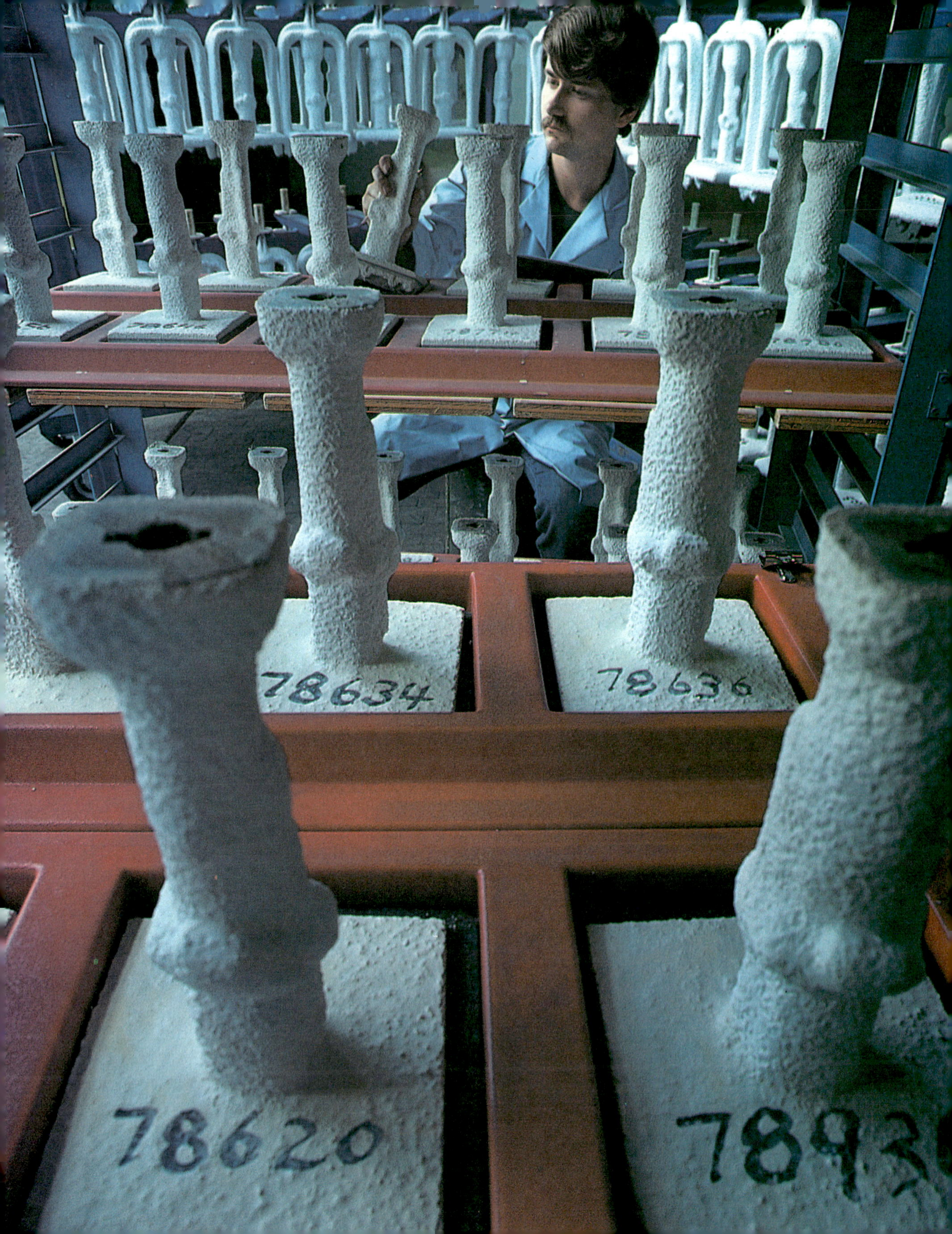
78634
78636
78620

PART TWO
Entering the Work Force

Part Two helps you identify the job you want and tells you how to go about finding it. You will first learn about how different businesses operate and what roles people play in making a business a success. The advantages of different kinds of career training are outlined, as are various sources of job leads. You will learn successful ways of applying for jobs, including how to write effective resumes. You will discover what to do and what not to do in an interview. Finally, you will examine your rights and responsibilities once you enter the work force.

Chapter **5**

How Business Works

OBJECTIVES

This chapter will enable you to:

- define business and describe the three general types of business.
- explain profits and losses.
- outline the way in which businesses combine resources.
- identify the four vital roles people play in business and describe each one.
- point out the advantages and disadvantages of each of the five major organizational forms of business.
- give reasons for the important economic role played by small businesses.
- describe the characteristics of nonprofit organizations.

Calvin

Last summer, I really had to make some money, but I couldn't find a summer job—not even a part-time one. Then one day, I was mowing the lawn when my neighbor came over. He told me that he and his family were going on vacation for a month, and he wanted to hire me to mow their lawn while they were gone. I said, "Sure!" Suddenly, I had a brainstorm. Lots of people in my neighborhood go away in the summer. I figured they would need their lawns mowed—and I also figured that I was just the guy to do it for them.

Well, it didn't take long before things started happening. I put a couple of signs for Calvin's Custom Lawn Care on the bulletin boards in the local supermarkets, and the calls started coming in. The first day, I got three customers. The next day, I got three more. It was becoming too good to be true. Pretty soon, I was swamped with work. Calvin's Custom Lawn Care needed more than Calvin.

I got my friends Paula and Darryl to help out. I was going to pay them an hourly wage that would give me some profit, too. They said, "No fair. After all, we're using our lawn mowers and our cars. We think we should be your partners—all you did was put up a couple of signs."

"But I had the idea," I said.

"Your idea isn't pushing those lawn mowers. We are!" they answered.

I ended up making them my partners. My profits are somewhat lower, but the work load is lighter. We share the responsibility for doing the paperwork, getting gas for the mowers, and arranging for repairs. It's good experience learning what it's like to run a business. I like it. This could help me decide what I want to do after high school, and even beyond that. I've always been good at fixing things. Now I know I'm good at dealing with people and at doing a good job that pleases them. Maybe someday I'll start up my own business, as some sort of repair person. That's an idea I like.

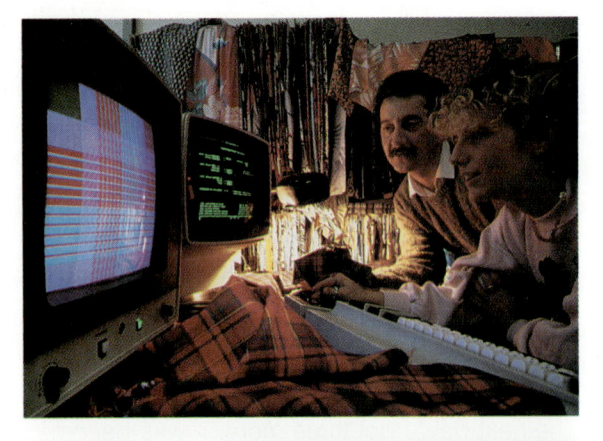

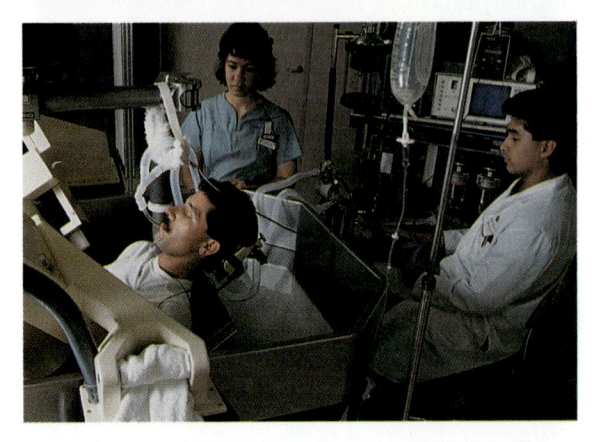

All businesses fall into three broad categories. This textile worker is a producer who helps create goods. A supermarket is a distributor that makes goods available to consumers. Health technicians provide a service.

WHAT BUSINESS DOES

Calvin has already learned some important facts about business and what it takes to succeed at a job. A **business** is *a person or group that produces goods and services for profit*. There are so many goods and services that we could never think of them all. Many businesses require very special skills. They all reward work that is done efficiently and quickly. They also value workers who are friendly and willing to learn new methods.

Three Kinds of Businesses

All businesses can be placed in one of three broad categories. There are **producers** of goods, which are *businesses that actually make the goods*. **Distributors** are *businesses that help get goods to producers and consumers*. Finally, there are **services,** *businesses that perform actions of value for consumers or other businesses*. That is the kind of business Calvin's Custom Lawn Care is.

Producers. Extractors, processors, and manufacturers are all producers. **Extractors** *take raw materials from the earth, air, or water*. Miners, farmers, and fishers are all examples of extractors. **Processors** *change raw materials into a usable form*. There are, for instance, factories that remove minerals from ore. There are also some that remove bones and other nonedible parts from fish. **Manufacturers** *use raw materials and processed goods to make finished products*. This category includes factories that turn minerals into house paint and those that turn fish bones into fertilizer.

Distributors. Distributors make goods available to consumers and producers. Some distributors help producers make exchanges. A distributor may buy tomatoes from farmers to sell to makers of spaghetti sauce. Distributors are called wholesalers and retailers. A **wholesaler** *buys goods from producers to sell to other producers and retailers*. A furniture

Chapter 5 How Business Works

wholesaler, for example, first buys large amounts of furniture from many manufacturers and then resells it to retail stores. The **retailer** *sells the product directly to consumers*. Retail clothing stores and shoe stores are among the many retailers that buy goods from producers or wholesalers to sell to the general public.

Many businesses deal in actions instead of objects. These businesses are called services. They provide actions of value to other businesses or to consumers. Services aimed at helping other businesses include those that provide research and information. Other services transport goods. Still other service businesses supply and repair equipment.

There are also financial services that help businesses and consumers manage their money. Consumers also receive services directly. These consumer services include shoe repair, piano tuning, and hairstyling. Calvin's Custom Lawn Care is also a consumer service.

HOW BUSINESSES EARN PROFITS

You may deal with several businesses every day. You may eat in a restaurant, go to a movie, and buy a new record. Each business is comprised of an individual or a group of individuals who produce goods or services for profit. **Profit** is *the amount by which a business's income exceeds its expenses*.

Profits and Losses

All businesses have the same goal: They want to earn a profit. The owners of a business want to use part of the money they earn to satisfy their own needs and wants. They cannot spend all the money they take in on themselves. Part—often most—of it must go back into the business. The owners have to pay salaries, rent, utility bills, and other expenses to keep the business going or to help it grow when expansion seems wise. Calvin and his friends need to buy gas for the mowers they use, and they must pay sharpening and repair costs as well. They also need to buy rakes and plastic bags. Only after they do all that can they count their profits.

Someone always invests time and money to start a business. Sometimes, though, a business does not take in as much money selling a product or service as it spent to provide it. Then, the owner or owners suffer a loss. A **loss** is *the amount by which a business's expenses exceed its income*. The owner of a bookstore, for example, has a number of expenses. He or she must pay salaries, rent, heat, and electricity. There are also fixtures and equipment to buy. In addition, the owner must buy books to sell. If not enough books are sold, the owner will not take in enough money to meet expenses.

The risk of suffering losses does not apply just to small business. Even giant corporations have no guarantee of a profit. A new product they introduce can fail. A number of years ago, one large corporation introduced red facial tissues. Consumers did not buy them, and the company had to withdraw the tissues from the marketplace—at a loss.

Why do people accept the risk of starting and running a business? One answer is the possibility of profit. If someone really believes she or he can make a profit, then that person may start a business. Calvin was sure he could earn money mowing lawns. That belief prompted him to begin his business.

How Profits Benefit Society

Without the reward of profits, no one would be willing to start a business. Very few goods and services would be produced. There would be little for consumers to choose from. In addition, the desire for profits leads businesses to produce more and better goods and services at lower prices. This benefits consumers. When business owners use profits to make their businesses grow, the result is that more and more affordable goods and services are available.

This growth creates new jobs for more people.

Profits can benefit many people. A corporation may be owned by thousands of people. Each owner gets a share of the profits. Finally, federal, state, and local governments tax profits that are over a certain amount. These taxes are used to provide services such as road repair, school construction, and police protection as shown in Figure 5.1.

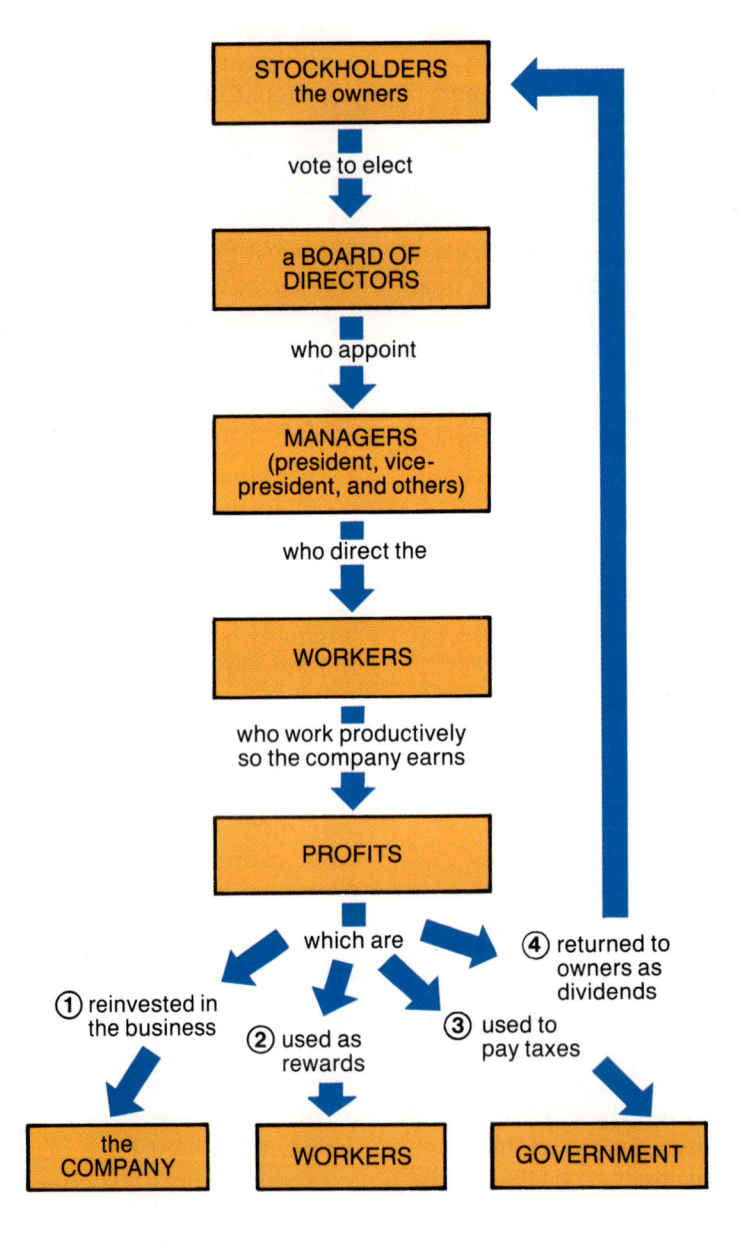

```
STOCKHOLDERS
the owners
        │
   vote to elect
        ▼
a BOARD OF DIRECTORS
        │
    who appoint
        ▼
MANAGERS
(president, vice-
president, and others)
        │
   who direct the
        ▼
WORKERS
        │
who work productively
so the company earns
        ▼
PROFITS
     which are
①reinvested in    ②used as    ③used to    ④returned to
 the business     rewards      pay taxes    owners as
                                             dividends
     ▼              ▼            ▼
   the           WORKERS      GOVERNMENT
  COMPANY
```

Figure 5.1 **How a Corporation Operates**

BUSINESSES NEED RESOURCES

All businesses need three kinds of resources to produce goods and services.

- **Human resources** are *people who use their time, energy, and skills to produce what is offered to the public.*
- **Natural resources** are *the raw materials that can be taken from the earth, air, or water.*
- **Capital resources** are *tools, machines, and buildings.*

Businesses use money to acquire these different kinds of resources. *Money used in trade, manufacture, or business* is often called **capital**. (Be careful not to confuse money, or capital, with capital resources. Money is used to get *all* resources.)

Though bigger businesses use more resources, all businesses, even the smallest and simplest, use the same kinds of resources. At Calvin's Custom Lawn Care, the human resources are Calvin, Paula, and Darryl. The main natural resource is the gasoline used to fuel the mowers and the cars they use to transport themselves and their equipment. Their capital resources are the mowers, lawn edgers, rakes, and cars. Larger businesses have far more extensive capital resources. These often include buildings and land as well as equipment.

WHERE PEOPLE FIT IN

No business can exist without people. It takes people to extract minerals from the earth and fish from the sea, and it takes people to turn these raw materials into useful products. It also takes people to sell and distribute what other people make. Even in factories where robots are being used to perform certain tasks, people are needed to keep the robots functioning. There are four vital roles that people can play in any kind of business.

No business can operate without people. These workers are some of the millions who help extract natural resources from land and sea.

Entrepreneurs

Calvin's business did not exist until he had an idea about how to combine the three kinds of resources—human, natural, and capital. By doing so, Calvin played the important role of entrepreneur. An **entrepreneur** is *someone who has an idea, takes risks, and combines resources to produce goods or services for profit.* Entrepreneurs, then, are the people who start businesses.

The idea of a successful entrepreneur can grow. Jean Nidetch began Weight Watchers by holding meetings with a few women in her home. Today, Weight Watchers has branches in countries around the world. The same kind of story can be told about dozens of other entrepreneurs.

All successful entrepreneurs, including Calvin, share three qualities. The first is the imagination and knowledge to come up with an idea for a product or service that people will

Many local businesses are started by entrepreneurs who combine resources to provide goods or services people want.

want to buy. He or she must also believe it can be produced and sold at a profit. The idea may be so new that no one else offers a competing product or service, or it may be a new solution to an old problem, as with Calvin. He realized that people in his community needed to have their lawns cared for while they were away on vacation.

The second quality all successful entrepreneurs must have is their willingness to take risks. There is never a guarantee that enough customers will want to buy a lawn care service, a weight-loss program, or anything else. Entrepreneurs believe that if they plan carefully and work hard, they will find people who will want their product or service.

The third quality all successful entrepreneurs must have is an ability to combine human, natural, and capital resources. This ability requires knowledge and money. Entrepreneurs must know how to combine resources to create goods or services people will want. The giant cosmetics firm of Helena Rubenstein began when she mixed a skin cream in her kitchen. People liked the product, and the company was launched. However, the company could not have been started without money. An entrepreneur must either have the money or be able to raise the money needed to produce the product or service.

Businesses require the work of other people besides an entrepreneur. In order to function,

Chapter 5 How Business Works

businesses also need owners, managers, and workers.

Owners

Owners are *people who invest money in a business*. Entrepreneurs often own the businesses they start, as Calvin did for a while. Often, though, a business needs more money than the entrepreneur alone can provide. This is especially true if the business is going to grow. Once others invest money in a business, they become part-owners. They gain the advantage of a share in the profits, but they also have the disadvantage of sharing in the responsibility for any losses.

Managers

Managers are also a necessary part of any business. **Managers** are *the people who turn the goals of a business into directions for the workers to follow*. Managers take care of four functions: planning, organizing, directing, and controlling. Sometimes, they perform more than one function at a time.

- **Planning** means *finding the best way to meet the goals of the business.*
- **Organizing** means *arranging resources to carry out the plans*. It involves thinking through tasks and assigning personnel to perform them. Calvin and his partners, for example, must figure out who is going to mow which lawns, and when.
- **Directing** means *coordinating how the different resources are used*. Directing may involve teaching workers how to perform their tasks. Managers must also motivate workers to take pride in the business and do their jobs well.
- **Controlling** means *examining results to be sure goals have been met*. Managers also consider how to improve the quality of the good or service that is produced.

Part of a manager's job may be to teach workers how to perform their tasks.

Workers

Businesses depend heavily upon workers. **Workers** are *people who make the product or provide the service that a business sells*. The workers make it possible for a business to meet its goals, but only if they have the following qualities:

- Workers should be competent. They should be able to do assigned tasks well.
- Workers should be reliable. They should be at work on time and work well on a steady basis.
- Workers should be productive. They should do a reasonable amount of work.
- Workers should be efficient. They should use resources wisely and not waste time.
- Workers should work safely. They should use equipment properly and carefully.
- Workers should have initiative. They should be able to see that something needs to be done and be willing to start the task on their own. (In some companies, this is known as being a *self-starter*.)
- Workers should be adaptable. They should be open to learning new things.
- Workers should be cooperative. They should be able to work well with others.

- Workers should be honest. They should deal truthfully with other workers and with superiors.

HOW BUSINESSES ARE ORGANIZED

There are five ways of organizing a business. Each has a different legal definition. Each also has different advantages and disadvantages for owners and workers.

Sole Proprietorships

When Calvin decided to start mowing lawns to earn some money, he put ads on some local bulletin boards and got customers. That, simply, was how he started a business. For a short while, Calvin's Custom Lawn Care was a **sole proprietorship**—*a business owned by just one person.*

There are no legal requirements for forming a sole proprietorship. No contracts need to be drawn up or official papers signed. Some local governments do require sole owners in some businesses to get a license. Calvin could not open a hot dog stand or any other place that sold food without getting a license.

Sole proprietorships have many advantages. Clearly, they are easy to form. Often, you need only a small amount of money to start one. Profits are taxed at the rate for personal income, because they make up your income. (This rate is usually lower than that for corporate income.) You are free to make all the decisions. You also get to enjoy all the profits.

Problems can result when a business is owned by just one person. He or she may have a harder time raising money than owners of other types of businesses. The firm's success may be limited because it depends on only the owner's abilities. That is something Calvin realized when more jobs came in than he could handle on his own. Also, the company may end if the owner dies or becomes too ill to operate the business. The biggest disadvantage is that the owner has **personal liability,** which means that *the owner is responsible for all business debts*. If the business fails, the owner's personal car or house or bank account can be used to pay its bills.

Partnerships

When Paula and Darryl became co-owners of Calvin's Custom Lawn Care, the business became a partnership. A **partnership** is *a business owned by two or more persons*. At least one of the partners has personal liability for the firm's debts. Partners usually enter into a legal agreement that explains how the partnership will work. It may say exactly how much money and work each partner will contribute to the business.

Partnerships have a number of advantages. They are almost as easy to form as sole proprietorships. Their earnings are also taxed at the individual rate. And each partner contributes her or his skills. Partnerships often can raise more money than sole proprietorships. One reason is that more than one person may put money into the firm.

Yet, partnerships have disadvantages, too. None of the partners has complete control of the business, and all must share the profits. Like sole proprietors, at least one of the partners has personal liability for debts. Also, if one quits the business, the remaining partner or partners may be forced to go out of business if they do not have enough funds to pay the departing partner for his or her share of the business. The business may also end if one partner dies and the others do not have the money to buy the deceased partner's share of the business from his or her heirs. Finally, strong disagreements among partners can paralyze the business.

A limited partnership solves some of the problems of partnerships. In a **limited partnership**, *the liability of some partners is limited to the amount of money they invested in the business*. Their personal property cannot be

Chapter 5 How Business Works

used to pay the firm's debts. At least one partner, however, must have unlimited liability.

Corporations

Calvin's parents work for a large corporation that has a branch in a nearby town. A **corporation** is *a business owned by stockholders*. It is run according to its **charter**, which is *a legal document that states the corporation's name, its business, and its procedures*. The charter is filed with the state in which the business is incorporated.

A corporation raises money by issuing and selling stock. **Stock** is *a share or shares of ownership in a corporation*. These shares can be transferred from one person to another. *People who own the stock* are called **stockholders**. The stockholders own the corporation. A corporation may have just a few stockholders, or it may have many thousands. The price of individual shares of stock varies greatly. You can buy stock in some companies for under $10 a share, while in others, they cost more than $100 per share. The stockholders do not run the corporation directly. Instead, they elect a board of directors to oversee the business. The directors appoint managers to run the company. Figure 5.1 illustrates how a corporation is organized.

Stockholders hope to receive dividends from their investment. A **dividend** is *the part of the profits of a corporation that its directors decide*

Figure 5.2 Comparing the Three Main Ways of Organizing a Business

	Sole Proprietorship	Partnership	Corporation
Ease of formation	Very easy	Fairly easy	Fairly complex
Money needed to form	Very little	Fairly little	Large amounts needed
Ability to raise money	Can raise little	Can raise more	Can raise large amounts
Ease in making decisions	Very easy	Fairly easy	Fairly easy
Amount of owner control of business	Complete control	Partial control	Little control
Number of people whose skills can be used	One	Few	Many
Extent of owner's liability for business debts	Unlimited personal liability	Unlimited personal liability for at least one partner	Limited for all owners
Taxes due	Personal income	Personal income	Corporate and personal income

to pay the stockholders. Dividends are based on the number of shares that have been sold. The more shares someone owns, the more money she or he receives. All profits do not automatically go to stockholders. Taxes must first be taken out. The board of directors may decide to use some of the profits to buy more resources for the company. There are even times when stockholders may not receive any dividends at all. This may occur when the corporation does not make a profit for a year or when the directors decide to use all the profits to improve the company. That is a risk people take when they buy stock. Also, individual stockholders of a huge public corporation have little control over its actions.

There are two kinds of corporations in business to make a profit. In a **public corporation**, *stock is traded on the open market.* Anyone can buy shares, but people do not buy shares directly. Instead, they use the services of a stockbroker. Most major corporations, such as IBM and Mobil, are public ones.

In a **private corporation**, *stock is held by only a few people.* Often, they are members of the same family. The general public cannot buy shares. One well-known private corporation is Mars, Inc., the manufacturer of M & M's and other candies. Many businesses start as private corporations and then become public.

Corporations have certain disadvantages. Profits are taxed twice, first as corporate income and then again as personal income. Corporations must obey many legal restrictions and reporting requirements.

There are advantages, too. Corporations can raise far more money than the simpler forms of business. That is why most of the country's largest businesses are corporations. Also, corporations have an ongoing life. The shares of a stockholder who dies can be transferred to someone else. Finally, stockholders have only limited liability for a company's debts. If the business fails, they lose only what they invested. Their personal property is safe.

Figure 5.2 compares the three main ways of organizing a business.

Cooperatives

A **cooperative** is *an enterprise, owned by more than one person or business, that acts for the benefit of its members.* Many small businesses form **selling cooperatives**, which *act as agents to help members sell their goods.* A large cooperative may have sales representatives who visit markets throughout this country as well as overseas. Many farmers are members of cooperatives. **Buying cooperatives** are made up of *businesses or consumers whose purpose is to save money by buying products in large quantities.* Your local health food store may be a *co-op,* as such groups are often called.

Franchises

You are probably a customer of several franchises. If you eat at a McDonald's, you may be eating at a franchise. In a **franchise**, *one business sells another business the right to use its name and sell its products in a certain area.* The buyer of the franchise is called the **franchisee**. The seller of the franchise is the **franchisor**. The franchisee pays the franchisor a fee or a percentage of the sales, or both. A legal contract defines the terms of the agreement and the duties of each party.

Operating a franchise is a good way for a person with little money to gain some of the advantages of running a business. The franchisor may provide useful training and advice. The franchisee is not entirely free to act as he or she wishes, though. The franchisor requires certain procedures and standards to be followed to make sure that each hamburger, for example, is exactly the same as every other one sold by the franchise.

The Importance of Small Businesses

Small businesses, on the order of Calvin's Custom Lawn Care, make up more than 95 percent of the businesses in the United States. They produce over 45 percent of the nation's goods and services.

The Small Business Administration classifies a **small business** as *any firm that employs fewer than 500 people*. As you can see in Figure 5.3, retailers make up the largest portion of small businesses.

Most businesses start small. Some stay small, at times because their owners do not want to expand. Others grow to enormous sizes. Apple Computer, Inc., is an example of a small company that quickly grew into a large corporation.

We buy many goods and services from small businesses. Local dry cleaners are often small

This restaurant is a franchise. The company requires that certain procedures be followed to ensure that the food is always prepared the same way.

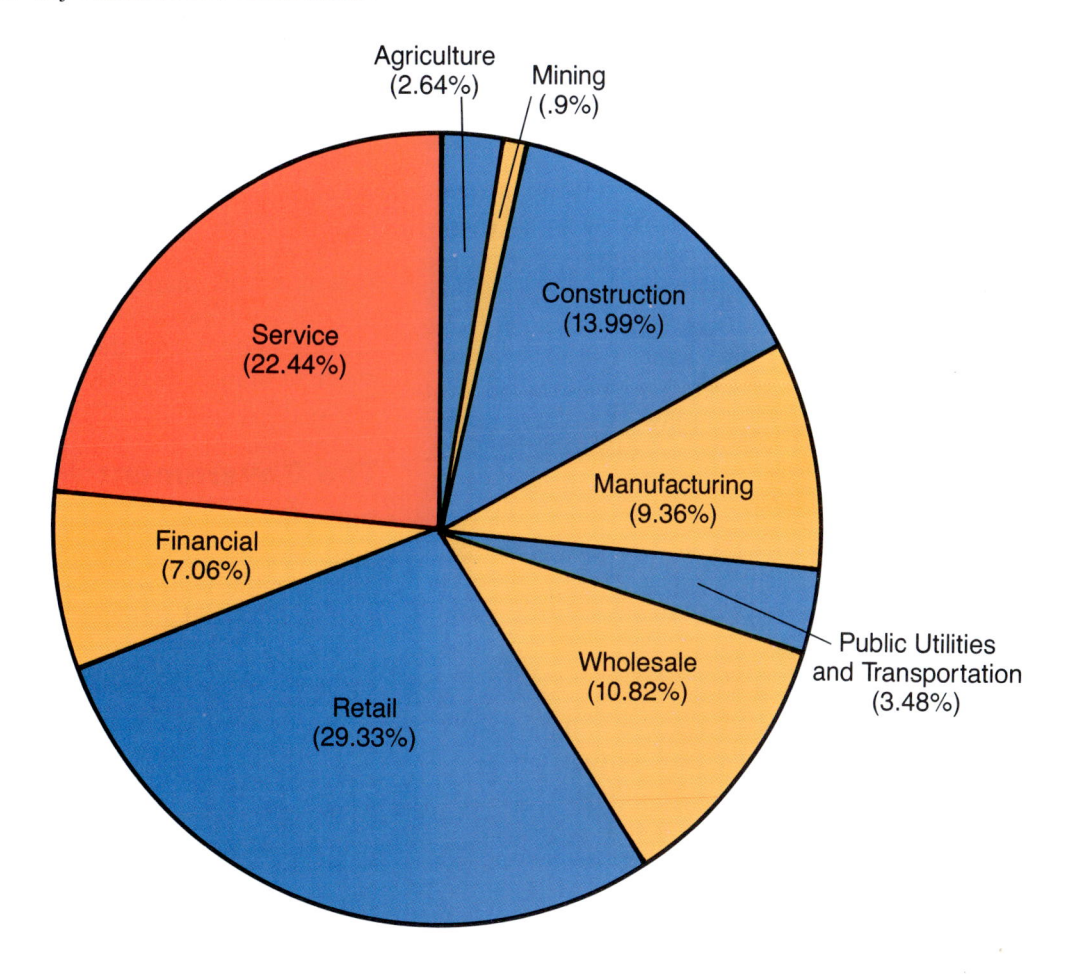

Agriculture (2.64%)
Mining (.9%)
Construction (13.99%)
Manufacturing (9.36%)
Public Utilities and Transportation (3.48%)
Wholesale (10.82%)
Retail (29.33%)
Financial (7.06%)
Service (22.44%)

Figure 5.3 The Proportion of Each Type of Small Business

service firms, as are auto repair shops, locksmiths, and Calvin's Custom Lawn Care. Other small businesses are retailers, such as the corner delicatessen or the Army surplus store. Small construction companies build new homes and offices. Small manufacturers often sell parts to larger ones—buttons to a clothing company or light fixtures to a restaurant.

Small businesses are a large part of our economy, and they create many jobs. In fact, almost 60 percent of all jobs are provided by small businesses.

Small businesses also increase competition, which results in more goods and services at lower prices. They often introduce new products as well. Small firms have produced much of the new computer software and have developed many video games, just to name two examples.

Probably, though, what most of us think of first when we think about small businesses is the personal touch they can provide. Often, local retailers know their customers by name and provide an extra measure of service. They may also have an extra measure of knowledge about the products they sell.

The government recognizes the important role small businesses play in our economy. Keeping them running smoothly is the work of the Small Business Administration (SBA), which Congress set up in 1953. The SBA is an agency of the federal government that provides loans, advice, and information to small businesses. It has about 110 offices throughout the country. The SBA gives small business owners several forms of assistance:

- It guarantees bank loans and makes direct loans to small business owners.
- It works to provide small businesses with a fair share of government contracts.
- It provides information and advice on efficient and profitable ways to run a business.
- It connects small business owners with knowledgeable business people who can advise them.

Nonprofit Organizations

There are organizations that are set up and run like private businesses, but there is one important difference. They are not run to make a profit. A **nonprofit organization** *aims to perform a public service rather than to make a profit.* Any income not used for expenses is used to further the work of the organization. (In a regular business, you will remember, extra income may become profits that are shared by the owners.)

Many familiar organizations are nonprofit. A number of them, such as CARE (the Cooperative for American Relief Everywhere), aim to improve the standard of living of underprivileged people, often on an international basis. There are also health-oriented groups such as the American Cancer Society. Many private schools are nonprofit organizations.

Like a regular business, nonprofit organizations need managers and workers. Like a business, a nonprofit organization can fail if it is not well managed. This can occur if an organization's expenses greatly exceed its operating budget or if the organization does not succeed in raising sufficient funds to continue its work.

The Government

The government of the United States is also a nonprofit organization. There are actually three different levels of government: federal, state, and local. The federal government serves the entire country. There is also a state government for each of the 50 states. There are local governments for many communities within a state. Taken together, the various types of government employ about 18 million people in a wide range of career areas.

The government offers jobs in almost all areas found in private business. There are jobs in publishing, printing, research, transportation, and sanitation, to name a few of the many areas. There are also certain jobs that are found only in government. Many of the jobs in the military, for example, do not exist elsewhere.

Chapter 5 How Business Works

MAIN POINTS

- The purpose of a business is to make a profit. To do this, businesses produce goods and services for consumers to buy.
- There are three kinds of businesses. Producers make the goods. Distributors get the goods to consumers. Services perform actions of value.
- Businesses create goods and services by combining human resources, natural resources, and capital resources. Money is used to buy all resources.
- People play four vital roles in business. Entrepreneurs have the original ideas about how to combine resources. Owners invest money in a business. Managers turn the goals of a business into directions for workers to follow. Workers make the product or provide the service that a business sells.
- A business can be organized as a sole proprietorship, a partnership, a limited partnership, a public corporation, a private corporation, a cooperative, or a franchise.
- Small businesses make up more than 95 percent of the businesses in this country. They produce over 45 percent of the nation's goods and services. Almost 60 percent of all jobs are in small businesses.
- Nonprofit organizations are set up and run like businesses. Their aim is to perform a public service. The government is the largest nonprofit organization of all.

Terms to Know

Use the following terms to fill in the blanks of the sentences below.

business	franchisee	private corporation
buying cooperative	franchisor	processor
capital	human resources	producer
capital resources	limited partnership	profit
charter	loss	public corporation
controlling	manager	retailer
cooperative	manufacturer	selling cooperative
corporation	natural resources	service
directing	nonprofit organization	small business
distributor	organizing	sole proprietorship
dividends	owner	stock
entrepreneur	partnership	stockholder
extractor	personal liability	wholesaler
franchise	planning	worker

1. If a business's expenses exceed its income, the business suffers a(n) _____.
2. A business that has no more than 500 employees is called a(n) _____.
3. A business that helps producers get goods to consumers is a(n) _____.
4. When Calvin put his idea for producing a new service to work, he acted as a(n) _____.
5. The person who is responsible for all of a business's debts has _____.
6. A person who owns shares of stock is called a(n) _____.

7. A person or group of persons who produce goods or services for profit is known as a(n) _____.
8. If you invest money in a business, you become a(n) _____ of the business.
9. The person who turns the goals of a business into directions for the workers is the _____.
10. A person who makes the product or provides the service a business sells is called a(n) _____.
11. An enterprise, owned by more than one person or business, that acts for the benefit of its members is called a(n) _____.
12. A share or shares of ownership in a corporation is called _____.
13. A business that has the right to use the name and sell the products of another in a certain area is a(n) _____.
14. When the income of a business exceeds its expenses, the result is a(n) _____.
15. A business owned by stockholders is a(n) _____.
16. When Paula and Darryl became part-owners of Calvin's Custom Lawn Care, the business became a(n) _____.
17. Directors may vote to pay stockholders less _____ from a corporation's profits.
18. A group that has public service instead of profits as its goal is called a(n) _____.
19. A business that actually makes goods is called a(n) _____.
20. A mining business is an example of a(n) _____.
21. A lawn care business is a type of _____.
22. A factory that removes minerals from ore is a(n) _____.
23. A store that sells goods to consumers is a(n) _____.
24. When Calvin owned his business alone, it was a(n) _____.
25. A business that buys goods from producers to sell to other producers and retailers is called a(n) _____.
26. Workers are also known as _____.
27. Examining results to be sure goals have been met is known as _____.
28. In a(n) _____, not all partners have complete liability.
29. The raw materials used to make goods are called _____.
30. Money is also called _____.
31. The legal document that describes a corporation is its _____.
32. A corporation owned by members of a single family is an example of a(n) _____.
33. Coordinating the use of different resources in a business is known as _____.
34. The person who buys a franchise is the _____.
35. The person who sells a franchise is the _____.
36. A corporation in which anyone can buy shares is a(n) _____.
37. A business's equipment is part of its _____.
38. When farmers band together to sell their crops they form a(n) _____.
39. Consumers can form a(n) _____ to try to save money by purchasing goods in bulk.
40. Finding the best way to meet the goals of a business is known as _____.
41. Arranging resources to carry out tasks is known as _____.
42. A factory that turns fish bones into fertilizer is a(n) _____.

Chapter Review

1. Describe the three different kinds of producers. What is the difference between a wholesaler and a retailer?
2. Can all the money a business takes in be considered profit? Why?
3. In what ways can profits benefit people?
4. Explain the four roles people can play in a business.
5. What are the three qualities that all successful entrepreneurs possess?
6. List five qualities that a worker must possess.
7. What are the advantages and disadvantages of a sole proprietorship? Of a partnership? Of a corporation?
8. What is the purpose of a buying cooperative?
9. List four ways in which small businesses benefit the economy.
10. What is the aim of nonprofit organizations?

Activities

1. Obtain a copy of current federal government job listings at your local library. Make a list of the different types of jobs available, and post it in your classroom.
2. Think of a brand new product or service that you believe people would buy. Describe in writing why you think there is a need for this product or service. How would you go about promoting it?
3. Talk to the owner of a small business in your neighborhood. Ask why she or he started the business, and find out the advantages and disadvantages of owning a small business.
4. Discuss what you think would be the differences between working for a sole proprietorship, a partnership, or a corporation. Which do you think you would prefer? Why?
5. Identify 15 businesses in your community. Identify the form under which each one operates, and classify each as a profit-making or nonprofit organization.

Chapter **6**

Preparing for the Job You Want

OBJECTIVES

This chapter will enable you to:

- explain the value of a high school diploma.
- define a cooperative education program.
- explain the purpose of a training agreement and a training plan.
- identify the advantages of part-time work.
- discuss the learning opportunities of on-the-job training and apprenticeship programs.
- describe the alternative of a career in the military and the training it can provide for a civilian career.
- describe formal education programs beyond high school, such as private vocational schools, community colleges, four-year colleges, correspondence schools, and adult education programs.

Rhonda

Next week, I start work as a chef. Well, not really—more like a chef-in-training. I'm going to be working in that fancy restaurant on Main Street. Can you see me as a head chef someday? I'll be planning the menu, hiring the staff, cooking the dinners. . . .

You know how I got the position? Through the school's cooperative education program. I've wanted to become a chef for several years, but I always thought I would have to apply after high school to one of those hotel and restaurant schools—and *everyone* wants to get into them. I was sure I'd have to graduate from high school before getting a job in a restaurant kitchen. Then, my friend told me about her co-op program. She said I should go talk to the teacher-coordinator, and he would tell me if I could get training while still going to school.

I went to see him, and did he ever open my eyes! He gave me a sheet of paper listing the jobs being offered through the program. Photographer, salesperson, printer—there were over 20 different listings. One of the listings was chef!

After school, I went with the coordinator to the restaurant on Main Street where a co-op student was working. I talked to him, and I was really impressed by what he has learned in a year. Best of all, he has a great job offer from one of the other chefs who is opening her own restaurant. I'll be taking his place when he leaves. I hope I'll get a job offer like his someday.

SCHOOL OR WORK?

What is a diploma? It is a piece of paper with official-sounding words on it. What is a diploma worth? Why is there so much emphasis on graduating from high school?

The Value of a Diploma

First of all, graduating from high school is an important step on the way to a career. For many employers, a diploma is a basic requirement for any job applicant. Although you can get a job without a diploma, you will have many more choices if you are a high school graduate. Newspaper ads often spell it out: "High school grad needed."

Second, studies show that people who graduate from high school make more money during their lifetime than those who do not graduate. The reasons are simple. Graduates receive more training than nongraduates and so are more likely to get higher-paying jobs. Graduates are likely to get jobs with more responsibility than nongraduates. By completing school, graduates have shown the ability to work steadily and complete a project.

Third, employers usually have more than one applicant for any job opening. A high school diploma may be the qualification that tips an employer's decision in your favor. As one employer explained: "Suppose I've got to choose between Griff and Cindi. Griff has a diploma, but Cindi dropped out in her junior year. I'll start wondering about Cindi. Does she have the ability to stick with something? I don't want to have to train another new person in six months. I'd better hire Griff."

A high school diploma is good insurance for many reasons. Perhaps it is not required for the job you currently have in mind, but in a few years, you may decide to pursue a career that calls for a diploma. Another possibility is that you may want additional schooling at a later date. Technical schools, community colleges, and four-year colleges almost always require that you be a high school graduate.

As you can see, there are many advantages to earning a high school diploma. Having one will ensure that your opportunities will not be limited.

COOPERATIVE EDUCATION

For Rhonda, her school's cooperative education program combines the best of two worlds. In **cooperative education**, *students go to school part of each day and work at a business part of each day*. Rhonda will get the training in a restaurant that she wants so much. She will also be able to earn her high school diploma.

A cooperative education program works because three parties cooperate—the school, an employer, and the student. At school, students take two types of courses. First, they take courses to fulfill their requirements for graduation. Second, they take courses that are related to their career interest.

At work, students are trained by the employer and more experienced employees. They also receive support and direction from their **teacher-coordinator**, who is their *bridge between school and work*. The teacher-coordinator is usually the person who helps students find **training stations**, or *job assignments*. He or she is also the person students can go to if they have questions about or problems at their training stations.

The cooperative education program in your school may go by a different name. Perhaps it is called a *work experience program, cooperative occupational education,* or *distributive education*. Although the name may differ, each program has the same goal—to prepare you for the workplace. Generally, co-op programs have similar requirements. For example, you might have to be 16 years old and a junior in high school. All programs require that you have your own social security card.

In most high school co-op programs, students go to school part of the day and work at a business part of the day.

The Training Agreement

When you begin a cooperative education program, you are entering a business arrangement. Your new employer wants to make sure you understand your responsibilities. Your school wants to be certain that you will use your time away from school wisely. Your parents are concerned about what kind of training you will be getting. They also need to be assured that the work is safe and a worthwhile part of your education. You need to know what is expected of you and how you will benefit from the program.

Because the cooperative program is considered a businesslike arrangement, most schools have an official form governing the arrangement. This **training agreement** serves as *a contract between the student, the employer, the school, and the student's parents or guardians.* The agreement lists the duties and responsibilities of each party.

Although agreements may differ from program to program, there are certain responsibilities that are generally the same.

Employer. By signing the agreement, the employer is committed to training the student to do the job outlined in the agreement. The employer also usually agrees to pay the student a fair wage and to provide the student with the same workplace safety conditions given other employees.

Student. Most importantly, the training agreement outlines your responsibilities. By agreeing to these responsibilities, you are actually taking the first step in training—commitment. You are pledging to do your best both on the job and in the classroom. You are agreeing to abide by the same rules and regulations that other employees follow. This means being prompt, dressing neatly, having a good attendance record, and working hard.

```
                District 145, Waverly High School
                   Cooperative Education Program
                   Supervised Experience Agreement
                        School Year 19__ - 19__

Training Station _____
Address _____ Telephone _____
              (City)              (Zip Code)
Student Trainee _____ Date of Birth _____
Social Security Number _____ Telephone _____
Occupational Objective _____
Training Period _____ Beginning Wage _____
Name and position of on-the-job supervisor/instructor:
_____   _____
                                                      (Position)
1.  The student enters this program for the purpose of learning as much as it
    is possible for the employer to provide in the nature of job information,
    skill, and attitudes.
2.  The student will maintain regular attendance both at school and on the job.
    This includes days on the job when school is not in session such as
    Christmas, vacation, etc., if desired by the employer. The student cannot
    receive credit for work on any day that he/she fails to attend school unless
    it has been previously approved by the teacher-coordinator. The student
    is required to call both the school and the employer in advance for
    absences.
3.  Pay and hours are to be determined by the employer. The student shall
    work a minimum of 10 or 15 hours per week depending on the student's
    amount of release time. The employer is urged to keep the student on the
    job for at least the minimum number of hours agreed upon. Hours worked
    on weekends and holidays will count ½ time for the total minimum hrs.
4.  Related class attendance is required by all student participants.
5.  The employer expects honesty, punctuality, cooperation, courtesy, and
    willingness to learn on the part of the student. The employer reserves
    the right to discharge the student for just cause; however, the teacher-
    coordinator requests consultation with the employer prior to such action.
6.  The student shall conform to all regulations of the business establishment
    and the school while on the job.
7.  The student and/or parents are liable in all accidents to and from work.
8.  The teacher-coordinator will make periodic visits to supervise the student
    and/or to consult with the student's employer or immediate supervisor.
9.  An evaluation of job performance will be completed by the employer each
    grading quarter to determine student's grade for school credit. Evaluation
    forms will be provided by the teacher-coordinator.
10. A copy of the student's work attendance record will be provided each grad-
    ing quarter to the teacher-coordinator by the employer.
11. No regular employee shall be displaced by a cooperative education student.
12. Waverly cooperative education programs will not discriminate against any-
    one because of race, color, religion, sex, national origin, or handicap.

_____        _____
         Student                              Coordinator
_____        _____
      Parent or Guardian                     Administrator
_____        _____
         Employer                    Current Date      Employment Date
```

Figure 6.1 A Sample Training Agreement

Parents or Guardians. When they sign the agreement, parents or guardians are stating that they understand the program. They are not directly responsible for your conduct in the program. That is your responsibility.

Teacher-Coordinator. The teacher-coordinator agrees to help you when you have questions or problems that you want to discuss. She or he also agrees to do a periodic evaluation of your progress and to help you improve your performance on the job. Any classroom activities related to your job will be organized by the teacher-coordinator.

The Training Plan

In order to help you reach various job and career goals, a **training plan** is designed. This is *a plan that outlines the knowledge, skills, and attitudes a cooperative education student should develop at his or her training station*. You will learn about such things as the company's history, organizational chart, and procedures. Job skills, of course, will vary from position to position. Rhonda, for example, will be learning about where pots and pans are located, how to operate kitchen machinery, and how to use utensils. She will probably learn a lot about work habits in a kitchen and about how to best organize her work. Interpersonal relations are important as well. For example, Rhonda will have to learn how to take criticism of her work.

Every week, Rhonda will check her accomplishments at the restaurant against what is outlined in her training plan. She will ask her teacher-coordinator for specialized training material to help her achieve goals she has not reached. At the review conference, Rhonda's teacher and employer will meet with her to review her accomplishments, evaluate her progress, and set new goals.

The step-by-step method of the training plan is what sets cooperative education apart from other types of job training. With a training plan, you can keep track of your progress toward your goals. You can see your skills grow, which can help you gain confidence in the workplace. By the time you finish training, you will have gained a definite body of knowledge that will prepare you for the career you have chosen.

WORKING PART-TIME

Another way to get work experience while completing your education is to take a part-time job, either with pay or as a volunteer. About two-thirds of all high school students hold part-time jobs. As mentioned in Chapter 3, part-time work can be very beneficial. You can gain valuable work experience. You can also learn how a business operates. By watching other people, you can learn how to get along with supervisors, co-workers, and customers. You will get valuable practice working in a businesslike manner. If it is a paid position, you will make money.

Different Types of Part-Time Jobs

Many kinds of part-time work are available to students. The kind of job you are able to get will depend on your age and the laws of your state. Both federal and state laws protect the health and safety of people under the age of 18. These laws determine the age at which you can work—and the kinds of work you can do. (Chapter 9 will tell you more about these laws.)

For students younger than their state's minimum working age, there are jobs available through neighbors and friends. Baby-sitting, paper routes, and yard work are the most common. If you would like to increase your chances of getting work as a baby-sitter or yard worker, make yourself better known. Write a simple ad, and make copies of it. Ring your neighbors' doorbells, introduce yourself, and leave your ad, even if you already know the family well. Although you know you can do a job, others may still think of you as a 14-year-old not ready for a part-time job. Also, if your neighbors do not

```
                District 145, Waverly High School
                    Cooperative Education Program
                            Training Plan
                       School Year 1984 - 1985
```

Name: _Jane Smith_   Date: _November 1, 1984_

A. Title of your job: _Sales Associate_   DOT Code: _277-357-066_

B. Description of your job (job duties): _Being friendly and polite, receiving inventory, ringing up sales, stocking shelves when needed_

C. Name and address of your training station: _Brandeis - Gateway_
   Gateway   _Lincoln_   _68510_   _555-8361_
   (Address)   (City)   (Zip Code)   (Phone Number)

D. Name of your job sponsor or supervisor: _Ms. Deb O'Hanlon_

E. Your career objective after adequate experience and training: _I would enjoy being a sales associate supervisor someday._

F. Training activities:
   1. _Receive inventory_
   2. _Ring up sales on the cash register_
   3. _Be friendly and polite to the customers_
   4. _Close registers_
   5. _Make sure sale signs for the next day are up before I leave_

G. Detail or outline of training activities:
   1. _Receive inventory_
      a. _Make sure the right amount of merchandise is received_
      b. _Check for the correct class and department numbers_
      c. _Rearrange shelves so everything fits in an orderly fashion_

   _____ Date Completed _____ Acceptable _____ Not Acceptable
   Comments: _____

   2. _Ring up sales on cash register_
      a. _Push the correct kind of sale (charge, cash, etc.)_
      b. _Put in ID#, quantity, department, class, etc._
      c. _Complete sale_

   _____ Date Completed _____ Acceptable _____ Not Acceptable
   Comments: _____

   3. _Be friendly and polite_
      a. _Always help people find what they are looking for_
      b. _Always smile_
      c. _Make sure customers come first_

   _____ Date Completed _____ Acceptable _____ Not Acceptable
   Comments: _____

   4. _Close cash registers_
      a. _Make sure all the money is there_
      b. _Keep a count of all money - record amount_
      c. _Turn off machine_

   _____ Date Completed _____ Acceptable _____ Not Acceptable
   Comments: _____

   5. _Make sure all signs are up_
      a. _Put up all sale signs in correct areas before I leave_
      b. _____
      c. _____

   _____ Date Completed _____ Acceptable _____ Not Acceptable
   Comments: _____

Figure 6.2 A Sample Training Plan

need your services, they may know other people who do.

You may end up with steady work—lawn care once a week or child care Tuesdays and Thursdays after school. Leave yourself open to several kinds of work. Cleaning out garages is good daytime work on a weekend, but babysitting is a better job for a free weeknight. Some communities even have special employment services to help students find jobs as different kinds of helpers. Check to see if your community has such a service. You should be able to register for free.

If you meet your state's age requirement, there are many more jobs open to you. The following places often hire part-time student workers:

- restaurants
- stores and supermarkets
- gas stations
- recreation and child-care programs
- car washes and parking lots
- farms
- theaters
- amusement parks
- schools and offices (for maintenance and clerical work)

Employers look for certain qualities in part-time job applicants. John D'Ambrosio, the owner of a local fast-food restaurant, explains it this way: "The kids I hire are going to be working with the public. I look for students who are involved in student activities. That shows that they're interested in other people. I look for outgoing people, ones with a good attitude. I also find out what hours they're available. In my business, you have to be able to work weekends."

If your part-time job is in the career field you are considering, that is ideal. You may not be able to find a paying job in the career field you are thinking about, however. An alternative is volunteer work. Many volunteer jobs offer interesting work opportunities. You might get a

Volunteer jobs can offer interesting work opportunities. They can help you find out more about your career interests.

job where you are in charge of casting a play or helping with a crafts program for the elderly. Other jobs might give you the chance to use a word processor at a neighborhood newspaper or run a film projector for the Red Cross. Such jobs may be closer to your long-term career interests. They may even lead to full-time jobs after graduation.

Finding a Part-Time Job

You can start looking for a part-time job by asking relatives or friends who are already working if they know of any available jobs.

You may have the most success by simply inquiring at local stores and businesses. Dress neatly and ask to speak to the manager when you arrive. Explain that you are interested in part-time work. Ask if there are any positions available and if there is a job application you may fill out.

If a manager is interested in you, she or he will notify you when there is an opening. You should check back every so often. Managers receive many applications, and yours might get lost in the pile. By calling back, you are reminding the managers who you are, and you will demonstrate your interest. This will help you stand out from the other applicants.

To find out about volunteer jobs in your community, call local hospitals, Boys' or Girls' Clubs, or the Red Cross. Other possibilities are the YWCA and YMCA, local charities and arts groups, and school recreation programs. Your town may have a central office that matches volunteers with jobs. If so, one phone call will give you a list of places where help is needed. Your guidance counselor can help you begin this type of job search.

ON-THE-JOB TRAINING

What do the manager of a fast-food restaurant, an auto salesperson, and a hospital orderly all have in common? All three probably received their training on the job. Many businesses hire people and train them while they work. As trainees become more experienced and knowledgeable, they move up the career ladder. The training may consist of being supervised by a more experienced worker for a few days, or it may involve a formal training program.

Learning While You Work

Diana is an auto salesperson. When asked about her, the dealer who hired her explained: "Diana was really outgoing and enthusiastic. She knew something about cars, and she was a good listener. She didn't start selling cars from day one. She went through our training program. We use books and videodiscs provided by the automaker. Diana also watched other employees work. She's been with the company three years now, and she's been terrific."

Rod became a hospital orderly after just a two-week training period. There was no written material to study. When he was assigned to a floor in the hospital, the nurse in charge supervised his work for two more weeks. At first, Rod was pleased that his job required so little training, but he began to see that he had little chance for advancement. He then signed up for another hospital training program to become a nurse's aide. The six-week training program included classroom time plus time spent working with patients. Rod was paid for both.

There are many other training opportunities. Police and fire departments offer on-the-job training. Telephone companies teach their employees to be operators, installers, and repairers. National companies of different types offer on-the-job training. To find out more about companies that offer such training, contact the local branch of your state employment office.

Apprenticeship Programs

Apprenticeship is *a formal system for teaching people technical and/or manual skills*. The people in such programs are called *apprentices*. Apprenticeship programs usually last from two to five years and combine on-the-job training with classroom work. Apprenticeship programs are often administered through labor unions and vocational schools. Apprentices who complete the program in their trade are fully qualified to call themselves **journeyworkers**—*skilled craftspeople*.

There are apprenticeship programs for about 400 skilled occupations. These are some of the wide variety of jobs that you can learn through an apprenticeship:

Workers in many occupations receive their training on the job. This employee learned his tasks in just a few weeks.

- construction (carpenter, electrician, plumber, heavy equipment operator, painter)
- manufacturing (machinist, toolmaker, welder, patternmaker, molder, maintenance electrician)
- services (chef, cook, barber, auto-body repairer, auto mechanic, appliance repairer, dental technician)

When you begin as an apprentice, you will earn about 35 to 50 percent of a journeyworker's pay. Near the end of your apprenticeship, you will earn up to 95 percent of a journeyworker's wage. If you have completed an apprenticeship program, you will in many instances earn more money than workers in the field who have not had that training.

Some apprentice programs do not require a high school diploma. Many require applicants to take tests to determine if they have an aptitude for the field. Some programs also call for technical courses or some experience in the field. All apprenticeship programs are now open to women. Competition for apprenticeships is keen. Often, there are many applicants for each opening. There may be a waiting list as well. If you are interested in becoming an apprentice, contact the apprentice information center at your state employment office.

THE ARMED SERVICES

The armed services are a major source of careers and career training. In 1986, nearly 2.2 million persons were on active duty. Their jobs are with one of the five armed services—Army, Navy, Air Force, Marines, or Coast Guard. Although the mission of the military is national defense, only one person out of eight in the armed services is actually bearing arms. The others are working at support jobs. They help feed, clothe, transport, and supply those bearing arms.

Career Training in the Military

The armed services provide training for many kinds of jobs, either in their own schools or in others. The following list shows a few of the jobs for which the armed services will train you:

- air traffic controller
- baker
- cook or chef
- journalist
- mechanic
- machinist
- photographer
- computer programmer
- medical technologist
- accountant
- inventory controller
- pilot
- heavy equipment operator
- truck driver
- electronic equipment repairer

To match you with a career that suits you, the military will give you a series of 10 tests—the Armed Services Vocational Aptitude Battery (ASVAB). You can take this group of tests even before you decide to enlist.

You can learn one of about 400 skilled occupations through an apprenticeship program.

The military offers training in more than 2,000 occupational specialties. You can take an aptitude test before you enlist to match your strengths to the right career.

There are benefits to enlisting in the armed services. As already mentioned, you can receive on-the-job training for many interesting positions. There are ongoing educational programs and many chances for advancement. Under one enlistment option, you receive a written guarantee of an agreed-upon training program. You are also guaranteed work at the military base you choose.

The financial benefits provided in the military services are different from those given by other employers. In addition to salary, the armed services provide housing or housing allowances for their members. They also provide dining halls or food allowances for service people who live on base. These are provided because it is in the military's best interest to satisfy you. They hope you will reenlist and make the service your career.

Many people do not look at the armed services as a lifetime career. Instead, they consider three or four years in one of the services as a source of career training that will equip them for a good position in civilian life. An air traffic controller who is trained in the military can get a similar job at a city airport once his or her military duty is over. A nurse trained in the military can later work in a private hospital.

When considering training in the armed services, evaluate it as you would any career training. Find out if there will be civilian jobs available in the field you will train in. Talk to local employers in the field. What do they think of the training offered by the military? Ask recruiters for information about specific types of training. Can the training really prove useful in civilian life?

Compare the military to other sources of career training. Can you get the same training closer to home in an apprenticeship program? Do the armed services provide better on-the-job training? Will they train you for what *you* want to do?

HIGHER EDUCATION

You may decide that the best training you can get is through advanced schooling. Many technical careers require some kind of classroom training after high school. In most career fields, a high school education plus some kind of additional school training helps you get a more interesting, better-paying job. Additional education will also improve your prospects for advancement.

This section will introduce you to several types of higher education. You will learn about private vocational schools, community colleges, four-year colleges and universities, correspondence schools, and adult education programs. The aims and features of each type of educational training are different.

Private Vocational Schools

Private vocational schools *offer practical, intensive training in specific career fields.* These fields include the following:

- air conditioning
- aircraft mechanics

Chapter 6 Preparing for the Job You Want

- appliance repair
- blueprint reading
- bookkeeping
- computer programming
- cosmetology
- court reporting
- dental laboratory technician
- dog grooming
- interior design
- photography
- TV and radio repair
- word processing
- X-ray technician

Private vocational schools have one specific aim—to give you useful training so that you can get a job upon graduation. These schools do not require that you take general education courses. They emphasize hands-on laboratory training experiences. Programs are concentrated in order to train you quickly and get you into the job market. When you finish the required course of study, you will receive a certificate stating your achievement. This will show possible employers that you have a formal background in the field.

Vocational schools train students quickly through hands-on programs. Students may not be required to take any courses outside their fields.

Community Colleges

You can probably find low-cost, high-quality training close to home in a local community college. These schools are often partially supported by county or city taxes. Tuition may range from nothing to several hundred dollars a year.

Community colleges *offer students one- or two-year courses of study in many fields.* These colleges are sometimes known as *junior colleges* or *technical colleges.* Many community colleges have an open admissions policy, which means that all high school graduates are admitted. In California, anyone who is over the age of 18 can enroll in a community college, even without a high school diploma.

Community colleges typically offer two types of programs: academic and occupational. The academic program is for the student who does not wish to go directly into a four-year college from high school. The program offers courses that first- and second-year students would take at any four-year college.

When you complete a two-year course of study, you will receive an associate of arts (A.A.) or an associate of sciences (A.S.) degree, depending on whether you took courses in the humanities or the sciences. If you decide to continue your education at a four-year school, you can apply for a transfer of credits. If the four-year college accepts the credits from the community college, you can start at the four-year school in an upper class. Often, though, students who transfer from community colleges to four-year colleges do not get full credit at their new college for all the courses they took.

The occupational programs in a community college teach specific skills in a variety of career areas. They may be tailored to the job needs of the community or surrounding employment area. Therefore, not every community college offers the same job programs. The following are examples of programs offered at community colleges:

- health care (dental assisting, physical therapy assisting, nursing, X-ray technology)
- agriculture (horticulture, agricultural technology, animal sciences, forestry)
- business (computer programming, secretarial sciences, personnel management, hotel/motel administration, food services, sales and retailing)
- trades, industry, and engineering (construction, drafting, electricity and electronics, computer technology, air conditioning technology, small-engine mechanics, laser technology, microelectronics, hydraulics, pneumatics, telecommunications)

Credits from occupational programs generally cannot be transferred to a four-year college.

Community colleges offer many advantages, as Pete discovered. Pete was interested in the hotel industry, but he was not sure he wanted four years of college. He had heard he could probably work as a registration clerk without further education, but he wanted a job with a better chance for advancement. Pete enrolled in the hotel management program at his local community college. He was able to keep the part-time job he had in his senior year of high school. When he graduated from community college, he landed a desirable job in a management trainee program for a national hotel chain.

Four-Year Colleges and Universities

A four-year institution prepares you for a career that requires four years of education beyond high school. It also offers a place to learn and explore new ideas. **Four-year colleges** are *schools of higher education that provide a course of study resulting in a bachelor of arts (B.A.) or a bachelor of science (B.S.) degree upon graduation.* Such schools are often called undergraduate colleges. A **university** *combines an undergraduate college with several graduate colleges* that provide education beyond the bachelor's degree. At a university, you can earn graduate degrees—a master's (M.A. or M.S.) and a doctorate (Ph.D.) The names of institutions do not always reflect the degree programs they offer. For example, Dartmouth College offers bachelor's, master's, and doctorate programs.

In a college, you will have a tremendous choice of courses in many different topics. The topics are usually divided into three fields: humanities, social sciences, and physical sciences and math.

- humanities (literature, art, drama, foreign languages, religion, philosophy, music)
- social sciences (economics, geography, history, journalism, psychology, sociology)
- physical sciences and math (applied mathematics, biology, chemistry, geology, statistics, physics)

In order to earn a B.A. or B.S. degree, you must complete a certain number of courses. Most students do so in four years, although some students accelerate their programs to graduate sooner. Colleges require you to choose a major subject area, such as business or nursing. You will be required to take courses in other fields as well as in your own major field of interest. If you are a business major, for example, you may have to take courses in science and a foreign language as well as in business.

If you have chosen a highly specialized career, college may be a necessity. To find out the educational requirements of a job, check the *Occupational Outlook Handbook*. Here are some positions that require a college degree:

Chapter 6 Preparing for the Job You Want

- teacher
- scientist
- psychologist
- engineer
- computer systems analyst
- insurance underwriter
- lawyer
- health inspector
- librarian
- forester
- oceanographer
- astronomer
- physician
- veterinarian
- physical therapist
- pharmacist
- social worker
- architect

Correspondence Courses

Suppose you are interested in commercial photography, but there is no school nearby that offers classes in the field. You do not want to leave your own community. What can you do?

You can learn photography through a correspondence course. In a **correspondence**

Figure 6.3 Typical Program for a B.S. Degree in Business Administration

Freshman Year	Junior Year
ECON 101/102 Introduction to Economics	FIN 323 Financial Management
ENG 104 English Composition	MK 323 Marketing Management
MATH 121 Calculus I	OM 323 Operations Management
IS 113 Introduction to Information Systems	ME 321 Managerial Economics
MG 121 Management in Society	Liberal Arts electives (12 credits)
Liberal Arts electives (8 credits)	Free electives (4 credits)
Sophomore Year	**Senior Year**
AC 221/222 Financial and Managerial Accounting	MG 422 Management Policy
MS 221 Probability and Statistics	Management electives (16 credits)
MG 222 Management Science	Free electives (12 credits)
OB 221 Human Behavior in Organizations	
Liberal Arts electives (12 credits)	

course, *you receive lessons through the mail.* You complete the assignments and return them through the mail. They are graded by the school's instructors. Courses can range in length from two weeks to six weeks.

Correspondence courses are popular. They offer part-time schooling at a fairly low cost. Colleges, as well as correspondence schools, offer such courses. Close to 2 million people are currently studying subjects ranging from air conditioning repair and commercial art to computer programming and upholstering. The following list includes some of the courses offered by correspondence schools:

- agricultural resources
- apparel
- hotel management
- real estate
- data processing
- electronics
- automobile servicing
- drafting
- truck driving*
- woodworking
- radio and TV repair

There are some drawbacks to correspondence courses. If you sign up for a correspondence course, you will be working on your own. That requires self-discipline. There will be no teacher to answer your questions and no other students to talk to. Many home-study students find it difficult to make time to study. As a result, they continually put off studying and may not complete their courses. However, if you are determined to learn a certain skill and are enthusiastic about the subject, a correspondence course may be right for you.

Adult Education

Many communities have adult education programs. They are usually held at local schools,

*(requires hands-on training at the end of the program)

colleges, or community facilities. The programs do not lead to any sort of degree or certification. **Adult education programs** are generally *designed for post–high school adults who want to learn a new skill or refresh an old one.* They can also give people knowledge that is valuable in their jobs. Adult education programs are also called *continuing education programs.*

The courses offered make use of the facilities of the community and the people in the community who are experts in their fields. The following list includes some of the courses offered by adult education programs:

- photography
- volleyball
- tennis
- foreign language conversation
- automobile repair
- typing
- word processing
- computer programming
- cooking
- resume-writing and job-hunting techniques

COST AND FINANCIAL AID

In general, four-year colleges cost the most. Of these, private four-year colleges are the most expensive. Annual tuition, including room and board, can easily run upward of $13,000. State colleges are less expensive. Their cost varies from state to state and can range from $4,000 to $8,000 a year with room and board.

Community colleges are less expensive. Ordinarily, all of their students live off campus. Thus, there is probably no charge for room and board. Depending on the program, a community college can cost up to $2,000 a year.

Private vocational schools charge by the course or program the student takes. One course can cost up to $800. A full program can cost up to $4,000. Correspondence course fees de-

It is wise to learn about a school's facilities before you make your decision. Most schools are happy to arrange tours for prospective students.

pend on the school and the course taken. Fees can range from $250 to $1,700. Adult education programs are usually the least expensive—ranging from $20 to $75 per course.

Financial Aid

You will find that all four-year and community colleges offer financial assistance. They have financial aid officers who will help you apply for federal or state loans at rates that are often lower than other types of borrowing. Financial aid officers can also tell you if you qualify for scholarships offered by the school or through special scholarship funds. **Scholarships** are *grants of money that do not have to be paid back.*

Students enrolled in qualified vocational schools are often eligible for student loans. Some vocational schools also have scholarships or extended payment programs of their own. Correspondence schools are much less likely to offer financial aid. Adult education programs at best offer extended payment plans.

Making a Good Choice

How you are going to pay for your education is important. However, what you will be paying for is more important. As in purchasing any product or service, you have to be a careful consumer. Check the qualifications of the teachers. Are they knowledgeable enough to teach you what you need to know? Learn about the school's facilities. If you will be living on campus, what are the dormitories like? If you will be taking a technical course, what are the laboratories like? How large is the library? What hours are the facilities open? Are evening classes available?

If you can, visit the school and talk to as many people there as possible. Get a range of opinions from current and former students, teachers, and admissions staff. Do not be afraid to ask questions. If you are not satisfied with the answers you get, write to your state's accreditation department. This department grants **accreditation**—*certification that a school meets certain standards.* For out-of-state schools, check with the particular state's department of education.

The accreditation of private vocational schools and correspondence schools can be checked by writing to their national associations. For private vocational schools, the best known national organization is the National Association of Trade and Technical Schools (NATTS). For a list of accredited schools, you can write to this group at 2251 Wisconsin Avenue, NW, Washington, DC 20007. Good correspondence schools are accredited by the National Home Study Council, 1601 18th Street, NW, Washington DC 20009. You also can write to this association for a list of accredited schools.

TAKE THE FIRST STEP

As you have seen in this chapter, there are many avenues of education open to you. To find out more about schools and training programs, you can start by visiting your high school counselor's office or the local library. Many public libraries have special sections on career guidance. Often, these sections include catalogs from hundreds of different schools around the country. If you cannot find the information you need there, write or call the specific schools you are interested in. Most schools are eager for new students and will send you a catalog free of charge.

MAIN POINTS

- A high school diploma is a basic requirement for most jobs. Training beyond high school usually leads to better jobs.
- Cooperative education programs provide students with training in real-life, paid positions. A training agreement outlines each party's responsibilities. A training plan helps guide the student's step-by-step progress on the job.
- Paid or volunteer part-time work can provide students with valuable experience and can lead to full-time jobs. Part-time jobs are often available in stores, restaurants, hotels, and recreation programs. Hospitals and other service areas usually need volunteers.
- On-the-job and apprenticeship training provide the opportunity to earn while you learn. Apprenticeship programs train you to be a skilled craftsworker.
- The armed services offer training programs that can lead to military or civilian careers.
- Vocational schools offer intensive hands-on training. Programs are brief but concentrated.
- A community college offers low-cost technical and academic training. The two-year program leads to an A.A. or an A.S. degree.
- A four-year college or university education is required for certain jobs. The degree awarded is a B.A. or a B.S.
- Correspondence schools and adult education courses offer many learning opportunities. Correspondence courses require an extra measure of self-discipline.

Terms to Know

Use the following terms to fill in the blanks of the sentences below.

accreditation	correspondence course	teacher-coordinator
adult education program	four-year college	training agreement
apprenticeship program	journeyworker	training plan
community college	private vocational school	training station
cooperative education	scholarship	university

Chapter 6 Preparing for the Job You Want

1. John graduated with a B.A. degree in history from a(n) _____.
2. You can earn a degree in two years from a(n) _____.
3. Jim worked to save $2,000 so he could begin training as a welder at a(n) _____.
4. Larry took a course at night in word processing given by the _____.
5. You receive your assignments through the mail in a(n) _____.
6. The type of training program in which a student spends half a day in school and half a day at a job is called _____.
7. A business that provides training for cooperative education students is called a(n) _____.
8. Kim's parents understood their responsibilities in her cooperative education program by reading the _____.
9. Jamie learned plumbing by working with an experienced plumber in a(n) _____.
10. After Jamie finished his plumbing training, he became a(n) _____.
11. If you need financial aid in order to pay tuition fees, a college may give you a(n) _____.
12. Certification that a school meets certain educational standards is known as _____.
13. Nora knew exactly what she would learn at her training station because she had a detailed _____.
14. The person who acts as a bridge between school and your training job is your _____.
15. Lucy thought getting her B.S. in biology was so worthwhile that she decided to go on for a master's degree at the _____.

Chapter Review

1. How does a high school diploma improve your chances for a job?
2. What is the purpose of a training agreement? How does a training plan set cooperative education apart from other training programs?
3. Name ten kinds of businesses likely to hire part-time student workers.
4. How can volunteer work substitute for part-time paid work?
5. How does an apprenticeship differ from other kinds of on-the-job training?
6. How can the military be a source of career training?
7. What is the main purpose of private vocational schools? How can they help you in your career?
8. What two basic types of programs are offered by community colleges?
9. What kinds of careers require a college degree? List five such careers.
10. How do correspondence schools operate?

Activities

1. Obtain a copy of your school's co-op training agreement. Which statements describe the students' responsibilities? The employers' responsibilities? Are there statements listing responsibilities of the school or the parents? Describe them.
2. Choose a career field that interests you. By using catalogs from four-

year colleges, community colleges, vocational schools, and correspondence schools, find out what kinds of training are available. Compare the programs listed, their costs, and their convenience. Write a report explaining what you have found. Which school offers the best training for you?

3. Invite a military recruiter or panel of recruiters to visit your class. Ask them to explain the training programs currently being offered by the armed services. Find out the details about length of enlistment and the military's commitment to train you in a particular field.

4. Invite to your class several students who have gone through a cooperative education program. Find out such information as: Did the program meet their expectations? What kind of training did they receive on the job? How did the time at work affect their schoolwork and their attitude toward school? What did they feel was most worthwhile about their co-op experience?

5. Call the local offices of several labor unions to find out about their apprenticeship programs. Is there a test required? Is there a waiting list for training? If possible, interview an apprentice. Find out what the training was like. Write a one- or two-page description of your findings.

Chapter 7

Getting the Job You Want

OBJECTIVES

This chapter will enable you to:

- list places where you can find out about possible job openings.
- use private or public employment agencies wisely.
- organize your job search by keeping track of phone calls, interviews, and follow-ups.
- write an effective résumé.
- give reasons why neatness and accuracy are important when writing business letters or filling out application forms.
- make a good impression during an interview.
- follow up on interviews with an appropriate letter or phone call.

Barry

In order to get the job you want, you have to be more eager and more interested than your competition. That's what our school guidance counselor always told us. Now I know she was right. I decided to be a go-getter, and yesterday I got a terrific job! Here's how it happened.

About a month ago, the job placement service at school sent me for an interview with the Valley Company. The firm had a position open for a sales trainee. The job sounded interesting, so I made sure I was neat, organized, and on time for the appointment. I filled out the application form as carefully as I could. As Mr. Deane, the manager, talked about the job, I began to get excited. I told him I thought I'd really like the work. He said I seemed outgoing, which was a good quality for salespeople. I felt that I made a good impression. At the end of the interview, Mr. Deane said that he'd let me know Valley's decision by the end of the month—one way or the other.

The minute I got home, I wrote a follow-up letter thanking Mr. Deane for the interview. I also told him why I thought the job was for me. A few weeks went by, and I didn't hear anything. I began to lose interest, and I even got a little angry. If Valley doesn't want me, I don't want Valley, right? By the end of the month, I'd given up hope—until I talked to my sister, Ellen. "If you want to know the company's decision, call Mr. Deane and ask him," she said. "Be assertive. You have nothing to lose."

I was a little nervous, but I made the call. I told Mr. Deane that I had been waiting to hear from him and that I was very hopeful Valley would hire me. Mr. Deane said that he still hadn't decided and that he would get back to me soon. Two days later, the phone rang. It was Mr. Deane, telling me I got the job. He told me I was hired because I was the only applicant to call back. He also liked my follow-up letter. He said that kind of assertiveness was important in sales. By calling, I had shown him I would be good at the job. That's one phone call I'm glad I made!

GETTING JOB LEADS

When you graduate from high school, you may go on for advanced training in a field that matches your interests and aptitudes. You may enter the job market immediately. Either way, you will eventually be looking for the right first job. Finding—and landing—the right job requires a careful strategy that is outlined in this chapter. Mastering that strategy can help you get the job you want.

To begin your job hunt, you will need to search for **job leads**, *information about possible job openings*. There are a surprising number of sources for job leads. The more sources you know about, the greater your chance of finding a job that will suit you. You may even find a number of attractive job possibilities.

People Who Can Help You

Some of the people who can help you find a job are specially trained to do so. Others can help you in a more informal manner.

Teachers and Guidance Counselors. A good place to begin a job search is at your school. Your guidance department may have information about job openings at local companies. If your school is large, it may have a job placement service, as Barry's school did. Small schools often have a teacher or a guidance counselor who helps students find jobs. If you are in a cooperative education program, your teacher-coordinator may be a good source of job leads.

Get to know the guidance counselors at your school. Talk to them often, and give them the latest news about your job search. Marie wanted a job after graduation as a secretary. She made sure to stay in close touch with her guidance counselor about her job hunt. Even if she got a job lead on her own, she would write a quick note to her counselor about it. If she saw the counselor in the hall, she would always say, "Hi! Anything new for me?" When the counselor finally did get a notice about a secretarial job, Marie was the first person she thought of.

Remember, though, that schools must consider all their students. If the guidance department sends you on an interview, they are probably sending others as well. Competition may be stiff, so do not expect your school to do it all. Check other job leads on your own.

Family, Friends, and Neighbors. Many job openings are never advertised. They are filled by friends or relatives of company employees. Telling the people you know what kind of job you are looking for can result in a good job lead.

To make sure you do not forget someone who might be helpful, make a list of people you know, starting with your family. What does your aunt or uncle do? Whom might she or he know? What about neighbors, the owner of your local drugstore, the parents of your friends? What about the people your parents know? Think about some companies you might like to work for. Do you know anyone who works for them already? Some young people do not like to use "pull," but no company will hire you if you do not have the right skills, no matter who has recommended you. You should not pressure your family or friends to find you a job. Just tell them the kind of job you want. If they have a suggestion, they will get back to you.

A guidance counselor can be a good source of information about job openings in the area.

Personnel Officers. The **personnel department** is *that section of a company concerned with filling jobs within the company*. In some companies, this department is called the *human resource department*. Personnel officers are always looking for people with good job skills. Is there any company in your town that you would like to work for? If so, telephone the company, and ask for the name of the person in charge of personnel. Then, write him or her a letter. Indicate that you are interested in the company and request an interview, even if there are no job openings at the time. In that way, the personnel officer will get to know you, and you can get information about the company.

Employment Agencies

Employment agencies *match suitable people to available jobs*. There are many sorts of employment agencies, and each kind works slightly differently. **Public employment agencies** are *nonprofit employment agencies operated by state governments*. Each state has such an agency, with offices in most large cities and towns. The services of public employment agencies are free. To find the one nearest you, look in the telephone book under the name of your state. To register, go to the local branch of the agency, and fill out an application form. You will then be interviewed by an employment counselor. If a possible job comes up, she or he will notify you.

Private employment agencies are *profit-making businesses that help people find jobs and help companies fill jobs*. Some agencies specialize in just one career field, such as secretarial services. Private employment agencies charge a fee for their services, which they collect from you as the job seeker or from the company that hires you.

If you want to work with a private agency, you may be asked to sign a contract. Read it very carefully before you agree to its conditions. When the agency sends you for an interview, always determine whether the fee will be paid by you or by the employer. If you are expected to pay, make sure the amount is agreeable to you. You should not have to pay any money until you are actually hired.

Want Ads

Want ads are advertisements of job opportunities. They are important sources of job information. Want ads indicate the type of job being offered, the salary range, and the experience or skills required. They also indicate how an applicant can contact the employer by giving an address, a telephone number, or a post office box number. You can also place your own ad in the want ads to advertise your skills or services. Here are some of the places want ads may be found.

Newspapers. Your local newspaper contains want ads every day, with the Sunday papers usually containing the largest number. Want ads are usually grouped alphabetically by type of job; for example, accountants, construction, editorial, engineering, sales. Some want ads give you the name of the company that placed the ad. Other want ads are called blind ads. They do not list the company name. Instead, they give you a box number to write to. Often, private employment agencies will place want ads. The ads may tell you to contact a particular person at the agency. If an ad says "Fee Paid," the agency fee will be paid by the employer, not by you.

Want ads make use of a number of special abbreviations to save space. Figure 7.1 lists these abbreviations and tells what they mean. Getting to know them can help you understand what the ads are saying. Otherwise, they may look like a foreign language.

Bulletin Boards. Find out if your school has a bulletin board where job opportunities are posted. Is there a grocery or drugstore that has a community bulletin board? Many companies have bulletin boards that list jobs they want to fill. Do your parents' employers have such bulletin boards? You can also ask your parents' friends to watch their company bulletin boards. Do not forget to check store windows. Businesses often place Help Wanted notices in their display windows.

Trade Publications. Trade publications are *regularly published magazines or newspapers for members of certain trades and occupations*. Trade publications often have a want ad section. Because these journals are distributed nationwide, the jobs listed will be from all over the country.

Civil Service Announcements. These publications list jobs available in federal, state, and local governments. The announcements describe the jobs and the requirements. You can find these announcements in the local library, post office, United States Civil Service Commission office, and state employment agency. If you want to work for the govern-

Figure 7.1 Common Classified Ad Abbreviations

ACC TYP	accurate typing necessary	MGR	manager
ADM ASST	administrative assistant	NO EXP NEC	no experience necessary
ASST MGR	assistant manager	OFC	office
ATTR BNFTS	attractive benefits	O/T	overtime
BC/BS	Blue Cross/Blue Shield provided	PD VAC	paid vacations
BGNR	beginner	P/T	part-time
BKKPR	bookkeeper	RECEPT/TYP	receptionist and typist
CLK	clerk	REFS	references needed
CO	company	RN	registered nurse
COL GRAD	college graduate	SAL REQS	send your salary requirements
DICT	dictation	SECY	secretary
DP	data processing	S/H	shorthand
EXC OPTY	excellent opportunity	SPVR	supervisor
EXP PREF	experience preferred	STENO	stenographer
EXP REQ	experience required	TEMP	temporary
40 WPM NEC	typing speed of 40 words per minute necessary	TO $450	up to $450 a week
F/P	job placement fee paid by employer	TRNEE	trainee
F/T	full-time	VDT	video display terminal
IMED OPNG	immediate opening	WP	word processor
KP	keypunch	$1,000/MO.	salary of $1,000 a month
LITE TYP	light typing	$OPEN	salary open to negotiation
LPN	licensed practical nurse	$15K *or* $15M	salary of $15,000 a year

Many local businesses simply place signs in their windows when looking for part-time workers.

ment, you may have to take a civil service test to determine your abilities. Nine out of ten government employees must take competitive examinations. The applicants whose test scores are highest are contacted first for positions.

If you want to apply for a federal job, you must contact the United States Civil Service Commission. For local and state jobs, contact the personnel office listed in the telephone book under the name of your community, county, or state.

As you follow job leads from the want ads, remember that not all companies that place ads are reputable. Beware of an ad that promises you much more money than other beginning employees in the same career field are getting. Also, no employers should ask you for money as an employment fee. Be wary of companies that ask you to pay money for courses that will lead to a job. They are probably making false promises.

Organizing Your Job Search

You may envy your friends who get jobs right away, but they may not be so lucky after all. They may have taken the first job that came along instead of waiting until they found the right job. If you really want a good job, you may need to search for several weeks or even months. You may need to follow several job leads, go on several job interviews, and write several letters of application.

Because you may be dealing with a number of companies at once, you will need to keep track of a lot of information. That means you should develop a system for organizing your job hunt. Otherwise, you may lose important phone numbers, confuse the names of companies, or misspell people's names on letters.

One way to organize your material is to start a file of 3- by 5-inch index cards. Use one card for each company. On the front of the card, list the following items:

- the name, complete address, and phone number of the company
- the name and title of the person you contacted
- the source of the job lead, such as family friend, school placement service, or newspaper ad

Be sure all the material on these cards is spelled correctly; refer to those spellings when you write letters or address envelopes.

On the back of each card, write the dates and results of each contact and what should happen next. Here are some notes that Barry made on his index card for the Valley Company.

Apr. 14 Interview 11 A.M., 4th floor. Job involves sales. Mr. Deane seemed to like me. Will let me know at the end of the month.

Apr. 15 Follow-up letter to Mr. Deane.

Because Barry had an exact record of the dates of his contacts, he knew just when to make his follow-up phone call. You might want to use an appointment calendar in addition to the file cards. That way you will not forget any interviews or follow-ups.

Chapter 7 Getting the Job You Want

                        Christina S. Blancher
                        100 Old Line Road
                        Fairlee, Connecticut 10236
                            (203) 555-4441

JOB OBJECTIVE   Sales trainee in clothing or department store, leading to position of buyer.

EDUCATION   Fairlee Community College, Associate of Arts degree, June 1991. Graduated in top 10% of class, majored in fashion merchandising.

                    West High School, Fairlee, Connecticut. Graduated June 1989.

WORK EXPERIENCE   Salesperson, Rodman's Department Store, New Haven, Connecticut, holidays and summers 1989-1990. After my first summer behind the counter, I was often asked to train new salespeople. During the summer of 1990, I supervised three other sales employees in Rodman's College Shop.

                    Waitress, The Wagon Wheel Restaurant, part-time, 1991. I received a commendation from the owner of The Wagon Wheel on my speed and efficiency as well as on my ability to deal with customers.

HONORS AND ACTIVITIES   Organized Fairlee Community College fall fashion show, 1990.
Design prize for West High School cheerleaders' uniforms, 1988. (The uniform design has been used by West High School ever since.)
West High cheerleader squad, 1987-1989.
Candy striper, Providence Hospital, 1987-1989.

                        REFERENCES AVAILABLE ON REQUEST

Figure 7.2 A Sample Resume

PREPARING YOUR RESUME

A **resume** is *a brief written summary of a person's work experience, education, and other job qualifications.* A resume is also known as a *personal data sheet* or a *personal profile.* A resume is helpful because it highlights your qualifications. It gives interviewers a way to find out about you even before they meet you. A resume also helps an interviewer remember you after the interview is over. Items on the resume can be discussed and expanded during the interview. Finally, your resume will represent you to people who have never met you. For this reason, you should give your resume much thought and care. It is extremely important that it be neat, well organized, and accurate.

When you are just beginning a career, your resume should be about one typewritten page in length. On that sheet should be the following information:

- name, address, and phone number
- job objective
- education
- work experience
- honors and activities
- references

Christina's resume, shown in Figure 7.2, illustrates how your data sheet should be organized.

How to Write Your Resume

First, make notes of everything you need to include. Then, organize each item under the headings above. Use these notes to make a **first draft**, *a rough copy that can be corrected and changed.* Under "Education," you might want to include your grade average or your class standing, if it was high. Under "Work Experience," list any part-time or summer jobs you have held. Think of any ways that your temporary jobs may have trained you for the kind of job you are now looking for. Notice how Christina mentioned some compliments she had received from her former employers. Her ability to work with people and her speed and efficiency are desirable qualities for sales trainees or department store buyers.

Under "Honors and Activities," mention any school offices you have held or teams you were on. Do not forget to highlight any awards that you may have won. These items will show an interviewer that you are a responsible, active person and give her or him a better idea of your interests and abilities. When at all possible, tie these activities into possible job skills. Christina made sure to include that she had organized a fashion show and that she had won a clothing design award. These activities would impress the interviewer with her leadership ability and her fashion sense. Your resume is an advertisement for you. Although you should avoid bragging, do not be afraid to include any facts that make you look good.

References are *statements that people give to employers about your character and abilities.* Work references come from former work supervisors who know about your performance on the job. Personal references are provided by teachers, clergy, or friends of your parents. These people could mention such qualities as honesty, reliability, and eagerness to learn. The people who supply your references are important, and you should treat them well. Do not tell an employer that someone will give you a reference until you have asked that person's permission.

There are two ways to treat references on your resume. You can list the names and addresses of those who have agreed to give you a reference. Or at the bottom of your resume, you can type "References available on request," as Christina did. If you do what Christina did, you can choose which names to give when the interviewer asks for them. This technique also allows you to keep an up-to-date list of names. You can change the names on your list without having to redo your resume.

Chapter 7 Getting the Job You Want

As you begin your job hunt, ask three or four appropriate people to provide references for you.

Neatness and Accuracy Count

Employers may see hundreds of resumes each year. Their impressions of you are based on the information on your resume and also on the way it looks. As you make up a final copy, ask yourself if all the information is true. Is your English clear and correct? Be *concise*, which means stating much in few words. To be concise, you need to use short words and short sentences. Before you type your final copy, check spelling, grammar, and punctuation. You might have someone who is good with words read your resume to give advice or make corrections. To avoid extra work, catch all errors before making your final draft. If you find a mistake after you type the final copy, you will have to make a fresh copy. Resumes with words crossed out or written over do not make a good impression.

Resumes should be typed, and they should be typed perfectly. If you do not know how to type, perhaps a friend will type the resume for you. It may be worth the expense to have your resume typed by a professional typist. After you have a perfectly typed resume, you can make photocopies. For a bit more money, you can have your resume printed. Give out copies to interviewers, but save the original typed resume to use as a master for making new copies.

Check your spelling carefully before you type that final copy of your resume. A well-prepared resume can make your application stand out from the crowd.

APPLYING FOR JOBS

After you have gathered some job leads, it is time to contact companies that might be hiring. Here are a few ways to introduce yourself to a possible employer.

Applying by Telephone

If you get a lead from a school counselor or see an ad on a community bulletin board, you may wish to contact the company by telephone. There are advantages and disadvantages to applying by telephone. On the good side, you obtain immediate feedback about job openings. On the other hand, you will have to make a good impression by voice only, and in a very short time. For this reason, it is a good idea to write out an opening statement and practice it several times before making the call. Your statement should be brief but it should contain the following facts:

- your name
- which job you are applying for
- how you got the lead
- your best qualifications for the job
- when you would be available for an interview

If you want to contact a company by telephone, practice what you are going to say before you call. That can help you make a good impression on an employer.

A sample opening statement may go something like this: "Hello, is this Mr. Girard? My name is Roberta White. Mr. Rotan at the West High School guidance office mentioned that your restaurant has an opening for a chef trainee. I have worked for the last two summers in restaurant kitchens. During that time, I learned a great deal about food preparation, and I was regularly asked to sub for the head cook on his day off. I graduated from high school in June, and I'm ready to go to work right away. Do you think we could talk more about this job?"

When you talk about your qualifications, mention what you have to offer, not what the job could offer you. Do not say, "This kind of job could help me grow." Instead, say, "I was the fastest typist in my class at school" or "My former employer told me I have a good personality for sales."

After you make your opening statement, do not continue talking. Pause for feedback from the other person. He or she may ask a general question, such as "Tell me more about yourself." You may also be asked specifically about your work experience or educational background. At the end of the conversation, be certain about what you should do next. Does the interviewer want you to send a resume? If so, ask for the exact mailing address. Does he or she want you to call back in a week? If so, make a note on your calendar. Is he or she asking you to come for an interview? If that happens, be sure to note correctly the exact time and place (building, floor, room) of the interview. Write down the name (ask for the spelling) and title of the person who will interview you.

Writing a Letter of Application

A **letter of application** is *a letter you write to a potential employer, asking that she or he consider you for a job*. You will need to write a letter of application when you answer a newspaper ad. If you are interested in a particular company but you are not sure if the firm has a job for you, you might want to send the com-

Chapter 7 Getting the Job You Want **115**

```
                921 Great Road
                Lumberville, NJ  08530
                June 6, 1992


        Ms. Louise Sagan
        The Camera Store
        Three Corners Mall
        Hamlin, NJ  08648

        Dear Ms. Sagan:

        In response to your ad of June 6, 1992, in the Star, I am
        applying for your position as a full-time sales clerk.  My
        resume is enclosed.

        My last three jobs have given me much experience working
        with customers.  I have also learned how to take and process
        orders and handle basic bookkeeping tasks.  My experience as
        a photographer has familiarized me with basic equipment and
        film types, so I should be able to answer customers'
        questions knowledgeable.

        I am available for an interview any weekday after 3:00.  I
        could start working two weeks after notifying my current
        employer.  My telephone number is 555-3867.

        Sincerely,

        Martha Stone

        Martha Stone

        Enc.
```

Figure 7.3 A Sample Letter of Application

pany your resume. In this case, you should also include an application letter (sometimes called a *cover letter*). An application letter is more personal than your resume. You should write a slightly different letter to every company you send a resume to. Try to get the name of a particular person in each company to whom you can address your letter.

Letters of application follow the format for business letters. They should be neatly typed on good-quality white bond paper. Place your address and the date in the upper right-hand corner. Farther down, on the left-hand side, type the name, title, and address of the person to whom you are writing the letter. (See Figure 7.3 for a sample of an application letter.) As with a resume, make at least one rough copy before typing a final draft. Be sure that your ideas are clear and that your spelling and grammar are correct. This letter may be passed around to a number of people. If there are mistakes, your chances of being contacted by a potential employer may be greatly lessened.

Start the letter by stating what job you are applying for and how you heard about the position. In a second paragraph, mention your best qualifications. You do not want to repeat information in your resume, but you may want to give more specifics about those facts. You might also mention some information you have heard or looked up about the company. You could, for example, mention the quality of some of the products the company sells or the length of time it has been in business.

Keep the tone of your letter businesslike. It should be polite and warm, but it should not be witty, cute, or overly friendly. The purpose of the letter is to present yourself as a serious, professional person. You might mention in the last paragraph of your letter that you will call the employer in ten days or so to check the status of your application.

Completing an Application Form

Many companies and employment agencies ask job seekers to fill out an **application form**, *a standard questionnaire that all potential employees must complete*. These forms are used to screen applicants, so complete them with care. Take the time to read instructions and look over the form so that you do not have to cross out or erase anything. As with resumes and letters, neatness is important.

Application forms often ask for information you may not have at your fingertips. It is a good idea to put together a pocket resume, a sheet listing certain facts about yourself that you take to interviews. Here are some pieces of information regularly asked for on application forms:

- your social security number
- the names and addresses of your grammar school, junior high school, and high school and the dates attended
- the names, addresses, and telephone numbers of former employers and the dates you worked for them
- the names, addresses, and phone numbers of people who have agreed to give you a reference

You might be asked to state the salary you are seeking. A good answer to that question is "Open." It is best not to give specific salary requirements before you have discussed a particular job with an interviewer. You might disqualify yourself by asking for too much or cheat yourself by asking for too little.

You might be asked to list any previous jobs, even if they were part-time or temporary. A common question on application blanks is, "What was your reason for leaving the job?" Your answer may be, "School commitments" or "Summer job only." If you left for a negative reason, word your answer carefully. You do not want to lie, but you do not want to say anything unflattering about yourself or a previous employer. If, for example, you did not get along with a supervisor, you might state "Personality conflict" as your reason for leaving.

Some parts of the form, such as "Military

Chapter 7 Getting the Job You Want 117

Figure 7.4 A Sample Application Form

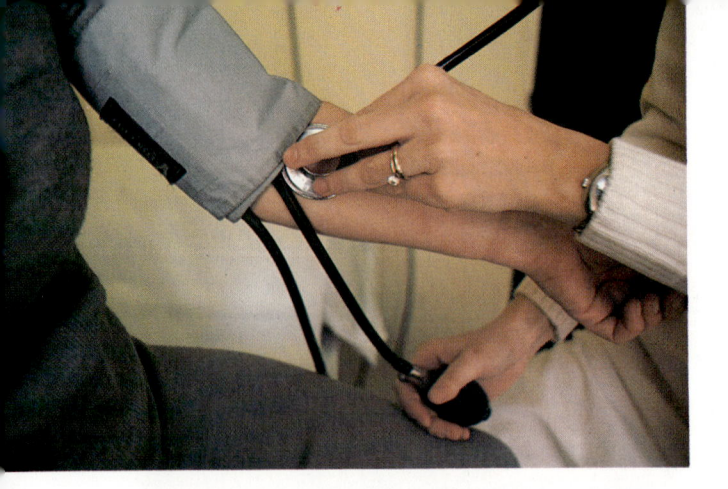

Companies often require job applicants to have physical examinations. For some jobs, an examination is required by law.

Service," may not apply to you. Instead of just leaving them blank, put in a dash or write "N/A" or "Not applicable." This shows that you did not overlook the section by mistake.

Taking Preemployment Tests

Many companies, large and small, give prospective employees some sort of preemployment test. Most government workers are tested before they are hired. Here are some examples of the kinds of tests you may be asked to take when you apply for a job.

Skills Tests. There are two kinds of skills tests. Hands-on, or practical, tests require demonstration of a certain skill. A typing test is a hands-on test. There are also written tests that measure your knowledge of a skill. Someone who applies for a bank teller job, for example, may be asked to take a math test.

Civil Service Tests. These are tests for government jobs. They are designed to help the government choose the best workers without considering race, religion, sex, or political affiliation. The civil service system offers all citizens a fair chance for a government job. Your test score will enable the government to compare your abilities with those of other applicants for the same position. Civil service tests are given all over the country. Look in the phone book under "United States Government, Office of Personnel Management" or the name of your state, for example, "Massachusetts, State of—Employment Service."

Psychological Tests. These tests help determine whether an applicant has the right personality for the company or the type of work. Psychological tests evaluate such traits as leadership abilities, loyalty, assertiveness, and the ability to work with others.

Polygraph Tests. Many employers use these tests (also called *lie detector tests*) to test the honesty of potential employees. Sensitive electrodes are attached to the subject's skin. The subject is asked a number of questions, including perhaps, "Did you ever steal from your last employer?" A machine records blood pressure, pulse rate, and perspiration. The person administering the test then reads what the machine has recorded and decides whether the person has been honest or dishonest during the test. Many people disagree with the use of polygraph tests. They believe such a test cannot truly measure a person's honesty. However, more and more companies are making use of polygraph tests.

Medical Tests. Companies often require job applicants to undergo complete physical examinations. They may wish to discover any major health problem that could keep an applicant from doing the job. If you wish to work in the medical field or the restaurant business, a physical may be required to make sure you have no disease that you might pass on to others.

BEFORE, DURING, AND AFTER THE INTERVIEW

Once you have been asked to come in for a job interview, congratulate yourself. It is a very good sign when someone in a company asks to see you. Now, you need to make sure you stand out among the candidates being interviewed. You may have a decision to make, too. Would you want this job if it were offered to you? You need to ask your own questions during the interview, as well as to answer those that are asked of you. What should you do to make the best impression during an interview? Here are some suggestions.

Learn About the Company

You can make a favorable impression on the interviewer if you know some facts about her or his organization. Before the interview, talk to people you know who work there. Your school career placement office may also have information. Call the company's receptionist, and ask if the company publishes an annual report. (An annual report is a published booklet describing the company's activities and financial situation in the past year.) The receptionist or public relations department may also be able to answer some of your questions about the company. Go to the library and ask for *Dun & Bradstreet Reference Book; Poor's Register of Corporations, Directors and Executives;* or *Moody's Industrial Manual.* Ask the librarian if you need help looking up the company. If the company is a small, local firm, you may be able to learn something about it through the Chamber of Commerce or the Better Business Bureau. You can also ask about listings of nonprofit organizations in which you might be interested. You can write to such an organization to obtain an application for employment. Most will also send you a brochure or booklet describing the work the organization performs.

When preparing for an interview, you may want to find answers to the following questions:

- In what year was the company founded?
- What products and services does the company provide?
- Is it a growing company?

Employers are impressed by applicants who are well dressed and well groomed.

- What is the reputation of the company in your community?

Practice for Your Interview

Make up a list of questions that an interviewer might ask you. Then, sit down with a friend or family member, and practice answering the question aloud. Here are some sample questions an interviewer might ask:

- Why are you interested in this kind of work?
- Can you tell me something about yourself?
- What are your best subjects in school? Your worst subjects?
- What have you learned from other jobs?
- Have you ever been let go from a job? If so, why?
- In what ways would your skills and abilities help you do this job well?

When you are being interviewed, your answers to questions should be related to the job. Do not discuss your personal problems, and do not criticize former employers. If you have some weaknesses, discuss with your parents or your school guidance counselor how best to handle them during an interview. Always tell the truth during an interview, but do not volunteer negative facts about yourself if you do not have to.

Think of ways to answer negative questions in a positive way.

You might also think of some questions to ask of your interviewer. Here are some suggestions:

- How will I learn my job duties? Is there a training program for this job?
- What are the biggest challenges I might face on the job?
- If I do well on this job, what are the possibilities for advancement?

Make a Good Impression

Choose your interview clothes carefully. The clothes you select should be just a bit dressier than the clothes you would wear on the job. For example, a young man being interviewed for an office job should probably wear a jacket and tie or shirt and sweater. A woman should wear a skirt or dress. Polished shoes are also a must. Keep makeup, jewelry, and perfume or after-shave cologne to a minimum.

To prepare for an interview, pay special attention to cleanliness and neatness. Bathe, wash your hair, and put on clean, well-pressed clothes. Make sure your hair is neatly combed before you meet the interviewer.

Be on time for your interview. Find out exactly where the interview will take place and the correct route to take. Figure out how long it will take you to get there. Then, add 15 or 20 minutes in case of a traffic jam or a stalled bus. It is much better to be early than late.

```
12A Harris Way
Maple Rapids, MI  48853
May 7, 1992


Mrs. Alice Van Pelt
Personnel Manager
Chelsea Art Supplies
64 Scott Road
Maple Rapids, MI  48853

Dear Mrs. Van Pelt:

Thank you for taking the time yesterday to give me a
thorough explanation of how Chelsea obtains art supplies
from international sources.  The interview made me eager to
put my secretarial skills to work for such an interesting
company.

I look forward to your reply regarding the position.  I
sincerely hope that I will be the one who fills it.

Sincerely,

Barbara Ressler

Barbara Ressler
```

Figure 7.5 A Sample Follow-Up Letter

Chapter 7 Getting the Job You Want

Gather together any items you will need ahead of time so that you will not be looking for them at the last minute. Keep your resume, pocket resume, a pen, a small notepad, and your list of questions all in one place. Check your appearance one last time before you leave.

When you meet your interviewer, introduce yourself clearly, shake hands, and look directly at him or her. Your handshake should be firm but not crushing. Remember that *your posture and movements will communicate a certain message about your attitude*. This message is called **body language**. If you sit upright, look alert, and respond with enthusiasm to what the interviewer is saying, you will appear interested and mature. If you slouch, chew gum, smoke, or stare out the window, you will leave a very different impression. Stay as calm as you can, and avoid making nervous gestures.

Allow the interviewer to lead the interview. If you practiced beforehand, you should have some good answers to her or his queries. Remember always to answer in a polite and courteous way. Avoid answering with just a yes or no. Explain your answer, or give an example. Always try to answer the questions in a way that shows your qualifications for the job. If an interviewer asks, "What is the most enjoyable thing you've done recently?" do not talk about a vacation to the Grand Canyon. Instead, mention a volunteer project or a school activity that involves some job skills.

Interviews are two-way communications. After the interviewer has finished questioning you, he or she will probably ask if you have any questions. Do not ask questions about salary, benefits, or vacation at this time. Ask about these matters only after you have been offered the job.

If you think you want the job, you should indicate your interest at the end of the interview. In most cases, the interviewer will want some extra time to consider your application and compare it with others. Maybe he or she will promise to call you. If you are not certain about what is to happen next, ask the interviewer. Be sure to write down the next step so that you will not forget it.

Write a Follow-Up Letter

Follow-up letters, as Barry discovered, can make an excellent impression. Writing a follow-up letter to an interviewer is courteous, and the letter will remind him or her of your talk and your qualifications.

In your follow-up letter, first thank the interviewer for taking the time to talk to you. Then, mention something you learned during the interview. You might also remind the interviewer about some of your strength or skills. Follow-up letters are a good way to bring up any points you forgot to discuss during the interview. Like Barry's, your follow-up letter may give you the edge in getting the job that you want.

MAIN POINTS

- There are a number of ways to obtain job leads in a career field. Tell family members, school counselors, and friends the kind of job you desire, and ask for their help. Make appointments with the personnel departments of local companies.
- Public and private employment agencies can help you find jobs. Private agencies charge a fee that is paid by either the employee or the employer.
- Want ads advertising available jobs appear in newspapers, trade publications, and civil service announcements. They may also be posted on school and company bulletin boards and in store windows.
- Good organization will help you get the job you want. A card file can help you keep track of company addresses and phone numbers, people's names, interview dates, and your follow-up.

- A well-written, factual, and neat resume will help present your qualifications to an employer in a positive way.
- If you are responding to a job lead over the telephone, practice in advance what you are going to say.
- Well-written application letters can impress potential employers. Study some model letters, make a first draft, and check grammar, spelling, and punctuation before and after typing the final draft.
- Many companies require job seekers to fill out an application form. Be sure to have the facts about your personal history with you when you attend interviews.
- Many companies require that applicants take preemployment tests prior to hiring. Preemployment tests may include skills tests, psychological tests, polygraph tests, and medical tests.
- Prepare carefully for interviews. Be clean, neat, and on time. Make a list of questions you may be asked and questions you want to ask the interviewer. Role-play your interview with a friend or parent. Remember that an interview is a two-way communication.
- Follow up an interview with a thank-you letter. A follow-up letter is a good way to remind an interviewer of your strengths or skills.

Terms to Know

Use the following terms to fill in the blanks of the sentences below.

application form
body language
employment agency
first draft
job lead
letter of application
personnel department
private employment agency
public employment agency
references
resume
trade publication

1. A profit-making business that matches people with jobs is called a(n) _____.
2. Slouching and chewing gum are examples of negative _____.
3. Anything that provides information about a possible job opening is called a(n) _____.
4. The division of a company concerned with finding new employees is the _____.
5. Statements by people telling an employer about an applicant's character and job skills are called _____.
6. The first version of a resume, which can be changed and corrected, is known as the _____.
7. When you write to a potential employer to ask for a job, you are writing a(n) _____.
8. Many companies use a standard _____ that asks for your job history and educational background.
9. A written summary of your work experience, education, and other job qualifications is called a(n) _____.
10. A magazine containing information devoted to a particular occupation is known as a(n) _____.
11. A free job-finding service run by a state is known as a(n) _____.
12. An organization that matches people to jobs is known as a(n) _____.

Chapter 7 Getting the Job You Want

Chapter Review

1. Name three or four sources of job leads.
2. What kinds of information do want ads usually provide? What are blind ads?
3. What is the difference between public and private employment agencies? What kinds of questions should you ask when you register with an employment agency?
4. List four reasons for organizing a job search.
5. What are the most frequently used categories of information on a resume?
6. Outline the proper steps to take when writing a resume or a letter of application.
7. Why is it important to practice your opening statement before applying for a job by telephone?
8. What kinds of preemployment tests are often given by companies, and what do they test?
9. List four or five things you can do to prepare for an interview.
10. Why is it important to write a follow-up letter?

Activities

1. Bring in the want ad section of the Sunday newspaper, and use it to answer the following questions:
   a. What kinds of companies are hiring in your area?
   b. What job category has the most openings? The fewest?
   c. What are the names of some local employment agencies? What kinds of jobs do they list?
   d. What are some of the abbreviations used in want ads, and what do they mean?
2. Role-play job interviews with friends or classmates. Pretend you are the owner of a restaurant. What qualities would you be looking for in a waiter or waitress? Make a list of questions you would ask an applicant. Conduct the interview with a classmate playing the applicant. Ask the rest of the class to evaluate the interview. Would this applicant be hired?
3. Write an opening statement for use when asking for an interview by telephone. Read your statement to the class, and ask for feedback. Listen to your classmates' opening statements, and offer suggestions for making them more concise and effective.
4. Extracurricular activities, clubs, volunteer work, and hobbies can often be used on your resume or in interviews as job-related experience. Make a list of all the organizations you belong to and the activities you like to do. Ask classmates to help determine how these activities can help prove to an interviewer that you would be a good employee.
5. Invite a representative from a public or private employment agency to speak to your class. Before the visit, prepare a list of questions about ways to make a good impression on prospective employers.

Chapter 8

Joining the Work Force

OBJECTIVES

This chapter will enable you to:
- explain the importance of being able to work well with others.
- relate workers' rights and duties to management's rights and duties.
- list ways in which a worker's status can change.
- define labor unions and explain what labor and management bargain about.
- summarize how being a good worker helps economic growth.

Jane

When I got my job at a fast-food restaurant a few months ago, I thought I had it made. I was really excited about the money I'd be making.

During my first few weeks, I found out there was more to the job than the paycheck. First, I learned how to clean up the dining area. Then, Betty, the manager, decided it was time for me to cook. She gave me a general introduction to the process. When she finished, I realized I still didn't know how to turn on the grill, so I asked her to show me.

Then, she assigned me to work with Mark, who had a few years' experience. He taught me how to cook the burgers and fries. Mark had even figured out a better way to set up the plastic dishes and told Betty about it. Betty told the whole crew, so now we all stack the dishes Mark's way.

I also found out how important it was for me to do what was expected. If I got behind or confused at the grill, everybody got messed up. The food couldn't be cooked too little or too much. I was working with a stove and hot oil for the fries, so I had to be careful.

Finally, I learned that Mark and I had to work seriously if we were to get our work done properly. At home, I'm sometimes known to clown around, but at work, I stick to business. Working in a restaurant kitchen can create a lot of tension. It's a more comfortable place to be if people help each other. For instance, where I work, everyone is trained to do all the jobs, so we can make things run smoothly. By the end of my first few months, I had cooked, stocked the refrigerators, run the register, and tended the counter. After closing, everyone, even Betty, helps clean up. Betty explained that cooperation helps make the restaurant successful, which is good for the workers, management, and, of course, the customers.

When I got my first paycheck, I was excited about the money. In fact, I felt terrific. I also knew I'd learned a lot about what it means to have a job.

WORKING WITH OTHERS

Before she started working, Jane thought a job was mostly the excitement of a paycheck. Now, she is learning that working means communicating with others. It means doing what is expected, doing a good job, and working safely. It also means getting along with people, so fellow workers, managers, and customers are all satisfied.

Working means interacting with other people. Even if you open your own pizza shop and do everything yourself, you will need to buy cheese and sauce from a supplier, and you will have customers to please. Chances are, though, your first job will be for an organization. An **organization** is *a group of people working toward the same goal.*

All organizations have goals. For a business, the main goal is to provide goods or services at a profit. Burger King sells fast food. H & R Block sells help in preparing income tax forms. A nonprofit organization might want to reduce heart disease or prepare athletes for the Olympics. Whatever the goal, everyone in the organization needs to work toward it.

Organizations use managers so that all work will meet the goals of the organization. **Managers** are *the people who explain jobs to workers so that they will help the organization meet its goals.* As Jane's manager, Betty explained to her what was to be done and how to do it.

Without teamwork on the part of its workers, an organization would not be able to meet its goals.

Chapter 8 Joining the Work Force

Managers want jobs to be done efficiently and well.

Everyone gains when an organization meets its goals. Workers gain satisfaction when they do their jobs well. They may also earn praise, be promoted, or get a raise in pay. Society gains because more goods and services are produced. Increased production can lead to lower prices, as in the fast-food restaurant where Jane works.

Goals are met through working well with other people. Organizations are made up of groups of people. People must work effectively as individuals and as a group to meet goals. Each person in a group is like a link in a chain. Each person matters. Each person must communicate with others, do a good job, and get along with people.

Communicating. Communication is the key to a smoothly run organization. Managers must explain and listen carefully. As a manager, Betty's job was to tell Jane how to keep the orders straight and how long to cook the food. Workers must ask for help and instructions. When Jane, for example, did not know how to turn on the grill, she asked to be shown. Workers should tell managers when they figure out better ways to do their jobs, as Mark did when he told Betty about an easier way to stack the dishes. Finally, workers must communicate with each other. An experienced worker like Mark can teach a new worker like Jane.

Doing a Good Job. When one worker does not do what is expected, everyone else has to do more work. Jane found that if she was slow or got orders confused, everyone had a harder time. Customers might choose to eat somewhere else next time if they had to wait too long or received poorly prepared food. So Jane had to do what was expected and do her best. Also, Jane had to work with care, because there are many safety hazards in a restaurant kitchen. (Chapter 11 discusses methods for maintaining health and safety in any workplace.)

Getting Along With People. Finally, working means getting along well with co-workers and managers as well as with customers. This may mean being more serious than you would be with your friends. Jane tried not to kid around at work. She learned and did all the jobs that needed to be done, even those she did not especially like. Where Jane worked, people helped each other. Everyone cleaned up. The crew and the managers felt better when things ran well.

RIGHTS AND DUTIES IN THE WORKPLACE

Everyone in a workplace has both rights and duties. Federal and state laws spell out many of the rights of workers. These rights start as soon as you apply for a job.

Workers' Rights

When you apply for a job, you are protected by **antidiscrimination laws**, which *forbid employers from discriminating against you because of your race, color, national origin, age, sex, religion, or other traits*. The Civil Rights Act of 1964 made it illegal to exclude workers because of race. Other laws, court decisions, and rulings of the federal government have broadened this protection. Employers now cannot discriminate against you in the workplace because of your age, sex, or a handicap that does not prevent you from doing the job. For example, if you need to use crutches for walking, you do not have the qualifications to be a construction worker, but you cannot be refused a drafting job because of this physical handicap.

Another law, which was passed in 1935, forbids employers from refusing to hire union members. This law, sometimes called the Wagner Act, also says that employers must allow workers to form a union if they wish to.

Laws also limit the work that can be done by young people. Most states do not let em-

Servers receive income in tips. The law in some states does not require employers to pay minimum wage because of this.

ployers hire children under 14. Most states also require workers under 16 or 18 to get a work permit. A **work permit** *allows a person under the minimum working age in a state to be legally employed*. Special laws also limit the work allowed under such a permit, but the laws vary from state to state. Some states may allow 14-year-olds to do harvesting. Others may not. A work permit is not required for some part-time jobs that young people often do, such as baby-sitting, delivering newspapers, or mowing lawns. (In Chapter 9, you will learn more about child labor laws.)

Workers have rights that govern their pay. Federal law sets a minimum hourly wage that most workers must be paid. The minimum was 25 cents an hour in 1938, when the law was first passed. In 1985, the minimum wage was $3.35 an hour. Minimum wage does not apply to some jobs. Servers, for example, receive income in tips, so in some states employers do not have to pay them a base wage that equals the minimum.

Some critics say that minimum wage laws mean fewer jobs. Businesses would hire more workers, these critics argue, if the employers did not have to pay so much. Efforts continue to permit workers under 18 to be hired at less than the minimum. These efforts are aimed at opening more part-time jobs to teenagers.

Other laws state that most workers must be paid extra—at least time and a half—for **overtime**, which means *any time worked beyond the regular number of hours*. Other laws state that employers cannot pay different wages for the same job if the difference is based on race, sex, or age. A new female house painter must be paid the same as a new male house painter. An experienced or skilled painter would earn a higher wage than an apprentice, however.

Workers have a right to safe working conditions. The Occupational Safety and Health Administration (OSHA) was created by Congress in 1970. This agency sets standards for safety on the job. OSHA can inspect workplaces and order employers to correct unsafe conditions. Loud, constant noise from a jackhammer might be considered a hearing hazard. OSHA might tell an employer to provide hearing protectors for workers.

Some workers' rights come from a contract between the worker and the employer. A contract exists automatically even if nothing is written down on paper. Employers must pay workers the promised wage for their work at the promised time because of this contract.

Chapter 8 Joining the Work Force

Workers can expect employers to explain any rules, including codes of dress and behavior on the job. The performance of workers must be reviewed fairly. Being reviewed gives workers the chance to find out if they do not measure up and the opportunity to improve. It also lets them know if they are meeting standards or perhaps doing better than is expected. If so, they might want to ask for a raise.

Management's Rights

Managers have the right to expect workers to work toward the organization's goals. These management rights, then, are workers' duties. Here is what managers expect from workers:

- Productivity. Productive workers do as much good work as possible.
- Initiative. Workers with initiative find out what needs to be done. Then, they do it without waiting to be assigned. They also tell managers about ideas for better ways to do a job.
- Quality work. Workers who do quality work make the product or provide the service in the best way possible.
- Cooperation. Cooperative workers share special skills or knowledge with other workers. They do whatever is possible to make everyone's job easier and more pleasant.
- Honesty. Honest workers respect an employer's property; they do not steal or lie about the time worked.
- Adaptability. Adaptable workers are willing to learn new jobs or new ways of doing a task.
- Reliability. Reliable workers strive to do the job the right way all the time. They arrive on time except under special circumstances such as illness.
- Good attitude. Workers with a good attitude think well of the job, other workers, and the organization.
- Efficiency. Efficient workers use materials or machines wisely and make good use of time.
- Safety. Workers who are safety-conscious use equipment properly and take care to protect themselves and their co-workers.

Workers who perform well do themselves a favor. A strong organization stays in business, which means job security. A successful organization rewards the workers who help it succeed. These workers may receive raises and promotions.

BARGAINING IN THE WORKPLACE

Ideally, workers and employers should be able to bargain as equals. The supply of workers and the demand for their skills should determine wages for different kinds of labor, but workers do not always feel they can bargain individually as equals. For instance, at the fast-food restaurant, Jane, Mark, and their co-workers might band together to approach Betty about scheduling holiday work hours. They would be united by their interest in having a more flexible schedule. They might feel Betty would pay more attention to them as a group.

To have more say over their job conditions, many workers form organizations of their own. These organizations, called **labor unions,** are *groups of workers who have joined together for better bargaining.*

Labor Unions

Members of some labor unions have the same skill, such as those in the Screen Cartoonists Guild. Members of others have the same craft, such as the Sheet Metal Workers' International Association. There are also unions that unite many kinds of workers in one industry or in a few related industries. The International Ladies' Garment Workers' Union is of this type.

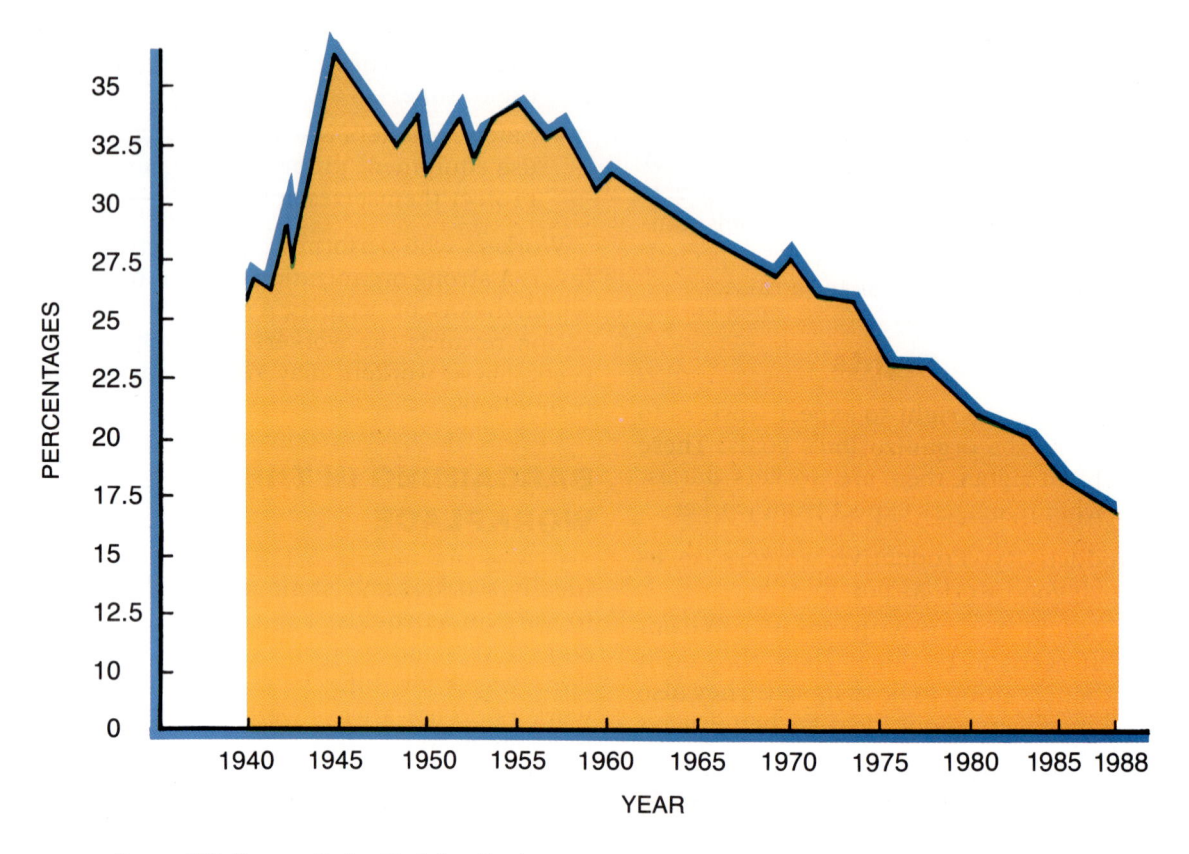

Source: U.S. Bureau of Labor Statistics, *Employment and Earnings*, January issues.
Figure 8.1 The Percentage of Workers Who Belong to Unions

Although the Wagner Act gave workers the right to form unions, fewer than 20 percent of American workers now belong to unions, as you can see in Figure 8.1. This percent is lower than at any time since passage of the Wagner Act.

Still, some unions are growing. More and more white-collar workers, government workers, and people in service jobs, such as hospital workers, are joining unions. Figure 8.2 lists the largest unions in the country.

How Bargaining Works

Perhaps Jane, Mark, and their co-workers discuss the holiday work schedule among themselves. They decide what they think a fair and flexible schedule would be. Then, Mark is chosen to represent the group's concerns to Betty, who will represent the needs of management. Through give-and-take, Betty and Mark will try to reach an agreement both sides can live with.

Similarly, unions and employers engage in **collective bargaining**, which is *negotiation over the terms of employment between officials of the union and representatives of the employer*. The officials bargain to create a contract both sides can agree upon. Then, union members vote to accept or reject the contract.

Both sides must bargain in *good faith*, which means they must be sincere about reaching an agreement. Good faith is hard to define. If one

Figure 8.2 The Ten Largest Unions in the Country

Union	Membership
International Brotherhood of Teamsters	2,000,000
National Education Association	1,700,000
Food and Commercial Workers	1,300,000
American Federation of State, County, and Municipal Workers	1,200,000
United Steelworkers of America	1,200,000
United Automobile Workers	1,150,000
International Brotherhood of Electrical Workers	1,100,000
International Association of Machinists and Aerospace Workers	943,000
Carpenters and Joiners of America	820,000
Service Employees International Union	650,000

side suspects the other of not bargaining in good faith, the courts may be asked to decide the case.

Sometimes, no agreement can be reached. Then, the two sides may ask an outside mediator for help. A **mediator** is a *neutral person who joins labor negotiations to help bring about an agreement.* The two sides may seek help from an **arbitrator,** *a neutral person who looks at the proposals of the negotiating parties and decides what they must accept.* A federal agency has a staff of mediators, as well as a list of skilled arbitrators from which unions and management can choose.

WHAT UNION CONTRACTS SAY

Contracts between unions and management cover pay, benefits, working conditions, and job security. Contracts also set up ways to settle disputes.

Contracts set workers' hourly wages, raises, and overtime. They state what benefits workers will get, such as vacations and pensions.

Contracts set working conditions. These include the length of a workday and the number and length of breaks. Health and safety rules may also be stated in a contract. Some union contracts state the kind and amount of work required of workers. A worker, for example, may be required to sew a certain number of shirts each day.

Contracts may also protect the job security of workers. Contracts have rules employers must follow when they hire, promote, lay off, or fire workers. For example, hiring rules might say an employer must try to fill job openings with workers who already work for the company before looking outside.

Contracts also state whether workers must join the union. There are several types of membership agreements. These range from an open shop to a union shop. In an **open shop**, *employees do not have to be members of a union with which the shop may have a contract*. In a **union shop**, *workers must join a union within 30 days of being hired*. Other kinds of membership agreements exist as well.

Finally, union contracts set up **grievance procedures.** These are *steps workers can take to protest and appeal any employer decision they think breaks the contract*. These rules set up an orderly way to settle disputes between workers and managers. The first step usually calls for the worker's supervisor and a union official to settle the problem. If they cannot, the matter is sent to higher-level managers and union leaders.

When There Is No Agreement

Sometimes negotiators cannot agree on a contract. Then, both workers and managers have ways to try to make each other change positions or to speed up the agreement.

One method unions have is the strike. A **strike** is *an organized refusal by workers to continue working*. Strikes slow down or halt an employer's production. Strikers may set up picket lines outside the workplace. The pickets often carry signs stating their views. Strikers may also ask members of other unions and the general public not to do business with the employer.

Some unions pay strike benefits to members during a strike because strikers do not get paychecks. Unions may pay them out of the union treasury so they will not give up the strike before reaching a satisfactory agreement.

Going on strike is a serious action. Before striking, workers must think about the effect of their actions. Is there something to be gained from a strike? Will the benefits be greater than the wages lost? Will the strike or the terms of the settlement hurt the union or even kill it? Will the company go out of business? Will nonstriking workers be harmed? For instance, a strike at a steel plant can lead to layoffs at a car factory.

Unions also try to get other workers and consumers to **boycott** the employer's products. This *refusal to do business with an organization or to buy its products or services* might force an employer to settle. For example, in a dispute with grape growers, the United Farm Workers asked consumers to boycott grapes from 1965 to 1970. Unions can also seek injunctions from

Workers sometimes strike when there is no agreement on a contract. Going on strike is a serious action.

the courts if they think employers are acting illegally. An **injunction** is *a judge's order that a person or organization stop an illegal action.*

Employers can also seek injunctions against unions. Employers have other ways of influencing workers. If workers strike, employers can hire nonunion workers or use supervisors to do the strikers' work. If employers think workers might strike, they can close the workplace. This is called a *lockout*. Some businesses buy strike insurance. Then, if workers strike, the company receives money to replace its losses. If a business feels that strike threats happen too often or that actual strikes are too severe, it can close permanently or move elsewhere.

employer time to consider your request.

Another kind of reward for work well done is a promotion. A **promotion** is *an advancement to a higher position.* A promotion brings more responsibility. It may also mean a raise. In the new job, you may have to do more difficult work. You may also have to supervise the work of others. (Chapter 10 discusses the qualities of a good supervisor.)

Your status can also change through a transfer. A **transfer** is *an assignment to a job in a different place.* Transfers allow employers to make the best use of employees. However, a transfer requires an employee to uproot his or her family. If a worker is part of a dual-career

CHANGES IN YOUR STATUS

There are several ways your status as a worker can change. You can receive a raise, a promotion, or a transfer. You may also leave a job by resigning, being laid off, being fired, or retiring.

A **raise** is *an increase in a worker's pay.* A raise can be a reward for good work, or it may be called for in a contract. An employer may offer you a raise after reviewing your work. If that does not happen, you may need to take it upon yourself to ask for a raise. First, you will have to review your own performance. Are you doing your best? Are you doing as much as your co-workers? And are you doing it as well? Is your work above average? If so, you may have grounds to ask for a raise.

The key word is *ask*. You should never demand a raise. Instead, you should persuade your employer that you deserve a raise. You can do this by listing your past achievements. You can also suggest ways you can help the organization in the future. When you do ask for a raise, request a reasonable amount. Do not demand an answer immediately. Give your

Pointing out your past achievements can help persuade your employer that you deserve a raise.

Now is the time to start developing interests and hobbies that can make your retirement years busy and fulfilling.

family, he or she may be less likely to accept a transfer. Think about how a transfer will affect you and your family before you accept or reject it.

You may decide to leave a job. You might **resign**, or *give up your position*. There are many reasons for resigning. A job may not match your goals. There may be little chance for advancement. You may be offered a better job by a different employer. You may decide to go into business for yourself. The way you resign a job can affect your future jobs. If you leave in haste or anger, your former employer may give a poor recommendation to a prospective employer.

You need to give advance notice when you resign. Your employer will need to replace you, and it can take time to find a new worker. One pay period is standard. You should give more notice if you are a supervisor. Your employer will also need extra notice if you are leaving at a busy time. It is best to give your notice in writing. During the weeks before you leave the company, be sure to work cooperatively and well.

You may not receive unemployment benefits if you resign. Check the laws of your state to find out if you are eligible. Do not resign until you have a new job or some savings.

You will probably be eligible for unemployment benefits if you are laid off. A **layoff** is *a temporary or permanent end to employment because of poor business*. If you are laid off, you might receive extra pay called *severance pay* from your employer. If you belong to a union, you may receive payments from the union treasury during the layoff. You should also consider learning new job skills that will enable you to enter a different career area.

There is also the chance that you might be fired from a job. **Firing** is *the permanent dismissal of a worker*. If you are fired, it is important to find out why. Then, it is important to correct the problem so you can succeed in your next job. You may receive severance pay when you are fired. You may also receive unemployment benefits.

Retirement is another way to leave an organization. **Retirement** is *withdrawal from work at the end of your career*. Even though you are many years away from retiring, you can begin planning for it. You will need to think about gaining financial security through insurance, savings, and investments. You will also need to

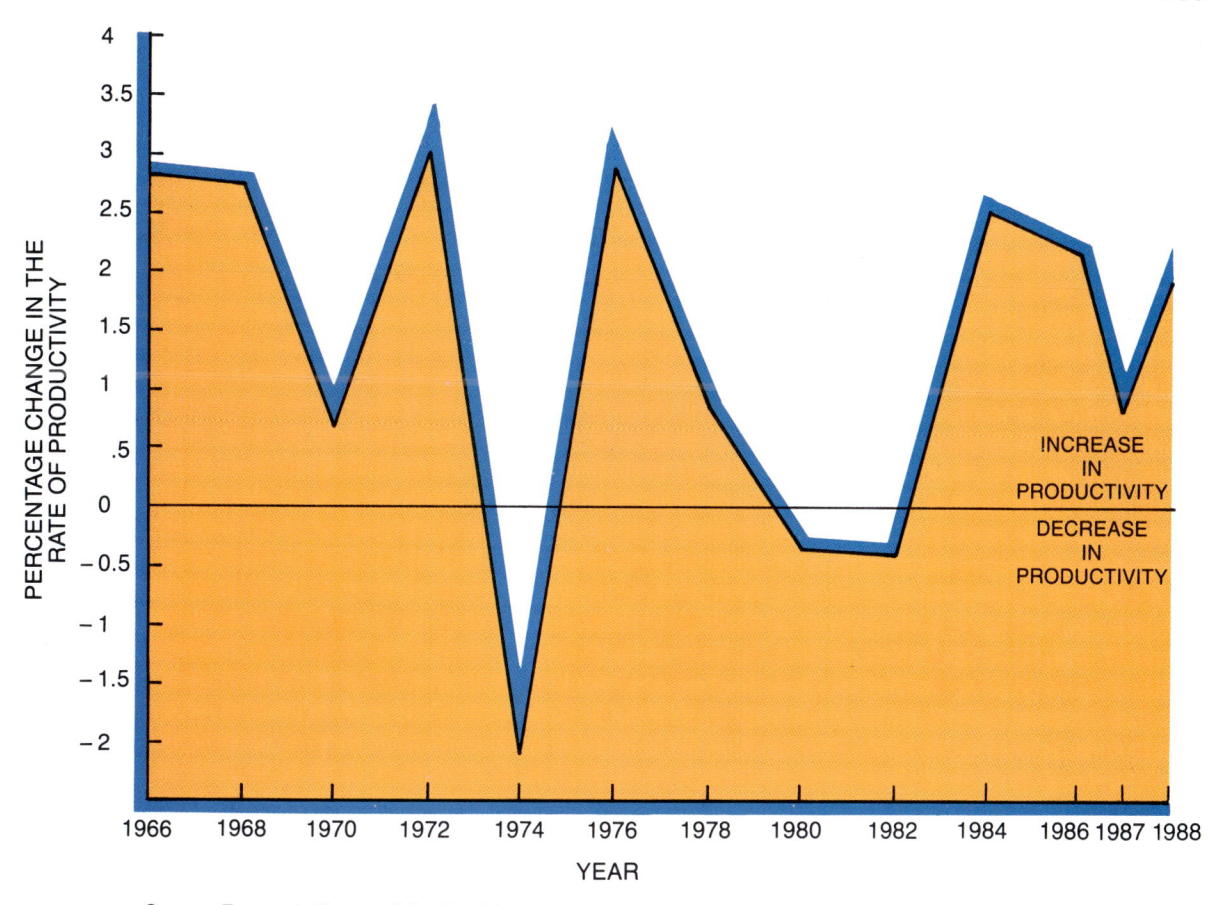

Figure 8.3 Changes in the Rate of Business Productivity

Source: Economic Report of the President

plan for your emotional well-being. Now is the time to start developing interests and hobbies. They will help you enjoy the leisure time that comes with retirement.

PRODUCTIVE WORKERS HELP ECONOMIC GROWTH

The economy grows when producers can use the same amount of resources to make more goods and services. It also grows when fewer resources can be used to make the same amount of goods and services. Growth is spurred by **productivity**, which is *a measure of how many goods or services can be produced with a given amount of resources.* The Bureau of Labor Statistics measures productivity by estimating how much each worker produces per hour. Figure 8.3 shows how the rate of productivity of American workers has changed in recent years.

Everyone benefits from higher productivity. Consumers can choose from more goods and services. Businesses can compete more effectively and make higher profits. Workers feel good about their work. They may also receive rewards such as raises. Certainly, they get more job security.

New technology can create jobs; workers are needed to build new machines and to repair them.

When productivity goes down, everybody loses. Workers find their jobs in danger. Money buys less. Businesses find it harder to compete, and some may be forced to close. Society suffers because many workers lose their jobs. Also, fewer goods and services are produced.

What can you or Jane, as workers, do to boost productivity? Here are a number of ways to help:

- Work more efficiently. Do not waste your employer's resources, one of which is your time on the job.
- Work more creatively. Find better ways to do tasks, as Mark did. If those new methods save time and resources, tell your employer about them.
- Adapt to new technology. You can learn new skills and find new ways to use old skills. Many organizations pay bonuses to workers who develop new methods and learn new skills.

Productivity does have its costs. This is especially true if it is based on new technology. New equipment costs money. In the long run, though, the equipment earns back its cost through increased efficiency. Some workers believe that technology has human costs. They see machines performing tasks once done by workers, but new machines can also create jobs. Workers are needed to build the machines, to operate them, and to fix them. New technology can be an opportunity for workers. They can learn new skills and use their old skills in new ways.

Chapter 8 Joining the Work Force

MAIN POINTS

- Workers must cooperate with others to help reach the goals of the organization where they work. Working with others means communicating, doing a good job, and getting along with people.
- Management must recognize workers' rights. These include the rights to be hired and to work without discrimination, to earn a fair wage, to earn extra for overtime, to work in a safe place, and to be paid the stated amount on time.
- Workers must recognize management's rights. These include the rights to expect productivity, initiative, quality work, cooperation, honesty, adaptability, reliability, good attitude, efficiency, and safety.
- Workers may form a union to bargain with management. Contracts agreed to in collective bargaining state the terms of employment and some of the rights and duties of workers and management.
- When they cannot reach an agreement, workers or managers may ask a mediator to help them settle their differences. They may also ask an arbitrator to create an agreement.
- To try to influence management, unions may ask other workers and consumers to boycott the employer. They can also seek a court injunction or go on strike.
- Management can seek court injunctions against unions. Employers can lock out workers who threaten to strike. During a strike, a company can hire nonunion employees or have supervisors do the work.
- A worker's status may change through a raise, a promotion, or a transfer. A worker may also leave a job by resigning, being laid off, being fired, or retiring.
- Workers can help improve the economy by improving productivity. They can do this by working more efficiently or by helping find new ways of doing their work.

Terms to Know

Use the following terms to fill in the blanks of the sentences below.

antidiscrimination laws
arbitrator
boycott
collective bargaining
firing
grievance procedures
injunction
labor union
layoff
manager
mediator
open shop
organization
overtime
productivity
promotion
raise
resign
retirement
strike
transfer
union shop
work permit

1. Many employees receive extra pay when they work _____.
2. The union members protested their employer's decision following the _____ set up in their contract.
3. A judge's order that a person or organization stop an illegal action is a(n) _____.
4. Only union members are hired in a(n) _____.

5. An increase in a worker's pay is a(n) _____.
6. A group of people working toward the same goal is a(n) _____.
7. A neutral person who looks at the proposals of the negotiating parties and decides what they must accept is a(n) _____.
8. Advancement to a higher position in an organization is a(n) _____.
9. If you are offered a better job by a different employer, you may decide to _____ your present position.
10. A person who explains jobs to workers so that their work will meet the organization's goals is called a(n) _____.
11. A temporary end to employment because of poor business is a(n) _____.
12. A business where employees do not have to be members of a union with which the business has a contract is a(n) _____.
13. The permanent dismissal of a worker is known as _____.
14. If you are under the minimum working age in your state, you must obtain a(n) _____, which allows you to work.
15. An employer who refuses to hire workers because of their race is disobeying _____.
16. Withdrawal from work at the end of your career is _____.
17. Even though it meant uprooting his family Larry was pleased with his job _____.
18. A group of workers joined together for better bargaining is a(n) _____.
19. A neutral person who joins labor negotiations to help bring about an agreement is a(n) _____.
20. A refusal to do business with an organization or to buy its products or services is a(n) _____.
21. When officials of a union and representatives of an employer negotiate, it is called _____.
22. A measure of how many goods or services can be produced with a given amount of resources is _____.
23. An organized stoppage of work by workers is a(n) _____.

Chapter Review

1. What is the key to a smoothly run organization?
2. How can a person work well with others? Give an example.
3. Who is required to get a work permit?
4. What rights do workers have about their pay?
5. List three traits managers can expect of workers. Choose one, and tell why it is important.
6. What is a labor union? Why do workers organize?
7. What kinds of employment conditions are covered in a union contract?
8. What questions should union members ask themselves before going on strike?
9. How does everyone—workers, businesses, consumers—gain when productivity rises?
10. How can workers boost productivity?

Activities

1. Do some research on working conditions in factories at the turn of the century. In a brief report, describe typical working hours, health and safety conditions, employee benefits, workers' rights, and the use of child labor.
2. Learn the requirements for a work permit in your state. What kinds of jobs are young workers restricted from performing? For what kinds of jobs do young workers not need a permit?
3. Do you think it is a good idea to repeal the minimum wage laws? Why or why not?

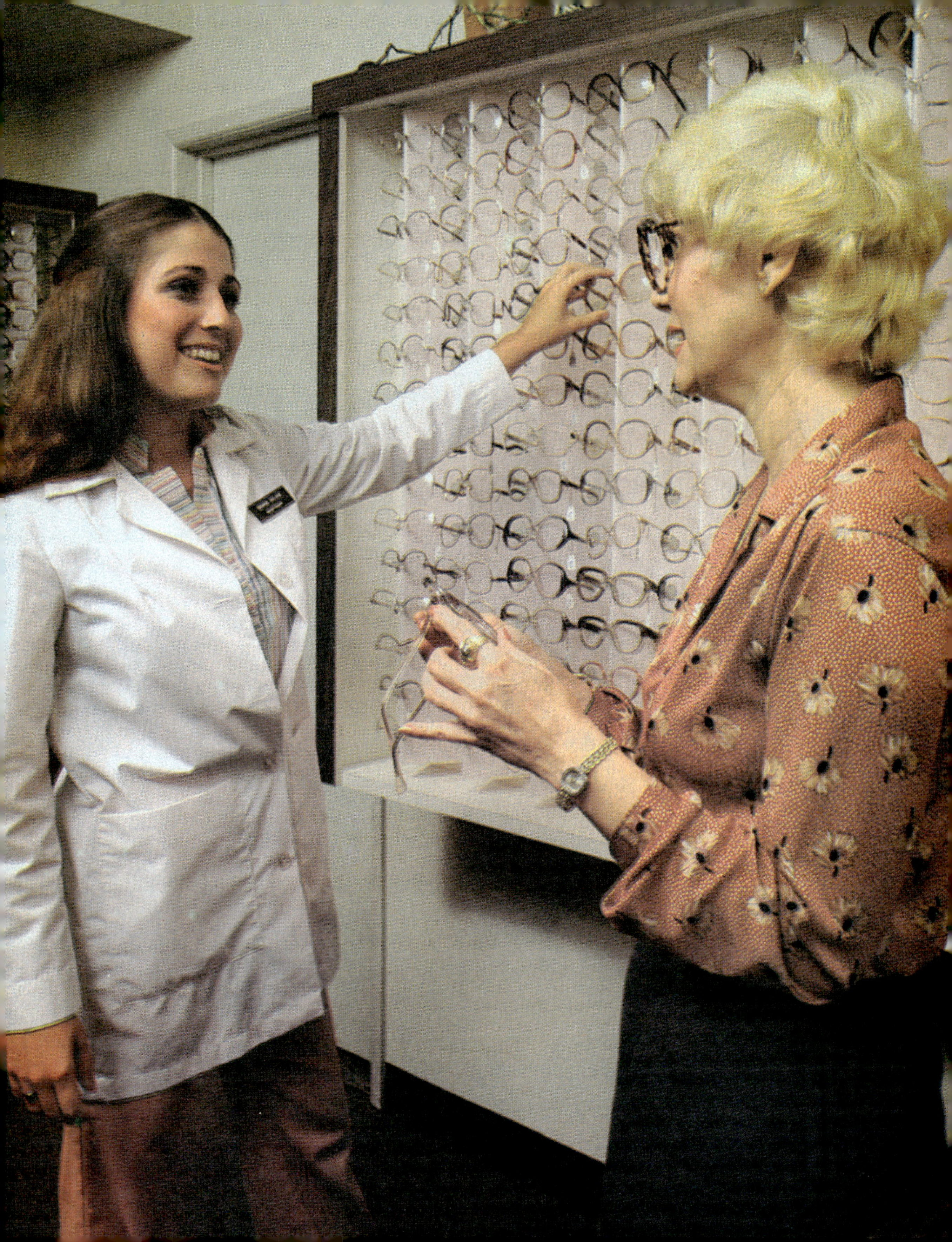

PART THREE
You as a Worker

In Part Three, you will explore the most important aspects of being on the job. Different methods of earning income are compared, and the various deductions subtracted from a worker's pay are described. You will also consider how your decisions affect your income. You will learn the value of a positive attitude on the job and techniques for working well with others, including ways to cope effectively with stress and conflict. You will also discover valuable guidelines for protecting your health and safety in the workplace.

Chapter **9**

Earning an Income

OBJECTIVES

This chapter will enable you to:
- compare the benefits of various ways of earning income.
- list the various deductions subtracted from a worker's pay.
- outline the process involved in filing an income tax return.
- explain how decisions made by workers affect the amount of income at their disposal.
- describe some important social insurance plans supported by income taxes.
- describe the ways in which child labor laws protect the health and safety of workers under the age of 18.

Molly

Sometimes it's hard to make a decision, especially when it involves money—and your future. You see, I'm trying to save money so I can go to an electronics school after I graduate from high school, so I need a part-time job. I've got several possibilities, which is great. The problem is, each one would pay me in a different way, and I don't know which would be best.

I've been delivering newspapers since sixth grade, and my circulation manager is leaving to take another job. I've got a chance to take his place. He gets a small salary each month, plus commissions on new sales that he makes in the area.

Then there's the Old Carriage Inn. That's a really nice restaurant on the outskirts of town that's been advertising for a busperson. Someone I know used to work there. She made an hourly wage, but most of her income came from tips. It's the kind of place where everybody puts their tips into a pot, and the tips are then divided equally among all the employees. Sometimes, the tips are great. But sometimes, they're pretty slim. You can't count on making a definite amount each week.

While I was thinking about those two jobs, my father told me that the owner of the service station where we get our gas was looking for an attendant. That job pays an hourly wage. Maybe I would get a bonus at the end of the year.

To further complicate matters, my mother just handed me a want ad from the newspaper. There's a farmer who needs people to grade and package eggs at his farm. He pays his workers a certain amount for every dozen eggs they package. The faster they work, the more they make.

Now the question I have to answer is, Which kind of payment will give me the best deal?

WORKERS EARN MONEY IN DIFFERENT WAYS

Molly has to choose one of four different jobs, each of which has a different method of payment. There are, in fact, even more ways of earning income—a total of six methods of payment.

Whichever way a worker is paid, the same transaction takes place. Workers sell their labor to producers. Producers use this labor to create goods and services. In exchange for their labor, workers receive money.

The money a worker is paid for his or her labor is called **earned income**. In addition, workers often receive fringe benefits. **Fringe benefits** are *other forms of payment for labor, such as insurance coverage, vacation time, sick days, and pensions*. Earned income is usually taxed by different levels of government, whereas fringe benefits are not. Let us compare the different kinds of income.

Wage. If Molly takes the job at the gas station, she will receive a wage. A **wage** is *an hourly rate of pay for work*. Let us say the owner agrees to pay Molly $4.50 an hour. If she works 5 hours a week, she will earn $22.50 before taxes. If she works 10 hours a week, she will earn $45 before taxes. The owner is not allowed to pay her less than the federal minimum wage if the business is covered by the Fair Labor Standards Act. Otherwise, the state minimum wage would apply. (One exception to this law is a job that involves tips.)

Hourly wages are paid most often in manufacturing, maintenance, and service jobs. These are the kinds of jobs in which employers have a good idea of the amount of work a worker can do in an hour.

Piecework. The job at the egg farm would pay Molly in a different way. Instead of being paid by the hour, she would be paid at a **piecework rate**. This is *a set rate of pay for each unit of work produced*. The more eggs Molly packs, the more money she earns. Like wage earners, pieceworkers are protected by law. They cannot be paid less than the minimum hourly wage. They must also be paid extra for *overtime*—time worked beyond the regular number of hours. Pieceworkers usually do not receive any paid days off, such as vacation days. They get paid only when they work.

Salary. The job as local circulation manager for the newspaper offers Molly a salary. A **salary** is *a rate of pay for work that is figured by the week, month, or year*. Workers usually receive payments every week or every two weeks. Their salary must equal at least the minimum wage for a normal workweek.

Salary is a common form of payment for managers and office workers. These are workers whose duties can vary greatly. That makes it difficult for an employer to predict how much work an employee will do each hour or day.

Workers on salary usually receive paid vacation days. However, they must often work many hours of overtime without extra pay. This is often the case with jobs in the middle and upper management levels of a company.

Commission. The newspaper job also paid **commission**, *a form of payment made up of a*

Garment workers are among those paid at a piecework rate. The more units they produce the more they earn.

Chapter 9 Earning an Income

Many salespeople are on commission. Their earnings depend on how much they sell.

percentage of sales made. The more sales made, the higher the commission. Many salespeople are on commission. Some receive a base salary plus commission. Others receive only commission. A commission can encourage workers to make more sales.

Tips. The busperson job Molly is considering is typical of many jobs in service industries. Workers in these jobs receive much of their income in tips. **Tips** are *small sums of money given to workers by satisfied customers*. Customers often tip food service workers, taxi drivers, hairdressers, and hotel employees. Tips are usually voluntary. That means customers decide how much to tip. Some restaurants, though, automatically add 15 or 20 percent to customers' bills for tips.

In the restaurant where Molly might work, the workers pool their tips each day. The tips are then divided evenly among the workers, including some who do not deal directly with customers. Most buspersons, for example, would not ordinarily receive tips. Yet servers depend on them to do a good job setting and clearing tables. That helps satisfy customers, which can improve tips received by servers. For this reason, it is common practice for them to share their tips with the other members of the food service team.

There are also restaurants in which servers do not pool their tips. Whatever they receive,

Fringe benefits such as paid vacations improve workers' morale.

they keep. Still, it is common practice for them to voluntarily give a share of their tips to other workers.

Bonus. If Molly works at the gas station and does a good job, her employer might give her a bonus. A **bonus** is *an extra payment given to a worker for excellent work or as a share in the profits*. Some employers give bonuses to all workers at the end of a good year. Others use bonuses as a reward for good work or for a cost-saving idea.

Fringe Benefits

Molly, as a part-time temporary worker, did not consider fringe benefits in weighing the advantages of each job. When she seeks a permanent position after school, fringe benefits will be an important consideration. Because they are not direct cash payments, fringe benefits do not appear in a worker's paycheck. However, these benefits can make up a large part of a worker's income. In many large corporations, fringe benefits add more than 35 percent to the cost of workers' income. This means that for every $100 employers pay workers, employers are paying another $35 into funds for various fringe benefits.

Why do employers provide fringe benefits? One reason is to improve workers' morale. A paid vacation can refresh workers and help them think well of their employers. (In many companies, workers get longer paid vacations as their time on the job increases. Workers may receive two weeks' vacation each year for the first five years. After five to ten years of employment, they may receive three weeks' vacation. After that, their vacation may increase to a month or more.)

Other fringe benefits increase workers' economic security. Life and health insurance fall into this category. If a worker is injured or suffers a major illness, insurance payments will take care of most medical costs. Workers may also receive disability payments during the time they are unable to work.

Some kinds of fringe benefits help employers as well as workers. Many companies pay all or part of the tuition for courses in work-related subjects. When workers improve their skills and learn new ones, they can do their jobs better. Profit-sharing plans encourage workers to boost their productivity so there are more profits to share.

Fringe benefits help make a company attractive to future employees. In addition to the benefits just listed, many companies provide day care for workers' children. A growing number of companies are now building gyms, tennis courts, and running tracks for their workers to use. Many companies offer their employees discounts on the products and services they produce. If Molly works at the egg farm, for example, she may be able to buy eggs at a discount.

Two kinds of fringe benefits supply income for workers. **Pension plans** are *retirement funds.* The money in them comes from employer contributions. Workers may also pay money into the plan. In **profit-sharing plans,** *businesses share part of their profits with workers.* In some companies, workers receive a share of profits directly in the form of annual bonuses. In others, the money is paid into an investment fund. Workers receive their share when they leave the company. Profit-sharing plans may also work like pension plans.

Different businesses offer different benefit packages. Benefits may also vary according to a worker's position. As a worker moves up in a company through promotions, benefits may increase.

What should you look for when you consider the benefits a company offers? That depends on your particular wants and needs. If you have children, you may consider a company day-care center to be an important benefit. If you value fitness, a company gym may attract you. And if you want to continue your education, tuition reimbursement may be a valuable benefit.

Because workers have different wants and needs, some companies have flexible benefits. These companies offer **cafeteria plans**, which *allow workers to select a benefit menu that suits their individual needs.*

DIFFERENT FORMS OF PAYMENT

Depending on where she works, Molly may receive her pay in different forms. She is most likely to receive her income by check. There are many advantages to this form of payment. Checks are safer than cash payments. If Molly loses $20 in cash, she is out of luck. The chances of her getting her money back are very slim. If she loses a check for $20, the check can be replaced easily. For one thing, it would be difficult for someone else to cash Molly's check. If Molly reports the lost paycheck to her employer, the employer can tell the bank to stop

If you value fitness, a company gym may be a fringe benefit that attracts you.

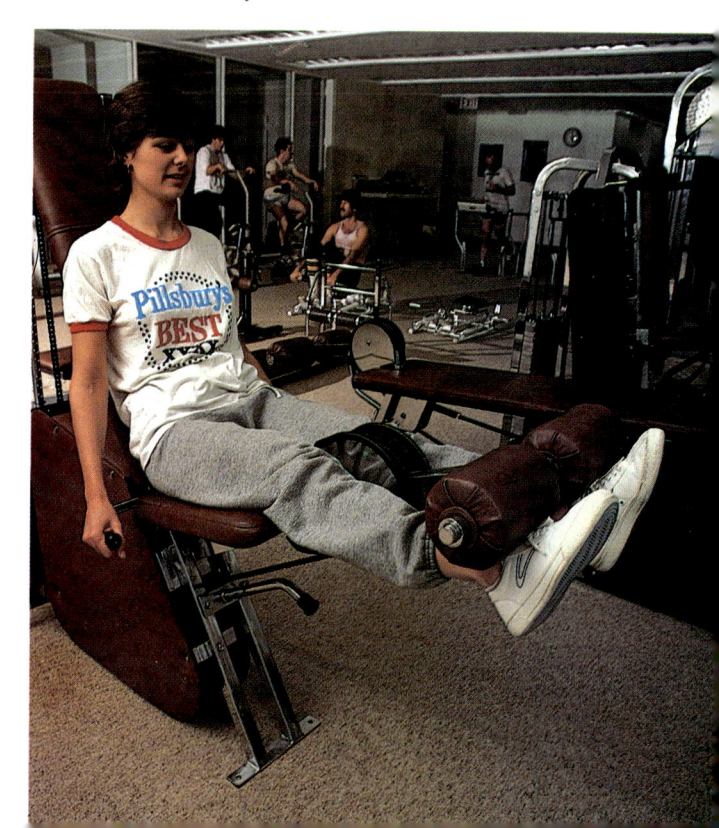

payment on the check. That means that the check cannot be cashed at all. Her employer will then issue her a new check for $20.

Payment by check also creates written records, which benefit employers and employees. Employers can show proof of the amount of money they have paid out to employees. Employees can document their income. That is valuable for tax purposes and in case of errors.

It is also possible for Molly's earnings to go directly to her bank on payday. With this kind of payment, called **direct deposit,** *funds are transferred electronically from the employer's bank account to the worker's.* Each person receives a printed record of the transaction. This type of deposit, also called *automatic deposit,* is the safest form of payment.

If Molly decides to work at the restaurant, she will receive cash payments in the form of tips. The law requires workers to declare their tips for tax purposes. Because there is no written record of cash payments, the Internal Revenue Service (IRS) ensures honest reporting in the following manner. Any restaurant with ten or more workers who receive tips must provide the IRS with information about sales. If workers report tips that total less than 8 percent of sales, the restaurant must give the IRS an estimate of each worker's income from tips.

Usually, workers do not receive the full amount they have earned. *The total amount of income an employer owes a worker for a given period* is called **gross pay**. Workers usually receive less than that amount because of **payroll deductions**. These are *amounts subtracted from gross pay to cover certain kinds of regular payments.* Some deductions are required. An employer must hold out money from workers' income for government taxes and for social security taxes (called FICA, which stands for Federal Insurance Contributions Act). There may be other deductions as well, such as union dues, charitable contributions, pension payments, and insurance premiums. *The amount left after subtracting various deductions from gross pay* is called **net pay.** That is the amount a worker actually receives. Usually, a pay stub is attached to each paycheck. The stub lists gross pay, deductions, and net pay. (Figure 9.1 shows a sample stub.) Workers should keep those pay stubs as records.

INCOME TAXES

As you can see from the sample stub, the biggest deduction from a worker's pay is for federal taxes. In addition to having this tax deducted regularly, workers must also file a federal income tax return on or before each April 15 for the previous year. The **income tax return** is *the form people use to state their income and figure the tax they owe*. Recently, the federal government simplified the tax forms. There may be additional changes in the future. Income limits also change periodically. The basic procedure for filing will probably stay the same.

Who Has to File?

Anyone who earns above a certain income is required to file a tax return. Workers below that level must also file if they are due a refund. Income includes wages, tips, and bonuses. It also includes interest or dividends from savings and investments.

Employers are required to send all their workers a **W-2 form** at the beginning of each year. This form *lists gross pay and payroll deductions for the previous year*.

You can see a typical W-2 form in Figure 9.2. Banks also have to send special forms to all depositors who earn interest. Corporations have a similar responsibility. They must mail forms to all their stockholders stating the amount of dividends earned. Finally, each source of income—employers, banks, corporations—must send a copy of each form to the IRS. That way, the government has a record of each person's yearly income and can assess each citizen's fair tax share.

Chapter 9 Earning an Income

EMPLOYEE NAME	SOCIAL SECURITY NUMBER
Betty Hernandez	683-210-7886
EMPLOYEE NUMBER	DEPARTMENT
412	6
PAY PERIOD	GROSS WAGES
Jan. 5 – Jan. 18, 1992	400.00

PAYROLL DEDUCTIONS TYPE	AMOUNT	NET WAGES
FEDERAL INCOME TAX	16.90	334.37
FICA TAX	24.19	
STATE INCOME TAX	4.04	
OTHER		

CODE	AMOUNT
3	2.50
1	18.00

CODE
1—Health insurance contribution
2—Savings bond purchase
3—United Way contribution
4—Union dues

Figure 9.1 A Sample Pay Stub

Figure 9.2 Sample W-2 Form

1 Control number 6P2		For Paperwork Reduction Act Notice, see separate instructions OMB No. 1545-0008	For Official Use Only ▶	
2 Employer's name, address, and ZIP code The Clothing Company 789 Broad Street Jamesburg, NJ 08831		3 Employer's identification number 92-444-2367	4 Employer's state I.D. number 37-33-220	
		5 Statutory employee ☐ Deceased ☐ Pension plan ☐ Legal rep. ☐ 942 emp. ☐ Subtotal ☐ Deferred compensation ☐ Void ☐		
		6 Allocated tips	7 Advance EIC payment	
8 Employee's social security number 683-210-7886	9 Federal income tax withheld $439.40	10 Wages, tips, other compensation $10,000	11 Social security tax withheld $628.94	
12 Employee's name (first, middle, last) Betty Hernandez		13 Social security wages $10,000	14 Social security tips	
		16 (See instr. for Forms W-2/W-2P)	16a Fringe benefits incl. in Box 10	
21 Greenview Avenue Jamesburg, NJ 08831				
		17 State income tax $105.04	18 State wages, tips, etc. $10,000	19 Name of state NJ
15 Employee's address and ZIP code		20 Local income tax — —	21 Local wages, tips, etc. — —	22 Name of locality — —
Form **W-2 Wage and Tax Statement 1989**		Copy A For Social Security Administration	Dept. of the Tresury—IRS	

How Do You File?

There are three basic federal tax forms. Each one is designed for a specific group of taxpayers.

Form 1040EZ. This form is for the use of single taxpayers under the age of 65 who are not blind and claim no dependents. The upper income limit for this form is $50,000 in taxable income. The limit on interest earned is $400. In addition, the taxpayer must receive no dividends and claim only one personal exemption. **Exemptions** are reductions in taxable income given to taxpayers for themselves and their children. In the case where a taxpayer is claimed as a dependent on another's tax return, no personal exemption is allowed. Form 1040EZ is, as its name suggests, easy to use. There is just one sheet to fill out. This form is often referred to as the *short form*.

Form 1040A. This expanded short form can be used by taxpapers who take tax deductions for payments to an individual retirement account (IRA). (A **tax deduction** is *an expense that reduces the income on which taxes must be paid*.) Married taxpayers filing separately or jointly may also use Form 1040A, as may taxpayers filing as heads of households. This is also the form for people who claim credit for child- and dependent-care expenses. As with Form 1040EZ, taxable income must be less than $50,000.

Form 1040. Form 1040 is often called the *long form*. All taxpayers may use this form if they choose. You must use this form if you are self-employed or if you wish to take more than the standard tax deductions. Form 1040 enables you to itemize deductions, or list each one separately. Itemizing deductions may allow a taxpayer to pay lower taxes, providing the deductions are over a certain amount. If, for example, you have had medical and dental expenses above a certain level, on Form 1040 you may deduct part of these expenses.

Whichever form you use, you need to add up your total income and then subtract deductions and other adjustments to income. What is left is your taxable income. That is the amount on which you pay taxes. You can then find out how much tax you owe by checking the tax tables in the back of the instruction booklet that comes with each form. You may be able to take a credit for child-care expenses.

The next step is to check your W-2 form to see how much tax your employer has withheld. Your employer is required to hold back a certain amount of your pay to cover federal taxes. In some states, employers must also deduct state taxes.

The amount of federal tax withheld depends on the number of allowances claimed and the level of income earned. You claim your allowances by filling out a **W-4 form** when you start a new job. This is *the form a worker uses to tell an employer how much money to withhold for income tax*. The basic rule of thumb is to claim the same number of allowances as you plan to claim exemptions. The amount withheld will then roughly equal the amount of tax you will owe.

Some people use different methods. There are those who claim many allowances so they will have more income available to them during the year. These people usually owe tax money at the end of the year. That means they have to plan carefully and save enough to pay their taxes.

Other people claim no allowances at all. That means more money is withheld than they will owe at the end of the year. The government will then issue them a refund. The people who do this often think of it as a way of forcing themselves to save money.

If you do end up owing less than your employer withheld, the government owes you a refund. The only way you can obtain this refund, though, is to mail in your completed tax return. If you owe taxes that add up to more than the amount withheld, you owe the government money. You must then send a check or money order made out to the IRS along with your completed tax return. All tax returns must be accompanied by a copy of each of your W-2 forms.

As mentioned above, there is a deadline for filing federal income tax returns. Your return must be postmarked no later than midnight of April 15 of the year after the income was earned. If you file after that date, you have to pay a penalty fee.

If You Need Help

If you have trouble filling out the tax form, you can get help from the IRS' Tele-Tax service. You can listen to recorded tapes on about 140 topics by calling certain IRS phone numbers. These numbers are listed in your local telephone directory. Local IRS offices offer special help to the handicapped, the elderly, people from lower-income households, and those who do not speak English. These sources of information are free of charge. You can find out more about these IRS services at your local library, post office, or bank.

Most people can fill out their tax forms by following IRS directions. People with complicated tax matters may pay to have their taxes prepared by someone who specializes in that service. It is important to hire someone who knows the tax laws well. Otherwise, the return may not be filled out correctly. Whoever prepares a tax form must sign it, but the final responsibility for the form is the taxpayer's.

State and Local Taxes

You may also owe income taxes on the state level. Forty-three states have income taxes. Their rates vary greatly. Figure 9.3 shows how one state determines the amount of income tax residents must pay. If you live in a city of more than 50,000 people, you may have to pay a local income tax as well. Some 45 cities of this

Anyone who earns above a certain income is required to file a federal income tax return.

size have income taxes. Local tax rates also vary; the highest is a little more than 4 percent of taxable income. In most cases, the deadline for state and local taxes is the same as for federal taxes—April 15. You can find out the details of filing by contacting your city and state departments of revenue or taxation. Professional tax preparers can fill out state and local returns, too.

DISPOSABLE INCOME

On the average, one dollar of every five dollars you earn will go to taxes. *Once you pay your taxes, the money you have left makes up your* **disposable income**. This is the money you can use to satisfy your needs and wants. How will you use this income? That is up to you. Even for necessities such as food, shelter, and cloth-

Figure 9.3 A Sample of a State Income Tax System: Ohio

Income	Tax Rate	Income Tax
$ 5,000	0.74%	$ 37.00
$ 10,000	1.48%	$ 148.00
$ 15,000	2.97%	$ 445.50
$ 20,000	3.71%	$ 742.00
$ 40,000	4.45%	$ 1,780.00
$ 80,000	5.20%	$ 4,160.00
$ 100,000	5.94%	$ 5,940.00
Over $100,000	6.9%	$ 6,900.00

ing, there are many choices. Will you have an expensive steak for dinner, or will you have an economical dish of spaghetti? Neither choice is right or wrong. Each choice affects the amount of disposable income you can put toward other wants and needs.

There are other decisions you make that affect your disposable income. The career you enter and the job you choose have a great effect on your income. Most experienced plumbers, for example, earn substantially more money than most experienced hairdressers. Potential earnings are not the only reason for selecting a career, but they are an important consideration.

The political choices people make also affect disposable income. Tax rates are set by the people elected to office. Therefore, citizens should pay careful attention to the economic policies of the candidates in an election.

What you decide to do with your disposable income is another kind of economic policy. When you buy a product or service, you are choosing one business over many others. In a sense, you are voting with your dollars. Your choice helps determine which businesses succeed—and which fail.

WHERE DO YOUR TAXES GO?

What do governments do with the taxes collected from you and other workers? They provide important services. Some of these services are in the form of direct payments of money to people. In many cases, these payments make up the only income these people receive.

Social Security

Social security is a **social insurance plan**—*a federal plan that provides retirement, disability, survivors', and health insurance*. The plan is financed by a tax on workers' salaries and on the income of those who are self-employed.

In order for you and your family to receive benefits from the Social Security Administration (SSA), you need to pay into the plan while

The way you choose to satisfy your wants and needs affects the amount of disposable income you have to put toward other wants and needs.

you are employed. The deduction shown on the pay stub (Figure 9.1) under FICA is the social security tax. The tax rate and qualifications for benefits have changed often in recent years. They are sure to change again. For up-to-date information, contact the local office of the SSA.

Before Molly starts her first job, she must get a social security number. You do, too. You can apply for this number by getting the form shown in Figure 9.4 from a local SSA office. Post offices also have these forms. The number you will receive is one-of-a-kind. No other person has the same number. This number will enable the SSA and other government agencies to identify you. They can keep track of the taxes you have paid and of the benefits you are eligible for.

When you start to work, your social security tax will be deducted from your pay. This tax is a percentage of your yearly earned income—up to a certain amount. In 1989, the rate was 7.51 percent of incomes up to $48,000. Your employer pays a matching amount. If you are self-employed, you must pay both amounts, or 15.02 percent of your yearly income.

The benefits you will one day receive will be based on your lifetime average of earnings. Your eligibility is based on the number of quarters you have worked. (A quarter is a three-month period.) You can check the SSA's records of the quarters you have worked, as well as the amount you have paid. All you have to do is fill out a simple postcard form and mail it to the SSA. You should check every three years. The SSA's records become permanent after that period and cannot be changed even if in error.

What kinds of benefits does the SSA pay? There are four different kinds of payment.

Retirement Benefits. The largest amount goes for retirement benefits. In one recent year, the SSA paid almost $124 billion in such benefits. You become eligible for these benefits when you retire at age 62 or later.

The amount you receive depends in part upon the exact age at which you retire. If you wait until you are 65 or older, you will receive higher benefits than if you retire before 65. If you work after retirement, however, your work income can lower your benefits. In 1990, a retired person 65 to 69 years old lost $1 in benefits for every $3 of work income over $9,360 a year. Currently, any income from sources other than work does not affect social security payments.

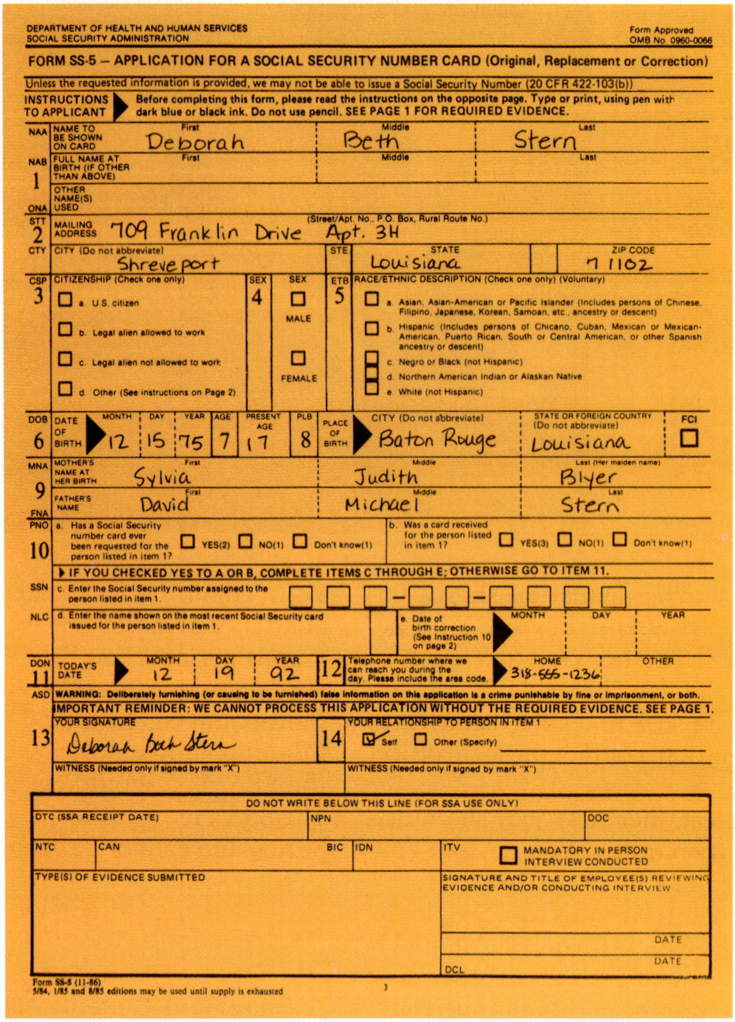

DEPARTMENT OF HEALTH AND HUMAN SERVICES
SOCIAL SECURITY ADMINISTRATION

Form Approved
OMB No. 0960-0066

FORM SS-5 – APPLICATION FOR A SOCIAL SECURITY NUMBER CARD (Original, Replacement or Correction)

Unless the requested information is provided, we may not be able to issue a Social Security Number (20 CFR 422-103(b))

INSTRUCTIONS TO APPLICANT ▶ Before completing this form, please read the instructions on the opposite page. Type or print, using pen with dark blue or black ink. Do not use pencil. SEE PAGE 1 FOR REQUIRED EVIDENCE.

NAA 1 NAME TO BE SHOWN ON CARD — First: Deborah; Middle: Beth; Last: Stern

NAB FULL NAME AT BIRTH (IF OTHER THAN ABOVE) — First; Middle; Last

ONA OTHER NAME(S) USED

STT 2 MAILING ADDRESS (Street/Apt. No., P.O. Box, Rural Route No.): 709 Franklin Drive Apt. 3H

CTY CITY (Do not abbreviate): Shreveport — STE STATE: Louisiana — ZIP CODE: 71102

CSP 3 CITIZENSHIP (Check one only)
- a. U.S. citizen
- b. Legal alien allowed to work
- c. Legal alien not allowed to work
- d. Other (See instructions on Page 2)

SEX 4 — SEX: MALE / FEMALE

ETB 5 RACE/ETHNIC DESCRIPTION (Check one only) (Voluntary)
- a. Asian, Asian-American or Pacific Islander (Includes persons of Chinese, Filipino, Japanese, Korean, Samoan, etc., ancestry or descent)
- b. Hispanic (Includes persons of Chicano, Cuban, Mexican or Mexican-American, Puerto Rican, South or Central American, or other Spanish ancestry or descent)
- c. Negro or Black (not Hispanic)
- d. Northern American Indian or Alaskan Native
- e. White (not Hispanic)

DOB 6 DATE OF BIRTH ▶ MONTH 12 | DAY 15 | YEAR 75 | AGE 7 | PRESENT AGE 17 | PLB 8 | PLACE OF BIRTH ▶ CITY (Do not abbreviate): Baton Rouge | STATE OR FOREIGN COUNTRY (Do not abbreviate): Louisiana | FCI

MNA 9 MOTHER'S NAME AT HER BIRTH — First: Sylvia; Middle: Judith; Last (Her maiden name): Blyer

FNA FATHER'S NAME — First: David; Middle: Michael; Last: Stern

PNO 10 a. Has a Social Security number card ever been requested for the person listed in item 1? YES(2) NO(1) Don't know(1)
b. Was a card received for the person listed in item 1? YES(3) NO(1) Don't know(1)

▶ IF YOU CHECKED YES TO A OR B, COMPLETE ITEMS C THROUGH E; OTHERWISE GO TO ITEM 11.

SSN c. Enter the Social Security number assigned to the person listed in item 1. ☐☐☐–☐☐–☐☐☐☐

NLC d. Enter the name shown on the most recent Social Security card issued for the person listed in item 1.
e. Date of birth correction (See Instruction 10 on page 2) ▶ MONTH | DAY | YEAR

DON 11 TODAY'S DATE ▶ MONTH 12 | DAY 19 | YEAR 92

12 Telephone number where we can reach you during the day. Please include the area code. ▶ HOME 318-555-1236 | OTHER

ASD WARNING: Deliberately furnishing (or causing to be furnished) false information on this application is a crime punishable by fine or imprisonment, or both.

IMPORTANT REMINDER: WE CANNOT PROCESS THIS APPLICATION WITHOUT THE REQUIRED EVIDENCE. SEE PAGE 1.

13 YOUR SIGNATURE: Deborah Beth Stern

14 YOUR RELATIONSHIP TO PERSON IN ITEM 1: ☑ Self ☐ Other (Specify)

WITNESS (Needed only if signed by mark "X")

WITNESS (Needed only if signed by mark "X")

DO NOT WRITE BELOW THIS LINE (FOR SSA USE ONLY)

DTC (SSA RECEIPT DATE) | NPN | DOC

NTC | CAN | BIC | IDN | ITV | MANDATORY IN PERSON INTERVIEW CONDUCTED

TYPE(S) OF EVIDENCE SUBMITTED

SIGNATURE AND TITLE OF EMPLOYEE(S) REVIEWING EVIDENCE AND/OR CONDUCTING INTERVIEW

DATE

DCL DATE

Form SS-5 (11-86)
5/84, 1/85 and 8/85 editions may be used until supply is exhausted

3

Figure 9.4 Sample Application Form for Social Security Number

Other sources include dividends, interest, and pension funds. A retired person can also receive support from her or his family without having social security benefits reduced.

Disability Benefits. Workers who become disabled on the job are eligible for social security benefits, no matter what their age. However, they must have paid a certain amount into social security before they become disabled. Payments may also be made to the spouse and dependent children of a disabled worker.

Survivors' Benefits. The SSA may pay benefits to the spouse and dependents of a worker who dies. These benefits may include a special payment for burial costs. The monthly amount that survivors receive is a percentage of the amount the eligible worker would have received. The percentage depends in part on whether the survivor is employed. It also depends on the number of children involved. Children of retired, disabled, or deceased workers may receive monthly benefits until the age of 18. These benefits continue until the

Chapter 9 Earning an Income

age of 22 for children who are unmarried, full-time students.

Medicare Benefits. A substantial portion of social security funds is used to support Medicare. Medicare is a federal hospital insurance program for people who are over 65 or disabled. To receive full Medicare coverage, you must be eligible for social security benefits or railroad retirement benefits.

State Government Plans

State governments also have social insurance plans supported by workers' taxes. The most important of these plans are unemployment compensation and workers' compensation.

Unemployment Compensation. If you are laid off from your job someday, you may be eligible for unemployment compensation. This plan provides payments to workers who have lost their jobs and cannot find new ones. To be eligible, you must have worked a certain number of months. Unemployment payments are temporary. You cannot receive payments beyond a certain number of weeks. The size of your benefits will depend on your previous income. The benefit fund is also supported by contributions from all the employers in your state.

Unemployment payments are meant to tide workers over until they find other jobs. Any worker who turns down a job that is similar to his or her previous job stops receiving payments. Also, a worker's lack of employment must not be voluntary. In other words, workers who quit their jobs are not eligible for unemployment compensation.

Workers' Compensation. This social insurance plan provides payments to cover the medical costs and lost income of workers who are injured on the job. Some states require employers to make payments into a state plan. Others require employers to buy workers' compensation insurance. Workers who may be disabled for a year or more may also receive disability payments from the SSA.

CHILD LABOR LAWS

There is another kind of protection the government provides young workers that will not appear on Molly's paycheck. This protection consists of child labor laws to guard her health and safety. Such laws restrict the kind and

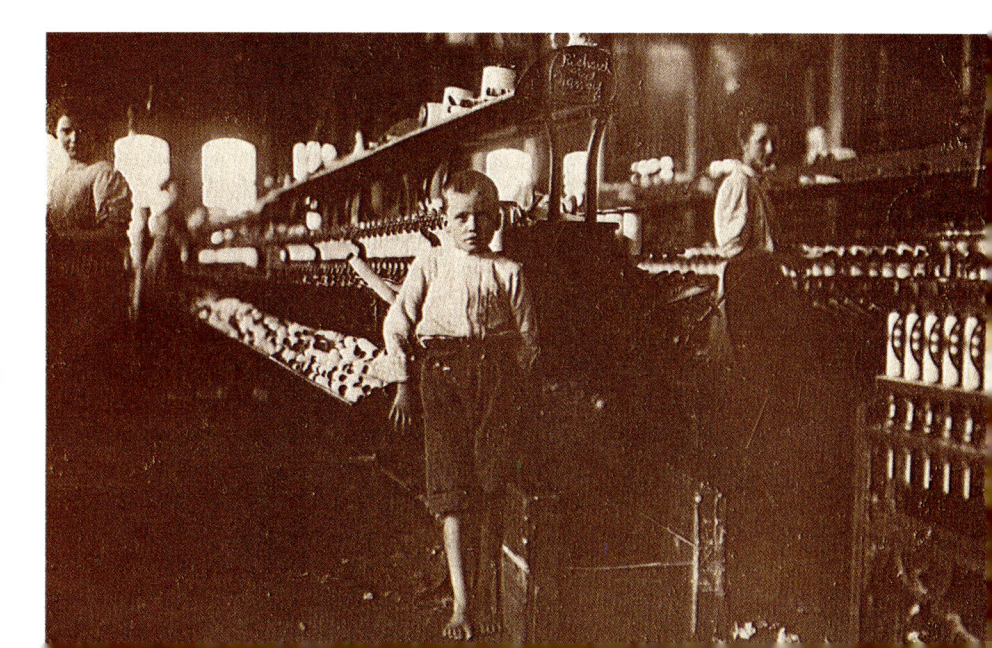

Until the early part of this century, children as young as 7 and 8 worked in mines and factories throughout the country.

amount of work anyone under the age of 18 is allowed to do.

This protection did not always exist. Until the early part of this century, children as young as the ages of 7 and 8 worked in mines and factories throughout the country. Conditions were terrible. Children often had to work 12 hours and more a day. Many lived at their place of work 24 hours a day. At night, they would sleep on a makeshift bed at their work station. Some were beaten or whipped if they did not produce as much work as their employers demanded. Sometimes, epidemics broke out that claimed the lives of many of these young workers.

Some state laws to protect children were passed in the nineteenth century. Federal laws passed by Congress in the early part of the twentieth century were declared unconstitutional by the Supreme Court. The court ruled that such laws restricted personal freedom. It was not until 1938 that a law called the Fair Labor Standards Act (FLSA) provided effective protection. Under this act, youths have to be at least 14 to 15 years old in order to work in certain jobs. These jobs cannot be dangerous to their health. Also, these jobs cannot prevent them from obtaining an education.

If you are 14 or 15, you can hold various jobs in stores, offices, restaurants, and service stations. These are the tasks you are allowed to perform at those jobs:

1. You can process goods for sale. Allowable jobs include pricing, labeling, weighing, cleaning, stocking, assembling, shelving, and bagging.
2. You can sell goods and operate a cash register.
3. You can run errands and deliver goods, but not in a car or truck.
4. You can wash, polish, and clean automobiles and trucks. You can also fill them with gasoline and oil.
5. You can prepare and serve foods and beverages.
6. You can rake, weed, mow, and maintain grounds. However, you cannot use motorized tools.
7. You can type, file, and answer the telephone in an office.

If you are 14 or 15, this is one of the various jobs you are allowed to perform in a store, office, restaurant, or service station.

Chapter 9 Earning an Income

8. You can do art work. Work in this area includes window dressing and advertising.

The hours you can work are also regulated. Until you are 16, you can work:

- no more than 3 hours on a school day during nonschool hours (if you are enrolled in an approved cooperative education program, you can work during school hours).
- no more than 18 hours during a school week (if you are enrolled in an approved cooperative education program, you can work up to 23 hours).
- no more than 8 hours on a nonschool day.
- no more than 40 hours during a nonschool week.

The time you can work is also set by the FLSA. When you are under 16, your workday may not begin before 7 A.M. and may not end after 7 P.M. The exception to these hours is during the summer months from June 1 through Labor Day. Then, the evening hours are extended to 9 P.M.

When you are 16 and 17, you can work any number of hours you choose. However, you cannot work at a hazardous occupation. The federal government has determined 17 hazardous occupations orders in jobs that do not involve farming. The orders deal with the following types of work or equipment:

1. manufacturing and storing explosives
2. motor vehicle driving and helping outside
3. coal mining
4. logging and sawmilling
5. power-driven woodworking machines
6. exposure to radioactive substances
7. power-driven hoisting apparatus
8. power-driven metal-forming punching and shearing machines
9. mining, other than coal mining
10. slaughtering, meat-packing, processing, or rendering
11. power-driven bakery machines
12. power-driven paper products machines
13. manufacturing brick, tile, and kindred products
14. power-driven circular saws, band saws, and guillotine shears
15. wrecking, demolition, and shipbreaking operations
16. roofing operations
17. excavation operations

If you are in a cooperative education program, you may be allowed to work in some of these occupations as a student-learner. However, the following conditions must be met:

- You must be enrolled in a cooperative vocational training program that is recognized by a state or local educational authority.
- You must be employed under a written training agreement that makes four promises. First, your work in a hazardous occupation must be only a minor part of your training. Second, you can do such work only occasionally and for short periods of time. You must also be closely supervised by a qualified person. Third, you must have thorough safety training. Fourth, your training must be organized so that your tasks become harder by successive steps.

In a number of states, a high school graduate from such a program can be employed in a hazardous occupation before the age of 18.

There are some kinds of jobs that do not have minimum age restrictions. You can work for your parents in certain jobs that do not involve farming. You can also be a performer. And you can deliver newspapers.

The laws in your state may place additional restrictions on or make additional exceptions to the FLSA. It is a good idea to find out what these laws say before you start to look for a job while you are under 18.

MAIN POINTS

- There are six methods of earning income: wage, piecework, salary, commission, tips, and bonus. A worker may also receive fringe benefits.
- Various deductions from a worker's gross pay leave a worker with net pay. Everyone who earns above a certain income must file an income tax return. Workers must pay income tax to the federal government and sometimes to state and local governments.
- Workers' disposable income is affected by the ways they satisfy their needs and wants, the careers they enter, and their political choices.
- Federal taxes pay for social insurance plans. Social security provides retirement, disability, survivors', and health insurance for workers and their families.
- State governments use taxes to provide workers with unemployment compensation and workers' compensation.
- Workers under 18 are protected by federal and state child labor laws. These laws regulate the kinds of jobs young people can do, the hours they can work, and the tasks they can perform.

Terms to Know

Use the following terms to fill in the blanks of the sentences below.

bonus
cafeteria plan
commission
direct deposit
disposable income
earned income
exemption
fringe benefits
gross pay
income tax return
net pay
payroll deductions
pension plan
piecework rate
profit-sharing plans
salary
social insurance plan
tax deduction
tips
W-2 form
W-4 form
wage

1. When you start a job, you must fill out a(n) _____ to tell your employer how much money to withhold for income tax.
2. You can select the benefits you want in a(n) _____.
3. Workers who receive a set rate of pay for each unit they produce are paid at a(n) _____.
4. Paid vacation time and sick days are examples of _____.
5. If your employer gives you extra money because you are doing good work, you receive a(n) _____.
6. A retirement fund for workers is called a(n) _____.
7. The money you receive for your labor as a worker is _____.
8. Many salespeople are paid a(n) _____ for the sales they make.
9. An expense that reduces the income on which taxes must be paid is a(n) _____.
10. If you are paid $5 an hour for your labor, you are receiving a(n) _____.
11. The money you have left after you pay your taxes is your _____.
12. In January, your employer sends you a(n) _____, which lists your gross pay and payroll deductions for the previous year.

Chapter 9 Earning an Income

13. A worker who receives a rate of pay figured by the year is paid a(n) _____.
14. Satisfied customers give waiters and waitresses money as _____.
15. Unemployment compensation is an example of a(n) _____.
16. The full amount of money you earn at a job is known as your _____.
17. If your earnings go directly to a bank on payday, you are paid through _____.
18. Workers usually receive less than their gross pay because _____ are subtracted from their pay.
19. April 15 is the latest date on which your federal _____ can be postmarked.
20. A reduction in taxable income for a dependent is known as a(n) _____.
21. The amount you receive after payroll deductions have been subtracted from your gross pay is called _____.
22. Some companies offer workers _____, in which the employer puts money into an investment fund for the worker.

Chapter Review

1. Compare the six forms of earning income.
2. Give some examples of fringe benefits. Why do employers provide such benefits?
3. Explain the advantages of being paid by check.
4. Briefly describe how to fill out an income tax return.
5. What is the purpose of asking for many tax allowances on your income? No allowances?
6. What are three sources of help with your income tax return?
7. What kinds of decisions affect your disposable income?
8. Describe the four different kinds of benefits paid by social security.
9. Name two social insurance plans supported by taxes on the state level.
10. What are the limits on your working hours when you are 14 and 15? When you are 16 and 17?

Activities

1. Which form of payment do you think is best: wage, salary, or piecework? What psychological advantages and disadvantages does each have? Which kinds of jobs are most suitable for each form of payment? Least suitable?
2. Do you think instituting a bonus plan in schools for students who earn high grades is a good idea? Why or why not?
3. In recent years, many companies have added physical fitness programs or centers to their fringe benefit package. Using current magazines for research, write a two- or three-page report describing these programs. How do they benefit employees? Employers?
4. At your local library or post office, obtain copies of the various types of income tax returns mentioned in the chapter. Discuss in class the ways in which the forms differ and the possible reasons for these differences.
5. Based on library research, give a talk or write a report on the plight of child workers in this country before child labor laws were passed.

Chapter **10**

Working With Others

OBJECTIVES

This chapter will enable you to:

- list the characteristics of a negative attitude and explain why it could hurt your work.
- list the characteristics of a positive attitude and explain its importance.
- describe various skills that can help you get along with others on the job.
- explain the positive and negative effects of stress and conflict on the job.
- describe the possible outcomes of conflict.
- use assertiveness skills to handle conflicts.
- list qualities needed for promotion.
- discuss how youth groups help develop leadership skills.
- participate in meetings conducted by parliamentary procedure.

Latoya

Jean used to gripe all the time. She complained about the restaurant customers, about the cooks, about her sore feet. Every night, we heard about what low tips her cheap customers gave her.

We all knew there was a reason for her low tips, and it wasn't her customers' lack of generosity. Jean's poor attitude toward the job was showing in her work. She was really short with customers, and she never smiled. She did only the bare minimum, always trying to save a few steps and make things a little easier for herself. She was always the last one to get to work and the first one to leave. Because of her attitude, no one else felt like helping her out when she was extra busy.

About a week ago, I couldn't keep my mouth shut anymore. For Jean's sake—and for ours, too—I talked with her after work. I told her that working as a server is hard and that it's harder when your customers are poor tippers. But then I said that it could be pretty good work, if she would look on the bright side of things.

More important, I showed her how she could please her customers. I explained that if she gave them good service, they would be more generous. She could greet the customers cheerfully and smile pleasantly. She could ask customers if they needed any more water, or bread, or butter. I gave her a couple of other suggestions. At the end of our talk, she said she would think about what I said. But I knew I had gotten through to her.

During the first week, I watched how Jean was doing. I complimented her when she did something well. By the second week, her tips were about the same as everyone else's. Jean is smiling a lot more now, and she even gets to work on time. In fact, the whole staff seems happier. It's amazing how one person's attitude can affect a whole group.

THE IMPORTANCE OF ATTITUDE

Someone once asked employers to list their reasons for firing young employees. The reason they listed most frequently was poor attitude.

Your **attitude** is *your outlook on something, or how you feel about a situation*. Your attitude is not determined by your job. You create the attitude. It is up to you whether your attitude is positive or negative.

Thinking Negatively

You have probably been around someone with a negative attitude at work or at school. People with such an attitude often have these traits:

- They do not smile very often.
- They complain and criticize.
- They are selfish with their time and their possessions.
- They blame other people for their own mistakes.

Jean's gloomy outlook about her job was making herself, her customers, and her co-workers unhappy. If Latoya had not spoken to her, it probably would not have been long before customer complaints would have forced the manager to do something. The manager might have told Jean that she would be fired if she did not improve her attitude.

Workers with negative attitudes seem to infect their co-workers, too. It can be hard to feel cheerful when the person sitting next to you is frowning all day. By changing other workers' feelings about work, a person with a negative attitude can hurt an entire staff.

Jean's poor attitude at the restaurant was affecting everyone at work. Before Jean was hired, the employees had been very close-knit. They enjoyed working together and spent leisure time together, too. After Jean started working, this unity fell apart. Going out together was no longer fun, because Jean would always be there complaining. Working at the restaurant was less enjoyable because Jean was leaving parts of her work for others to do. Only after Jean changed her attitude did she realize that her negative attitude had affected others.

Thinking Positively

Latoya's positive attitude toward her job helped Jean see the good side of serving. Latoya liked her co-workers and enjoyed meeting customers. She understood that her attitude was the major factor in how well she was paid. She did not blame anyone else for the hard work she had to do. She did her work and was proud of it.

Workers with positive attitudes set examples for others. They show by the way they work that they respect themselves and take pride in what they do. They get along well with others. Workers with good attitudes usually have the following traits:

- Cheerfulness. Cheerfulness is a basic characteristic of a positive attitude. The smiles and pleasant greetings of cheerful workers make others respond warmly to them. Cheerful workers create a good atmosphere in a workplace.

- Adaptability. Workers who are adaptable do not mind certain changes and often welcome them. In the short run, change disrupts people's work. In the long run, however, many changes open up new career possibilities or make work more efficient. For example, computerizing a company's filing system takes months and causes many headaches. But once the system is completed, it saves secretaries so much time that their jobs become easier.

- Acceptance of others. Workers with good attitudes respect and appreciate the different kinds of people they meet on the job. For instance, Stephen seemed pushy and loud to Cynthia. However, he was also the best project supervisor in the com-

Chapter 10 Working With Others

pany. Cynthia knew she could learn from him, even though his personality bothered her.

- Generosity. Workers with positive attitudes are generous in a variety of ways. They do more than their jobs call for. Latoya, for example, gave time and effort to help Jean become a better server. Generous workers are also quick to praise others.
- Responsibility. Workers with good attitudes take responsibility for their actions. They do not try to blame others for their own errors. One day, for example, Jean found that she had forgotten to charge customers the new higher price for pie. She worried what would happen if she admitted her mistake to the manager, but she decided that she had no choice. The manager was upset, but pleased that Jean accepted responsibility.

Getting Along With Others

If you have a positive attitude, you will find it much easier to get along with people on the job. When you begin work, you come into contact with new acquaintances. You may be working with people in different age groups. There may be people from a variety of backgrounds. You may also meet people you find unlikable. An important part of your job responsibility is to be able to work successfully with those around you. There are several things you can do to get along well with others.

Good Communication. Communicating well is one of the most important interpersonal skills. To communicate well, you need to know how to listen as well as how to talk.

Listening does not mean merely taking part in a conversation. There are specific skills needed to be a good listener. To be a good listener, you need to follow these guidelines:

To communicate well, you need to listen as well as to talk.

- Let the other person talk. It is sometimes difficult to keep from finishing another person's sentences, especially when the other person pauses often to search for a word. Patience in conversation is important. It is natural for people to hesitate while they are thinking of how to express themselves. Conversations are more enjoyable when each person has the chance to complete a thought.
- Concentrate on what the other person is saying. Many people think about what they are going to say next while the other person is talking. If people would listen carefully, they would have a better grasp of what the speaker is saying. That would allow them to reply more intelligently.
- Understand the other person's position. Understanding the other person helps the listener see the other side of things. To do this, the listener must imagine himself or herself in the speaker's situation.
- Give feedback. To give feedback, the listener restates the speaker's message in the listener's own words. Feedback allows the listener to check his or her understanding. Providing feedback can greatly increase listening skills because it requires the listener to concentrate on what the other person is saying.
- Ask questions. Asking questions creates better communication. The speaker's answers will clarify his or her points for the listener. By asking questions, the listener shows a genuine interest in what the speaker is saying.

Willingness to Learn. A worker with a positive attitude is willing to learn. A worker with a negative attitude, in contrast, often has the attitude that she or he knows everything. When Lisa started working at the Colonial Diner, she already had some experience in food service. She had been a co-op student in the school cafeteria and had helped prepare hot lunches there, but working as a short-order cook was new to her. She listened carefully to what Stan, the other cook, had to say. Although the diner's meals were made differently from those Lisa had made in the past, she learned the new method quickly. Lisa's willingness to learn new skills, combined with her related experience, helped her move smoothly into her new job.

Empathy. Empathy is *the ability to share another person's emotions or feelings*. Sondra knew that Tom, her fellow customer relations officer, was having a hard time in his personal life. At one point, Tom shouted at her for not getting a form he needed. Instead of becoming angry or upset, Sondra realized that Tom was really shouting out of frustration over his personal life. This enabled Sondra to take Tom's outburst in stride. When Sondra felt that Tom had calmed down, she asked him if he would like to have lunch with her to discuss his problems. Tom appreciated Sondra's empathy.

Courtesy. Courtesy—the ability to be considerate of other people—is vital in the workplace. Courteous workers treat co-workers and the public politely. Courteous workers thank others for doing certain tasks, even though the tasks may be part of the job. When Steve, for example, finished typing Sharon's report so she could meet a deadline, she thanked him for his efforts.

Humor. Having a sense of humor helps people work well together. A sense of humor goes far beyond telling jokes. It enables people to see humor in difficult situations. It also enables them to have a sense of humor about themselves. This ability helps people deal well with problems on and off the job.

Impartiality. Impartiality means *being fair and refusing to take sides in someone else's argument*. Jumping into a quarrel on one person's side creates a no-win situation for you. The other person is likely to resent your interference for a long time.

Chapter 10 Working With Others

For example, two of your co-workers may be arguing over how certain undesirable tasks should be divided between them. If you throw in your opinion, it really will not help. The two people have to work out the problem themselves.

STRESS AND CONFLICT

How do you react to changes in your life? Were you nervous on the first day of high school? Did your mouth get dry the first time you spoke in front of a group? Were you excited just before running in a track meet? If you have experienced these feelings, you have known stress. **Stress** is *the body's reactions to change.*

Stress can be positive or negative, depending on how you react or adapt to it. For example, weight lifting can be positive stress. You are challenging your muscles, and they are adapting by developing. Weight lifting can turn into negative stress, however. If you lift too much weight at one time, you can injure your muscles.

Anything that causes stress is called a **stressor.** Stressors can be external, coming from forces outside you, or internal. For example, you might have felt stressed by trying to decide between two job offers that you found equally attractive. Some stressors, such as receiving a promotion, are positive. Others, such as illness, are negative. Many can be either, depending on your reaction to them. This is especially true of stressors on the job.

Stress on the Job

A deadline for a project can make you feel either panicked or challenged. The holiday rush can make you feel either overworked or excited by all the extra activity.

Being a new worker can have special stresses, as Jeremy discovered. Jeremy had waited a long time for his apprenticeship as an electrician. However, two months into the apprenticeship, he was thinking of quitting. He felt as though his supervisor did not trust him. After all, she was always checking his work. The work was difficult to learn, and the pace of the shop made him feel overwhelmed at times.

Jeremy was experiencing job stress. He did not realize that it often takes new workers a few months to feel really comfortable in a position. It takes time to master new tasks and learn the routines of the workplace. Until then, it is a supervisor's job to constantly check the work of a new employee like Jeremy.

After a while, most new workers become accustomed to their jobs and skilled at their tasks. Supervisors allow workers more independence as they become better at their jobs. New workers eventually make friends with the other workers, which makes them feel more a part of the group.

However, stress never disappears completely. Some stressors are a basic part of the job. People who work for a newspaper, for example, have constant deadlines to meet. Workers in the customer service department of a department store must deal daily with unhappy customers.

Managing Stress

As noted before, stress can be positive or negative. Stress can make you work faster or better. A stressful situation can force you to come up with new solutions to problems and can show that you have abilities you did not know about.

Stress can also cause problems. If it is not managed well or if there is simply too much of it, your mind and body can react negatively. You may become depressed or nervous. You may get frequent headaches. And you may get sick often.

There are several things you can do to be able to cope well with stress.

1. Eat right. Good eating habits keep your body and your mind functioning well. That can help you ward off the negative effects of stress.

Exercise is an excellent way to fight stress. A vigorous bike ride can let you release mental tensions.

2. Get enough sleep. Your mind and body renew themselves during sleep. Lack of sleep can lower your physical and mental resistance to stress.
3. Exercise. Exercise is an important stress-fighter. Regular exercise increases your strength and energy. It also lets you release mental tensions.
4. Take time to relax. Like sleep, relaxation helps you recuperate from stress. Try to set aside some time each day to listen to music, read, or just do nothing.
5. Talk out your problems. Talking to someone about a problem can have several benefits. You may find new ways to cope with the situation. You may also be able to put the situation in better perspective, rather than letting it grow out of proportion. And just the act of talking things out can help you feel better.
6. Learn your limits. Stress can occur if you are overworked. Be aware of just how much you can handle. If someone is asking too much of you, explain the situation. There may be another way to get the work done.

Dealing With Conflict

What if your stress is caused by genuine conflict? A **conflict** is *a sharp disagreement about an idea or a procedure.*

The first step is to review the problem calmly. To do that, you need to step back from the

Chapter 10 Working With Others

conflict and ask yourself several questions: Why does it bother you? Who is involved? What can be done about it?

Next, you have to assert yourself. **Assertiveness** means *standing up for yourself and letting others know how you feel*. You do not have to be pushy or aggressive to do this. Being assertive is the best way to deal with a conflict with another person. If you are honest with the person, you have provided the basis for solving the problem.

If you are not assertive, what can happen? First of all, nobody hears about the problem. The person with whom you have the conflict may think that everything is fine. And the continuing conflict will cause stress to build up inside you.

After you have stated your feelings, though, you must make constructive suggestions. Without suggestions, your feelings are simply complaints. Then, you must work sincerely with the other person or people involved to end the conflict.

Susan has a well-paying job as a travel agent. She also has two school-age children. Until recently, her schedule allowed her to be home in the evenings with them. However, the agency's owners decided to keep the agency open in the evenings, too, in order to compete with other agencies. They wanted Susan to work

The first step in being assertive consists of stating your feelings. The second involves making constructive suggestions.

two evenings a week and have two mornings free. With this schedule, Susan would have less time with her children.

Susan could have accepted the new hours without telling the owners about her dissatisfaction. She could have kept her feelings bottled up inside until the stress began to affect her work. Or she could have marched into the owners' office and demanded that the owners change the plan. This approach might have gotten her fired.

Instead, Susan thought about the situation. She knew the agency had to stay open at nights or it would lose a lot of business. The owners would not change their minds about the new hours, so Susan did not waste time thinking about that. She thought about how she could adapt to the new schedule and still have time for her children.

When Susan had carefully worked out a plan, she calmly asked to speak with the owners. She outlined her plan for them. Instead of working from 1 P.M. to 9 P.M., she would work from 9 A.M. to 3 P.M., go home to be with her children for dinner, and then return at 6:30 P.M. and work until 9 P.M. One of her co-workers had already agreed to cover her afternoon hours.

The owners agreed to Susan's plan in part because it was thoughtful and seemed to satisfy everyone's needs. They were also cooperative because Susan had proved herself to be a hard worker. Susan had stood up for what she wanted—her job *and* time with her children. She had dealt with the conflict by thinking of a plan, presenting the plan, and convincing her employers to accept her solution.

Possible Results of Conflict

Susan's employers accepted her solution to the conflict. It would be unrealistic, however, to expect your solution to a conflict to be accepted every time. In actuality, there are several ways for a conflict to work out.

You Change Your Mind. If you listen to the other point of view with an open mind, you may come to agree with it. If you are suggesting a change in a work procedure, you may feel differently once you learn the reasons for the current system.

Other People Change Their Minds. You may be able to convince the other person to agree with your point of view. It is not always realistic to expect this. Susan, for example, did not even try to convince the agency's owners to drop the plan for evening hours. She knew there was a good reason for expanded hours.

You Compromise. What Susan suggested was a compromise. In a **compromise**, *each side gives up something in order to reach an agreement*. Susan agreed to work two evenings a week, and the owners agreed to adjust another worker's schedule.

You Get Help From a Third Person. *Having a third person step in to help work out a solution to a conflict* is called **mediation**. The person must be impartial. The mediator does not have to be an official. If you and a co-worker disagree on something, you can ask for the help of another employee whom you both respect.

GETTING AHEAD IN YOUR JOB

After you have been at a job for a while, you may begin to look for advancement. Step back and think about your job. Do you like the work? Do you want to continue with the company? What can you do to ensure that you will be promoted?

Self-Evaluation

How good do you think you are at your job? Are you learning what you need to know? In order to get promoted or get a raise in pay, you must demonstrate above-average work

An impartial mediator may be needed to help work out a solution to a conflict.

skills, good work habits, and the ability to deal with others.

Good Work Skills. People who are ready for advancement know what they are doing on the job. They have shown that they can learn new skills. They have mastered the procedures of their jobs.

Good Work Habits. Good work habits start with taking pride in your work. If you are proud of your work, you will want to do anything that will help you work better. This includes arriving on time, not wasting time or supplies, and consistently trying to do your best. It also involves showing **initiative**, or *the ability to begin work on a project without a specific order or instruction from someone else*. Workers with initiative see what needs to be done; then, they go ahead and do it.

Good Interpersonal Skills. Workers who can deal effectively with others get their jobs done better. This ability depends on listening to people, thinking about what they have said, and explaining what needs to be done. Impartiality, a sense of humor, empathy, and courtesy are all interpersonal skills. These skills help people work together in close quarters and under stressful conditions. They keep the workplace running smoothly.

Performance Reviews

Usually, after three to six months on a job, you will have a **performance review**. This is *an official evaluation of your work*. For the review, your supervisor may fill out a special form to describe your work habits and skills. Then, the supervisor will discuss your strengths and weaknesses with you. Wage increases and promotions are usually based on performance reviews.

Both you and your employer can learn from the performance review. The review helps your employer take a good look at your work and answer these questions: How do you fit in at the company? Do you need extra training? Is the organization making the best use of your skills? A good employer tries to make the most of each employee's talents.

Discussions of employees' weaknesses are not meant to hurt employees. They are designed to give workers the chance to improve. Workers who then make an effort to better their performance are often rewarded with higher pay or more responsibility.

Moving Up

If you have demonstrated above-average work skills, good work habits, and good interpersonal skills, you may receive a promotion. Your job may become more complex, or your employer may feel you have leadership qualities and make you responsible for training or supervising others.

QUALITY WORKERS

Employers look for a combination of employability and academic skills when hiring a new employee.

Employability Skills

Employers pay attention to an employee's enthusiasm, responsibility, cooperativeness, self-discipline, flexibility, and willingness to learn. Employers favor employees with a general understanding of the business world. Young employees should know how to work cooperatively in today's workplace because many employers take a team approach to doing business.

Work-related social skills are important. This means knowing what behavior is expected of you at work and in small-group meetings. If your employer asks you to participate in a work meeting, it is your responsibility to come to the meeting prepared to take notes or ask questions where appropriate. If you will be giving a brief presentation, make sure you have rehearsed in advance what you are going to say.

Academic Skills

Today's employers want quick learners. The most important academic skills are reading, math, writing, listening, and problem solving.

Math skills come into play when you are asked to perform basic calculations, estimate quantities, and apply numerical values from charts and tables. A survey of employers reveals that using fractions, decimals, and formulas are trouble spots for young employees.

Written job applications are often the testing ground for assessing a young applicant's writing skills. However, once you are hired, you may be asked to take lengthy telephone messages, write memos, or draft a letter for your supervisor. You should be able to write legibly and complete forms accurately. Be able to write clear, concise English that is grammatically correct and proofread your writing.

Employee Involvement

Employers want employees who are cooperative in the workplace and who can help solve business-related problems in a team atmosphere. Employers realize that if they want to improve the quality of their service or product and the productivity of their workers, they are going to have to pay attention to the morale of their employees. Getting and keeping valuable employees involved in the company builds high employee morale.

Many companies use **quality circles** as a way of bringing employees together to solve mutual problems. The quality circle concept, adopted from Japanese business practices, involves workers coming together voluntarily, usually on company time and at company expense, to solve business problems. The workers in a quality circle share similar work tasks. A trained expert may lead the quality circle. The concept of quality circles is also known as employee involvement, team building, work teams, and work groups.

Companies have many ways of soliciting employee involvement. For example, employees may be consulted about changes in technology or work schedules. Other ways of soliciting employee involvement include:

- Open-door policies. Managers who have an open-door policy welcome visits from employees who wish to discuss business concerns, make suggestions, or offer useful information.
- Employee suggestion box. Employees can write suggestions to management on a special suggestion form and place it in a box. Managers review the suggestions received and may respond in a company-wide memo or newsletter.
- Employee incentive programs. Some companies award cash prizes to employees who come up with better, time-saving ways of doing things or improved product designs.
- Employee surveys. Some companies hire a consultant to measure how happy employees are with their company and jobs. Employees may be asked to complete a lengthy written survey or agree to be interviewed one-on-one by a highly trained neutral interviewer.
- Community involvement. Many companies take an active interest in their workers' quality of life. Companies support business-school partnerships, health and human welfare, the environment, and the arts with grants of money and other resources.

Drugs in the Workplace

Drug abuse presents a very real challenge to organizations and society. How widespread is the problem of drug abuse within the workplace? We know the highest drug-using part of the population is the young working adult. Experts claim that as many as 65 percent of the young people just entering the workforce have used drugs and that between 10 and 23 percent of all workers use drugs on the job.

The cost to employers — of lost productivity, absenteeism, increased health benefits, direct treatment, accidents, and other losses — is enormous. Many companies have written policies that address drug use in the workplace, and some offer employee assistance programs for counseling and referrals to other agencies. Drug testing is another tool that is used to reduce drug abuse in the workplace. Drug testing tells employees that drug use in the workplace is not tolerated.

Although there are other issues surrounding drug testing in the workplace, such as invasion of privacy and the accuracy of testing, it is

Workers who are ready for advancement have mastered the procedures of their job.

clear that more and more employers now require drug testing of new applicants and will continue to do so in the future. In fact, one recent study found that 47 percent of the employers surveyed required drug testing of new college graduates.

WHAT IT TAKES TO BE A LEADER

When Eric was promoted to data processing supervisor, he was surprised and delighted, but also nervous. Could he do a good job in his new position?

Eric had a lot to learn in his new job, but he already had a lot going for him. He was good at his work, dependable, and respected by those who worked with him. He set good standards for the other workers, and he had other leadership qualities.

Eric was developing a thorough knowledge of the various jobs in the data processing office. He also knew how data processing related to the rest of the company. Therefore, he was able to understand the needs of other departments and translate those needs into effective action in his department.

He was also able to give clear and thorough directions, an important leadership quality. His workers knew exactly what he expected of them. Thus, they could do the best job possible. Eric also **motivated** his workers, or *gave them the desire to work to the best of their abilities*. He made sure they understood the reason for their work and why it was valuable. He complimented workers when they did well. That helped make the workers enthusiastic about their tasks.

Another reason Eric was promoted was his ability to make good decisions. He did not keep changing his mind, nor did he put off making decisions. When he had to make decisions concerning his workers, he was always fair and **consistent**—he *acted in the same way each time a certain thing happened*.

Eric also gained new skills in his new job. He learned to **delegate** work, or *to assign it to others*. He realized that no matter how good a worker he was, he could not do the entire group's work. Because he had a good relationship with his workers, he was confident they could do the job. Thus, he did not become overworked, and projects moved quickly through the department.

Eric also found that he had to change how he related to his workers. There were times when he had to be firm with some of them. Part of his job was to correct workers who made mistakes or who had poor work habits. If he did not do this, the good workers would begin to resent him. At the same time, Eric had to make the workers feel he was on their side. He was genuinely concerned about their welfare. He looked for quicker, better ways for the workers to do their jobs. He listened to workers' thoughts on changing procedures. And he was sympathetic to his workers' problems.

Developing Leadership Abilities

Eric was obviously a good choice for supervisor. How can you gain these abilities? One way is to join organizations that emphasize group action. You will be able to develop your interpersonal skills first. Then, as you become more confident, you can begin taking on leadership roles.

The following national organizations all offer leadership training:

Through the activities of a youth group, you can develop both your interpersonal skills and your leadership ability.

- American Industrial Arts Student Association (AIASA). The members of this organization are enrolled in industrial arts courses. The AIASA helps students develop leadership abilities in relation to the industrial-technical world.
- Distributive Education Clubs of America (DECA). These clubs are for students interested in marketing and distribution occupations. Members learn about marketing, merchandising, management, and other related subjects.
- 4H. 4H is no longer limited to youths living in rural areas. Today the focus of 4H programs is on the development of the total person. The Cooperative Extension Service at the local, state, and federal levels administers the 4H program.
- Future Business Leaders of America (FBLA). The members of this organization are students pursuing careers in business or business education. The FBLA's goals include promoting competent, aggressive business leadership; understanding business enterprise; developing character and self-confidence; and easing the transition from school to work.
- Future Farmers of America (FFA). The members of the FFA learn how to develop their skills in agriculture, use cooperative techniques, and finance their own projects. In addition, they also have the opportunity to speak in public and assume civic responsibilities.
- Future Homemakers of America/Home Economics Related Occupations (FHA/HERO). The FHA emphasizes consumer homemaking education but also explores careers related to home economics. HERO emphasizes careers. Both organizations recognize that people fill roles in the home and in the workplace and that they need to know about both areas.

Meetings run by parliamentary procedure are fair and orderly and enable everyone to participate.

- Health Occupations Student Association (HOSA). Members of this organization are usually enrolled in health and related courses. HOSA helps its members develop into competent health care workers and leaders.
- Office Education Association (OEA). The OEA is for students enrolled in vocational courses dealing with business and office occupations. The organization fosters leadership abilities and interest in free enterprise, and it works to help its members become competent office workers.
- Vocational Industrial Clubs of America (VICA). VICA is for students enrolled in vocational trade, industrial, technical, and health education courses. VICA members develop their skills and personal abilities, enjoy leadership opportunities, and work together with professionals in their fields.

Club Activities

The groups you can join will probably have several functions. They may provide activities related to careers or intended to improve the school or community. They might plan social activities, such as dances or picnics, or specialize in service—helping others in the community. Most of the organizations will have fund-raising activities. Thus, there will be many ways to develop your abilities.

Membership in these clubs will prepare you for the work force in another way. You will learn about how groups operate and how they get things done. You will also learn how to work with other people.

Parliamentary Procedure

All truly organized groups have one thing in common: They are run by **parliamentary procedure**. This is *a system of rules for organizing and conducting the formal business of groups*. It is designed to be orderly, fair, and efficient. It also encourages cooperation. The rules of the system are described in a well-known book called *Robert's Rules of Order*. Knowing the basics of parliamentary procedure will help you be a more effective group member.

Suppose you are chosen to represent your class in the Student Vocational Association (SVA). Here is what you might find at a meeting that follows the ten steps called for in parliamentary procedure.

Step 1: Call to Order. The president of the SVA calls the meeting to order. If a **quorum**—or *majority of the membership*—is present, the meeting proceeds.

Step 2: Reading and Approval of Minutes. The president asks the secretary to read the **minutes**—*offical notes*—of the last meeting. After the secretary reads the minutes, the president asks, "Are there any additions or cor-

Being a leader can be a rewarding activity. By doing your best, you can help other people reach their potential.

rections to the minutes of the last meeting?" Any group member can stand and make a correction or addition. These are added to the minutes.

Step 3: Reports of Officers. Now, the president asks the vice-president, secretary, and treasurer to give reports if they have any. Usually, the treasurer's report is the only one regularly made.

Step 4: Standing Committee Reports. The president next asks each standing committee—regular, permanent committees—for a progress report. The head of each committee stands up and tells what the committee has been doing and what is still to be done.

Step 5: Special Committee Reports. Special committees are set up for special purposes. These committees are temporary. They disband after their business is done.

Step 6: Unfinished Business. Next, the president asks, "Is there any unfinished business?" At the last meeting, someone may have proposed a motion to sell T-shirts to raise money. A **motion** is *a suggestion that the group do a particular thing*. When someone makes a motion, another member should **second** the motion, or *indicate a desire to have the motion considered*. (If there is no second, the motion is dropped.) Discussion of the motion follows the seconding. During the discussion, someone might make a motion to **amend**, or *change*, the original motion. If this is seconded and agreed to by a vote, the original motion is changed.

Step 7: New Business. "Is there any new business?" asks the president. New business consists primarily of future plans for the group. As a result of group discussion, special committees may be formed. If no decisions are reached, this new business will probably be discussed again at the next meeting as unfinished business.

Step 8: The Program. The president next says, "The program committee will now present the program." Perhaps, the program committee arranged to have a graduate of the cooperative education program, now a successful entrepreneur, come to speak. After the speech, the president takes over the meeting again.

Step 9: Announcements. Now, the president asks for announcements. Members might announce the date and time of a committee meeting or remind members to wear their club jackets to the awards assembly.

Step 10: Adjournment. Finally, the president ends the meeting by calling for a motion to adjourn. When the motion is seconded and agreed to by the members, the meeting is adjourned.

Leadership Satisfaction

Leadership of a group does not appeal to all people. Some people work best when they receive direction from others. Everyone can use some leadership abilities in their lives. Being assertive can help you at work, no matter what your job. Developing good interpersonal skills will make you a better group worker. Taking pride in your work is necessary for good self-esteem.

You may not realize it, but you may have many leadership qualities already. If you do choose to become a leader, you may find it very fulfilling. By doing your best, you can help other people reach their potential. By helping other people, you can make your office, shop, home, or school a better place in which to live and work.

MAIN POINTS

- A positive attitude is essential on the job. Someone with a positive attitude is uncritical, generous, helpful, cheerful, and accepts responsibility.
- A person who gets along well with others does better on the job. Getting along well calls for good listening skills, a willingness to learn from others, a sense of humor, empathy, and courtesy.
- Stress and conflict exist on any job, and you must learn to deal with them. Ways to manage stress include good nutrition, adequate sleep and exercise, relaxation, and talking out problems. Assertiveness skills can help you resolve conflicts.
- Good work skills, good work habits, and good interpersonal skills can lead to job advancement.
- It takes many skills to be a good leader. These include the ability to motivate workers; to delegate work; to be fair; to make consistent decisions; and to listen to employees.
- National youth organizations, such as DECA, FBLA, and VICA, help students develop their leadership abilities.
- Youth clubs operate like other groups outside of school. They use parliamentary procedure to accomplish things through group action.

Terms to Know

Use the following terms to fill in the blanks of the sentences below.

amend	empathy	parliamentary procedure
assertiveness	impartiality	performance review
attitude	initiative	quorum
compromise	mediation	second
conflict	minutes	stress
consistent	motion	stressor
delegate	motivate	

1. Your outlook on your job is your _____.
2. A neutral attitude toward the two sides in a conflict is known as _____.
3. The ability to put yourself in another person's shoes is called _____.
4. A sharp disagreement between workers is a(n) _____.
5. When calling our meetings to order, the president of our club follows _____.
6. When you stand up for yourself without accusing the other person, you are practicing _____.
7. Juan wanted to change the original motion, so he made a motion to _____ it.
8. A solution in which both people give in a little is called a(n) _____.
9. A conflict can be solved by a third person through _____.
10. The official notes taken by the secretary of an organization are called _____.
11. When good workers finish their assigned tasks, they have the _____ to find other tasks that need to be done.
12. A worker's skills are evaluated in a(n) _____.
13. A leader who makes workers enthusiastic about their jobs is able

Chapter 10 Working With Others

to _____ them.
14. A supervisor cannot do all the work alone, so he or she must _____ some of the tasks.
15. A meeting cannot be called to order unless a(n) _____ is present.
16. A leader who always handles similar conflicts in the same way is _____.
17. The body's reaction to change is called _____.
18. Anything that causes stress is a(n) _____.
19. A suggestion for the members of a group to consider is a(n) _____.
20. When someone makes a motion at a meeting, another person who wants it to be considered should _____ it.

Chapter Review

1. List four characteristics of a positive attitude.
2. How can you change a negative attitude?
3. Give three examples of good listening skills.
4. Describe positive and negative stress. What are some ways of managing stress?
5. How can conflict be helpful?
6. Is it a good idea to keep a problem to yourself? Why or why not?
7. What steps does an assertive person take to resolve a conflict?
8. Describe four possible results of a conflict.
9. Name three traits needed for a promotion. List five skills a good supervisor must have.
10. Explain the purpose of parliamentary procedure.

Activities

1. Invite an employer to speak about positive and negative attitudes on the job. Suggest that the speaker give specific examples of both attitudes.
2. Write a paragraph describing a time in your life when a conflict led to a good solution to a problem.
3. Imagine that you are working as a teacher's aide. When you were hired, you were told that you would occasionally have the chance to work with students. Instead, the teacher expects you to spend the entire time correcting papers and running the copy machine. You have some ideas that you would like to try with students. Role-play the meeting in which you discuss this conflict with the teacher. Use assertiveness skills to discuss and resolve the problem.
4. List three student organizations that you think might help you in a career that interests you. Attend the groups' meetings, or write to the national organizations for more information.

Chapter **11**

Health and Safety on the Job

OBJECTIVES

This chapter will enable you to:

- describe health and safety hazards that exist in the workplace.
- explain how lack of knowledge and lack of skill cause accidents and health hazards.
- give examples to show how anger, worry, drugs, alcohol, fatigue, and illness can cause accidents.
- explain unsafe attitudes and their results.
- list the most common types of work injuries and the most common work-related causes of death.
- follow nutritional and exercise guidelines to take care of your health.
- dress for safety on the job.
- explain the importance of training in first aid and fire safety.
- explain the importance of the Occupational Safety and Health Act.

Armand

I can't believe this is happening to me. This morning, I was thinking about going camping this weekend. Now, here I am in the hospital—in traction, too!

I had just a few hours more to work at the sporting goods store before the weekend. I had these boxes of barbells to move to the front of the store. I was carrying one at a time, but then I thought if I could finish faster, maybe I could leave early. No one was around to help, so I decided to haul two boxes at a time. I stacked two boxes, but when I tried to pick them up I felt this pain shoot through my lower back. It hurt so much I could hardly breathe. A friend brought me to the emergency room. I couldn't sit still during the ride because of the pain.

I'll be here for at least two weeks — all because I didn't lift those boxes the right way. If I had squatted down and used the strength of my legs to lift, I would have been all right. Well, maybe not. I never should have rushed and tried to lift two boxes in the first place.

Now I'm flat on my back for two weeks, maybe a month, according to the doctor. I hope I can get my job back when I'm better. I hope I *get* better. To think this all happened because I wanted to save a few minutes. I ended up paying a big price for my carelessness.

HOW GREAT IS THE DANGER?

What are the chances that you will be exposed to a serious health or safety **hazard**—or *danger*—in the workplace? You may be surprised at how high the chances are. About one in every four workers is exposed to known health hazards on the job. That is more than 21 million workers. It is estimated that up to 40 percent of all cancer cases are work-related. As for safety hazards, the National Safety Council estimated that about 10,600 Americans died in work-related accidents in 1988. Another 1.8 million suffered occupational injuries that made them miss work. Health and safety hazards can be quite similar. In general, though, health hazards cause disease, and safety hazards lead to injury.

Where Are the Hazards?

Health and safety hazards exist in almost every kind of job and every kind of workplace. The kinds of hazards that exist depend in large part upon the nature of the job. If you become a construction worker on a high-rise building, for example, you will be more in danger of falling than if you worked in an office. Figure 11.1 shows you the death rates in various industries in 1988. There are some surprises on the chart. You might, for example, expect aircraft workers to have a much higher accident rate than they do. One reason for the low rate is the strict health and safety practices in that industry. How risky a job is, then, depends on both the nature of the work and the health and safety practices in the workplace.

For a workplace to be as safe as possible requires the cooperation of three groups: government, employers, and workers. Government is responsible for setting health and safety standards. Employers are responsible for seeing that workplace conditions meet those standards. Workers themselves have the responsibility of following health and safety precautions both on the job and off. As you will see in this chapter, being a safe and healthy worker is a 24-hour-a-day job.

WHY ACCIDENTS HAPPEN

"My sister is accident-prone. Everything happens to her." You have heard people make such statements. It does seem that some people are more likely than others to spill their milk, trip on the stairs, or slam a door on their fingers. What have these people done to deserve such disasters? Are they just unlucky? Are they truly accident-prone—somehow more likely than others to get hurt?

Certain people may have more accidents than others. Accidents at home and on the job are not just a matter of bad luck. They happen for specific reasons. They are usually caused by one of the following five factors:

- lack of knowledge
- lack of skill
- physical limitations
- unsafe work behavior
- fatigue and illness

In addition, an unsafe work environment can make anyone appear accident-prone. Most accidents can be avoided with careful job training and a high level of safety awareness.

Lack of Knowledge

The machines and materials in many jobs can be hazardous to your health. If you work in a delicatessen, you might use an electric meat slicer daily. If you become a machinist, you would operate a lathe, a drill press, and other powerful equipment. If you become a medical technician, you may handle blood containing disease organisms.

Having complete knowledge about the tools of your trade is essential to job safety. Tools, machines, and materials are made to be used or operated in certain ways. As long as they are used correctly, they are generally safe. If

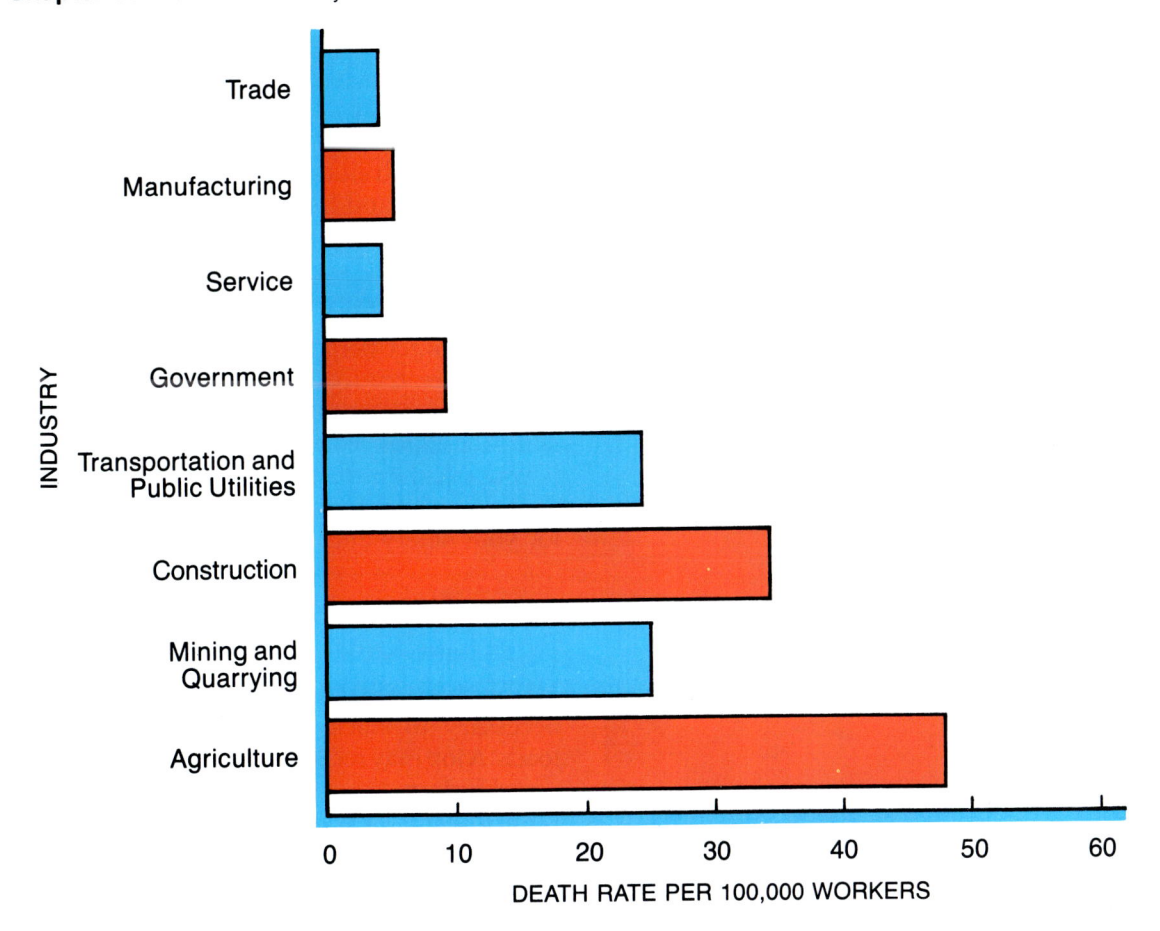

Chapter 11 Health and Safety on the Job

Figure 11.1 Death Rates for Major Industries in 1988
Source: U.S. Bureau of Labor Statistics

used improperly, they can cause injury. For example, a hairdresser must follow specific guidelines when giving a customer a permanent. These include wearing rubber gloves. Otherwise, the strong chemicals used in permanent wave lotions can cause severe skin irritations.

Tools can become dangerous in ways that are not obvious. For instance, as you drill a hole with a power drill, friction heats up the drill bit to a temperature hot enough to burn your hand if you touch the bit. The only way to know *not* to touch the bit is through training, either on the job or in the classroom.

Employers should provide adequate training for their employees. However, workers are then responsible for putting that knowledge into action. It is up to workers to help guard their own safety by learning as much as possible about what the tools of their trade can do.

Lack of Skill

Power tools, such as electric saws, drills, and grinders, are essential in many industries. Tractors, backhoes, rollers, and other heavy equipment are necessary in modern farming

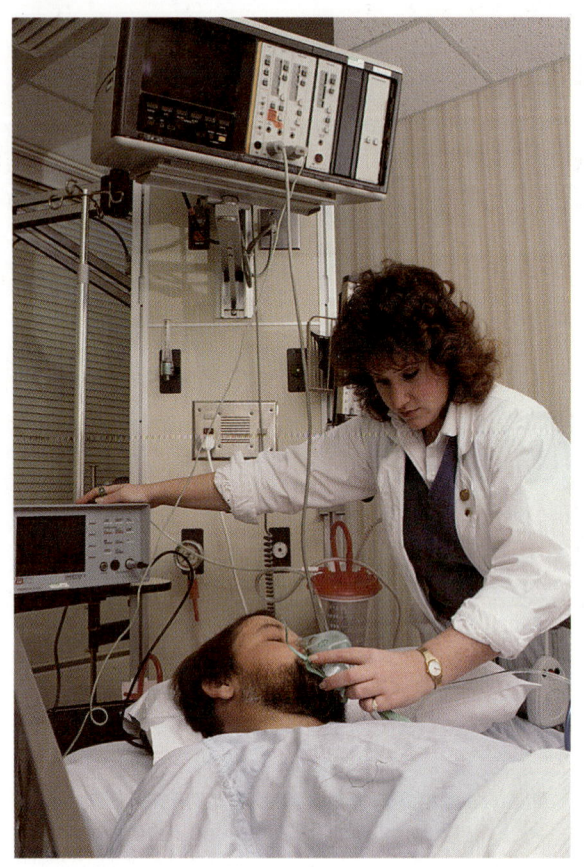

Health hazards for patients and hospital employees alike may result if a medical technician lacks knowledge about the equipment and procedures of the job.

and manufacturing. It takes skill and training to use such tools and equipment, however. Good power tools and heavy equipment are designed to be safe for the operators. However, their designers usually have highly skilled users in mind for the tools. Workers who lack the skills to use the machines properly are endangering themselves and others.

In order to gain the necessary skills, read the directions before you operate any equipment for the first time. Then, learn the skill from an experienced worker in these four steps:

1. Watch the skilled person operate the machine.
2. As the skilled person performs the task, have her or him explain it to you step by step. Ask questions about anything that you do not understand.
3. Do the job slowly while the skilled worker watches and instructs you.
4. Practice the job with the skilled worker nearby until you can do it skillfully enough to work safely on your own.

Be sure to get help from co-workers if necessary. Never try to show what a good worker you are by taking on jobs you do not have the skills for. Other workers will respect you more if you ask them to train you. This will show that you are responsible enough to look out for your safety and the safety of others.

Physical Limitations

All jobs have physical requirements. It may be necessary to stack crates or to carry heavy loads. A job may require a high level of eye-hand coordination. If you cannot meet the physical requirements of your job, you may be endangering yourself.

For example, Gerald's job at the computer shop required him to stack the new computers on high shelves. Gerald was of average height, but the highest shelves were beyond his reach. One day, he could not find the stepladder he usually used to reach the top shelves. Instead of looking for it, he decided to climb up the shelves. He lost his balance and fell, suffering cuts and bruises.

Gerald was quite capable of doing his work safely *if he used the right equipment*. Without that equipment, the task was beyond his physical limitations.

Before taking on a task for which you will have to perform physical feats, think about what you can do. If you find that you will have to reach too high, lift too much, or stay in one position too long, get help. You should be able to find some equipment that can help you or some other way to do the task.

Unsafe Behavior

Accidents occur when workers act in unsafe ways. Some types of unsafe behavior are obvious. Playing with dangerous tools is one example. Leaving boxes in a busy corridor and leaving file drawers open are two other examples. There are other kinds of behavior that are unsafe but less obvious.

Steve was a maintenance worker for the town. One of his jobs was to drive the truck that sanded the streets when the roads were icy. One day, Steve had an argument with his wife. When he got in his truck, he was still furious. He was concentrating on his anger rather than his job. As a result, he took a curve too fast, and the heavy truck skidded sideways into a ditch. The load of sand shifted, and the whole truck went over. Steve suffered a concussion in the accident.

Steve's behavior was unsafe because he let outside factors affect how he worked. Anger is one factor that affects work behavior. Another factor is worry. Worrying about how she would make the next payment on her car distracted Liz, and she burned herself while soldering. Of course, it is not always possible to keep your mind off personal problems at work, but it is important to realize that your emotions can affect your safety and the safety of others. You need to do your best to put your personal problems out of your mind while you are on the job.

Unsafe Attitudes. Unsafe attitudes cause accidents, too. Some people have the attitude that "It can't happen to me." They think that accidents happen to the other person—the one who is not as experienced or as skilled or who just has bad luck.

The most dangerous piece of work equipment is the motor vehicle. In 1988, 35 percent of all work-related deaths resulted from motor vehicle accidents.

An unsafe attitude can creep up on a worker. For example, Jennie followed all the safety rules for the first few weeks at her new job. Then, she began to take a few shortcuts, for example, not putting on her safety glasses if she only needed them for a minute. No one said anything about her not wearing the glasses, and she did not get hurt. Jennie began to believe that the glasses were not necessary, at least not for her, because she was so careful. She began to wear the glasses even less frequently.

However, the past is no indication of what will happen in the future. Jennie was making her job more dangerous by not wearing her glasses. She went on for months without them, and nothing happened. Then one day, her hand slipped, and a speck of metal flew up from the piece Jennie was smoothing. It scratched her eye, and Jennie came close to losing most of her vision in that eye. Fortunately, there was no permanent damage.

Jennie learned that a safe attitude means *always* protecting yourself. You can think of safety equipment as being a nuisance—hot, uncomfortable, or hard to put on. For your protection, however, you should think positively about the equipment. Putting it on should become a habit; wearing it should be part of the job. And the time spent putting it on will become part of your routine.

Alcohol and Drugs. What you put into your body can also lead to unsafe behavior on the job. Using alcohol or drugs such as tranquilizers, marijuana, or amphetamines can create any or all of the attitude and behavior problems described above. Some people say they can "handle" their liquor or drugs. The fact is

Unsafe attitudes lead to accidents. Workers who have a positive attitude toward their safety equipment make wearing it a habit.

alcohol and drugs, even in relatively small amounts, affect people's judgment, behavior, and reaction times.

Drugs and alcohol slow down reflexes and increase reaction time. They affect sense of balance and reduce ability to concentrate. If a worker under the influence of drugs starts to slip off a ladder, he or she may not be able to react quickly enough to avoid a fall. Drugs and alcohol make workers less alert, more apt to fall asleep or to misjudge what they are doing. Some experts say that 40 percent of all industrial accidents are caused by people who have been drinking.

If an accident occurs, a person who has been drinking may have trouble escaping from the dangerous situation. She or he may not be able to think clearly and may be unable to get help. What might have been a simple injury can become more serious.

Common medications also create hazards. Cold and hay fever medications often contain substances that can make the user sleepy or less alert. The labels on these products warn people against driving or using heavy machinery while using the drug. If a person drinks alcohol while taking a cold remedy, the effects of the drug will be even stronger.

Fatigue and Illness

Fatigue and illness can cause accidents, too. When you are tired or sick, you may not give full attention to your work. Because Phil had a bad headache, he was less careful than usual in carrying a pot of hot soup across the restaurant kitchen. He dropped the pot and scalded his legs.

A tired worker may also make careless mistakes. Tanya had gotten very little sleep over the weekend. Because of her lack of sleep, she was inattentive at work on Monday. She did not bother to put away an electrical cord and left it trailing across a walkway. A co-worker tripped over the cord and sprained his ankle. Tanya's carelessness, brought on by lack of sleep, caused injury to someone else.

Unsafe Work Environment

By law, employers must provide a workplace that is free of physical hazards. Dangerous conditions can occur, however, if workers or employers take shortcuts that bypass safety rules. Watch out for these workplace hazards:

- Inadequate machine safety guards. Sometimes, workers remove safety guards to make a task quicker or easier to do. For example, someone might lift the safety shield on a grinder for a better view of the substance in the machine. That exposes the moving parts, which can trap the worker's hand.

- Poor condition of equipment. Eventually, all equipment begins to wear out and must be repaired or replaced, but repairs may not be done when needed. For example, typewriters with frayed cords can give workers shocks or even start fires.

- Poor design or construction. Some machines, especially older models, were not designed with safety in mind. Workers may be endangered, even though they are as careful as possible. Management should be notified about such situations.

- Dangerous processes. Feeding wood into a table saw with your hand instead of a pushing stick is an example of a dangerous process. Some jobs, by their nature, involve dangerous processes. For this reason, logging is one of the most dangerous professions. A chain saw can kick back, or a tree can fall in an unexpected direction. Observing safety rules, however, can reduce the risks.

- Poor lighting. For anyone from a fabric cutter to a gardener, poor lighting increases safety risks. In poor light, a gardener may not see the obstacles in the lawn mower's path. A fabric cutter may not be able to guide the cutting tool correctly. Employers should be told if lighting is not adequate.

- Poor ventilation. Fumes and dust in the

air can endanger workers. The fumes from operating a gas forklift in an enclosed area can make workers sick. Adequate ventilation in the workplace is vital. When this is not possible, workers must wear respirators (breathing masks).

Health hazards are also created by unsafe products used in work environments. There are many products that were once thought safe that are now known to be **carcinogenic**—*cancer-causing*. However, people worked with these substances for years without knowing their effects.

One example is asbestos. For years, asbestos was considered a wonderful substance. It was used as insulation and fireproofing in thousands of schools and other buildings. Then, in the early 1970s, researchers discovered that asbestos workers who had been in the industry for 20 years or more had especially high rates of cancer. There were few safeguards against breathing asbestos particles because nobody knew the dangers. Experts now predict that about 2 million workers will eventually die from cancers caused by asbestos particles that they breathed over the years. For these workers, discovery of the hazards of asbestos arrived too late.

The workplace is no longer as dangerous as it once was. As you can see in Figure 11.2, the rate of work-related accidents and deaths has been dropping in recent years. Knowledge of health hazards is greater, and companies are

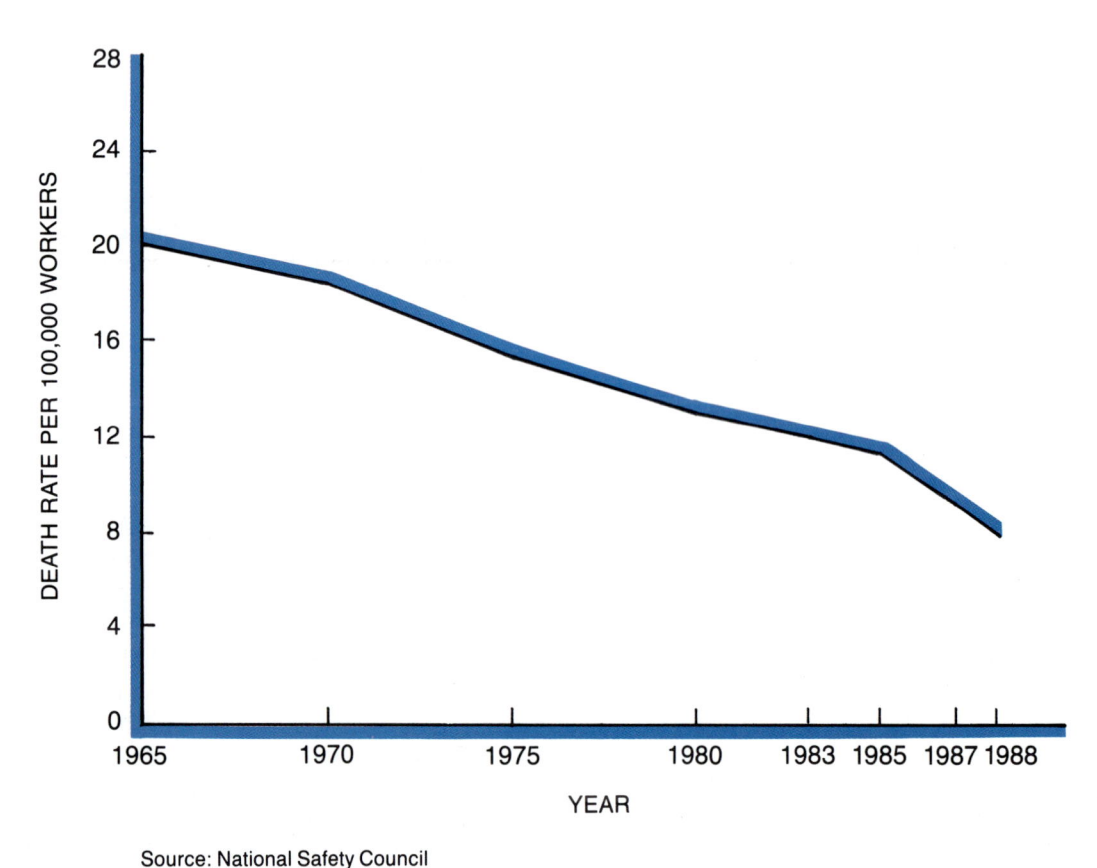

Source: National Safety Council

Figure 11.2 Changes in Work-Related Death Rates Since 1965

now much more health-conscious. New hazards are constantly appearing. For example, new chemicals are being produced every day. Many are being used in the workplace, although few have been thoroughly tested for their effects on people. It is still not known which ones are **toxic**, or *poisonous*.

THE MOST COMMON TYPES OF ACCIDENTS

The injuries and deaths that result from on-the-job accidents fall into specific patterns. Knowing these patterns can help you raise your level of safety awareness.

Common Injuries

When Armand hurt his back trying to lift two boxes of barbells, he suffered the most common work-related injury. Four out of ten on-the-job accidents cause injuries to the trunk, or midsection, of the body. Frequently, these injuries are to the back. What causes so many back injuries? Very often, like Armand, workers do not use proper technique when lifting things. Sometimes, the injury is due to lifting something too heavy. Other times, the problem comes from doing too much lifting in one day.

About 30 percent of work injuries are to the arms, hands, or fingers. Most of these accidents happen to people using large machinery. A recent study showed that almost three out of every four of these injuries occurred to people who were not wearing safety gloves. (Figure 11.3 shows the injury pattern for on-the-job accidents.)

Common Causes of Death

The most dangerous piece of work equipment is not something unusual. It is the common motor vehicle—the car or truck. In 1988, 35 percent of all work-related deaths were due to motor vehicle accidents. The victims were driving company trucks, buses, or cars. They were making deliveries or traveling from one work site to another. In most cases, the causes of the accidents were the same as for motor vehicle accidents off the job. The workers had been drinking, driving too fast, or not paying attention to the road.

Falls are another common cause of death. In 1986, 13 percent of all work deaths were caused by falls. Naturally, some job groups are more at risk. Falls accounted for almost 30 percent of the deaths in construction, but they caused a very small percentage of the deaths in office jobs.

Industrial vehicles and equipment accounted for about 10 percent of work deaths in 1983. People working in mining and manufacturing occupations are most apt to die in such accidents. They work with tools and equipment that make their jobs hazardous.

COSTS OF ON-THE-JOB ACCIDENTS AND ILLNESSES

Work-related accidents and illnesses have human, as well as financial, costs. In 1988, 10,600 people died in job-related accidents. In addition, about 1.8 million people were injured.

Based on these numbers, some authorities estimate that 1 out of every 100 new workers will die as a result of a work-related accident. Six of the 100 will suffer a permanent injury or handicap. Seventy of the 100 will be injured at some time.

The government estimates that about 100,000 people die from job-related illnesses each year. Coal miners die of black lung, a disease caused by breathing coal dust. Cotton mill workers die of brown lung from breathing cotton dust. Both of these diseases make breathing difficult and eventually destroy the lungs. Workers in a number of different fields, such as construction and auto repair, die of asbestos-caused cancers. Many of these people were working at their jobs long before the danger was clearly known and before the government stepped in.

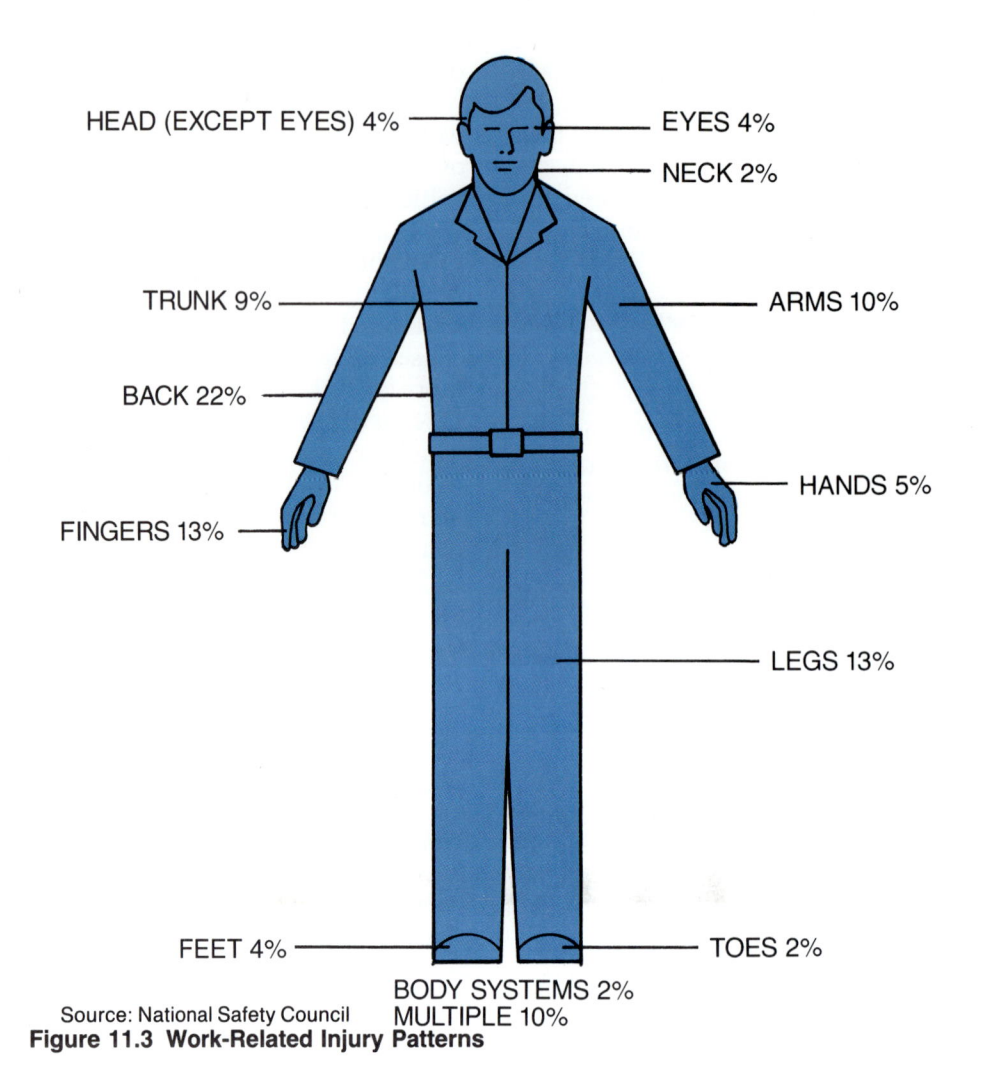

HEAD (EXCEPT EYES) 4%
EYES 4%
NECK 2%
TRUNK 9%
ARMS 10%
BACK 22%
HANDS 5%
FINGERS 13%
LEGS 13%
FEET 4%
TOES 2%
BODY SYSTEMS 2%
MULTIPLE 10%

Source: National Safety Council
Figure 11.3 Work-Related Injury Patterns

Financial Costs

In addition to the human suffering, work injuries cause many workers to miss days from work. The accidents of a single year cost 35 million lost workdays in the work force. This does not count the workdays lost by people whose injuries in past years disabled them for life. These disabled workers account for 40 million more lost workdays each year. Many million more days are lost through work-related diseases.

Accidents on the job cost both workers and employers money. Injuries cost the U.S. economy $180 billion in 1988, according to a study done for the federal government. That figure includes both the direct cost of health care and the indirect costs of lost work time, disability, and premature death. Work-related illnesses added billions of dollars to that total.

PREVENTING ACCIDENTS AND ILLNESSES

Your body is your own machine. It is a finely tuned instrument that must be well maintained to stay in good running order. You have

Chapter 11 Health and Safety on the Job

a responsibility to yourself to stay in shape and stay healthy.

Eat Properly

Part of taking care of yourself consists of eating the right foods. Ellen learned that the hard way. When she finished school, she got a job as a data processor. Every morning she rushed to work, so she usually had only coffee for breakfast. At lunch, she grabbed a hamburger or a hot dog. Afternoon coffee break meant more coffee and a sweet snack. When she came home at night, she ate a big dinner with her family.

Ellen saw nothing wrong with her eating habits. But they were actually affecting her work. She made quite a few mistakes in the afternoon. She usually became irritable toward the end of the day. She felt tired, even after a full night's rest.

One night, Ellen watched a television program about good nutrition. She learned that her behavior resulted from her poor eating habits. The next morning, she ate a healthful breakfast—juice, whole-grain toast, and cereal with milk. At lunch she went to a salad bar to add vegetables and fruit to her diet. During her afternoon coffee break, she bought some crackers and an apple. She was trying to cut down on sweets. She had learned that a candy bar could give her quick energy by increasing the sugar in her system, but that it could actually leave her feeling more tired in

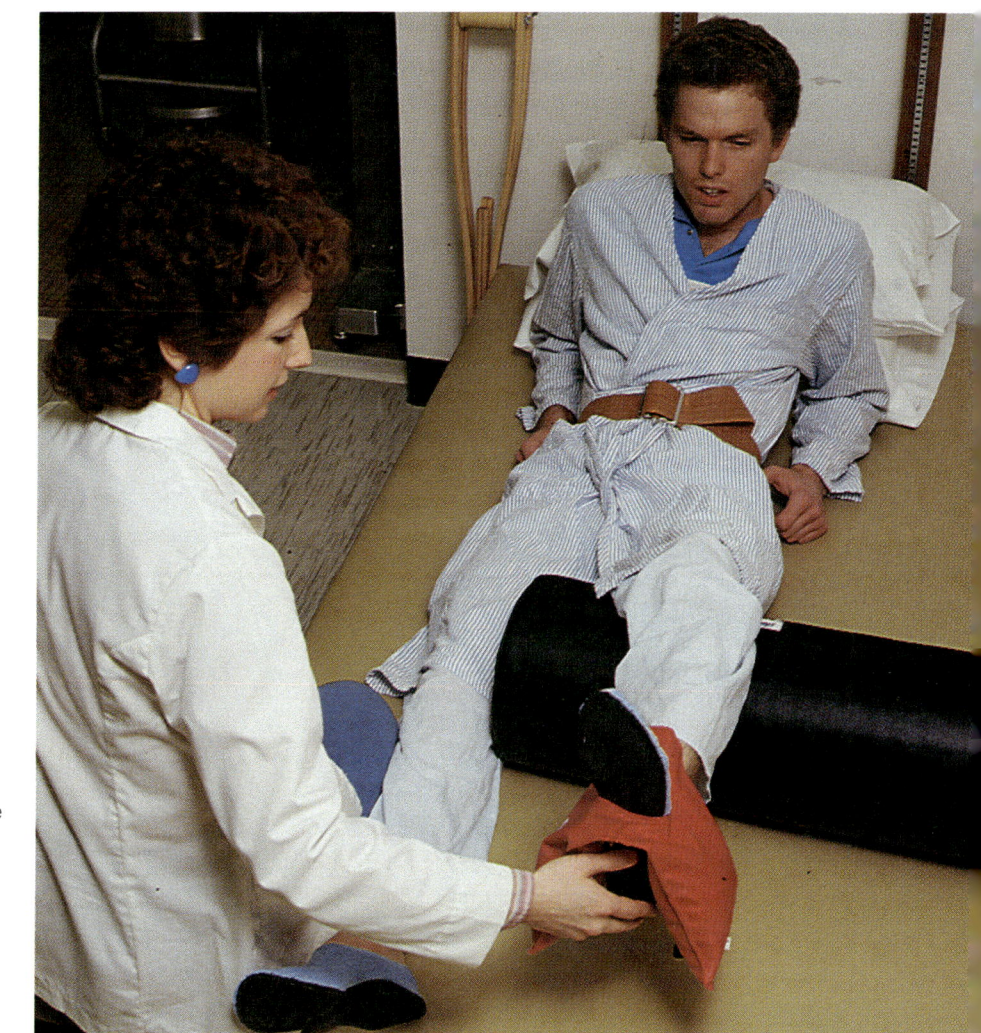

Accidents on the job cost both workers and employers money. Medical expenses, insurance costs, and lost work time added up to more than $47 billion in 1988, according to the National Safety Council.

Exercising regularly will give you renewed energy—both on and off the job.

an hour or so. That night, Ellen had less appetite for dinner because of her healthful eating during the day. She ate a lighter meal.

After a short time of healthful eating, Ellen began to notice some changes. First, she was more alert at work. She made fewer errors, and she was more cheerful with her co-workers and friends. Her fatigue disappeared. After work, she still had plenty of energy. Instead of complaining about getting home too late to do anything, she began taking a pottery class.

Get Adequate Sleep

Along with eating well, getting enough sleep is important to feeling good and staying alert. If you are not getting enough sleep, your body will probably tell you. You will feel tired and irritable. You may also get a headache. Most people need between seven and eight hours of sleep a night, although some do very well on five or six hours.

Many people have trained themselves to get by on less sleep than they need. Not realizing how much sleep they require, they gradually become victims of constant **fatigue**, or *tiredness*. Their energy levels drop, their work suffers, and their safety awareness is reduced. Drowsiness can cause accidents. If you are alert, you can make those quick decisions that can avoid accidents.

Exercise Regularly

Many workers find that regular exercise helps them work better. Exercise raises energy levels, reduces muscle strain, and produces a better state of mind. It also helps ward off illness. Vigorous exercise will make your heart and lungs stronger and lessen the chance of heart disease.

Exercise gives you more, instead of less, energy. Workers who swim or jog during their lunch hours have much more energy in the afternoon. In fact, people who exercise find they have more energy off the job as well as on it.

Many employers realize the benefits of regular exercise for their workers and have instituted company-wide physical fitness programs. Physically fit workers are more productive, take fewer sick days, and are better able to handle on-the-job stress.

Wear Safety Clothing and Equipment

To avoid accidents, workers must wear the right clothing and equipment for the job. For many jobs, this means special protective clothing. Welders wear heavy gloves and aprons to prevent burns. People working in noisy areas wear earplugs. Those with jobs near dust or hazardous gases use masks and respirators. Hard hats and safety shoes help prevent injuries to people in manufacturing and construction. Gloves protect against cuts in many lines of work, and safety glasses protect the eyes from injury.

Chapter 11 Health and Safety on the Job

In most cases, these protective devices are required by law. You may need some time to get used to wearing them. These devices are absolutely necessary for your safety and health. Going without them is unsafe—and may be illegal.

Even where special safety equipment is not required, think carefully about what you wear to work. For example, a bracelet or loose hair can get caught in a piece of equipment.

Comfortable clothes make a difference in your work. You will be distracted from your tasks if your wool collar is scratchy or if your waistband is too tight. A pair of shoes selected especially for work also may make sense. Even if your position does not require steel-tipped safety shoes, some type of work shoes may make your job easier and safer. Rubber-soled or low-heeled shoes can help you avoid falls. If you are on your feet most of the day, comfortable shoes are a must. Look at the shoes that hairdressers, nurses, dentists, and food servers wear. Usually, they are comfortable shoes with thick soles and plenty of support. Such shoes come in many attractive styles. These shoes are not glamorous, but workers have learned that they are well worth wearing for the comfort they provide. The right shoes can help you avoid falls, muscle strains, and fatigue.

Learn Your Job and Your Workplace

To avoid accidents, learn all you can about your job. Do not be afraid to ask questions about a process you do not understand. Invest time in practicing the skills your job requires.

Learn the safety procedures of your workplace. If you are working with chemicals, learn the locations of emergency showers in case chemicals are spilled on you. Know fire exit routes and the locations of fire extinguishers.

Find out what to do in case of other emergencies on the job. If you handle money, learn how to act in case of armed robbery. You should also learn what to do if a power failure or natural disaster occurs.

Use Good Safety Habits

As you learn about your job, make safety skills a habit. Put on your safety equipment before you start work. Keep your work area free of clutter. Follow the safety rules posted by each machine. Be alert for possible hazards, and report any hazardous conditions to management. Show that you are concerned for the safety of others.

If you are working with a hazardous substance, understand the importance of the right safety clothing. Use your respirator correctly. Stay alert for warning signs such as a cough or burning eyes. If you believe that you have been exposed to a hazardous substance, speak to your supervisor immediately. If she or he takes no action, file a complaint with the government. In a later section of this chapter, you will learn how to do that.

Learn First Aid

Quick thinking and first-aid training can decrease the seriousness of injuries and save lives. **First aid** is *emergency medical care that can be given before a doctor or other trained medical person arrives*. When a co-worker lost a fingertip in a table saw accident, Becky stayed

Learning first aid can help you save a life. Many free classes are available in first aid and CPR.

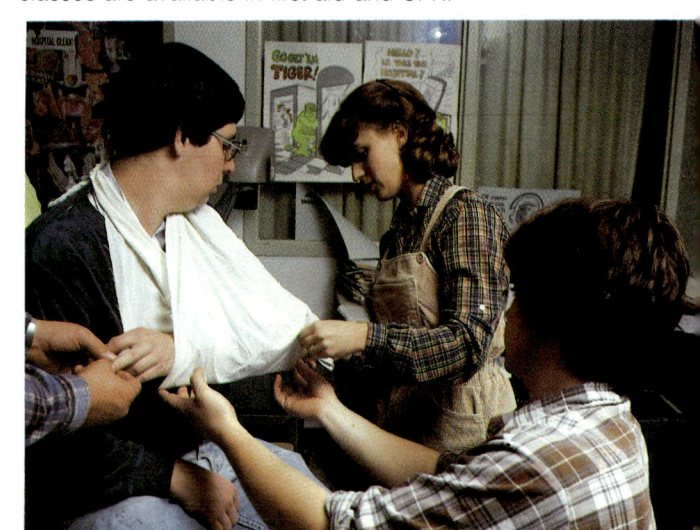

calm. First, she had another worker call an ambulance. Then, she made the victim sit down and try to relax. She stopped the bleeding by bandaging the finger and applying pressure below the injury. She directed another worker to find the fingertip, wrap it in a clean cloth, and put it on ice. Thanks to Becky's knowledge, doctors were able to reattach her coworker's fingertip.

In other cases, workers have saved lives with **cardiopulmonary resuscitation (CPR)**. This procedure is *a way of restoring the heartbeat by applying rhythmic external pressure.* You must have the right skills to be a lifesaver. Many schools and businesses offer first-aid classes. The American Red Cross offers classes in both first aid and CPR.

THE THREE-WAY PARTNERSHIP FOR SAFETY

Until 1970, the responsibility for making workplaces safe was left to state governments. Workplace conditions had improved steadily during the twentieth century, but in the 1960s, accident rates suddenly began to climb. At the same time, new occupational diseases were being discovered. In 1970, there were about 14,000 worker deaths, and 2.5 million workers were injured. An untold number were being made ill by the materials they worked with. Many workers feared they would lose their jobs if they complained to the government about the conditions. Others were not aware of the hazards in their workplaces. In response to these problems, Congress passed the Occupational Safety and Health Act.

This act set up the **Occupational Safety and Health Administration (OSHA)** *to create health and safety standards for business and industry.* The act also established each employer's legal responsibility to provide a safe and healthful workplace.

OSHA is the watchdog that checks businesses to make sure they are following the rules, but the system of safety and health regulation is actually a three-way partnership. OSHA makes regulations for businesses to follow after careful study. OSHA receives much of its information about workplace conditions from employers and workers. The Administration encourages workers and employers to cooperate in making workplaces safer.

Health and Safety Inspections

If workers feel that management is not doing its best to remove a safety or health hazard, workers can ask OSHA to inspect their workplace. OSHA will not tell the employer which workers asked for the inspection if confidentiality is requested. An OSHA inspector will check the workplace in the presence of representatives of the employer and the workers. During the inspection, the worker representative should do the following:

- Point out hazards.
- Describe accidents or illnesses that have resulted from hazards.
- Describe past worker complaints.
- Tell the inspector if working conditions are not normal during the inspection.
- Help the inspector evaluate the records the employer must keep of employee deaths, injuries, illnesses, and exposure to dangerous substances.

Correcting Hazards

After the OSHA inspector has inspected the workplace and has evaluated the company's records, he or she meets with the representatives of the workers and management. This meeting is designed to point out hazards and suggest solutions. The inspector then reports to the OSHA area director, who decides if any citations for violations will be issued. An OSHA citation states the nature of the hazard, what should be done about it, and the date by which it should be corrected. Employees then work

Chapter 11 Health and Safety on the Job

with management to correct the problem. Workers should do the following:

- Make sure the citation remains posted until the violation is corrected.
- Make sure that the violation is corrected by the deadline.
- Work with the employer to be sure that changes really remove the hazard.
- See that the corrective measures are maintained.
- Ask for progress reports on the work.
- Make sure that any personal protective equipment required during work is used and maintained properly.

Sometimes, however, correcting hazards is not this simple. If the employer disagrees with OSHA's findings, a long legal fight may follow. There may be hearings before an OSHA Review Commission or informal hearings with Department of Labor lawyers. The case may even go to court. All along the way, workers must stay involved to make sure their side of the case is heard.

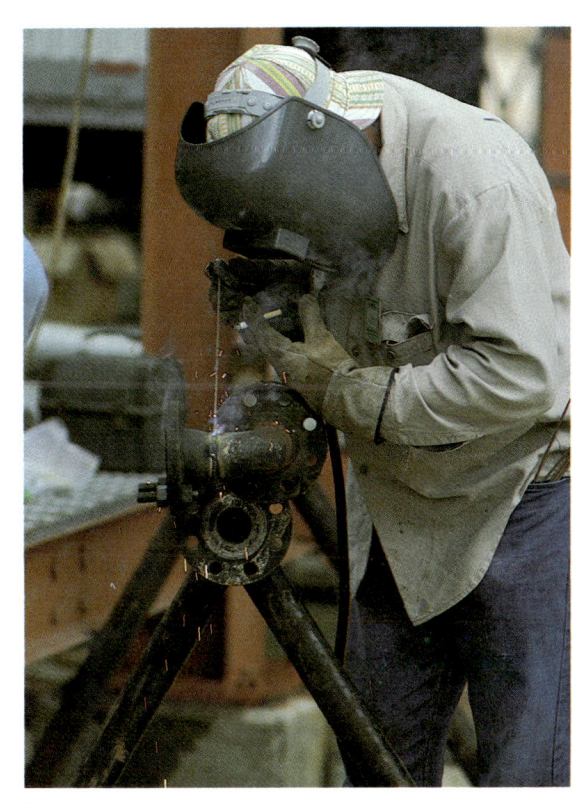

A safe workplace requires cooperation among workers, employers, and government. A worker who smokes in a restricted area endangers the entire workplace.

Your Right to Know

In order for you to know if there are hazards in your workplace, you need to know the OSHA guidelines for your industry. Your employer must make these standards available to you. If you need more information on hazards, you can contact the **National Institute for Occupational Safety and Health (NIOSH)**. This group *collects data about accidents and illnesses and recommends new standards.* The Institute does research into the effects of new substances on workers. It also funds studies that examine links between chemicals and cancer.

If you want to find out about possible health hazards, you can send a form to NIOSH. An expert will visit your workplace to see if there are any health hazards.

Safety and Health Standards

The purpose of safety and health standards is to provide information that will help prevent injury to employees and damage to property. Standards are minimum, basic, safe procedures that must be followed to the letter in every case. Certain personal freedoms — wearing jewelry or loose-fitting clothing, for example — are no longer an option in the industrial environment, but this is necessary to protect employee well-being and to keep safety performance consistent throughout the United States. Most standards result from hard lessons learned from past industrial accidents. Industry does not want these lessons to be repeated.

It is the employee's responsibility to know and to follow mandatory safety and health standards. This requires a dedicated and consistent personal effort on the part of the employee. Safety and health standards are not considered just guides, and employees must not intentionally ignore any safety or health standard.

The bottom line is that managers are ultimately responsible for the overall health and safety of their employees and work area. They must ensure that up-to-date job knowledge, continual training, sufficient protective devices, and well-maintained equipment are available.

MAIN POINTS

- Work-related accidents and illnesses cause thousands of deaths and millions of injuries each year.
- Accidents result from lack of knowledge or skill, physical limitations, unsafe work behavior, fatigue and illness, and unsafe work environment.
- Health hazards in the workplace, such as chemicals and asbestos, can bring on illnesses many years later.
- The most frequently injured parts of the body are the midsection, fingers, hands, and arms.
- Workers can help prevent accidents by taking care of their health. Good nutrition, enough sleep, and plenty of exercise keep workers alert and less prone to illness.
- Dressing for safety on the job means wearing safety equipment if needed, safe and comfortable clothing, and the right shoes.
- Learning safety skills, such as fire procedures, will help you be safe on the job.
- Learning first aid may enable you to save someone's life.
- The Occupational Safety and Health Administration (OSHA) and the National Institute for Occupational Safety and Health (NIOSH) are federal organizations that set and enforce safety standards and study safety problems.
- The responsibility for occupational safety and health is a three-way partnership that includes the government, employers, and workers.

Terms to Know

Use the following terms to fill in the blanks of the sentences below.

carcinogenic
cardiopulmonary resuscitation (CPR)
fatigue
first aid
hazard
National Institute for Occupational Safety and Health (NIOSH)
Occupational Safety and Health Administration (OSHA)
toxic

1. A workplace condition that threatens workers' safety or health is a(n) _____.
2. A substance that is proven to be a cancer-causing agent is called _____.
3. If you are feeling extremely tired, you are suffering from _____.
4. If a substance is poisonous, it is called _____.
5. The government organization that

studies workplace safety is known as the _____.
6. Setting national health and safety standards for business and industry is the responsibility of the _____.
7. A trained person can restore a victim's heartbeat by using _____.
8. Emergency care given before a trained medical person arrives is called _____.

Chapter Review

1. Explain the general difference between a safety hazard and a health hazard.
2. Describe some ways that lack of knowledge can hurt you on the job. How can an employer's lack of knowledge cause workers' illnesses?
3. List the four recommended steps for learning a new job skill.
4. How can the poor condition of equipment cause accidents?
5. List six types of unsafe behavior on the job.
6. Which part of the body is most often injured on the job? What is the most common cause of death?
7. How are good nutrition and exercise related to on-the-job safety?
8. What is the purpose of safety clothing? Give some examples of such clothing.
9. How does OSHA safeguard workers?
10. Who shares responsibility for workplace safety and health?

Activities

1. Research the effect of OSHA on an industry that is important to your area. For example, if you live in a mining area, find out what mining safety standards are required by OSHA. Call someone connected to the local industry to answer your questions. Report your findings to the class.
2. Invite a safety engineer from a local factory, plant, or research center to visit your class. Ask her or him to explain and demonstrate the safety equipment used at that company.
3. Arrange with an industrial arts or home economics teacher to tour a shop or classroom. Have the teacher or an experienced student explain safety rules. Have the teacher explain how the design of the equipment and the layout of the room help to prevent injuries.
4. Write a brief report about a safety hazard currently in the news. Examples might be oil or chemical spills, problems with nuclear waste or nuclear power plants, or toxic waste storage.

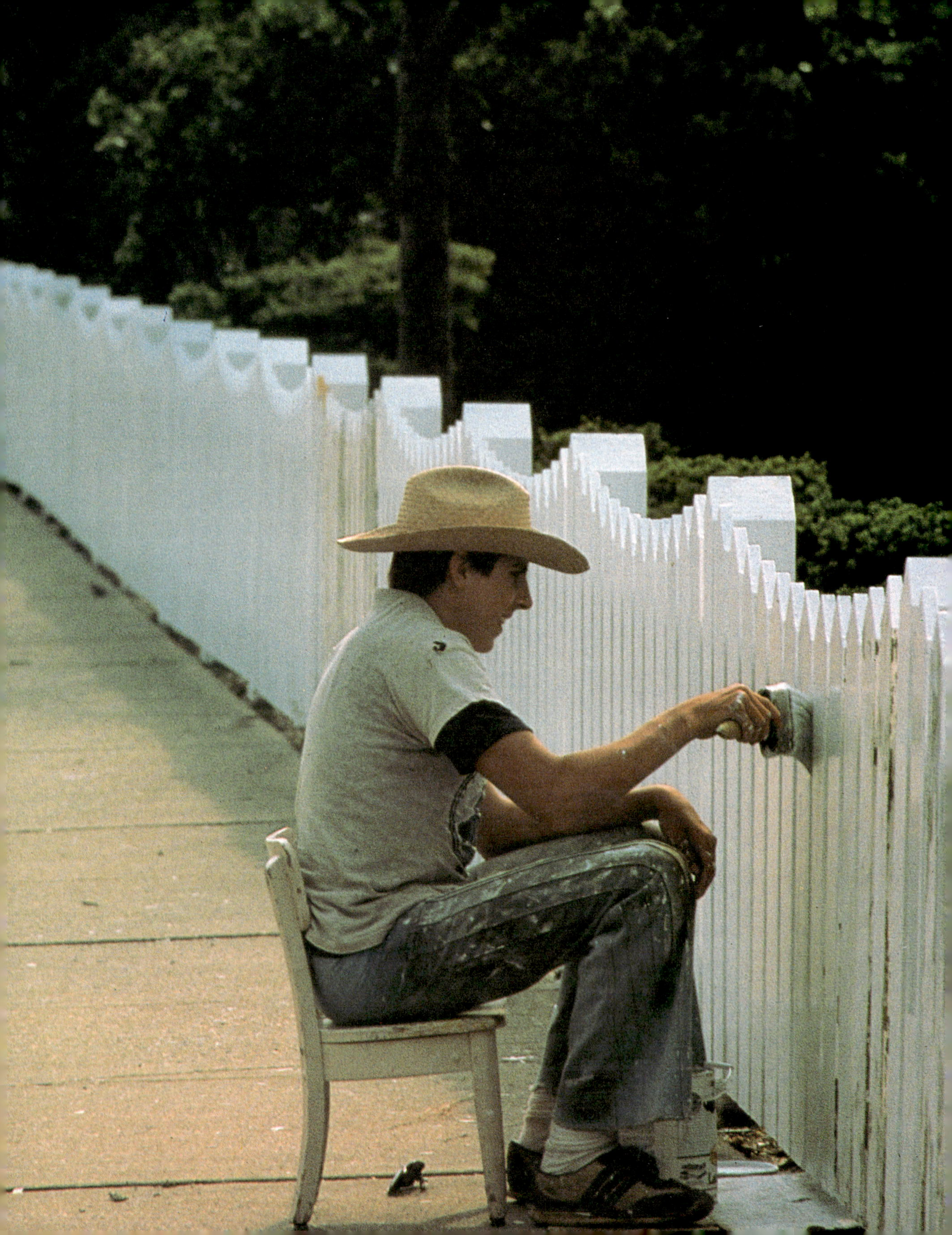

PART FOUR
You and Your Resources

Part Four presents the consumer skills you will need in order to use your resources effectively and wisely. You will find out how planning can help you achieve your goals, and you will discover alternatives to buying goods and services. You will learn where to go for consumer information and how to judge its value. You will find out how to analyze the appeals and techniques used in advertising. You will also explore comparison-shopping techniques that will help you decide when, where, and what to buy. Finally, you will examine the advantages and disadvantages of buying with cash, credit, or savings.

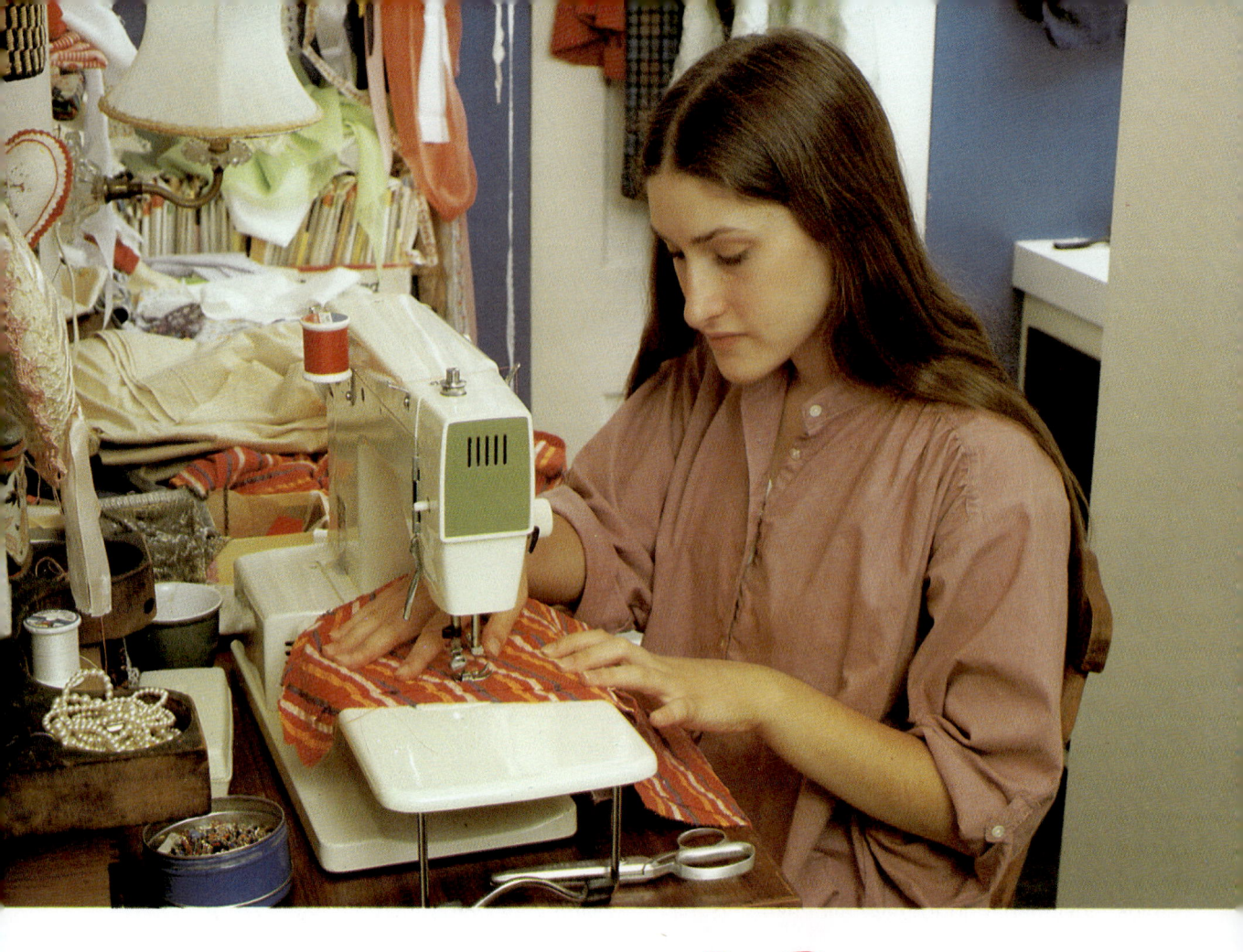

Chapter **12**

Planning to Use Your Resources

OBJECTIVES

This chapter will enable you to:
- explain the steps to take in order to be a satisfied consumer.
- list the alternatives to buying goods and services.
- give examples of how planning can help you use your resources to achieve your goals.
- develop a strategy for budgeting your time.
- give reasons for developing consumer skills.
- outline techniques for maintaining or increasing your energy.
- discuss the effects that inflation and deflation have on budgets.

Rachael

I think I just managed to have my cake and eat it too. Careful planning really works. I needed some new clothes, so I took a job on Saturdays from 9 to 5 and three nights a week.

In a few weeks, I discovered that working plus going to school took a lot out of me. Often, I would cancel my Saturday night plans with my friends because I was just too tired to do anything but sleep.

Then one day, I started to tell my friend Karen exactly what I was planning to buy at the Trend Shop with the money I was saving. She asked me if I had looked anywhere else, and I told her I didn't want to spend the extra time needed to shop around.

Then, Karen told me I could get the same clothes a lot cheaper at an outlet store that she knew about on the other side of town. That's where she had been buying her own clothes, and she always looked great; so I figured she knew what she was talking about. If the outlet was as low-priced as Karen said, I already had enough money for a few outfits.

Well, I did get some outfits, for a lot less money than I had originally planned to spend. As I was thinking about what I was going to buy next, I realized that there was no point buying new clothes if I was going to be too tired to go anywhere to wear them. So I cut back on my buying plans—and on my hours at my job. That way, I gained some time and energy for other things.

Now, I have a few new outfits—plus the time to go places to wear them. I've learned that checking prices in different stores can save you time and money in the end.

THE CONSUMER PROCESS

Like Rachael, you often act as a consumer when you make decisions. You buy things to satisfy your wants. You also wish to get the most out of your **personal resources**, which are *your time, energy, and skills, as well as your money*. Getting the most out of your resources requires planning, as Rachael started to realize. Once she did a little comparison shopping and decided to juggle her time, energy, and money in a particular way, she began to use the consumer process.

The **consumer process** is *a step-by-step method for making decisions about how to use your resources*. Using these seven steps can help you become a satisfied consumer:

Step 1: Make a Plan. Determine your wants. Become aware of your resources and decide which ones to match to which wants. Rachael, for example, decided to use some of her free time to earn money for new clothes. The rest of her free time she decided to use for going out with her friends.

Step 2: Learn the Facts. Gather information about those products that might satisfy your wants. There are a number of consumer magazines that rate a large array of products and services. You can use these magazines to help you select a new toothpaste or a new radio. Friends and relatives can also be sources of information.

Step 3: Shop and Compare. Do some comparison shopping to decide what to buy and where to buy it. Prices can vary widely from store to store, so do return and exchange policies. It is a good idea to check them out before you buy anything. You can visit stores to comparison-shop. You can also use newspaper ads and catalogs, as well as requesting information over the phone.

Step 4: Decide How to Pay. Will you use cash, credit, or savings to make your purchase? The method of payment you select can make a difference in the final cost of your purchase. (Chapter 15 will tell you more about these alternatives.)

Step 5: Decide When to Buy. Is it best to buy what you want now or later? If you know there is a sale coming up, for example, it might make sense to postpone your purchase for a while.

Comparison shopping can help you get the most for your money.

Step 6: Make Your Purchase.

Step 7: Evaluate your Purchase. Does it live up to your expectations? If it does not, what can you do to improve your consumer skills?

The seven steps of this process are closely related. Let us say you decide to buy a new stereo that costs $600. That decision can determine how you will pay for the stereo, because it is quite likely you will not have $600 in cash. You will then have to decide if it is wise to buy on credit or if you should wait until you have saved $600.

Deciding to wait for a better time can also affect the outcome of the consumer process. While you are waiting, another want may become more important to you. You may decide not to buy the original item at all.

The consumer process is closely related to the decision-making process. When you make a plan (Step 1), for example, you are defining a problem. When you make a purchase (Step 6), you are putting your decision into action.

You can get the most out of your resources by managing all of them carefully. One important thing to remember is that there are alternatives to buying goods and services: You can use other resources besides money to get what you want.

Alternatives

Most people have the same initial thought when they want or need something. They try to think of a way to buy it. Buying is not always the best way to achieve a goal. In actuality, there are six alternatives to buying. **Alternatives** are *choices between two or more things.* A number of these alternatives were in existence long before people started to use money:

1. Substituting. You may have your eye on a new moped to get you to school. You could, instead, take a bus, walk, or use your brother's old bicycle.

2. Doing it yourself. Obviously, it would be pretty hard to build yourself a moped. If you needed new bookshelves, however, you might be able to build them for much less than it would cost to buy them.

3. Bartering. The barter system has been in use for centuries. When you **barter**, you simply *trade goods or services with someone else.* You might, for instance, give your neighbor's dog a bath in exchange for some books on photography your neighbor no longer wants.

4. Making it last. Most things wear out sooner or later. Items that are properly cared for and maintained will last a lot longer than those that are not. Cleaning and oiling your sewing machine will keep it in working order for years, allowing you to use your money for something else.

5. Renting. Many people have discovered the benefits of renting certain items that they will need only once or for just a short time. When you **rent** an item, you *pay a fee for using it temporarily.* You do not need to buy a canoe if you want to go on a two-week camping trip. You can rent a canoe, along with a tent and other gear, from a camping goods or rental service store. Before renting anything, you should comparison-shop to make sure you get the lowest price and to make sure it is cheaper to rent the item than to buy it.

6. Doing without. Sometimes, deciding not to buy something is the wisest alternative. Rachael made that choice when she decided not to buy all the outfits she had originally planned to buy. The cost in time and energy was just too great.

THE BENEFITS OF PLANNING

When you make a plan, you use time and energy, but you can earn big dividends on this investment. The following benefits make planning worthwhile:

It may make sense to rent an item you will use only for a brief while.

- A plan offers you ways to reach your goal. Wishing you could go on the class trip to the mountains will not get you there. Planning may.
- A plan helps you make the most out of what you have. Otherwise, you may waste your resources. If you earn $10 an hour giving guitar lessons and you need to paint your room, it does not make sense to cancel some lessons to do the painting yourself. You would be better off hiring your sister for $5 an hour to do the job for you.
- A plan helps you stay within your limits. You are less likely to get in over your head if you know exactly what your resources are. If you know that you have 15 hours a week to spare, you will not take on a part-time job for 20 hours a week.
- A plan helps you take care of upcoming needs. Making a plan involves looking at your future wants. That gives you a better chance to use your resources in ways that will enable you to satisfy tomorrow's wants as well as today's.
- A plan helps you decide which needs to satisfy first. When you rank your wants, you can develop your priorities; lesser wants will be satisfied after more important ones.
- A plan helps chart your progress. With a plan, you know how close you are to reaching a goal.
- A plan helps you avoid impulse purchases. **Impulse purchases** are *unplanned purchases made on the spur of the moment.* Impulse purchases can keep you from reaching your goal. A plan prompts you to think before you act.
- A plan simplifies making choices. When you know the cost of various alternatives, you will have an easier time deciding what to give up.

YOUR TIME

You need to start somewhere when you make a plan to manage your resources. It is best to start with a resource you are always spending—time.

Setting Goals

Time is a valuable resource that can never be regained. You can use time in many ways, some more productive than others. Everyone needs to "waste" time now and again. In general, though, it is more satisfying to manage your time in ways that will help you better use your other resources. Doing that takes planning.

The first step is to identify your goals—to decide what you want to achieve. Then, you need to break down your goals into short-, medium-, and long-range goals. **Long-range goals** are *goals that may take three years or longer to achieve*. Graduating from college is one example of such a goal. **Medium-range goals** are *goals that take six months to three years to achieve*. Saving enough money to buy a personal computer would be a medium-range goal. **Short-range goals** are *goals you can reach in one day to six months*. Baking a cake for your sister's birthday tomorrow and finishing a report for Friday are both short-term goals.

In most cases, you plan how to spend your time according to your short-range goals. The choices you make on a short-range basis, however, can affect your medium- and long-range plans. If Rachael, for example, spends a lot of time at her part-time job, she may spend less time studying. That could hurt her grades. Lower grades could, in turn, affect her chances of going to college or getting a job that she wants.

Looking at things on a long-range basis can also help you make certain choices about short-range goals. Tim, for example, could not decide whether to join the track team or the wrestling team at school. He enjoyed both activities equally, but he did not have time for both sports. Eventually, Tim based his choice on thoughts of the future. He chose track because he knew running, unlike wrestling, was something he could do to keep fit for many years. For Tim, track offers the possibility of more long-range rewards than wrestling does.

Budgeting Your Time

It is best to start small when you begin to budget your time. First, you need to write down everything you want to do in a short period of time—a week would be a good unit of time to use. Write down *everything* you want to do during that week. Do not leave anything out because you think you are trying to accomplish too much. Also, write down everything you have to do, such as schoolwork, chores, and club meetings and activities.

The next step is to figure out how much time it will take to accomplish each goal. Be careful here. Do not make unrealistic estimates. Now, determine your available time by subtracting the number of hours you spend sleeping, eating, and going to school. Subtract that amount of time from the number of hours in the week. You now know how much free time you have at your disposal.

Next, you need to rank your goals according to their relative importance. This step can involve some conflict, because you will not be able to do everything. You may find yourself selecting short-range goals that fit in with your long-range goals.

You also need to consider time limits; a birthday present has to be purchased before the person's birthday. The leaves need to be raked during daylight hours so you can see what you are doing.

Tips for Using Time Well

Here are some more guidelines to help you plan your sequence of activities:

- Alternate your activities. A change of pace will keep you fresh. Alternate physical work with mental work whenever possible. You might, for example, study for a math test for a few hours, then refresh yourself by playing basketball.
- Do not rush. Trying to save a few minutes now can cost time later if you have to correct mistakes. Take the time, for example, to read directions carefully before you assemble anything. Working at a comfortable pace will also make you feel more relaxed.

- Do not put things off. Letting things go until a later time can cause a variety of problems, which may prevent you from achieving a number of goals.
- Use time efficiently. Grouping activities together, for example, can save you time. Stop off at the dry cleaner's on the way to the supermarket instead of making two separate trips.
- Save the best until last. Do the things you do not like to do first. Then, you will not have the feeling that they are hanging over your head. You will also be more likely to get them done.
- Think ahead. If tomorrow is the only time you have to mow the lawn, check today to make sure you have enough gas for the mower. While you are in the clothes you wear for yard work, you could schedule another messy job, such as washing the car.
- Be good to yourself. Everyone needs time for fun. Be careful not to plan so many activities that you feel overworked. That can take the pleasure out of everything.

Make sure you include everything you have to do in your time budget—as well as everything you want to do.

YOUR SKILLS

Skills are another valuable resource. A **skill** is *the ability to do something well*. One benefit of your skills is that you can use them to promote your other resources. If you are skilled at fixing your car, for example, you save the money you would pay someone else to repair it. You might also earn extra money by fixing other people's cars. Skills also save time and energy. Someone who is skilled at typing can finish a term paper faster and more efficiently than someone who types poorly.

Improving Your Skills

Skills are one resource that can increase as time goes on. You can improve existing skills and develop new ones in a number of ways. You can go to school; there are many types of schools offering courses in a great variety of skills. In a school, you can learn skills ranging from karate to cooking.

You can also learn skills from those around you. Your mother might share her knowledge of baking with you, and you may learn how to refinish furniture from a neighbor. There are also a number of skills you can teach yourself by reading how-to books or articles or by taking how-to lessons on a home computer. The list of how-to topics is practically endless, including auto repair, gardening, sewing, dancing, and weight lifting.

"Practice makes perfect" is an old saying that holds true with skills. The more you do them, the better you get. It is important, therefore, to budget time for practicing skills. It is usually best to schedule a number of short practice sessions on a regular basis than one long session occasionally.

Your practice time may yield a number of long-term benefits. You may be able to earn money by selling your skill, or you may be able to save money by doing something yourself that you would otherwise have to pay someone else to do. In addition, you will have the pleasure that comes from doing something well.

Chapter 12 Planning to Use Your Resources

YOUR ENERGY

In order to achieve your goals, you need energy. You need energy, in fact, to do anything at all. **Energy** is *the body's capacity to do work.* Work includes every one of your daily activities, ranging from combing your hair to running for the bus.

In recent years, scientists have discovered that it is possible to increase your store of energy by the way you take care of yourself. Because food supplies the raw materials that the body needs to produce energy, it is vital that you eat the right kinds of food. A good diet is especially important during your teenage years because your body is still growing. Growth means that your body is creating new cells. To do this, the body needs certain foods to use as building blocks for the new cells. It may take a little extra time to plan well-balanced meals, but the energy rewards make the effort worthwhile. You can find information on nutrition in many different books and magazines. You may also be able to take a nutrition class at school.

You probably already know how important sleep is to your energy level. If you miss a few hours of sleep one night, you usually do not feel like doing very much the next day. That is because your mind and body renew themselves during sleep. A well-rested body can resist infection better than one that becomes rundown from lack of sleep. A well-rested mind is better able to cope with the stresses of daily life. Including enough time for a good night's sleep in your day-to-day planning will enable you to accomplish your goals.

Regular exercise is a proven method for increasing your energy. Spending energy through exercise makes your heart, lungs, and muscles work more efficiently. That means you will be far less tired after vacuuming the house or chopping firewood than you would otherwise be. Exercise can also help you to maintain a desirable weight. Exercise, then, is another must in your weekly time budget. When you make your exercise plan, remember that experts recommend at least three 30-minute exercise sessions per week.

YOUR MONEY

Your money is another valuable resource. And it is very important to have a budget for your money. A **budget** is *a plan for spending, saving, and investing your income.* A budget can help you reach your short-term and long-term goals by giving you control over your money.

There are several steps in the budget process. The most important aspects of this process are determining your spending pattern, preparing the budget, balancing the budget, and making the budget work.

Determining Your Spending Pattern

You cannot make a budget until you know how much you are spending—and on what. In other words, you need to discover your spending pattern. To do this, keep a written account for a few weeks of the ways in which you spend

Regular exercise increases your energy, making you better able to complete the other activities on your time budget.

your money. A week is a good budget period because it usually coincides with a pay period. Some people prefer a two-week budget period because they are paid every other week.

If you ask people without a budget how they spend their money, you will find that often they do not know where a lot of their money goes. Ben, for example, did not know why he could never reach his goals. For over a year, he has wanted to buy a new 35-mm camera. He has not been able to save enough money, even though he supplements his weekly allowance with money he earns at a part-time job as a cafeteria helper. He also baby-sits for various neighbors.

In addition to his short-range goal of buying a camera, Ben has a long-range goal. He has just received his driver's license, and he wants to buy a car after he finishes school. To do that, he has to save a certain amount of money each week to have enough when he graduates.

Now, Ben has decided to take charge of his spending, and he has discovered that a large part of his income is in the question-mark category (Figure 12.1). If he can save some of that money, he will be able to meet his goals of buying a camera and later on a car.

A budget will also give Ben a chance to set and reach other goals as well. Once he has his camera, for instance, he will have to set another goal—buying and processing film for the camera. A budget will also give Ben a better idea of whether his goals are realistic to begin with. He may find that he cannot save enough for a car without supplementing his income somehow.

Figure 12.1 Ben's Spending Pattern Before Making a Budget

	Week 1	Week 2
Weekly Income	$60.00	$64.75
Bus Fare	8.00	8.00
School Lunches	6.25	6.25
School Supplies	8.00	2.50
Clothes	0	14.00
Savings for Camera	5.00	0
Movies	7.00	11.00
Books and Magazines	6.00	3.00
Snacks	5.25	4.00
???	14.50	16.00
Total Expenses	$60.00	$64.75

Preparing the Budget

When you prepare a budget, you have to be able to predict the future to a certain extent. You have to make a fairly accurate estimate of your income for the budget period.

Estimating Income. Ben, for example, knows how much his allowance and his paycheck will be each week. That is his fixed income. A **fixed income** is *usually the same from week to week and month to month.* His income from baby-sitting is less predictable. Some weeks he has more jobs than others. Baby-sitting, then, provides Ben with a variable income. A **variable income** *changes from week to week and month to month.* Still, Ben can base his estimate on past experience. He knows, for example, that he earns more during school vacations and holidays than at other times.

Ben also knows that he is likely to receive cash as gifts on his birthday and at holiday time. He cannot really count that money as part of his budget, because it is too hard to predict the amount. Cash from gifts should be counted only after it has been received.

Estimating Expenses. Once Ben estimates his income, he needs to estimate his expenses. First, he must look at his fixed expenses. **Fixed expenses** are *those that stay the same and that must be met, often by a certain time.* For Ben, school lunches are a fixed expense. They cost the same each day, and he has to pay for them when he purchases them in the cafeteria.

Ben's other fixed expense is bus fare to and from school and work. Eventually, his fixed expenses will include car insurance and gasoline. For the time being, Ben's fixed expenses are relatively few.

The second category of expenses is made up of variable expenses. **Variable expenses** are *those that change from week to week and month to month.* They are also less likely than fixed expenses to be necessities. Ben's variable expenses include books, magazines, and movies. Because they are not necessities, they are under Ben's control. He can adjust the amount he spends on them to fit his budget plans.

Another variable expense, clothing, falls somewhere in between necessity and luxury. It is necessary for Ben to spend a certain amount on clothing. He is responsible for buying his own uniforms and shoes for work. If he buys a new sweater when he already has five others, that could be considered a luxury.

Whether something is a luxury or a necessity depends in part upon a person's life-style. For Ben, a camera is a luxury. He does not need one to earn a living. A professional photographer, in contrast, needs a number of cameras in order to function well on the job. It is important to your budget for you to decide which of your expenses are luxuries and which are necessities.

Starting Your Budget. As you might imagine, you begin your budget by subtracting fixed expenses from your expected income. It is important to remember fixed expenses that occur infrequently, too. Club membership dues, for example, usually must be paid once or twice

Packing a lunch may help you cut down on expenses.

a year. That means you need to figure out how much you need to put aside each week to meet the payments.

The next step is to decide how much to save. **Savings** are *dollars put aside for use in the future.* Savings are a must for reaching goals, whether short-range or long-range. Even if you do not have a particular goal in mind, saving money is a good idea. Savings are a reserve fund that can make it possible for you to meet unexpected expenses. If your typewriter breaks and you need to have it repaired, your savings can enable you to meet the expense. You can also put savings toward other long-range goals as they occur. No matter how small the amount you put aside each week, you should get in the habit of making saving part of your budget plan.

Ben wants to buy a camera before summer vacation. That goal can help him decide how much he needs to save each month. That amount, in turn, can help Ben figure out what adjustments he needs to make in his expenses.

Finally, you need to deduct your variable expenses. This is the step that will tell you if your budget will work. If the total of your estimated expenses and savings does not exceed your income, you have drawn up a realistic budget. For Ben, his known variable expenses are snacks, movies, books, and magazines. He also has a question-mark column. Ben knows he has to reduce that amount, which goes mainly for small impulse purchases. He can probably reduce some of his other variable expenses, too. In Figure 12.2, you can see the trial budget Ben came up with and how it worked.

Figure 12.2 Ben's Trial Budgets and His Final Budget

Trial Budgets Week 1	Trial Budgets Week 2		Final Budget (per week)
$64.00	$64.00	INCOME	$64.00
		FIXED EXPENSES	
8.00	8.00	Bus Fare	8.00
6.25	6.25	School Lunches	6.25
		VARIABLE EXPENSES	
5.00	6.00	School Supplies	6.00
8.00	10.00	Clothes	8.75
4.00	5.00	Snacks	5.00
0	5.00	Movies	5.00
3.00	6.00	Books and Magazines	6.00
2.00	4.75	Other	4.00
20.00	12.00	SAVINGS	15.00
$56.25	$63.00	TOTAL EXPENSES + SAVINGS	$64.00

Chapter 12 Planning to Use Your Resources

Balancing Your Budget

If your planned expenses and savings turn out to be larger than your income, there are a number of guidelines that can help you bring your budget in line. These guidelines will also protect your goals:

- Go over your math. You may have made an error that threw off your budget.
- Look at your estimates carefully. Are they reasonable? Do they really reflect your spending patterns?
- Look for ways to save money through substitution. Can you ride your bike to school instead of taking the bus? Can you pack a lunch instead of buying it?
- Do not make budget cuts based only on the size of the expense. Some important budget items are costly. That does not mean they should be reduced. Instead, reduce the amount you spend on less important items. That is what Ben did when he cut variable expenses such as movies.

A trial budget is just that—a trial. Often, a trial budget had to be fine-tuned to be satisfactory. In the first week of his trial budget, Ben got carried away with reducing his variable expenses. He left almost nothing for entertainment. His drastic reductions turned out to be unrealistic. His second week's budget proved more satisfactory. Ben achieved a balance that is allowing him to work toward all his goals without sacrificing any.

Making Your Budget Work

Once you make a budget, you need to put it to work, which means a little effort on your part. You may decide to follow Ben's example. He started to carry a small notebook with him. In the front of the book, he wrote down his budget, which he looked at before spending any money. He also used the notebook to record the amounts he spent.

Some people like to keep their records differently. They keep a notebook at home and bring their budget up to date at night. You need to have a good memory to use that technique. Once you get used to your budget, it becomes easier to make mental notes of how you spend your money each day.

Adjusting Your Budget. Even a final budget will need some adjustment now and again. If Ben lost his sunglasses, for example, he would have an emergency expense. That means he would have to adjust his budget so he could buy a new pair.

Other adjustments may be more permanent. When Ben looks at his spending patterns over the next few months, he may find that he had overestimated some expenses. Maybe he will spend less on school supplies than he had expected. That would free up some money to put toward other expenses or toward savings.

It is also possible that Ben's income will change. Maybe one of the families he often baby-sits for will move away. That would eliminate one source of income, and Ben would have to rework his budget. On the other hand, he might get a raise at his part-time job. Then, his income would go up. Again, he would have to redo his budget.

Goals change, too, over time. After Ben buys his camera, he may decide he wants to take a photography class at the Y. That means he would have to come up with the money to pay for the course by a certain date. You, too, will find the different elements in your budget changing as time goes on.

The Family Budget

You are involved in still another budget beside your personal budget: your family's budget. A family budget is more complex than a personal budget. However, it involves the same procedures. Family members have to determine their spending patterns, prepare the

A family budget is more complicated than a personal budget because the needs and wants of all family members must be taken into account.

budget, balance it, and make it work. The various expenses in a family budget are far more extensive than in a personal budget. After all, the needs and wants of all family members have to be taken into account. In a family budget, for instance, there are expenses such as rent or mortgage, utilities, insurance, home repairs, medical and dental care, food, transportation, and vacations. There may also be birthday parties and allowances. The salaries of several family members may be combined to make up the income and meet the expenses.

To make a family budget work successfully, family members must cooperate. Through his personal budget, Ben is getting practice that will help him handle a more complicated budget later on. He can also gain a greater appreciation of the budgeting skills his parents have developed—and of his own part in the family budget.

YOUR BUDGET AND THE ECONOMY

As you read before, budgets involve predicting the future. You estimate future income and expenses. Your estimates of tomorrow's expenses, though, are based upon today's prices, and prices can change.

Inflation

During the past 20 years or so, there has been a marked upward trend in the prices of almost all goods and services. *A general increase in the level of prices* is called **inflation**. Inflation lowers **buying power**, or *the amount of goods and services a dollar can purchase*. Since 1967, prices have more than tripled in many cases. That means it now takes $3.75 to buy what $1 would purchase in 1967. That is a big drop in buying power. Workers often receive raises during inflation, but inflation may increase at a greater rate than wages. Inflation can cause problems in any budget, from the government's down to the individual's.

No one knows for sure why inflation occurs. Experts suggest at least two causes. The first is rising costs. During the 1970s, for example, the price of oil skyrocketed. That meant it cost more to produce most goods and services, many of which rely on oil. Producers passed their increases on to consumers in the form of higher prices. Prices can also be pushed up when workers demand higher salaries.

The second possible cause of rising prices is greater consumer demand. In prosperous times, people want to buy more goods and services. People must then compete for the goods and services available. This creates a sellers' market, and prices go up.

Certain expectations also contribute to inflation. If people expect prices to rise, they will often try to buy what they want before prices go up. They are less likely to save money because the value of their dollars will go down. They are also more likely to buy on credit in order to obtain the products and services they want before prices rise.

The government has used a number of measures to try to stop inflation. The aim of these measures is to make people less eager to buy. Common anti-inflation tactics include higher taxes and a tighter money supply. When people must pay out more in taxes and find it harder to borrow money, they cut back on their spending.

210

INDEX, 1982-84 = 100 (RATIO SCALE)

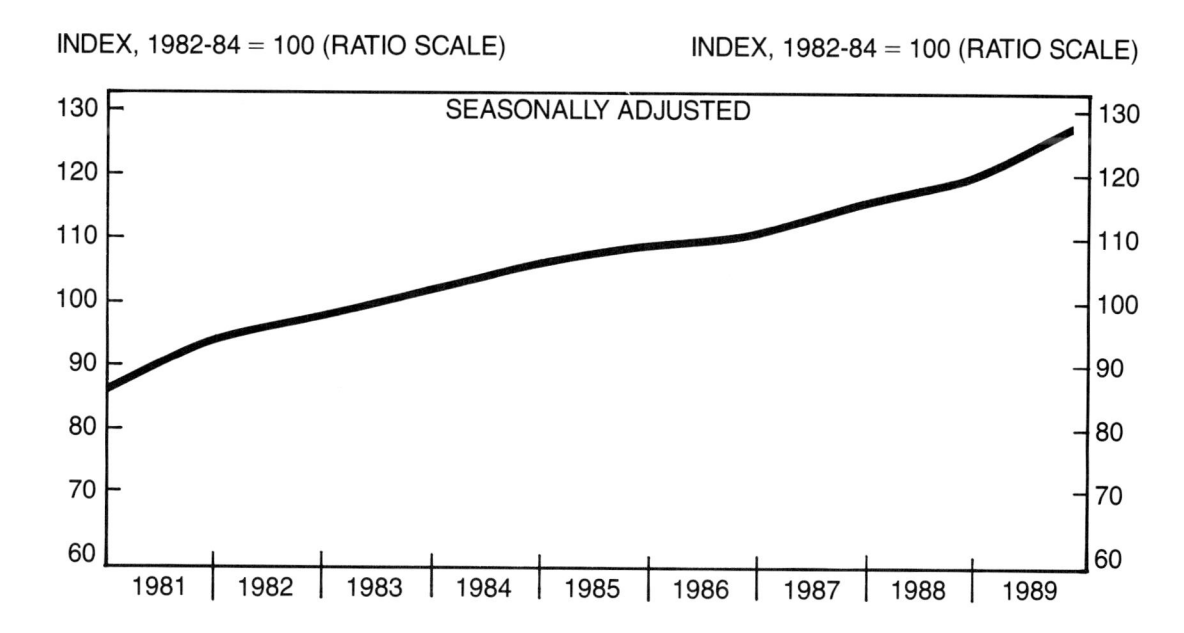

[Chart: Seasonally adjusted consumer price index rising from about 86 in 1981 to about 126 in 1989. Source: U.S. Department of Labor]

Figure 12.3 The Rise in Consumer Prices Since 1981

What You Can Do. There are a number of measures you can use to protect your personal buying power. Do not, for example, buy anything until you have compared prices at different stores. Do your buying from discount sources whenever possible. Check the newspapers for coupons that offer reduced prices on goods you need.

Timing can help your budget, too. Wait for sales, which often occur at predictable times. Many stores, for examples, have big reductions during holidays such as Washington's Birthday. And seasonal items such as winter gloves are usually reduced near the end of the season.

Quantity is another factor to consider. If there is a sale on your favorite shampoo, it is a good idea to stock up. However, if lettuce is on sale at three heads for $1, will you be able to use all three heads before they spoil?

Whatever you buy, make sure you match the quality to your needs. It would be wasteful to buy sirloin steak to chop up and put into a stew. A top-of-the-line racing bike would be much more than you need for occasional Sunday bike rides. You may also find what you are looking for secondhand at yard sales or flea markets. Buying used items can be a good way to save money—if the items are in good condition or if you are good at fixing things.

There are other methods for stretching your dollars. Avoid unnecessary convenience items. It is a lot cheaper to buy a large bag of pretzels and wrap some for your lunch each day than to buy single-serving packs. You should also avoid waste. That means turning off lights when you leave a room. It also means repairing things instead of throwing them out. If you buy on credit, plan your purchases so you can pay the entire bill before you have to pay interest. Finally, avoid impulse purchases. Plan what you will buy, and buy only what you have planned.

Deflation

Sometimes, the economy goes through a period of deflation. **Deflation** is *the reverse of inflation: Prices go down.* Reduced prices means greater buying power. Consumers may buy more if they think prices will go up again. If they think deflation will continue, consumers will save their money, hoping to buy when prices drop even further.

Deflation can cause a slowdown in the growth of the economy. At first, businesses may cut back on production because of reduced prices. Fewer workers are needed, and layoffs occur. Production costs may drop, too. That drop may then encourage businesses to produce more, boosting economic growth. Because deflation can cause unemployment, the government may step in to try to increase production. Periods of deflation have been far less common than periods of inflation.

MAIN POINTS

- We can manage our personal resources through the consumer process. The seven steps in the process are: making a plan, learning the facts, shopping and comparing, deciding how to pay, deciding when to buy, making the purchase, and evaluating the purchase.
- There are alternatives to buying goods and services. They are substituting, making or doing things yourself, bartering, making things last, renting, and doing without.
- Planning enables you to reach your goal and use your resources wisely. A plan also helps you stay within your limits and take care of upcoming needs. You can decide which needs to satisfy first and chart your progress. You can also avoid impulse purchases and make choices more easily.
- Budgeting your time is an important step in managing your resources. Most time budgets are made according to short-term goals.
- Your skills can be used to promote your other resources. Skills can be acquired by going to school, by learning from others, and by reading how-to books and articles. Skills can increase over time, through practice.
- Energy enables you to reach your goals. You can maintain or increase your energy level through good nutrition, sufficient sleep, and regular exercise.
- A budget can give you control over your money and help you reach your goals. To make a budget, you need to estimate your income and keep track of your spending. Budget items include fixed and variable expenses. Your budget should enable you to put money aside as savings. Budgets need adjusting when income, expenses, or goals change.
- The economy affects your budget. In times of inflation, prices rise. In times of deflation, they fall. To protect your budget during inflation, you can look for sales, comparison-shop, and match the quality and quantity of your purchases to your needs.

Chapter 12 Planning to Use Your Resources

Terms to Know

Use the following terms to fill in the blanks of the sentences below.

alternatives
barter
budget
buying power
consumer process
deflation
energy
fixed expenses
fixed income
impulse purchases
inflation
long-range goals
medium-range goals
personal resources
rent
savings
short-range goals
skill
variable expenses
variable income

1. When prices go down, we are in a period of _____.
2. Your body's ability to do work is called _____.
3. The money you put aside for future use is your _____.
4. A plan for saving and spending your income is a(n) _____.
5. When you trade a book for a record with a friend, you are using the _____ system.
6. Income that changes from week to week is _____.
7. Goals that you plan to reach within a week are _____.
8. The amount of goods and services a dollar will purchase is known as _____.
9. Your money, time, energy, and skills are your _____.
10. Goals to reach five years in the future are _____.
11. A seven-step method for making decisions about how to use your resources is called the _____.
12. Choices between two or more things are known as _____.
13. Income that stays the same over a period of time is called _____.
14. When you pay a fee to use something temporarily, you _____ it.
15. When prices go up, we are in a period of _____.
16. Expenses that change frequently are _____.
17. Purchases made on the spur of the moment are _____.
18. Expenses that stay the same over a period of time are called _____.
19. The ability to type quickly and accurately is a valuable _____.
20. Goals that you plan to reach in a year are _____.

Chapter Review

1. What is the first step of the consumer process? The last step?
2. List the six alternatives to buying a product or service.
3. What is the first resource to budget when you start managing your personal resources? What must you identify before you budget this resource?
4. Describe three ways to help develop or improve your skills. What could be the benefits of developing your skills?
5. What are the benefits of exercise?
6. Describe the four most important steps of the budget process.
7. Which kind of expense is usually under the budgeter's control? Why?
8. Why is it important to include savings in your budget?
9. List four ways to balance a budget.
10. Explain two of the causes of inflation. What do consumers tend to do in times of inflation?

Activities

1. Visit a rental service store, and make a list of 25 items for rent. Discuss your findings with the class. Are there any items that could have saved you money if you had been able to rent them in the past?
2. List your short-range goals in order of priority. Explain why they are in the order in which you have placed them. Do the same for your medium- and long-range goals.
3. Obtain brochures describing local adult education courses, which are usually offered by public school systems. Most such courses welcome high school students. Which of the enrichment courses would help you advance your skills? Post the brochures in your classroom.
4. Make a pie graph that shows how you spend your time during the week. Make another pie graph to show how you spend your time on weekends. What changes do you think you could make in the way you use your time? Make a third pie graph to illustrate your plan.
5. Keep a record of the ways in which you spend your money during a one-week period. At the end of that period, analyze your expenses and make a budget similar to Ben's. Try using that budget for a week. Evaluate your budget at the end of the week.
6. Interview one of your parents about your family's budget. Make a list of all the fixed-expense items, such as rent and heat, that your family must meet each month. Also make a list of the variable-expense items. (Do not include the amounts of money budgeted for each category.)

Chapter **13**

Becoming an Informed Consumer

OBJECTIVES

This chapter will enable you to:

- locate sources of consumer information.
- evaluate information and its source.
- identify the appeals and techniques of advertising.
- compare the costs and benefits of advertising.

Kim

I've been thinking about buying a new turntable to go with my new speakers. About a week ago, I saw an ad that this department store had a really great deal—you could save $50 on a turntable.

When I told my brother, he said, "Slow down. It would be a mistake to buy that turntable." That stopped me in my tracks because I respect his opinion. My brother works for a radio station and seems to know what he's talking about. He told me to investigate different turntables before I made a decision.

"Why don't you just tell me what kind to buy?" I asked him. He said I couldn't afford the one he would recommend, and he was right. Turntables can cost a lot. He showed me some of his stereo magazines, though, and told me to look at some of the articles and the ads. I found some really good prices, but there were so many kinds of turntables that I got confused.

Then, my dad found out that I was looking for a turntable. He said he was looking for a lawn mower and maybe we could help each other.

I said, "Sure," but I secretly wondered what he was talking about. If there's one thing I know about turntables, it's that they aren't anything like lawn mowers.

My dad took me to the library and showed me a couple of magazines that test and rate consumer products. One issue had a whole list of turntables. It gave them grades for all kinds of things and put the grades on a chart. He found another issue that did the same thing with lawn mowers.

Then, we talked about what we wanted. I told him I wanted a turntable that would stack a bunch of records and then play just some of the songs on each record. He said he wanted a lawn mower you could start by pushing a button. He also wanted one that was pretty quiet. The one he has now makes a real racket.

We both found out a lot in those consumer magazines—even more than we had planned. The articles on lawn mowers reminded my father of ways to use power mowers safely. A couple of articles on stereo equipment made me realize that stacking records on a turntable could harm them. That made me change my mind about the features I wanted.

Now, we've learned enough to know just what we want. I'm waiting for a sale on the kind of turntable that seems to be best for me. In the meantime, I'm checking around for more information on stereo equipment.

THE VALUE OF INFORMATION

Kim has the right idea about making her purchase. She wants to use her resources wisely. In order to spend her money well, she is first using time and energy to find out more about turntables. She is gathering information about goods and services. She will then use her time and skill to evaluate the information. That is an important step in the consumer process. The more Kim knows about different turntables, the better she can evaluate her options.

What kind of decision could Kim make without information? She could have bought the turntable she first saw advertised. Once she used it, she may have discovered it was difficult to operate. She may also have discovered

Chapter 13 Becoming an Informed Consumer

that she did not need all the features the machine had. She would have paid extra for features she would never use. She may have paid extra money anyway. It is possible that the turntable would have cost less in a different store. It is also possible that Kim would have been completely satisfied with the turntable. Without information, she would be relying on luck.

Information is vital to the consumer process. You cannot make a good decision without it. While gathering information is a separate step in the consumer process, it overlaps with the other steps. Finding out the prices of items can help you plan a budget. Comparison shopping provides information about products, stores, and prices. Gathering information about cash, credit, and savings can help you decide the best way to pay.

Evaluating Information

Not all information is equal. Some kinds have more value than others. It is important, then, to evaluate the information you get. To judge information, you need to ask the following:

1. Is it reliable? In other words, can you depend on your source? A reliable source has a fund of knowledge about different options. If Kim's brother was familiar with just one kind of turntable, he would not have been a reliable source.
2. Is it objective? A source should not be partial to one option. The salesperson in a store might suggest that Kim buy a certain turntable. The salesperson might get a higher commission on that brand than on another one. If the salesperson would benefit from the recommendation, he or she is not objective.
3. Is it complete? To be useful, information needs to be accurate and detailed. It should compare different brands. It should show both strong and weak points. And it should cover a variety of concerns. A good source of information for Kim might include the repair records of different turntables.
4. Is it appropriate? The information should cover the areas appropriate to your needs. Finding out that one kind of turntable is used by some rock stars does not mean the same one would be good for Kim. She may want to use the turntable in a different way.

Influences or Information?

You also need to recognize the difference between influences and information. Information consists of facts. **Influences** are *forces that appeal to the emotions as well as the mind*. Both information and influences affect our choices. Kim may favor one turntable because a friend has one. She may also like the advertisements for that brand.

Influences and information can come in the same package. A manufacturer's pamphlet on a turntable will praise that turntable. The pamphlet can also contain useful facts about the turntable. Kim needs to be able to separate fact from advertising appeals. Consumers who are aware of various influences can avoid being affected too much by them.

Comparison shopping provides information about products, stores, and prices. Such information is vital to making good consumer decisions.

HOW INFLUENCES AFFECT WHAT YOU BUY

Most people are swayed by two kinds of influences. Some come from within. Others are external.

Internal Influences

Your values shape your wants. Values are beliefs about what is important in life. Someone who values music is more likely to spend more money on records than someone who does not. Someone who values sports will buy tickets to sports events. Knowing your values can help you make satisfying decisions.

The amount of money people earn also shapes their wants. When income goes up, people can satisfy more of their wants, but managing their money becomes a more complicated task.

Changes in living patterns can affect wants. Once you move away from home, for example, you may need to buy furniture and other household items. If you change your habits, your wants may change, too. You may decide to start running two miles a day. That could mean you want a new pair of running shoes.

The wish to impress people can also affect your wants. If you think others will admire a certain item, you may want to buy it. That can range from a certain car to a certain shirt to a certain pen.

Outside Influences

The state of the economy greatly influences people's wants. In times of prosperity, people are willing to spend their money. When the economy is not doing well, people want to save their money. They buy fewer consumer goods and services.

Culture is an important influence. Your family background affects you, too. Your family may have special favorite foods or habits. Your ethnic background is another influence. People from different ethnic groups may enjoy different kinds of food or clothes.

As fashion changes, so do people's tastes. Clothes, hairstyles, furniture styles, even car designs, are all affected by fashion. What looks right one season may look wrong the next.

Friends also influence your wants. Peer pressure can be very strong. **Peer pressure** *makes you want to act the same way as your friends do in order to be accepted by them.* To gain that acceptance, you may choose to buy the same clothes or do the same things your friends do.

Sales pressure is another kind of external influence. This is *the use of certain tactics by salespeople to convince consumers to buy.*

Our tastes change as fashion changes. What looks right one season may look wrong the next.

Chapter 13 Becoming an Informed Consumer

Salespeople can be a great help. They may also try to pressure you into buying something. Watch for these signs of sales pressure:

- "If you wait until tomorrow, it probably will be sold." Do not let a salesperson push you into buying something before you are ready.
- "Here's Helen to tell you more about it." A second salesperson may come over to increase the pressure on you to buy. You will not hurt a salesperson's feelings if you do not buy.
- "That woman over there has her eye on this stereo, too." The salesperson may hint that someone else is going to buy the item if you do not make up your mind fast enough. Remember that most stores have a generous supply of every item.
- "You have very good taste." Beware of salespeople who try to flatter you.
- "Everyone will envy you." A salesperson may try to appeal to your wish to impress others.

Do not let a salesperson put pressure on you. You can resist these tactics by knowing your own mind and by simply stating that you need time to think. If the pressure continues, shop elsewhere.

MAJOR SOURCES OF INFORMATION

There are four major sources of information. You can ask people you know. You can also learn about goods and services from businesses, consumer groups, and the government. Whatever the source, you need to evaluate the source as well as the information you receive from it.

Family and Friends

People often go to family and friends first for information. After all, they are readily available. For example, you may ask a neighbor how he likes his new tennis racket. You may ask a cousin what she thinks of the new hairstylist in the shopping center. Because they know you, family and friends have a good idea of what you like. They can tailor their responses to fit your individual needs and preferences. Your cousin, for example, might point out that the new hairstylist has a knack for working with curly hair.

If you ask around, you might be surprised at how often you can find a person who has recently bought the very item you are interested in purchasing. These informal connections are sometimes called networks. Any group of people you can talk to and get information from can be a network. All the students in your class at school are a network. All the members of a club or team form a network. By asking around, you can sometimes come up with a surprising amount of information about almost any subject.

Family and friends should not be your only sources. They may have limited knowledge, or they may buy according to deep-seated habits and prejudices. A friend may buy only one brand of shoes because that is what his family has always bought.

Salespeople can be very helpful. They may also try to pressure you into buying. You can resist sales pressure by knowing your own mind.

Businesses

Businesses want you to buy from them. They will usually provide you with a lot of helpful information. This information comes in various forms.

- Labels provide many useful facts. Food labels, for example, tell you a great deal about the product. They list the name, weight, ingredients, and nutrients. They also list the maker's name and address. Clothing labels tell you what the fabric is made of and how to care for it.
- **Warranties** are *promises that goods meet certain standards.* The maker or seller promises to repair or replace an item at no charge if it breaks. Usually, there is a time limit on warranties. Some products have warranties that last as long as you own the item. It is important for Kim to check warranties when she compares turntables. (Chapter 16 contains more information about warranties.)
- Advertisements let you know when new products come on the market. They tell you where to buy products and services and how much they cost. Ads tell you when there are sales. Ads may also tell you how to use a product. You need to be able to analyze ads, though. As you will see later in this chapter, you need to separate facts from influence.
- Salespeople can be a valuable source of information. Some have a great deal of knowledge about the goods they sell. This is especially true of salespeople who work in stores devoted to one type of product, such as bicycles or camping gear.
- Pamphlets put out by manufacturers and sellers to describe their products can be helpful. As with ads, though, you have to separate facts from emotional appeals.
- Use-and-care manuals that come with many products are more than helpful. They are necessary for proper use and maintenance of the products. Before Kim uses the turntable she decides to buy, she needs to read the use-and-care manual thoroughly. Otherwise, she may damage the machine.
- **Trade and professional associations** are *groups of people or businesses that join together to promote their common interests.* These associations can tell you a lot about specific types of products. The American Wood Council, for instance, publishes pamphlets that explain why you should buy products made of wood. Trade associations usually do not recommend actual brands, just the general product. Several associations have offices that provide product information. They may also list local sellers. You can find local offices in the *Encyclopedia of Associations.* This book is located in the reference section of most libraries.
- **Better Business Bureaus (BBBs)** are *groups set up by businesses to regulate themselves.* BBBs promote fair advertising and selling practices. They do not compare products or give out prices. You can check with a BBB to see if any complaints have been made against a business. There are BBBs in 41 states. The only states without them are Alaska, Maine, Montana, North Dakota, South Carolina, South Dakota, Vermont, West Virginia, and Wyoming.
- Underwriters' Laboratories (UL) is concerned with safe electrical products. UL tests products and awards a seal of approval to those that are safe. When Kim looks at turntables, she needs to check for the UL seal of approval.
- The mass media are major sources of information. Newspapers are filled with consumer information. They print columns to tell readers about good buys and ways to save money. There are often do-

Magazines offer information about the cost and qualities of many kinds of products and services.

it-yourself features. News items provide information about consumer laws and other topics of consumer concern. Radio and television programs and magazines provide similar information. Some magazines deal only with consumer topics. There are also magazines devoted to testing and rating consumer goods and services. Kim and her father used such magazines when they needed information on turntables and lawn mowers.

Consumer Organizations

Some of the magazines that Kim and her father looked at are published by consumer organizations. Some of these organizations test competing products and services. In just one issue of a consumer magazine, you might find articles that rate canned soups, insurance policies, shampoos, air conditioners, and movies. Some products are tested often. Cars, for example, are tested every year.

Consumers Union is the primary independent consumer testing organization in the United States today. The Underwriters Laboratories, an independent organization, establishes safety certification programs for manufactured products and develops nationally recognized safety standards. Some government agencies also test, but like the UL, products are limited to a specific area.

Many publications provide consumers with an abundance of information on products and services so the consumer can be well equipped to make an intelligent buying decision:

- *Consumers' Research.* This publication is published by Consumers' Research.
- *Consumer Reports.* This magazine is published by Consumers Union. The annual *Buying Guide* summarizes test results for the previous year.
- *Changing Times* and *Money*. These publications offer information about money

matters such as saving, investments, insurance, and financial planning.

When you use consumer publications for the purpose of comparing different products or services, remember to evaluate the information. Make sure it is appropriate to your needs. If is also possible for you to be interested in a brand or model not tested in a consumer organization or reviewed in a publication. You can still use the publication as a guide.

Figure 13.1 Units of the Federal Government That Provide Consumer Information
Specific offices or divisions to contact are in parentheses.

Cabinet Departments

Agriculture (Agricultural Marketing Service; Animal and Plant Health Inspection Service; Extension Service; Food and Nutrition Service; Food Safety and Quality Service; Office of Consumer Advisor)

Commerce (National Bureau of Standards; National Marine Fisheries Service; Office of Consumer Affairs)

Education (Office of Bilingual Education and Minority Language Affairs)

Energy (Energy Information Administration)

Health and Human Services (Food and Drug Administration; Public Health Service; Social Security Administration)

Housing and Urban Development (Fair Housing and Equal Opportunity Division; Federal Housing Administration)

Interior (Fish and Wildlife Service; National Park Service)

Justice (Citizen Complaint Center)

Labor (Occupational Safety and Health Administration; Women's Bureau)

Transportation (Federal Aviation Administration; National Highway Traffic Safety Administration; Office of Information)

Treasury (Internal Revenue Service; U.S. Savings Bond Division)

Non Cabinet Offices

Consumer Product Safety Commission (Office of Public Affairs)

Environmental Protection Agency (Office of Public Affairs)

Equal Employment Opportunity Commission (Office of Public Affairs)

Federal Communications Commission (Office of Consumer Assistance and Small Business Division)

Federal Deposit Insurance Corporation (Office of Consumer Affairs; Corporate Communications)

Federal Home Loan Bank Board (Division of Consumer Affairs and Civil Rights)

Federal Reserve System (Division of Consumer and Community Affairs)

Federal Trade Commission (Bureau of Consumer Protection)

General Service Administration (Government Printing Office; Consumer Information Center)

Interstate Commerce Commission (Office of Compliance and Consumer Assistance)

National Credit Union Administration (Office of Public and Congressional Affairs)

National Transportation Safety Board (Public Inquiries Section)

Nuclear Regulatory Commission (Consumer Affairs Officer; Office of Public Affairs)

Pension Benefit Guarantee Corporation (Office of Public Affairs)

Securities and Exchange Commission (Office of Consumer Affairs)

Small Business Administration (Office of General Information)

United States Postal Service (Consumer Advocate; Office of Consumer Affairs)

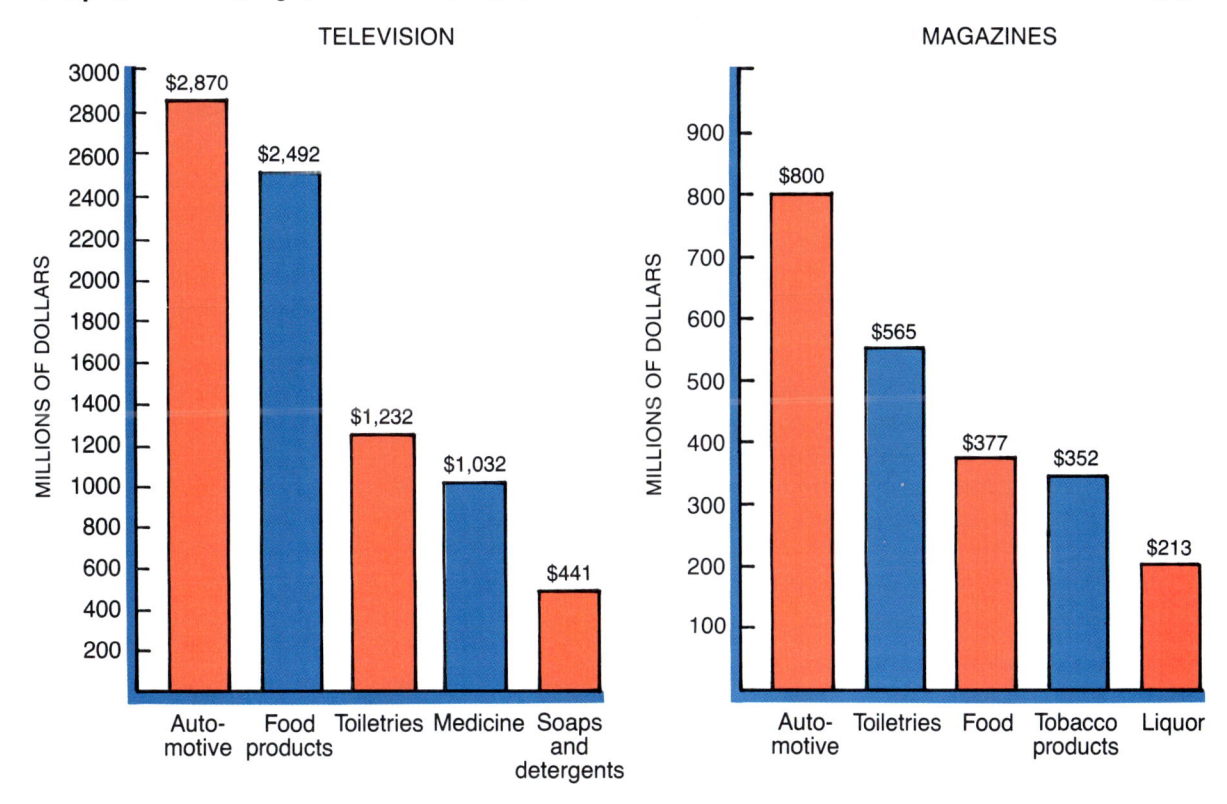

Figure 13.2 Consumer Product Types That Advertise in Different Media

TELEVISION (Millions of Dollars)
- Automotive: $2,870
- Food products: $2,492
- Toiletries: $1,232
- Medicine: $1,032
- Soaps and detergents: $441

MAGAZINES (Millions of Dollars)
- Automotive: $800
- Toiletries: $565
- Food: $377
- Tobacco products: $352
- Liquor: $213

The Government

The government is concerned with helping consumers act wisely in the marketplace. Agencies in the local, state, and federal levels distribute information. Often, this information appears in special pamphlets available for little or no charge. Some government agencies have toll-free 800 numbers. Operators are on hand to answer your questions or to tell you where to go for answers. You may also be able to visit a local office of the agency. The *U.S. Government Manual* provides a complete list of government agencies, including addresses and phone numbers. The manual is located in the reference section of most libraries. You can also ask a librarian about listings of current government pamphlets on consumer topics. (Figure 13.1 provides a partial listing of government agencies that provide consumer information.)

ADVERTISING

American businesses spend more than $188 billion a year on advertisements. **Advertisements** are *messages meant to persuade consumers to buy certain products or services.* Ads appear in newspapers and magazines, on television and radio, on billboards, and in mailboxes. There are now ads on video cassettes as well. In Figure 13.2, you can see five product types that appear most often in magazine and TV ads. All ads, no matter what the product, use the same methods.

Ads Provide Information

Ads can tell you a lot. Without ads, you would never know about many new goods and services. Ads also tell about various features. From ads, you can learn what a product looks like and how much it costs. You can check ads to see which stores have the best prices. Ads also tell you about the characteristics of a product. Ads for cars list gas mileage. Ads for answering machines tell you what kinds of messages the machine can take. Newspaper ads can tell Kim about the kinds of turntables available and where to buy them. She can also compare prices through ads.

Ads Use Persuasion

Advertisements are a form of persuasion. Store merchants want you to buy their goods. An exclamation point after a price adds little information, but it attracts attention. It tries to create excitement. The seller wants you to rush down there and buy.

Advertisers have many ways to persuade you:

- The *rational appeal* uses facts and logic. An ad for turntables may talk about lack of harmonic distortion and noise-to-signal ratios. Facts can be persuasive.
- *Emotional appeals* play on emotional desires and needs. Ads with emotional appeals show a product bringing love or success. Others show products meant to ward off disaster and keep you safe.
- An ad that says a product is wonderful uses a *positive appeal*. A positive appeal tells you all the good things about a product and none of the bad. An ad that says a certain sweater is dangerous uses a *negative appeal*. Your curiosity is aroused. When you read the ad, you discover that the danger consists of your liking the sweater so much you will want to buy one in every color.
- Ads with *humor* are meant to stick in your mind. Advertisers hope you will be so amused that you will tell your friends about the ad—and about the product.
- Ads for many kinds of products use *sex appeal*. Sex appeal plays on your desire to be attractive. A perfume ad may show a handsome man kissing a beautiful woman. The suggestion is that her perfume made her irresistible. Sex appeal is also used to sell spark plugs and watches.
- Some ads use *fear appeal*. They remind you of natural fears and suggest the product or service will somehow protect you. An ad for insurance might show a family watching their house burn down.

Often, one ad uses several appeals. Most ads use some rational appeal. Many ads use both humor and negative appeals. In order to be helped by ads, you need to screen out the emotional appeals.

Advertisers use certain techniques to make the different appeals work. Knowing these techniques can help you evaluate the usefulness of ads.

- A **testimonial** *shows people saying how good a product is*. Five people in a supermarket say they always buy that brand. *A testimonial given by a famous person* is called an **endorsement**. A well-known football player might announce that the wrench he is holding is his favorite brand.
- In a *problem-solving ad*, a product is shown as a solution to some difficulty. A C student becomes an A student when he gets a computer.
- The *scientific ad* gives the favorable results from a test. An advertisement for a battery shows two cars frozen in a giant block of ice. One car's headlights still shine.
- A *demonstration ad* shows how a product works. An animated close-up of a man's face shows how a shaving cream makes his whiskers stand up.
- When two competing products are shown, the ad is probably a *comparison ad*. Two paper towels are dipped into a liquid, and one absorbs the liquid more quickly. The advertised brand always wins. Sometimes, the competing brand is named. Other times, it is not.
- *Life-style ads* connect a product with a

Figure 13.3 Words to Look For in Advertising

Word	Explanation
Clearance	This should mean that the seller has reduced the usual price in order to sell its stock of the product.
Comparable value *or* Compare at	This advertiser implies that another business sells a product at a higher price. Ask yourself, How comparable are the two products?
Formerly sold at	The item was sold at the stated price in the past and is being offered for less now. Ask yourself, How long ago was the higher price charged? Are other stores selling it for even less?
Introductory offer	This should mean that a new product is temporarily being sold at a lower price than it will in the future.
Manufacturer's list price *or* Suggested retail price	The advertiser states the price that the maker suggests, but often all sellers offer the product for less. Ask yourself, Does anyone sell it for list price? Is a larger discount available elsewhere?
Regularly	The "regular" price should be the price the seller charged immediately before offering the sale.
Special	A temporary price reduction that is limited in some way, often in the number of units of the product that will be sold at this price. The product is often bought at a "special" price for the sale.
Up to _____ % off	Only some items will have the maximum price cut—others will be reduced less.

glamorous way of life. A beautiful woman in an expensive evening gown puts on a new kind of hand lotion.

- Advertisements that show lots of people using a product are using the *bandwagon* approach. In fast motion, a product quickly disappears from the shelves of a supermarket. Advertisers expect you to want what everyone else is buying.

In Figure 13.3, you can see explanations of some terms that often appear in ads. An advertiser may use these terms in misleading ways. This is known as deceptive advertising, and you can do something about it. There are laws to prevent such advertising.

REGULATING ADVERTISING

Business and government have made efforts to make sure advertising is used fairly. In addition, radio, TV, and print media may not allow certain ads that do not meet their professional standards.

Groups that set standards for the media include the National Association of Broadcasters and the Outdoor Advertising Association. The ads that appear in your mailbox are regulated by the Direct Mail Advertising Association.

Ad agencies also share some of the responsibility for the truth and accuracy of ads. The groups that watch over ad agencies include the American Advertising Federation and the American Association of Advertising.

Business also watches over itself through two groups that are part of the Council of Better Business Bureaus. The National Advertisers Division (NAD) accepts complaints from consumers and businesses about national ads. The NAD can ask a company to stop using a misleading ad. If the company refuses, NAD can send the complaint to the National Advertising Review Board (NARB). The Board appoints a panel of five to look into the problem. Most advertisers obey the panel's decision.

The federal government has several special agencies to protect consumers. One of the major responsibilities of the Federal Trade Commission (FTC) is to prevent deceptive advertising, packaging, and selling. The FTC accepts complaints from consumers, businesses, government officials, and trade groups about deceptive ads. Consumer complaints, in fact, are often the first sign of a problem. The FTC then gathers evidence about the ad. If it finds an ad deceptive, it can do one of several things. First, the FTC can fine the advertiser. Second, the FTC can order the ad to be stopped. Third, the FTC can order the advertiser to run a corrective ad. The FTC can also sue advertisers.

One type of ad that the FTC investigates is known as **bait-and-switch advertising**. This occurs when *a store owner advertises a low price on one product to lure shoppers into the store, then tries to talk them into switching to a more costly product.* Be wary of bait-and-switch if a salesperson will not show you the advertised item or tells you it is not worth buying. You may also be told that the advertised item has been sold out. If you suspect bait-and-switch, contact your local consumer protection office, your state attorney general, or the FTC.

Separate government groups oversee ads for certain consumer products. The Food and Drug Administration monitors promotional activities for prescription drugs. The United States Postal Inspector investigates problems with goods or services purchased through the mail.

ADVERTISING: GOOD AND BAD

Some people love advertising. Others hate it. Some feel conflicting emotions. They might like looking through magazine ads, but they resent ads that interrupt TV shows. Whatever their feelings, most people learn to live with advertising.

John Kenneth Galbraith, a famous economist, has claimed that ads take away consumers' power in the marketplace. He argues that producers do not respond to consumers' true wants. Instead, producers use ads to create consumer wants. These wants are those that will bring the most profit to the producers, not those that will satisfy consumers.

People who defend advertising deny Galbraith's charge. They say that beyond the basic needs for food, clothing, and shelter, wants vary. If ads persuade people to buy one brand of ice cream instead of another, what harm is done? After all, ads do not force consumers to buy. If consumers do not like a product, they will not buy it more than once.

People disagree about advertising on several other points. Critics say that spending more than $118 billion a year on ads is wasteful. They claim that people would buy the same amount of a product without advertising. Defenders say that ads provide valuable information. Only by having that information can consumers

Advertisements have been with us for many years. Defenders of advertising say that ads provide valuable information that can help consumers make wise choices.

make satisfying decisions. Without ads, consumers would not even know certain products exist. Defenders further claim that ads help people compare goods and services. By comparing, people can make more satisfying choices.

Another charge is that ads limit competition. Large companies have more money to spend on ads than small companies do. Therefore, large firms can place more ads in more places. That can put smaller companies out of the running, critics say. Defenders say the opposite is true. They claim that ads actually promote competition. Ads help small companies. By placing ads, small producers can let consumers know they exist. This helps prevent large companies from controlling a market.

Some critics charge that ads increase prices. Commercials and many print ads are expensive to produce. Critics say producers tack these costs onto the price of a product. Defenders reply that ads actually reduce prices. An ad can create a huge national market for a product. Millions of people may buy it. Then, producers can make more goods at a lower cost per item.

The most popular criticism is that ads are annoying. They interrupt TV shows and radio music. They take up space in newspapers and magazines. Advertisers point out, though, that income from ads pays for the music, TV shows, and articles that people enjoy. Without ads, there might be far less entertainment, and newspapers and magazines would cost much more than they do now. Such an increase would prevent many people from affording them.

MAIN POINTS

- Gathering information helps consumers use their resources wisely.
- Consumers need to evaluate both information sources and the information itself. Sources should be reliable and objective. Information should be complete and appropriate to consumer needs.
- Consumers need to be aware of the difference between information and influences. Some influences are internal. These include values, income, living patterns, habits, and the wish to impress people. Outside influences include the economy, culture, fashion, peer pressure, sales pressure, and advertising.
- The four major sources of information are people you know, businesses, consumer groups, and the government.
- Advertisements provide information and use persuasion. They try to influence you through rational and emotional appeals, positive and negative appeals, humor, sex appeal, and fear appeal.
- Advertising techniques include testimonials, problem solving, scientific tests, demonstrations, comparisons, attractive life-styles, and the bandwagon approach.
- Advertising is regulated by business, the media, the advertising industry, and the government. Business groups that protect consumers are the National Advertisers Division of the Council of Better Business Bureaus and the National Advertising Review Board. The Federal Trade Commission is the main federal government agency regulating advertising.
- Advertising has critics and supporters. Critics say ads create consumer wants, waste money, limit competition, and interrupt entertainment. Supporters say that ads do not force people to buy and that ads inform consumers, promote competition, lower prices, and support entertainment.

Terms to Know

Use the following terms to fill in the blanks of the sentences below.

advertisement
bait-and-switch
  advertising
Better Business Bureau
endorsement
influences
peer pressure
sales pressure
testimonial
trade and professional
  associations
warranty

1. A form of information that aims to persuade is a(n) _____.
2. A promise that a product meets certain standards is a(n) _____.
3. People or businesses that join together to promote common interests are known as _____.
4. If a salesperson tries to persuade you to purchase a more expensive product than the one you saw in the ad, you may be the victim of _____.
5. An advertisement in which a person or group proclaims satisfaction with a product is a(n) _____.
6. An organization of businesses that want to protect consumers and themselves by investigating improper practices is the _____.
7. Forces that appeal to the emotions as well as the mind are called _____.
8. A force that makes you want to be accepted by people your own age is known as _____.
9. The use of tactics by salespeople to persuade consumers to buy is called _____.
10. A testimonial by a famous person is called a(n) _____.

Chapter Review

1. List four sources of consumer information. What questions should you ask yourself when you evaluate this information?
2. Describe the internal and external influences that affect your buying decisions.
3. List five forms of consumer information provided by businesses.
4. What consumer groups test and rate products?
5. What is the name of the publication that gives a complete listing of government agencies?
6. What kinds of information do ads provide?
7. Describe the different advertising appeals.
8. Describe three different advertising techniques.
9. What federal government agency has the primary responsibility for regulating advertisements?
10. What do critics say is wrong with advertising? How do supporters reply to those charges?

Activities

1. How could you find out about products and services if there were no advertisements? Would these methods increase or decrease the costs of goods and services?
2. Choose a product you want to purchase someday. Collect information from friends, ads, and consumer magazines. Is the product UL listed? Did the government test

it? Choose the features most important to you. Which brand and model would you buy? Be prepared to explain.
3. Pick a product you wish you had. For one week, clip out every advertisement you see for this type of product. Try to find a mail-order catalog that offers the product for sale. Write down ads you see on TV or hear on the radio. At the end of the week, list everything you learned about the product just from ads.
4. Make up an imaginary product. Pretend you are the manufacturer and you want to persuade people to buy it. In what kinds of stores would you sell it? How much will it cost? Where will you advertise? Who will buy it? Create a magazine ad and a television or radio ad to appeal to the typical buyer.

Chapter **14**

Shopping Around

OBJECTIVES

This chapter will enable you to:
- compare competing products and services.
- choose the best place to buy something.
- judge the best time to buy.
- explain how your choices help determine the success or failure of a business.

Kevin

My friend Jan has a minicassette player. Last week, I saw her raking leaves in her yard. She had the player hooked on to her belt and was listening to music through the headphones. I hate to rake leaves, and I thought she did, too. When I saw how cheerful she looked, I went over and asked what was up.

She told me how great it was to be able to listen to her favorite music everywhere she went. She said it made the time seem to fly, even when she was doing work around the house. She let me try it out, and it sounded wonderful. I decided that I had to have a minicassette player of my own.

I've been shopping around for a few days now, trying to figure out where I can get the best deal. It's pretty complicated. There must be a couple of dozen different models. Some famous companies make them, and some companies I've never heard of do, too. I'm having trouble remembering which brand has which features. I can't believe all the different kinds of stores that sell them.

Some stores offer big discounts. The first time I saw a sign that said Half Price, I was tempted to buy right away. I have a lot of questions I want answered about which player is best for the money and about the various features each one has. The salespeople in that store didn't seem to know much about what they were selling. I also want to know what I can do if something goes wrong. Can I bring it back to the store for repairs, or do I have to mail it back to the manufacturer or a service center?

I can also get a minicassette player by ordering one through the mail. Maybe I can buy a used one at a flea market or a yard sale. At first, I was discouraged by the number of choices I have to make, but comparison shopping is turning out to be really interesting. I'm keeping a list of the features each cassette player has and of the services the different stores offer. I've even gone around to supermarkets and convenience stores to see where I can get the best price on tapes.

It's been fun, but the time has come now to make my decision. What kind of minicassette player should I buy, and where should I buy it?

COMPARING BEFORE YOU BUY

Kevin thought he had made a simple decision—to buy a portable cassette player with lightweight headphones. It is turning out to be far more complicated than he thought it would be. Before he buys a player, he has many choices to make. He is not sure how much money he wants to spend, and he has not decided what kind of player he wants. After he solves these problems, he still has to decide where to buy the player and when to do it.

In this chapter, you will learn how to make the same kinds of decisions Kevin is making. To decide what, where, and when to buy, you can do some **comparison shopping**, which is *comparing prices and quality to find the best value for your money*. When you shop, buying the first thing you see may not be the best idea. You should look around to see what kinds of products are available. When you find something you think you would like, you should shop around for the store with the lowest price. Then, you can check to be sure that the store offers the services you need.

You cannot always comparison shop. Some products and services, such as electricity, can be bought from only one company. If the product is very inexpensive, comparison shopping is not worth the trouble. For example, if you want to buy only one apple for a snack, it does not make sense to go from one store to another trying to save a few cents. However, if you often buy apples or buy a great many of them at one time, it would pay to find the store that offers the best price.

You could probably benefit from comparison shopping more often. Like Kevin, you may be tempted to take the easy way out. When you shop for the best deal, you will not only save money, but you will also enjoy your purchase more because you will have taken the time to get what you really want.

People buy thousands of different kinds of products and services. Even though they want different kinds of things, their shopping will be easier if they follow some general guidelines. When you shop, you can adapt these general guidelines to fit your own situation. Remember, some of them may work better for one kind of purchase than for another. You will probably also find that some of the guidelines are more important to you than others are.

How to Compare Products

You can compare products by considering eight standards.

Price. Like most people, Kevin will probably consider the price of a product first. Some of the best cassette players may cost more than Kevin can afford. Kevin needs to find the highest-quality player in his price range. He knows that the one that costs the most is not necessarily the best. He wants to be sure that the one he gets is worth what he pays for it. Price, of course, is not the only thing to consider.

Intended Use. The way Kevin plans to use the cassette player helps him determine the features he needs. He will be using the player during the day when he walks to school and late at night when his brother is sleeping. His intended use determines what he will look at when he starts to comparison-shop. He can

Price is an important consideration when comparison shopping. The product that costs the most, though, is not necessarily the best.

eliminate certain products right away, such as cassette players that are not portable or that do not have headphones.

Quality. A third consideration is the product's quality. Kevin may find that some mini-cassette players have such poor sound that he would not enjoy listening to them. He may eliminate others because they are inconvenient to use. Before he makes a final choice, he wants to be sure that the cassette player he buys will last. A quality product should last longer than one that is poorly made. When shopping for quality, Kevin needs to be wary of counterfeit consumer products. These are products made to look exactly like name-brand products, right down to the brand name. The quality of such products is extremely poor, however. Because these imitations can look exactly like the genuine items, they may be hard to spot. Counterfeit products are often sold at flea markets at prices far below those charged for the genuine articles.

Extra Purchases. A good comparison shopper also takes into account any extra purchases that she or he must make in order to use the product. Over the long run, the extras may end up costing a surprising amount of money. Some products come with everything you need, but others require many additional

Product safety is a consumer concern. The government has set minimum standards of safety for products such as motor vehicles and motor vehicle equipment.

purchases. Before he buys his cassette player, Kevin will ask the salesperson whether batteries are included. He may also check to see if a shoulder strap or belt clip comes with the player.

Care. Kevin also wants to know what he has to do to take care of the cassette player. He has heard that he will have to clean certain parts. He also knows that he will have to replace the batteries from time to time and that some players use up batteries faster than others. He wants one that is easy and inexpensive to take care of.

Safety. Another concern is product safety. Some products can be dangerous. Laws protect consumers against unsafe products, such as children's clothes that catch fire too easily or food containing harmful chemicals. Appliances and cars are some of the many items for which government has set minimum standards of safety. The cassette players Kevin compares should be made in such a way that consumers are not in danger of receiving an electrical shock if it starts to rain while they are using the player outside.

Consumer Protection. Kevin plans to examine the warranty that comes with the cassette player he chooses. He wants a warranty that covers both parts and labor and that stays in effect for as long as possible. (Chapter 16 contains more information about warranties.)

Service. The service reputation of the store and the manufacturer is also important. Some stores have a reputation for giving good service. Such a store would probably be able to answer Kevin's questions and fix his cassette player if he has a minor problem. If a more serious problem develops, he might have to send the player back to the manufacturer. He will feel better about doing so if the company has a reputation for reliable service.

Look at Figure 14.1. It shows how you can use the same standards Kevin is using to shop for two different products, a television and a pair of shoes. Notice that you ask the same kinds of questions for both purchases. With a more expensive purchase, you will probably want to do more comparison shopping.

How to Compare Services

You can comparison-shop when you buy services, too. There are six standards for comparing services.

Price. As you do with products, you also need to be sure of what you are getting for your money when you buy services. For example, one dry cleaner may charge less to clean a pair of slacks than another one does, but the dry cleaner who charges more may make minor repairs free of charge.

Nature of the Service. When you buy a service, you first decide exactly what you want done. Many services are custom-tailored to a consumer's individual needs. If you want a haircut, you probably do not tell the hairstylist, "Just cut it. I don't care how it looks." You are much more likely to be satisfied if you describe exactly what style you want.

Chapter 14 Shopping Around

Figure 14.1 Using Eight Standards to Compare Two Types of Products

Standard	Television	Shoes
Price	Compare prices of competing brands; compare credit cost.	Compare prices of competing brands.
Intended use	What type of TV do you want: color or black and white? console or portable? large or small screen?	What type do you want: dress or casual? winter? special-use (running, hiking)?
Quality	What is the quality of picture and sound? Does the maker have a history of quality work?	Are the shoes well constructed? Does the maker have a history of quality work?
Extra Components	Do you want model to connect to video recorder or cable? Do you want remote control? Is stand included for portable?	Shoe ornaments; shoe trees; shoe bags or racks for storage.
Care	What is probable frequency of servicing?	Any special care instructions?
Safety	Is model approved by Underwriters' Laboratories?	Does not apply.
Consumer protection	What warranties are offered? What do they cover? Is an authorized service center nearby?	Does not apply.
Seller services	Are service contracts offered? How much do they cost? Will the seller deliver?	Does not apply.

Quality. Although two businesses may offer the same service, one may do it better than the other. One shoe repairer might be able to repair and recondition shoes and leather goods so that they look almost new. Another may do sloppy work, such as sewing crooked seams on a belt brought in for repair. If possible, try to look at an example of a business's work before you make a decision.

Life Span. The better some services are performed, the longer they will last. If your parents have the basement waterproofed, they expect the job to last for many years. If water begins to leak in after a few months, they will feel they have been cheated. That is why people who have work done on their homes are wise to obtain written contracts.

Consumer Protection. Written contracts are important for certain services. With a written contract, both you and the person offering the service know what is expected. For example, if you sign up for dance lessons, you might sign

Figure 14.2 Using Six Standards to Compare Two Types of Services

Standard	Auto Insurance	Music Lessons
Price	Compare rates and coverages.	Compare fees for lessons and any extra charges.
Nature of the service	Find out what coverage is required by your state, and decide if you want more.	What instrument do you want to learn to play? What level of skill do you want to achieve?
Quality of the service	What is the company's record for settling claims? How helpful is the agent or company representative?	What is the training and background of the instructor? Are lessons group or individual?
Life span	Does not apply—insurers sell policies for the same length of time.	How long are the lessons?
Consumer protection	Check your state insurance laws.	Are there refunds of canceled lessons?
Supplier reputation	Talk to others who have been insured through the company or agent.	Talk to others who have taken lessons.

a contract that promises you money back if you cannot come to class for medical reasons. Then, if you break your leg before the lessons start, you will not lose all your money.

Supplier Reputation. You should check the reputation of the firm supplying the service. One car rental firm may be known for renting out cars in poor condition. A bus company may frequently lose luggage. You can find out about a supplier's reputation from other consumers or consumer magazines.

Figure 14.2 shows how to use these six standards to compare two common kinds of services—car insurance and music lessons.

DECIDING WHERE TO BUY

Deciding where to buy something is almost as important as deciding what to buy. Once Kevin has chosen the kind of minicassette player he wants, he still has to decide where to get it. He can choose from among different kinds of stores, and he could also buy from one of several other sources.

What to Look For

Anytime you have a decision to make, you need to know what your choices are. The more choices you have, the better your chances of finding exactly what you want. Kevin thinks he may locate a better deal on a tape player if he finds out about more places to shop. His friend Jan bought her player from Wolff's Department Store, but he hopes to get a good one at a lower price somewhere else. How can he find other places to shop?

First, he can go to the stores he already knows about. He can also ask friends and family members to suggest good places to shop. To

Chapter 14 Shopping Around

find out about other sources, he can read newspaper advertisements and look through the Yellow Pages in the telephone book. Other sellers might advertise in magazines or on radio or TV. They might also mail advertisements to his home.

Once Kevin knows all his options, he must evaluate them. People should consider the following standards when choosing a seller:

- Prices. Are prices reasonable?
- Quality. Is the quality of the merchandise good?
- Selection. Is there a wide variety of products from which to choose?
- Convenience. Is the store easy to reach? Does it stay open late? Can you order by mail?
- Payment. Can you pay by check or credit card?
- Courtesy. Are salespeople polite and helpful?
- Reputation. Is the business honest and reliable?
- Service. Does the seller service the product?

Different Kinds of Sellers

Kevin also needs to compare the advantages and disadvantages of the many different kinds of sellers that may offer minicassette players for sale.

Department Stores. *Department stores* are *large retail businesses that sell a wide variety of products.* These stores may sell clothing, furniture, gifts, and other products. Department stores offer special services such as home delivery and gift wrapping. Most accept payment by check, many issue their own credit cards, and some accept bank credit cards as well.

Some department stores are known all over the world. Tourists visit them just to see the lavish displays and the many products for sale.

Discount Department Stores. *Discount department stores* are *retail stores that sell a variety of products at lower prices than department stores.* These stores keep their costs by spending less on displays and services. Most accept bank credit cards and personal checks. Some issue their own credit cards.

Supermarkets. *Supermarkets* are *large self-service food stores.* In addition to food, they sell a wide variety of other products such as cleaning products and paper goods. Some supermarkets also sell housewares, plants, toys, cosmetics, and magazines. Larger supermarkets may have a pharmacy, a video tape rental service, and a film processing service. Customers may be able to pay for their purchases with personal checks.

Discount Supermarkets. *Discount supermarkets* are *large self-service food stores which charge lower prices than regular supermarkets but which offer fewer services.* They may be called warehouse stores or no-frills supermarkets. *No-frills* means that no extra services are provided in these stores. Such stores are unlikely to have special sections such as pharmacies and bakeries. They also may not take checks, accepting cash payment only. They spend little money on attractive displays. Some do not even supply bags or boxes for customers' groceries.

Convenience Stores. *Small neighborhood food stores that stay open all day and most of the night* are known as **convenience stores.** Some stay open 24 hours a day. They have a limited selection. Their prices are generally higher than those of the larger stores, but they do sell the foods people need most often, such as milk, eggs, and bread, along with newspapers and magazines, cleaning products, and other items. Convenience stores may accept personal checks.

Specialty Stores. *Stores that carry only one kind of merchandise* are called **specialty stores**. They can offer a wider selection of the products they handle than other kinds of stores do. Toy, computer, camera, and record stores are examples of specialty stores. Although other kinds of stores sell records, you might like shopping at a record store because of the wider selection. Another advantage of a specialty store is that the salespeople may know more about what they sell than salespeople in larger stores would. Specialty store salespeople can probably answer more of your questions about a product. Many specialty stores accept personal checks and credit cards.

Factory Outlets. Factory outlets are *stores that sell specialized products at discount prices.* A factory outlet that sells shoes might be located in or near the factory that makes the shoes. Different kinds of factory outlets can be found together in shopping centers or malls. Outlets sell clothing, dishes, furniture, and other kinds of products. They usually carry goods that are not selling well in regular stores. They also sell products that have flaws and styles that are no longer being made. Outlets usually do not provide extra services. There might not even be a place to try on the clothing offered for sale. Some outlets do not allow exchanges or returns. Most accept personal checks and credit cards.

Catalog Selling. Shopping at a store is not the only way to buy something. Many products are sold in other ways. For example, in **catalog selling**, *products are offered for sale through the mail.* Shoppers select what they want from catalogs and then mail or call in their orders.

Some catalogs are sent out by department stores. Others are issued by companies that sell only through the mail. The range of products offered in catalogs is enormous. Everything from cheesecake to an airplane can be ordered by mail. People can pay by check, money order, or credit card, but they should not send cash through the mail. If a delivery date is not specified, merchandise ordered by mail must arrive within 30 days. If the merchandise does not arrive on time, the buyer can cancel the sale and get his or her money back. Payment can be made by personal check, money order, or credit card.

Catalog buying can save time and money, but there are some disadvantages. People cannot examine merchandise until they have bought it, so it is important for them to look closely at catalog descriptions and warranties. Buyers should also consider possible extra costs. They might have to pay shipping charges and insurance. Another disadvantage is that catalog shoppers have to wait several days or weeks for their purchases to arrive.

Computer Shopping. Some people shop at home through *computer shopping.* They use their computers to get up-to-date information on products and prices. For this service, they pay a monthly or yearly subscription fee. Like ordering by mail, computer shopping can save time and energy, but buyers cannot look over products before they buy them. Because the

You need to read catalog descriptions carefully because you cannot examine merchandise until you have purchased it.

products ordered by computer arrive by mail, buyers still have to wait for delivery. They may also have to pay shipping costs.

Mail-Order Clubs. *Mail-order clubs offer one kind of product to members through the mail.* They accept payment by check, money order, or credit card. People become members of these clubs automatically by buying from them. The clubs sell books, records, and specialty foods. For example, one club sends a box of fresh fruit to members every few weeks.

Usually, people's first purchases from mail-order clubs are bargains known as introductory offers. Members are then required to make purchases at regular prices. Some clubs require a certain number of purchases within a specific time period. Kevin is considering joining a mail-order tape club after he gets his new tape player. His first four tapes would cost only $1, but he would have to agree to buy additional tapes at higher prices later. The club offers a new tape every month. If Kevin does not want the tape, he will have to send in a postcard. If he is forgetful, he may end up buying more tapes than he intends to.

Direct Selling. *Buying from someone who comes to your home* is called **direct selling**. Sometimes, direct selling is called *door-to-door selling* because salespeople go from home to home to make sales to individuals. Other salespeople arrange parties to sell their merchandise to small groups of people. Payment is usually made by cash or check. Plastic food containers, cosmetics, and clothing are among the many products sold directly to consumers. Some direct sellers hire consumers to do the selling. These consumer-sellers earn cash, discounts, or free products based on how much they sell.

Direct selling can save people time and money. Many people feel more comfortable shopping at home, but some people feel pressure to buy from someone they have invited into their homes. For this reason, the law gives

Buying at home through direct selling can save consumers time and money. But there may be more sales pressure involved.

consumers a "cooling off" period of three days to cancel any purchase made in the home if the price is over $25.

Flea Markets. Bargaining at a flea market is an interesting and different way to make a purchase. **Flea markets** are *gathering places where new and used merchandise is sold.* Some flea markets are held outdoors. People can rent space in a flea market and sell whatever they wish. The forms of payment accepted vary from seller to seller. Some accept cash only. Many accept personal checks, and a few accept credit cards.

Garage Sales and Yard Sales. Garage sales and yard sales are other places to buy things that other people do not want anymore. These sales are usually advertised in local newspapers. You can find many bargains at garage and yard sales, but you take some risks because the things you buy there are not guaranteed. Most sellers accept checks.

Auctions. Some people think it is exciting to buy at auctions. **Auctions** are *public sales where products are sold to the highest bidders.* If you plan to buy something at an auction, first get an idea of what it should cost and how much you can afford to pay. If possible, try to look at the item before the auction. Sometimes,

239

Figure 14.3 Advantages and Disadvantages of Different Sellers of Goods

Type of Seller	Advantages	Disadvantages
(1) Department store	Variety of products, prices, services, and payment methods.	Higher prices than (2); service in (6) may be better.
(2) Discount department store	Lower prices than (1); variety of payment methods.	Fewer services and less selection than (1).
(3) Supermarket	Variety of food and other products, brands, and payment methods.	Higher prices than (4); service in (6) may be better.
(4) Discount supermarket	Lower prices than (3); variety of packaged foods.	Less selection and fewer services than (3).
(5) Convenience store	Convenient location and hours.	Somewhat higher prices than (3) or (4); little variety.
(6) Specialty store	Variety of related goods; possibly knowledgeable salespeople.	Possibly not as many services as (1) or (3).
(7) Factory outlet	Low prices for related goods.	Few services; not all goods sold this way.
(8) Catalog selling	Saves time and energy; prices lower than in stores (shipping charge added).	Inability to inspect goods; wait for delivery.
(9) Mail-order clubs	Money-saving introductory offers; prices lower than in stores (shipping charge added).	Possibly required to buy more goods; wait for delivery.
(10) Direct selling	Convenient, possibly lower prices.	Possible pressure to make purchase.
(11) Flea markets	Often lower prices.	Often no warranties or returns.
(12) Garage sales and yard sales	Often lower prices.	Generally used goods; no guarantee on quality.
(13) Auction	Can purchase rare or unusual goods.	Bidding may send price high.
(14) Computer shopping	Saves time and energy; possibly wide selection in future; prices lower than in stores (shipping charge added).	Not yet widespread; inability to inspect goods; wait for delivery.

people get carried away by the excitement of bidding and end up paying more than they would have if they had bought the same product in a store. Items bought at an auction, like those bought at a yard sale, are not guaranteed. Some auctions accept only cash payments; others accept cash or checks.

Consumer Cooperatives. Buying through a consumer cooperative can be a good way to save money. A **consumer cooperative** is *an organization formed by consumers to save money by buying goods in bulk directly from producers.* Some health food stores are cooperatives. There are also consumer cooperatives for purchasing produce and fuel oil. Members pay by cash or check.

Figure 14.3 compares the advantages and disadvantages of all these different kinds of sellers.

An auction can be an exciting event. You must be careful, however, not to get carried away by the excitement of bidding.

THE MOST FOR YOUR MONEY

You know that prices can go up and down. Understanding why prices change can help you save money by timing your purchase wisely.

Why Prices Change

Prices go up or down because of changes in five areas:

- demand
- supply
- competition
- technology
- government regulations

Demand is consumers' desire for a product. Consumer demand determines the quantity of a good or service that can be sold. If demand increases, prices can rise. If fewer people want something, sellers may lower the price for it. Right now, many people want minicassette players. The demand for them is high.

This could mean that prices are quite high. However, because demand is high, more companies are making minicassette players. As supply catches up with demand, prices may drop, as they have in many instances. (Kevin will discover when he comparison-shops that prices for minicassette players range from under $15 to as much as $300.)

Supply is the quantity of a product that is for sale. Prices can change when supplies increase or decrease. The price of orange juice depends on the size of the orange crop. When the weather is good, more is produced and prices stay low. When freezing weather or plant diseases reduce the size of the crop, prices go up.

Another influence on price is competition. Usually, the more companies making a product, the lower the price will be. Companies lower prices to get consumers to buy their products instead of those of their competitors. An example is digital watches. The first ones cost hundreds of dollars. Then, more companies began to make them. As a result, prices fell.

Changes in technology also helped reduce the cost of digital watches. Advances in technology can greatly affect prices. As better ways to make products are found, prices come down. Sometimes, the drop is drastic. This happened with digital watches. Today, you can buy a digital watch for less than $2 because new ways to make them have been invented. The same story can be told about electronic calculators.

The government sometimes controls prices, either directly or indirectly, for the good of the public. Government regulations can make prices go up or down. Laws that do not directly control prices can also affect a company's costs. For example, laws requiring cars to get better gas mileage could raise car prices. Car makers might charge more if making fuel-efficient cars costs more.

Good Times to Buy

A few simple rules can help you take advantage of price changes:

- Shop at sales.
- Choose the best season to buy:
- Watch for rebates.
- Compare brands.

Sellers offer sales when they want to increase demand or reduce supply. In **promotional sales**, *stores lower prices to increase the demand for products.* For example, new products may be sold at low prices to persuade people to try them. A store may also hold a sale to encourage new customers to shop there. In **clearance sales**, *sellers offer lower prices to get rid of unwanted supply.* A car dealer may lower the prices of last year's models in order to make room on his lot before this year's models arrive.

Sales can save you money, but remember, buying something just because it is on sale is no saving if you will not use it. Also, just because one product in a store is on sale, it does not mean that everything is. Stores sometimes reduce prices on one item. That item is called a **loss leader** because it is *sold at or below cost to attract customers into a store.* Once the customers are there, the store managers hope they will buy other goods that are not on sale.

Be sure a sale is a true sale. Sellers often advertise a **suggested list price**. This is *the price a manufacturer suggests.* It is possible that no one actually sells the product at that price. Kevin does not take suggested list prices for minicassette players very seriously. He has seen ads for players at half off the suggested price. What one store calls a sale price on the players can be the regular price for them at most other stores.

Prices change from season to season. Figure 14.4 shows the months during which certain products are often on sale. Business is slow after Christmas and Chanukah, so stores have sales to bring in customers. In the late winter, demand for winter clothes is low, and sellers need to make room for spring shipments. The result is that prices go down. Food prices depend a great deal on local growing seasons. For example, fresh fruits and vegetables are cheapest during the summer. Out-of-season produce costs more because it must be shipped long distances.

You can also save money by taking advantage of rebates. A **rebate** is *the refund of part of the purchase price.* Manufacturers give rebates in order to increase the demand for their products. Analyze why the rebate is being offered to be sure you are getting a good deal. Maybe a newer and better model is coming on the market. Also, be sure you obtain the form to send in to receive a rebate. You must follow the instructions on the form exactly. It may take weeks or even months from the time you mail in the form for your rebate check to arrive in the mail.

Another way to save money is to compare brands. A **brand** is *the name or trademark that identifies a product.* Store brands may be less expensive than national brands. You can also save by buying **generic products**. These are *products not labeled with a store or company name.* Only the type of product is given. These are also called *unbranded products.* For example, a package might be labeled *Tea Bags* instead of having a national name like *Tearrific* or a store name like *Shopper's Choice.*

Figure 14.4 Months That Products Are Typically on Sale

Month	Products
January	Appliances, dishes, housewares, linens, stereos
February	Bedding, dishes, housewares, toys
March	Skates, ski equipment, winter coats
April	Coats, dresses, infants' clothing, men's suits
May	Blankets, linens, televisions, tires, towels
June	Building materials, dresses, televisions
July	Appliances, children's clothing, radios and stereos, refrigerators and freezers
August	Air conditioners and fans, bedding, gardening supplies, men's clothing, school clothing and supplies, tires
September	Batteries and mufflers, dishes, gardening equipment, housewares, new cars
October	Bicycles, glassware, school clothing and supplies
November	Children's clothing, dresses, men's suits, ranges
December	Blankets, shoes

YOUR CHOICES AFFECT BUSINESSES

Kevin finally decided to buy a SuperSound minicassette player. He liked the light weight and convenient controls of this brand. The company that makes it has a good reputation and offers a good warranty. Most important, the player has excellent sound quality. Kevin decided to buy the player at Dave's Discount Store. Dave's offered a low price, and Kevin liked the salespeople there. They did a good job of answering his questions. If he ever has a problem with his player, he thinks they will be willing to help. Another store Kevin visited sold the same tape player for a few dollars less, but the salespeople were not helpful. Kevin decided that service was important, so he was willing to pay the extra money.

Kevin's choice has a positive effect on two companies, SuperSound, Inc., and Dave's Discount Store. If many buyers made the same decision, these companies would do well. Other companies would need to change their products or their ways of doing business. If they did not change, they would make less money. Eventually, some of them would fail.

Businesses often make changes to attract more buyers. Fast-food chains expanded their menus to satisfy consumer demand. They added breakfasts, new sandwiches, and salads. Other companies make the same kinds of changes. When people want something new, such as soft drinks without caffeine, companies change their products.

When buyers do not like something, businesses react to their disapproval. Magazines that do not attract readers change their approach. Producers of ice cream stop making flavors that consumers do not buy. Businesses spend millions of dollars each year trying to find out what consumers want. Through market research, businesses evaluate consumer likes and dislikes. They then try to supply what consumers want.

Because businesses exist to make money, you, the buyer, have power. If you make your wants known by comparison shopping and by buying only when you have found a good deal, businesses will respond by offering better products and services. You can also tell your friends about stores and products that satisfy you and those that do not. Your consumer power means nothing if you do not use it!

MAIN POINTS

- Comparison shopping helps people decide what to buy and where and when to buy it.
- Before you buy a product, you should compare features, quality, price, extra purchases you might need to make, care, product safety, warranties, services offered, and the manufacturer's reputation.
- When buying services, compare the nature of the service, price, quality of performance, life span, contracts, and reputation.
- Finding out about different kinds of stores and other sellers can help you choose the right place to buy.
- To decide where to buy, consider a seller's prices, the quality of the merchandise, the selection available, your convenience, methods of payment, salespeople's courtesy and knowledge, the seller's reputation, and provisions for service.
- Department stores, supermarkets, convenience stores, specialty stores, and factory outlets provide varying products and services at different prices.
- Consumers can also buy products by mail, by computer, through direct sales, at flea markets and yard sales, at auctions, and through cooperatives.
- Prices change when demand, supply, competition, technology, and government regulations change.
- Consumers can save money by taking advantage of sales, knowing the right season to buy, watching for rebates, and choosing generic products.
- Consumers' buying decisions help determine which businesses succeed and which ones fail. Businesses conduct market research to find out consumers' likes and dislikes.

Chapter 14 Shopping Around

Terms to Know

Use the following terms to fill in the blanks of the sentences below.

auctions
brand
catalog selling
clearance sales
comparison shopping
consumer cooperatives
convenience stores
department stores
direct selling
discount department stores
discount supermarkets
factory outlets
flea markets
generic product
loss leader
mail-order clubs
promotional sales
rebate
specialty stores
suggested list price
supermarkets

1. The name or trademark that identifies a product is called the _____.
2. Comparing prices and quality to find the best value for your money is called _____.
3. Something sold at or below cost to attract customers to a store is known as a(n) _____.
4. Public sales where products are sold to the highest bidders are _____.
5. Selling to consumers in their homes is known as _____.
6. The price a manufacturer recommends for a product is the _____.
7. A jar labeled only as *Peanut Butter* is an example of a(n) _____.
8. Groups that sell products to their members through the mail are _____.
9. The refund of part of the purchase price of a product is a(n) _____.
10. Stores that sell specialized products direct from the manufacturer at discount prices are _____.
11. Gathering places where new and used merchandise is sold by various people are called _____.
12. Sellers lower prices to persuade people to try new products in _____.
13. Large self-service food stores which charge lower prices than regular supermarkets but which offer fewer services are called _____.
14. Stores that carry only one kind of merchandise are known as _____.
15. Products are offered for sale through the mail in _____.
16. When stores want to get rid of unwanted goods, they lower prices and hold _____.
17. Small neighborhood food stores that stay open all day and most of the night are known as _____.
18. Large retail businesses that sell a wide variety of products are called _____.
19. Large self-service food stores are known as _____.
20. Retail stores that sell a variety of products at lower prices than department stores are called _____.
21. Organizations of consumers who save money on products by buying them in bulk directly from producers are known as _____.

Chapter Review

1. How can comparison shopping help buyers?
2. When is it not a good idea to comparison-shop?
3. What questions should people answer when they shop for goods? For services?
4. How could you go about locating

a number of sources for a piece of merchandise?
5. What should people look for when choosing a store to buy from?
6. Why do some kinds of stores sell products at lower-than-normal prices?
7. If you decided not to shop in stores anymore, what are some alternative ways to purchase what you need?
8. What are five reasons why prices change? How can consumers take advantage of price changes?
9. Describe two kinds of sales.
10. How do the consumers' buying decisions affect businesses?

Activities

1. Choose a product that appeals to you, such as a home computer or a bicycle. Write product profiles describing each of three possible choices you could make. Include the advantages and disadvantages of each possibility. Conclude by choosing the one you consider the best buy. Explain your reasons.
2. Write radio or newspaper ads for three different kinds of sellers. Invent a name and a slogan for each one. Use your ads to dramatize the advantages of each seller.
3. Evaluate a store or sales organization using 10 points as a perfect score in each of the following categories: prices, variety of merchandise, quality, sales, variety of ways to pay, physical appearance, location, attitude of salespeople, hours, exchange and return policy. A perfect store would get 100 points.
4. List ten purchases you have made this year. Include products such as clothes, school supplies, and snacks. Circle the products for which you comparison-shopped. Then, mark the products using the following code:
E   spent too much money
V   good value for the money
$ bought on sale or at a discount
S   sorry I bought this
G   glad I bought this
What conclusions can you draw from your chart?

Chapter **15**

Deciding About Saving, Spending, or Borrowing

Objectives

This chapter will enable you to:

- decide whether to buy with cash, credit, or savings.
- compare interest rates on savings accounts, loans, and credit.
- use a checking account properly.
- use electronic banking and explain user rights and responsibilities.

Michael

I really wanted a home computer. I found out all I could, and I picked the one that looked the best. The price was $1,800, though, so I figured there was no way I could get it.

These days, my source of money is a part-time job. I work as a checker at the supermarket a few blocks from home. I have to pay for my own clothes, and I also spend money on movies and tapes and records. I've got $300 in my savings account, which took about six months to save. I don't have a checking account, and I don't think I could get credit. So that was that, unless my sister Debbie could help me out. She has a good job as a sales manager.

When I went to her apartment and asked my sister, she of course wanted to know why I wanted a computer. She thought I just wanted it for the games. I had to convince her I was serious about working in the computer field. I've already learned quite a bit at school, but I'd like to go further. In a couple of years, when I graduate, I'd like to land a good job in the computer area.

"So would a lot of people," said Debbie.

"That's why I want a home computer," I said. "So I'll have an edge."

Then, Debbie said, "Eighteen hundred dollars is more than I have in cash, but maybe the store gives credit. We could use your $300 as a down payment. Maybe I could put the computer on my credit card and you could make monthly payments to me. There's also the possibility of a bank loan. With all these ways, you'd pay more, because you'd pay interest, but you'd have the computer now. You wouldn't have to wait to save up the cash."

"Which is better—store credit, using your credit card, or taking out a loan from the bank?" I asked.

"You'll have to find out. You'll also have to decide if this is how you want to use your money. It'll be tied up paying off the computer for a long time. Can you handle that?"

I wasn't sure, but I decided to find out about loans and credit. At the same time, I decided to check to see if my savings account was earning the best interest rate available.

"Can we talk again when I know more?" I asked.

"Sure," she said. "If you come up with a good deal, I might be able to help you out a little. In exchange for access, of course."

DECIDING HOW TO PAY

When Michael wanted a computer, he discovered there was more to buying than meets the eye. Making a big purchase means making decisions.

One way to buy is to use cash. Like many people, Michael did not have enough cash saved for an item as costly as a computer.

Another method is to buy on credit, borrowing from a store or lending institution. The purchase is taken home now and paid for later. However, interest on the loan means paying more than the actual cost of the item.

A third way is to save—to put money into a savings account now and buy later. Michael saved $300 in six months, about $12 a week. It would take him more than two years to save the rest of the computer money, and he could not spend that $12 a week on something else.

Cash, credit, savings—each way to buy has pluses and minuses. Here is what a buyer has

Chapter 15 Deciding About Saving, Spending, or Borrowing

to consider in order to choose the best method of payment.

- Price. Is this a big item? Some people could buy a computer without credit, but most buyers must use credit for a house or car.
- Interest rate. What is the interest charged on the loan? Can you get a better rate? Can you afford to pay interest?
- Need. Do you need the item? Do you need it now? Suppose you have a job delivering flowers. You have to use your car. If your car breaks down, a loan might make sense because you need the car to keep the job.
- Frequency of purchase. Will you buy this item once in five years? Once in a lifetime? Once a week? Remember, regular costs, such as food and rent, have to be met before you can start to buy costly products on credit.
- Availability. Does the store offer credit? Will it take a check? If not, you will have to buy another way or buy elsewhere.
- Opportunity cost. Any method of payment has an *opportunity cost*. This means you must give up something else you want in order to use the method. If you pay cash, you give up expanding your buying power by using credit. If you save up for the purchase, you give up having the item right away. If you use credit, you may give up something else you want, because using credit costs you more than the purchase price.
- Convenience. Because a store wants to sell its goods, it may make credit easier to get than at a financial institution. In some stores, it is easier to charge a purchase than to pay by check.

These seven factors should be considered before you buy.

SAVING AND BORROWING INVOLVE INTEREST

Saving and borrowing are related because both involve **interest**, *a fee for the use of money*. Your savings account earns interest from the financial institution, which uses your money for making loans. In the same way, if you borrow, you pay interest for the use of the lender's money.

Financial institutions pay you interest on your savings account. The institution invests your money in different ways to make a profit.

Financial institutions lend money for profit. Their borrowers must pay a certain amount in interest. If you borrow $100, you might repay a total of $114. The extra $14 is interest. The lender pays costs, such as employees' salaries, with some of the interest. The rest is profit for the lender.

Many financial institutions offer savings accounts. Individuals can deposit their money into a savings account and the institution pays them interest for the right to use it. (The money you put into a savings account does not just sit there. The institution invests it in various ways to earn a profit.) If you put $100 into a savings account, you might have $105 at the end of a year. Interest rates on savings are lower than those on loans. Financial institutions must take in more than they pay out in order to make a profit.

The **principal** is *the sum of money saved or borrowed*. Interest is calculated on the principal. In the examples above, the $100 is the principal borrowed or saved. The interest charged is figured as a percentage of the amount lent. A financial institution pays you interest on your savings because in a sense you are lending the institution your money.

Figuring Interest on Savings

Here is how you find out the amount of simple interest your savings will earn. Multiply the principal by the interest rate by the time. Say you deposit $100 at 5 percent interest for 1 year:

Principal	Rate	Time	Interest
$100	× 0.05 ×	1 year =	$5

Suppose you left the $100 in the savings account for only half a year. Your money would earn less:

Principal	Rate	Time	Interest
$100	× 0.05 ×	0.5 year =	$2.50

Financial institutions often compound the interest on savings. **Compound interest** means *interest is added to the principal as it is earned*. So, the interest, too, earns interest. Thus, the account grows each time interest is added. *The net amount earned* is called **yield**.

The more often interest is compounded, the more money is earned. For instance, $100 saved at 5 percent and compounded once a year earns $5 a year. *Interest that is compounded once a year* is called **simple interest**. If the interest is compounded twice a year, or *semiannually*, you earn more.

Principal	Rate	Time	Interest
$100	× 0.05 ×	0.5 year =	$2.50
$102.50	× 0.05 ×	0.5 year =	$2.56

Total interest earned in 1 year when interest is compounded semiannually: $5.06. Some financial institutions may compound interest quarterly (every three months), monthly, weekly, or even daily.

Michael said he had a savings account of $300. He wants to make sure his money is earning the highest possible interest rate. To do that, he needs to compare the interest rates at several financial institutions.

It can be hard to compare savings plans. Interest rates may vary. The periods for compounding may vary. Financial institutions even differ on the date they start paying interest, depending in part on the nature of your deposit. Cash deposits will earn interest immediately. If you deposit a check, the institution may begin to pay on the day it receives the check, or it may wait until the check *clears*. (This means the institution has actually received funds from the one on which the check was written.) A financial institution can stop paying interest on the day you withdraw funds, or it can stop on the last day interest was credited to your account, which is usually whenever interest is compounded. You earn the most when interest is paid from day of deposit to day of withdrawal.

How can you compare interest rates? Ask the institution to tell you the effective annual yield. **Effective annual yield** is *the actual yearly*

When purchasing a costly product, the borrower often pays part of the purchase price as a down payment.

interest rate for savings. It is figured by dividing one year's interest by the principal. With this information, you will be able to place your savings where they will earn the most money.

Figuring Interest on Borrowing

Borrowers pay interest. They may also pay other fees. A **finance charge** is *the amount of interest plus any other fees charged for a loan*. Fees might include service charges or insurance. Lenders charge fees in part to cover their costs. Fees are usually charged for the time and paperwork involved in investigating your credit rating and keeping track of your payments.

Credit insurance covers the possibility of your being unable to finish repaying a loan. If you get sick and cannot work, for instance, insurance might cover some or all of the unpaid amount. Some lenders insist that you buy insurance. Others let you choose.

Buying on Installment

Closed-end credit is a common kind of consumer credit. It is also called an *installment loan*. When **closed-end credit** is given, *a fixed amount is borrowed at a fixed charge for a fixed period and repaid in fixed sums*. When purchasing a costly product, the borrower often pays part of the purchase price. This is called the *down payment*.

When Michael phoned the computer store, he learned about two credit plans. The computer cost $1,800. In Plan A, Michael could make a $300 down payment. Then, he would make 24 monthly payments of $75. He would pay a total of $2,100. Of this amount, $1,800 would be the cost of the computer. The other $300 would be finance charges. Plan B called for the same down payment. Then, Michael would pay $55 a month for 36 months. The finance charge in Plan B was $480.

How can Michael and his sister compare these two plans? After all, the plans cover different time periods. Plan A covers two years. Plan B covers three. To compare the plans, they must look at them in terms of the same amount of time. So they use the **annual percentage rate (APR)**. The APR is *the yearly cost of a loan, expressed as a percentage of the principal*. The APR translates the finance charge into a yearly interest rate.

The Truth-in-Lending Law requires lenders to tell borrowers the APR and finance charge before a borrower signs a credit agreement.

Michael found Plan A has an APR of 19.2 percent. Plan B's APR is 20.93 percent. Under Plan B, less of the monthly payment goes toward the principal. More goes into finance charges. Michael can see that Plan A is less expensive. However, at his present ability to pay, he cannot afford the higher monthly payments.

Suppose, then, that Michael chooses Plan B, with the lower monthly payments and higher interest. Michael has been able to save $12 a week in the past, or $48 a month. If he trimmed his budget a bit, he was sure he could come up with the extra $7 needed to pay under Plan B. Before he decides, though, he will look into charging the computer on his sister's credit card.

Open-End Credit

Many people use open-end credit when they make purchases with store charge plates or credit cards. Open-end credit is different from an installment loan, which is made up of a single borrowed sum that is then repaid in equal payments. In **open-end credit,** the amount owed goes up with each purchase and goes down with each payment. Store charges and credit cards are simply the means by which open-end credit is extended. Suppose the creditor bills you each month. If you charge a $200 purchase and make a $25 payment, how does the creditor figure the interest you owe?

There are three ways. One is the **adjusted balance method.** It means *the creditor subtracts payments made during the billing period.* A $200 charge and a $50 payment leave an adjusted balance of $150.

The second way is the **previous balance method,** in which *payments made during the billing period are not deducted.* You pay interest on the balance from the last billing period even if you made a payment, which makes this the method most costly to the consumer. With the previous balance method, the balance in the example would be $200.

The third way is the **average daily balance method.** *The creditor adds the balances for each day in the billing period and divides the total by the number of days in the billing period.* Suppose the billing period goes from August 1 to August 31. You begin the month with a $0 balance. On August 5 you charge a $200 purchase. On August 22 you pay $50. The balance is figured like this:

Time period	Number of days		Balance each day		Total
August 1–4	4	×	$ 0	=	$ 0
August 5–21	17	×	200	=	3,400
August 22–31	10	×	150	=	1,500
				=	$4,900

Total balance		Days in billing cycle		Average daily balance
$4,900	÷	31	=	$158.06

The method used makes a difference in how much interest is charged. This is true even if the interest rate is the same:

	Adjusted balance	Average daily balance	Previous balance
Monthly interest rate	1.5%	1.5%	1.5%
Balance	$150.00	$158.06	$200.00
Interest	$ 2.25	$ 2.37	$ 3.00

Creditors can use any of these methods to figure the balance. However, by law, they must tell which method they use. This information often is stated in the credit agreement. It also appears on the backs of bills sent to buyers.

CASH AND CASH SUBSTITUTES

Using cash to make purchases is simple and direct, but you cannot always carry cash with you. Cash substitutes are used for ease and safety. They are also used for keeping records.

Chapter 15 Deciding About Saving, Spending, or Borrowing

Personal checks are a popular cash substitute. Checks are safer to carry or mail than cash.

Five Cash Substitutes

Personal checks, certified checks, cashier's checks, money orders, and traveler's checks are substitutes for cash.

- **Personal checks** are *written orders drawn on a checking account to pay cash on demand.* Checks are safer to carry or send through the mail than cash. They also give you a proof of payment. Stores usually require identification before accepting a check. As a *drawer,* you write a check to a person or business for any amount up to the total in your account. The receiver of the check is called the *payee.* That person collects the money from your financial institution, which is called the *drawee.* The drawee then deducts the amount of the check from your account.

- **Certified checks** are *personal checks that a drawee guarantees an account has enough money to cover.* You make the check out for the exact amount and give it to your financial institution. For a fee, the institution then sets aside money from your account. This certifies to the payee that funds exist to cover the check. Stores sometimes ask for certified checks on expensive items. Michael might have to make his down payment on a computer with a certified check.

- **Cashier's checks** are *checks drawn on a financial institution's funds.* They are similar to certified checks. Anyone can buy a

Traveler's checks protect you against loss or theft. If a check is lost or stolen, you can get a refund simply by supplying the number of the missing check.

cashier's check, even without an account at that financial institution. A cashier's check costs the amount of the check plus a fee.

- **Money orders** are *cash substitutes bought from financial institutions or the post office.* You pay the amount of the money order plus a fee. You get the money order and a receipt. You fill in the name and address of the payee. Money orders are a safe way to pay by mail. If the money order is lost or stolen, your receipt will get you a refund.

- **Traveler's checks** are *checks for fixed sums protected by the issuer against loss or theft.* You sign each check when you buy it and again when you cash it. That way the payee can tell that the check is definitely yours. Traveler's checks come in fixed amounts from $10 to $500. If you spend less than the amount of the check, most stores will give cash as change. If a traveler's check is lost or stolen, you can get a refund. All you have to do is tell the issuing company the number of the missing check.

Checking Accounts

You can choose from different types of checking accounts. One is a **regular checking account**. This is *a demand deposit account offered by a financial institution.* Some institutions charge fees. A fee may be charged if the balance in the account falls below a certain amount. No fee is charged if the balance stays above that amount. Fees may also be based on the monthly number of deposits made and checks written.

You may choose an **interest-bearing checking account**. With this type of account, *the institution pays you interest on the balance.* You are required to maintain a certain minimum balance. Some institutions call such accounts *NOW accounts.* (NOW stands for negotiable order of withdrawal.) You may have to pay a fee based on the balance, as in regular checking. If so, you should see if the interest you expect to earn is more than the fee. If it is less, you might earn more interest in a different account.

SuperNOW accounts pay higher interest. They also require a higher minimum balance than regular checking accounts. There is no limit on the number of monthly transactions that can take place.

Using a Checking Account

You open a checking account by depositing money. You must also sign a signature card and select the type of blank checks you want. (There is usually a fee for a supply of blank checks.) The signature card lets the financial institution verify your signature on checks. Whenever you put money into your account, you must fill out a deposit slip with your name, account number, the date, and the amount deposited.

You must endorse any check you deposit or cash. An **endorsement** is *the payee's signature on the back of the check.* The money cannot be paid until the payee endorses the check. The payee must use exactly the same name that appears on the front of the check. For example, if a check is made out to Michael David Jones, Michael must sign his name that way. If his name is misspelled "Micheal" on the payee line, he must sign the check "Micheal" and then sign again with the correct spelling.

There are three ways to endorse a check. A *blank endorsement* is simply the payee's signature—Michael Jones. With a blank endorsement, the check is payable to whoever has it. That means a person who finds or steals it can cash it. So, a blank endorsement is not safe until you are in the bank. A *special endorsement* avoids this risk. The check is made payable to a specific person. For instance, Michael writes, "Pay to the order of Debbie Jones." Then, he signs "Michael Jones." Only Michael's sister Debbie can cash or deposit this check now. Payees can also limit the use of a check by writing a *restrictive endorsement.* An example is, "Pay to Debbie Jones only." A restrictive endorsement that says "For deposit only" must include the number of the account. (Figure 15.1 shows the different types of endorsements.)

When you make a deposit, be sure to enter the amount in the **check register**. This is *the record for a checking account.* Also add the amount of the deposit to the balance in your account. Figure 15.2 shows a sample page from a check register.

You can withdraw money from your account by writing a check. Always write checks carefully, as shown in Figure 15.3. Use ink, because checks written in pencil can be changed. Here is how to write a check properly:

1. Number the check, unless it has a printed number.
2. Fill in the current date.
3. Write the payee's name. Draw a line to the end of the blank. The line prevents anyone from changing the check. Do you want to withdraw cash from your account? Then write *cash,* the name of your bank, or your own name as payee.
4. Write the amount, in numbers, as close to the dollar sign as possible.
5. Write the amount, in words, as far to the left as possible. Use *and* to join dollars and cents. Write cents as a fraction. Draw a line to the end of the blank.
6. Sign the check the same way you signed the signature card. A check is valid only if signed. Never sign a blank check or one made out to cash until you are inside the financial institution. Otherwise if the check gets lost, anyone can cash it.
7. Fill in the "memo" blank. This reminds you what you wrote the check for.

Then, record the check in your check register. Subtract the amount of the check from the account balance.

Write out your checks with care. Checks with corrections on them may not be accepted. If you do make a mistake on a check, write "Void" in large letters across it. That prevents anyone from cashing it. Then, write a new check. If an uncashed check is lost or stolen, tell your financial institution at once to stop payment. A **stop-payment order** is *an instruction to the financial institution to refuse to make payment on a check.* You must give the institution the number of the check, the date, the amount, and the payee. You may also have to pay a fee.

Sometimes, people forget to enter a check in the register. They may also forget to deduct the amount from their balance. The next check they write could result in an **overdraft**. That is *a check written for more money than an account contains.* An overdraft is also known as a "bounced" or "rubber" check. (Some institutions cover overdrafts up to a certain sum for depositors who have a special credit service.) When a check bounces, the payee will not

256

BLANK ENDORSEMENT

Daniel Bevan

1½"

SPECIAL ENDORSEMENT

Pay to the Order of Gina Venturi
Daniel Bevan

1½"

RESTRICTIVE ENDORSEMENT

For deposit only
19-303398
Daniel Bevan

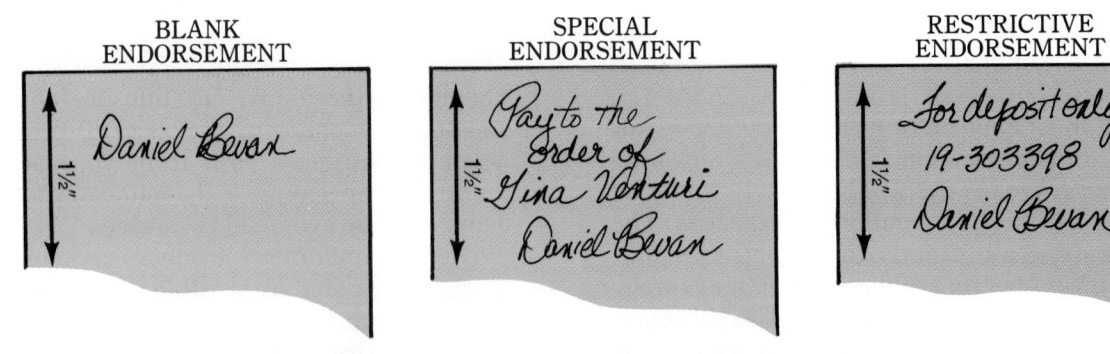

1½"

Figure 15.1 The Three Types of Endorsements

The endorsement signature, and any information put on the back of the check by the endorsee, must be within an inch-and-a-half of the top edge of the check.

ITEM NO.	DATE	DESCRIPTION OF TRANSACTION	AMOUNT OF PAYMENT	AMOUNT OF DEPOSIT	BALANCE FORWARD
					477 19
107	3/23	TO Allcity Insurance	128 00		128 00
		FOR Auto insurance			349 19
108	3/23	TO Cheap Food	23 15		23 15
		FOR groceries			326 04
—	3/25	TO Deposit		117 52	117 52
		FOR Paycheck			443 56
—	3/30	TO Withdrawal	50 00		50 00
		FOR Cash from Auto teller			393 56
109	3/30	TO Public Utilities	34 62		34 62
		FOR February electric bill			358 94

Figure 15.2 A Sample Page from a Check Register

```
                                                    1
          DANIEL BEVAN                   12-17      107
          3 EDGEMERE DRIVE               ────
          FORT WORTH, TEXAS 76101        1501
                                    2
                                       March 23,    19 92

PAY TO THE   3                                    4
ORDER OF   Allcity Insurance Co.              $  128.00
         5
         One hundred, twenty-eight and 00/100 ─────── DOLLARS

FIRST BANK OF FORT WORTH

         7                              6
    FOR  Policy # 61-79-20J               Daniel Bevan

    ⑆:231271174⑆:   19 303398 2⑆
```

Figure 15.3 A Check That Is Written Correctly

Chapter 15 Deciding About Saving, Spending, or Borrowing

receive the money. The institution will notify you and charge a fee. The institution may also return the check to the payee. You must then deposit enough money to cover the check—and the fee. You must also write a new check.

Your Statement

Once a month, a financial institution sends each depositor a **statement**. This is *the institution's record of monthly deposits and withdrawals, as well as the balance at the end of the statement period*. You will receive a list showing which checks were paid, as illustrated in Figure 15.4. You will probably also receive the checks themselves. The statement allows you to **reconcile your account**, which means *to match your own checking account figures with those from the financial institution*. The form on the back of the statement helps you do this, as shown in Figure 15.5. Here are the steps:

1. Adjust your register balance by subtracting any service charges or adding any interest shown on the statement.
2. Put the canceled checks in order by their numbers. Sorting can be easier if you hold the checks as though they were a hand of playing cards.
3. Compare the canceled checks to those in the register. If you forgot to record a check, do so now.
4. Did you write any checks that have not yet been canceled? If so, write an *o* next to each of them in your register. These are called *outstanding checks*. That means they are unpaid.
5. Compare the deposits on the statement to those in your register. If you forgot a deposit, record it now.
6. Add up all the outstanding checks.
7. Total any deposits you have made that are not on the statement. These are called *outstanding deposits*.
8. Add the total of outstanding checks to the balance in your register.
9. Subtract the total of outstanding deposits.
10. Match your final register figure against the balance on the statement. They should be the same. If they are not, retrace your steps.

- Make sure you did Step 1.
- Make sure you did not miss a check, a deposit, or a withdrawal from an automated teller machine (ATM).
- Redo the math in your register. You might have added a check by mistake, or subtracted a deposit. You may have misread a number.
- Redo the math of the reconciliation. If you cannot find the error, tell your financial institution. It is possible for a financial institution to make a mistake, too.

ELECTRONIC BANKING

Now consumers are able *to pay bills or make deposits electronically*. This is called **electronic funds transfer (EFT)**. There are different types of EFT systems. All involve certain rights and responsibilities.

An **automated teller machine (ATM)** is one type of EFT system. An ATM is a *computer-run unit that takes deposits, gives cash, transfers funds, and tells you your balance*. ATMs may be located in the lobbies of financial institutions or in shopping centers, offices, or apartment buildings. They are usually open 24 hours a day, 365 days a year. To use an ATM, you must get a plastic card and a personal identification number (PIN) from your financial institution.

Another type of EFT system is a point-of-sale terminal for shopping. These terminals also use a debit or checking card. **Debit cards** are *plastic cards that let holders get instant cash or pay instantly for purchases*. Debit cards look like credit cards, but they work in the opposite manner. Credit cards delay payment for something you buy until the bill comes. With a debit card, what you owe is deducted immediately from your account, as when you write a check.

```
FIRST BANK OF FORT WORTH
1476 FINANCIAL ROW
FORT WORTH, TEXAS 76101

                                    PERIOD ENDING 4/10/92
                                    DATE OF LAST STATEMENT 3/10/92
          DANIEL BEVAN              ACCOUNT 19-303398
          3 EDGEMERE DRIVE
          FORT WORTH, TEXAS 76101
```

DATE	ITEM	CHECK AMOUNT	DEPOSIT AMOUNT	BALANCE
	OPENING BALANCE			347.26
03/02	CHECK #102	17.04		330.22
	CHECK #104	36.34		293.88
03/08	ATM WITHDRAWAL	50.00		243.88
03/11	DEPOSIT		117.52	361.40
03/13	CHECK #106	10.00		351.40
03/17	CHECK #103	18.12		333.28
03/21	CHECK #105	15.25		318.03
03/25	DEPOSIT		117.52	435.55
03/29	CHECK #108	23.75		411.80
03/30	ATM WITHDRAWAL	50.00		361.80
04/02	CHECK #107	128.00		233.80
04/05	CHECK #109	34.62		199.18
04/08	SERVICE CHARGE	5.00		194.18

SUMMARY

PREVIOUS BALANCE	TOTAL DEPOSITS	TOTAL CHECKS	NO. OF CHECKS	NO. ATM TRANS.	NO. OF DEPOSITS	SERVICE CHARGE	NEW BALANCE
347.26	235.04	383.12	8	2	2	5.00	194.18

Figure 15.4 A Sample Bank Statement

A debit card is easier to use than a check because no other identification is needed. However, the money is deducted immediately from your bank account and cannot be stopped. If you use a debit card, you must be sure your account has enough money in it to cover the bill.

- Many financial institutions allow *direct deposit* of paychecks and social security checks. In this method, you do not personally receive your check. Instead, your employer or the government sends the funds directly to your account. You get a statement telling you that the financial institution received the money. You can also pay bills this way. If you wish, the institution can take money each month from your account and send it to the phone company or to a store where you have an account.

- Your financial institution may also offer *telephone transfers*. By using either a push-button or rotary phone, you can transfer money between accounts. You can use this system to pay bills as well.

- Finally, you can do *home computer banking* in some areas of the country. You can use your own computer to pay bills, transfer funds, or get information about your account. The number of home computers in use will determine how widely this kind of banking will be used. If Michael gets a

Chapter 15 Deciding About Saving, Spending, or Borrowing

FIRST BANK OF FORT WORTH

To reconcile your checking account:
1. Adjust the balance in your check register by subtracting service charges, if any, or by adding interest, if any.
2. Put the canceled checks in order, and check them off in your register.
3. Check off all deposits listed on the front of this statement.
4. List to the right all checks that you have written that are not returned with this statement.
5. Add the deposits you have made that are not included on the statement.

OUTSTANDING CHECKS

NUMBER	AMOUNT
110	32.19
111	16.20
112	24.93
ATM	50.00
113	20.00
TOTAL	143.32

Write the balance in your register here.   168.38
6. Add the total of outstanding checks.   143.32
   311.70
7. Subtract the total of outstanding deposits.   117.52
New balance — this total should match the balance on the reverse side of this statement.   194.18

Figure 15.5 A Sample Bank Statement

computer, home computer banking might be an area for him to explore.

Federal law gives EFT users many rights, but they involve responsibilities as well. For example:

- You should never lend your automatic teller card or debit card. You also should never reveal your PIN to anyone. Do not write your PIN on your card or keep it with your card. Keeping your card and PIN separate reduces the possibility that someone could illegally remove funds from your account. If you forget your PIN, the financial institution will give it to you if you identify yourself properly.

- Use the ATM with care. Do not leave it before the transaction is finished. Some financial institutions have a customer telephone that you can use to get help if you have trouble. When you use the machine, do not let others see your number or transaction. Take your receipt with you when you leave, and do not forget your card.

With an ATM card, you can make deposits and withdrawals at any time.

- Report at once a machine that is not working properly. Be sure to cancel the transaction, even if the ATM may be out of order.
- Record machine transactions immediately, and keep receipts. Write all transactions in your check register.
- Tell the financial institution immediately of any errors on your statement.

What should you do if you lose your EFT card? What if it is stolen? What should you do if the computer does not record a deposit?

The Electronic Funds Transfer Act of 1978 gives you some protection from such problems. However, your rights are based on your informing your financial institution at once of any error. If you do not, you receive less or no protection.

Under the EFT Act, you are responsible for no more than $50 in unauthorized withdrawals if your card is lost or stolen, but you must inform the financial institution within two business days of discovering the loss or theft of your card or code. If you do not notify the institution within that time period, your liability goes up to $500. There is also a time limit for errors on a bank statement. Your liability goes up if you fail to inform the institution within 60 days of the statement date. It is important to act fast.

MAIN POINTS

- There are three ways to pay for purchases. One way is to buy now and pay now with cash or a cash substitute. The second way is to buy now and pay later with credit. The third way is to put money aside now and buy later with your savings.
- When choosing a way to buy, consumers examine the price of the item, the interest they may have to pay, and their need for the item. They also consider the frequency of such a purchase and the availability and convenience of payment methods. They also weigh the opportunity cost.
- Financial institutions pay interest for the use of depositors' money. Borrowers pay interest to lenders for the use of lenders' money. The interest on borrowing is higher than on savings so lenders can cover their costs and earn profits.
- Most financial institutions offer compound interest on savings, which enables depositors to earn interest on their interest. The more often interest is compounded, the more money a saver earns.
- To compare interest rates on savings accounts, ask financial institutions their effective annual yield.
- The annual percentage rate (APR) is the percentage cost of credit on a yearly basis. The lower the APR, the less costly the credit. The finance charge is the total dollar amount you pay to use credit. Creditors must, by law, state all finance charges and the APR in loan and credit agreements.
- In open-end credit, creditors usually use one of three methods to calculate the balance on which they assess finance charges: the adjusted balance method, the previous balance method, or the average daily balance method.
- Consumers can use cash or cash substitutes. These include personal checks, credit cards, certified

Chapter 15 Deciding About Saving, Spending, or Borrowing

checks, cashier's checks, money orders, traveler's checks, and EFT systems.
- Some checking accounts pay interest. Some charge fees. Checks should be carefully written, recorded, and endorsed. Statements should be reconciled right away.
- Financial institutions offer several electronic funds transfer systems.

These include automated teller machines, debit cards, direct deposit, telephone transfers, and banking by home computer. Electronic services are fast but may also cost money. Consumers are protected by law from theft or fraud, but they must notify the financial institution promptly of the situation.

Terms to Know

Use the following terms to fill in the blanks of the sentences below.

adjusted balance method
annual percentage rate
automated teller machine
average daily balance method
cashier's check
certified check
check register
closed-end credit
compound interest
debit card
effective annual yield
electronic funds transfer
endorsement
finance charge
interest
interest-bearing checking account
money order
open-end credit
overdraft
personal check
previous balance method
principal
reconcile an account
regular checking account
simple interest
statement
stop-payment order
traveler's checks
yield

1. You can deposit funds and write checks if you have (an) _____.
2. Buying on the installment plan is an example of _____.
3. A store charge account or a credit card gives you _____.
4. The method of figuring store charges in which the lender finds the principal by subtracting payments made during the billing period is the _____.
5. The sum of money saved or borrowed is the _____.
6. If you go on a trip, a good cash substitute to use is _____.
7. Your signature on the back of a check is the _____.
8. A checking account that earns money is a(n) _____.
9. The method of figuring store charges in which payments made during the billing period are not deducted is the _____.
10. The amount of interest plus any other fees charged for a loan is called the _____.
11. If a check is lost or stolen, you can ask the financial institution to refuse payment with a(n) _____.
12. Funds can be transferred immediately from your account to pay for a store purchase if you have a(n) _____.
13. To compare a statement with a check register is to _____.
14. The yearly cost of a loan, expressed as a percentage of the principal, is the _____.
15. A percentage earned on savings or a percentage paid on a debt is

known as _____.
16. It is important to enter all automated teller transactions in your _____.
17. The method of figuring store charges in which the lender adds the balances for each day in the billing period and divides the total by the number of days in the period is the _____.
18. The record of deposits and withdrawals that your financial institution sends you each month is known as a(n) _____.
19. A store accepting your _____ as payment may ask for identification such as a driver's license.
20. Interest on savings accounts can be compared by using the _____.
21. If you do not have an account at a certain financial institution, you can still buy a cash substitute called a(n) _____.
22. A safe way to send funds through the mail is with a(n) _____.
23. A(n) _____ occurs when you write a check but cannot cover it with funds in your account.
24. A personal check that a financial institution guarantees an account can cover is a(n) _____.
25. A computer-run unit that accepts deposits and gives cash is a(n) _____.
26. The interest on a savings account will also earn interest if a financial institution pays _____.
27. Interest that is compounded once a year is called _____.
28. The net amount earned when interest is added to an account in a financial institution is known as the _____.
29. When you make a deposit electronically, the transaction is called a(n) _____.

Chapter Review

1. What are three ways a consumer can pay for a purchase?
2. What are the seven factors to consider before making major purchasing decisions?
3. How does interest work? What is compound interest? Why do depositors want interest to be compounded often?
4. What is a finance charge?
5. Why would Michael use APR to compare credit plans?
6. What is open-end credit?
7. What are two substitutes for cash?
8. How does a check work?
9. List the steps used to reconcile a checking account.
10. How does the Electronic Funds Transfer Act protect consumers?

Activities

1. Consider the purchase of a small portable radio and a large color TV. Decide on a way to pay for each product, and explain your choice.
2. Compare the effective annual yield of a $1,000 cash deposit for one, two, and three years at two financial institutions in your area.
3. Phone two stores where you would

Chapter 15 Deciding About Saving, Spending, or Borrowing

like to have a charge account. Find out:
   a. the procedure for opening an account.
   b. the method used to calculate the interest on the unpaid balance.
   c. the monthly interest rate.
   d. the annual percentage rate.

Which store offers the credit user a better deal?

4. Compare the automated teller machine systems of two financial institutions in your area. Consider location, services, fees, and customer assistance. Choose one, and explain your choice.

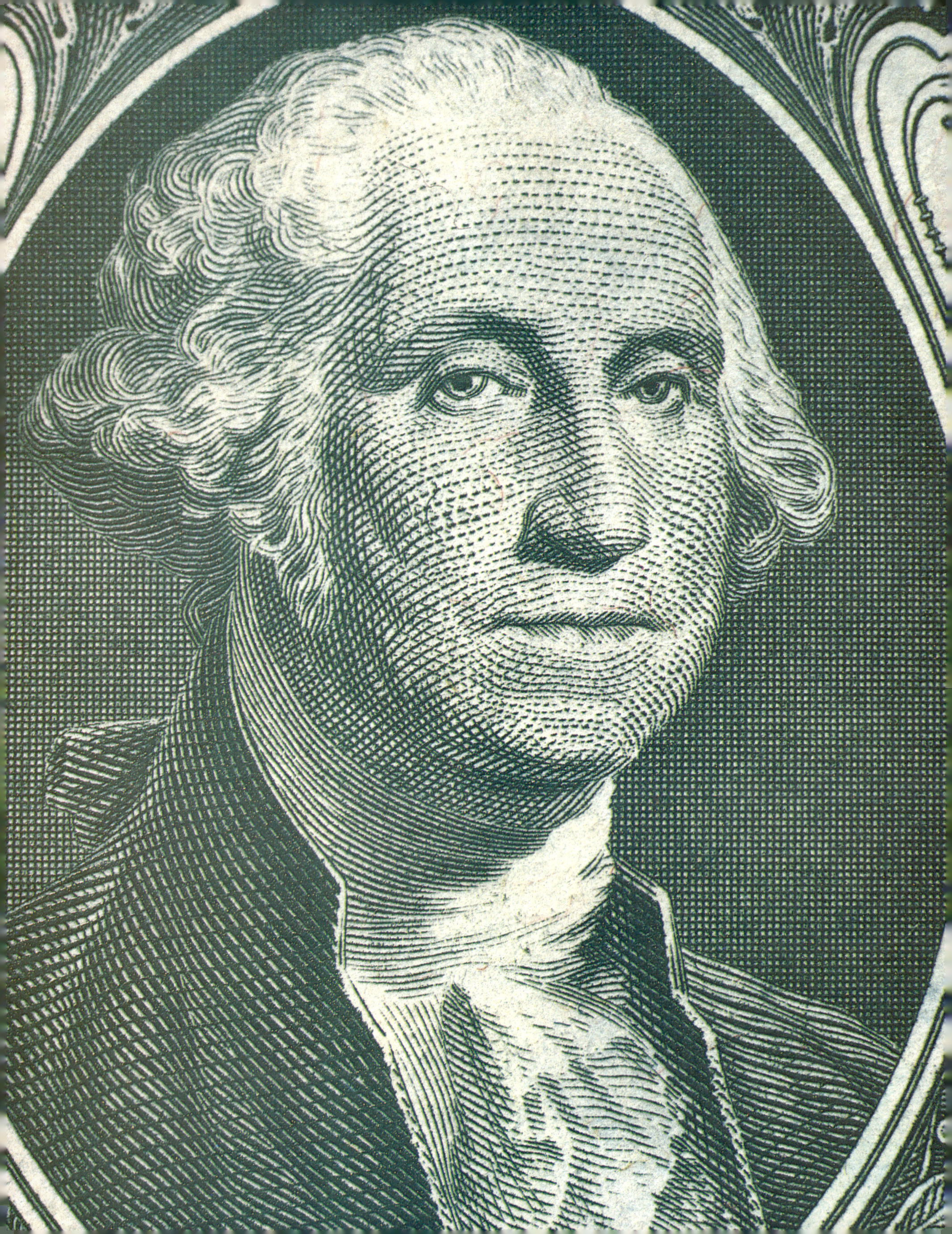

PART FIVE
Making Financial Decisions

Part Five provides you with the information necessary for exercising your consumer rights and responsibilities. Consumer contracts and warranties are explained, and the services offered by different financial institutions are compared. You will explore the sources and types of credit and learn effective methods for avoiding the trap of overborrowing. You will examine the different types of insurance and learn how to shop for the insurance that fits your needs. Finally, you will review the major themes of *Working: Today and Tomorrow* so that you can fulfill your roles as worker, citizen, and consumer to the best of your abilities.

Chapter **16**

Getting Consumer Satisfaction

OBJECTIVES

This chapter will enable you to:
- define consumer contracts.
- interpret warranties.
- stand up for your rights as a consumer.
- identify consumers' responsibilities.

Adam

I hate popcorn! Well, actually, I love popcorn. Soft and fluffy, with melted butter all over it—yum. Unfortunately, this new popcorn popper I bought this morning is driving me crazy! "Look, Adam," I said to myself. "You love popcorn, right? Now you have it only at the movies. Why don't you go downtown to Popcorn World and buy yourself a popper of your own? Then, you could have popcorn any time you want."

Sounds like a great idea, right? Well, I did it. Popcorn World is quite a store. Row after row of popcorn poppers—big ones, small ones, tall ones, short ones, ones that drip butter on the popcorn automatically, ones that use hot air to pop the corn, poppers costing hundreds of dollars, and poppers costing only about $15. That was just the kind I was looking for.

I told the salesperson what I wanted and what I could afford. He told me he had just the thing: the Prince Popcorn Popper. He said it was one of the best home poppers on the market. It was on sale this week, too, for $13.99.

It looked great, so I bought it. I couldn't wait to get it home to try it. I bought a jar of popping corn and practically sprinted all the way back, thinking of how I would soon be sitting in front of the TV with a huge bowl of hot, fluffy, buttered popcorn, with plenty more where that came from.

When I set the popper on the kitchen counter and tried to use it, I was in for a surprise. The corn popped all right, but not much of it stayed in the popper. The cover flew off and the popped kernels scattered all around the kitchen—a real popcorn blizzard. Some even shot up to the ceiling and got stuck in the light.

I've tried six times now to get the top to stay on, but no matter what I do, it keeps flying off, and the popcorn storm starts all over again. I'd sell this popcorn popper for two cents. Now I'm out $13.99 and stuck with a popper that doesn't work properly. What do I do now?

IT IS A CONTRACT

Adam did not realize it, but when he bought his popcorn popper, he was entering into a contract. In fact, whenever anyone buys or sells something, a contract is created. A **contract** is *an agreement that can be enforced by the courts.*

Adam had always thought of a contract as a complicated legal document, such as the one a professional baseball player signs. Many contracts are much simpler than the ones athletes sign. Some of them do not even have to be written down.

What Is a Contract?

All contracts are promises, but not every promise you make is a contract. Luckily, you do not have to face lawyers and judges every time you break a promise. For example, if you promise to take your brother to the movies but later decide that you cannot go because you have too much homework to do, your brother cannot take you to court.

Once a salesperson has made a definite offer to this customer, one of the requirements of a contract has been fulfilled.

For a promise to be a contract, it must meet four requirements. The four requirements of a contract are:

1. Both sides must agree.
2. Both sides must give up something.
3. Both sides must know what they are doing.
4. The purpose of the agreement must be legal.

Some contracts must also be written down. Adam's purchase met all these requirements. We will look at each of them.

Both Sides Must Agree. A contract begins when one side makes an offer to the other. An **offer** is made when *one person promises to do something in exchange for something that another person agrees to do.* When the salesperson pointed out a popcorn popper and said how much it cost, he was making an offer to sell it.

An offer must meet three tests:

1. The person making the offer must intend to make it.
2. The offer must be definite.
3. The offer must be clearly communicated.

The salesperson was serious when he made the offer. On the other hand, when Adam said, "I'd sell this popcorn popper for two cents," he was not serious. He did not really intend to offer the popcorn popper for sale. You could not insist that he sell you the popcorn popper for that price even though he had said he would.

The second requirement of an offer is that it be definite. The salesperson made a definite offer, not a vague one. He referred to a specific popcorn popper, a Prince Popcorn Popper, and named a specific price, $13.99. Adam understood the offer, which shows that it was communicated clearly.

Adam accepted the offer when he said, "I'll buy it." **Acceptance** is *agreeing to an offer and promising to do something in return.* Usually, what the person who accepts an offer agrees to do is to pay for what has been offered.

Money is the consideration most often asked for in a contract.

Of course, no one can force someone else to accept an offer. Adam could have turned down the offer. He could also have offered the salesperson a lower price or agreed to buy the popcorn popper only if the salesperson included a jar of popping corn with the popper. This is called a *counteroffer*. After a counteroffer is made, it is the salesperson's turn to accept it, refuse it, or make a second counteroffer.

Both Sides Must Give Up Something. When you said you would take your brother to the movies, you may have made a promise, but you did not make a contract. Your promise was given freely. However, you asked for nothing in return. In a valid contract, both sides must give consideration. **Consideration** is *something of value that a person must give up in order to get what she or he wants in return*. When Adam bought his popcorn popper, he offered to pay the purchase price—$13.99—and the store agreed to give him the popcorn popper in exchange.

Both Sides Must Know What They Are Doing. It would obviously be unfair to enter into a contract with a person who could not think clearly about what he or she was giving up or receiving in return. The law protects certain people from entering into contracts that they are unable to understand. One requirement of a contract is that both people be **competent**, which means *being capable of bargaining effectively with others*. People who were drunk, insane, or senile when they entered into contracts cannot be made to carry them out because they were not competent at the time they agreed to the contracts.

Minors, *people who are not old enough to be treated as adults under the law*, are also entitled to certain protections. Because Adam is 18 and thus legally an adult in his state, his contract with Popcorn World was legal. In some states, pepole must be 21 before they are considered legal adults.

Because minors are not old enough to enter into contracts, they can sometimes back out of legal agreements. When they do this, they cannot withdraw only from the parts of contracts that they do not like. They must call off the entire contract, and both sides must return what they have received.

If a minor lies about his or her age, he or she loses the right to back out of a contract. Also, if a minor lives with his or her parents, the parents might be held responsible for contracts the minor makes. However, minors who live on their own are responsible for certain kinds of contracts, such as those for food, clothing, shelter, and medical care.

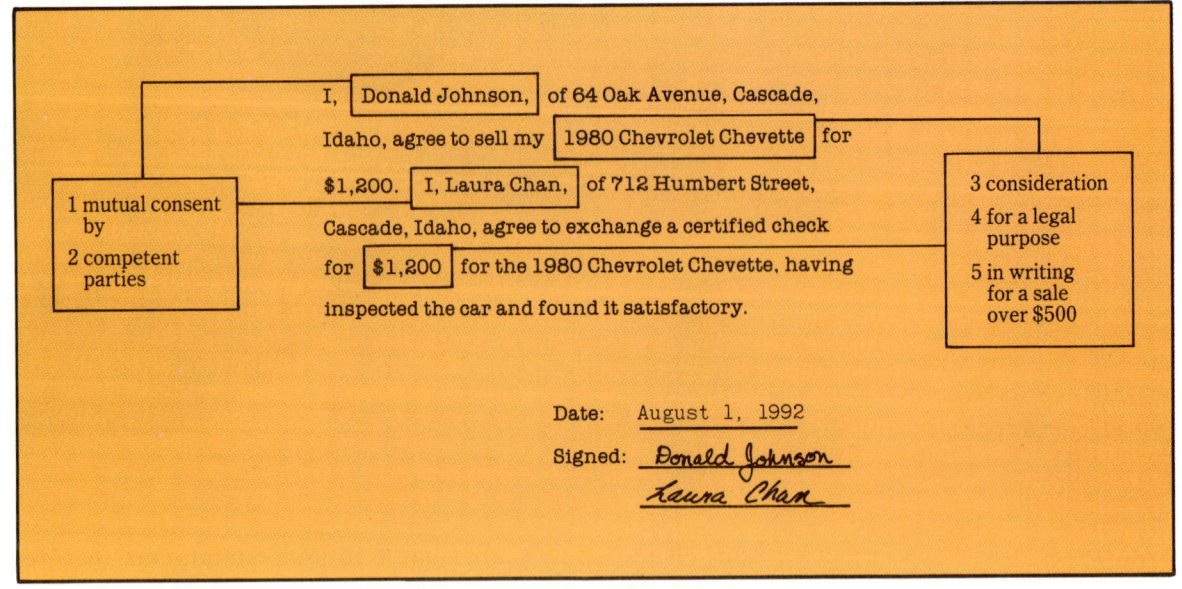

Figure 16.1 A Simple Contract That Meets All the Requirements

The Purpose Must Be Legal. No one can make a contract to do something that is against the law. For example, a contract to rob a bank cannot be legally enforced because bank robbery is illegal. Obviously, neither Adam nor Popcorn World was breaking a law, so their agreement was a legal contract.

Should It Be in Writing? Some contacts must be written down. Four types of contracts usually must be written:

1. contracts for the sale of land or buildings
2. contracts that will not be carried out until a year or more has passed
3. contracts for the sale of something worth more than $500
4. contracts to pay someone else's debt

Adam's contract did not have to be written down since it did not fit into any of these four categories.

A written contract does not need to be long or complicated. When Adam's older brother Donald decided to sell his car to a neighbor, Laura, they reached an agreement and wrote it down. Look at their agreement, which is given in Figure 16.1

A written contract should have the same kinds of information Donald and Laura put in their contract:

1. the purpose of the contract
2. a description of what is being sold
3. the price
4. the names and addresses of both people
5. the date

More complicated contracts may require additional information. Someone who lends or borrows money needs to have a written record of all the details, such as finance charges and due dates for payments. Other contracts describe the rights and responsibilities both people have. They might also name the penalty each person faces if she or he fails to fulfill the contract.

If Someone Breaks a Contract

Most of the time, when people have agreed to a contract, both sides fulfill the bargain. Sometimes, one person does not do what he or she has agreed to do. This failure to do what was promised is called breach of contract. *Breach* means "break," so **breach of contract** refers to *a broken legal agreement.*

Breach of contract can cause extra expense and other difficulties, but the person who is harmed can do something about it. He or she can sue the other person. To **sue** means *to bring a lawsuit against someone.* If the court decides in favor of the person who is suing, the person who failed to fulfill the contract can be forced to meet his or her obligations.

If after Donald signs the contract with Laura, he sells his car to someone else or decides not to sell it at all, he would breach the contract. Laura could accept Donald's decision and look for another car. On the other hand, she could sue to force Donald to sell her the car. If she has already paid for it, she could sue to get her money back.

SATISFACTION GUARANTEED

A business that sells goods has special contract obligations called warranties. A **warranty** is *a promise made by a store or manufacturer that its merchandise has certain qualities.* This kind of promise is also known as a **guarantee**. Some warranties exist whether businesses tell you about them or not. This means that even if you do not get a written warranty, you still have some rights.

Types of Implied Warranties

There are two types of implied warranties created by state law that do not need to be in writing:

1. merchantability
2. fitness for a particular purpose

Merchantability is a *guarantee that the product sold can do what it is supposed to do.* When used properly, popcorn poppers are supposed to pop popcorn neatly without scattering it all over the kitchen. Adam had the right to expect the lid of the popcorn popper to stay on while the corn was popping. In Adam's case, the implied warranty of merchantability was breached.

When a buyer needs something special, and a salesperson suggests a specific product to meet that need, the second type of implied warranty applies. **Fitness for a particular purpose** is a *guarantee that the product can be used for a certain purpose.* Suppose Adam had asked for a popper that would pop a pound of popcorn at one time. Then, suppose the salesperson promised that a particular popper would do what Adam wanted. If the popper could make only half a pound at a time, the implied warranty of fitness for a particular purpose would be breached.

These implied warranties apply only to purchases from regular businesses. A used popcorn popper bought from a neighbor at a yard sale would not be protected by any type of warranty. Sometimes, even retail stores sell goods that have no guarantee ("as is"), or they may be covered under other kinds of policies such as satisfaction guarantees or service contracts. If Adam's popcorn popper had been marked "as is" when he bought it, he would not be protected.

Spoken Warranties

Salespersons often make oral promises about a product's performance. These statements are known as spoken warranties. They can be created in three ways:

1. A seller makes a promise about what a product looks like or what it can do. If a salesperson promises that a sweater can be machine-washed, he or she is creating a warranty.
2. The buyer and seller agree on a detailed description of the product. For example, a watch that you buy from a catalog must

work and look the way the catalog says it will.
3. The buyer orders a product after having seen a sample. People often order cars after driving demonstration models. The cars they receive must be just like the ones they drove.

Sometimes, you hear statements such as, "This is the best bike you'll ever see!" or "It's a real bargain." *Exaggerated claims about a product* are called **puffery**. These claims are obviously based on the seller's own opinion. They do not create warranties.

Using Express Warranties

Express, or written, warranties on consumer products costing more than $15 must be available for you to see before you buy.

Some written warranties are full warranties. A **full warranty** is a guarantee that a store or company will fix or replace a faulty product free. This must be done within a reasonable amount of time. If a product cannot be fixed, the buyer can choose between a replacement and a refund. A full warranty may cover only part of a product. For example, it could cover only the picture tube of a television set. It may also be in effect for only a limited time, but the time limit must be clearly stated. In addition, a full warranty cannot force a buyer to do something unreasonable, such as ship a heavy piece of equipment somewhere.

A **limited warranty** is *an express warranty that offers the buyer less protection than a full warranty.* A limited warranty is shown in Figure 16.2.

The limited warranty in Figure 16.2 applies only to the first person who buys the radio. The purchaser must also mail the radio back to the company at her or his own expense. The warranty shows owners exactly what is covered and what is not. It also states what owners must do to maintain coverage.

Another type of limited warranty states that the company will supply free parts. However, the owner must pay to have the new parts put in. The coverage in limited warranties varies with each manufacturer.

You should read the warranty carefully before you make a major purchase. Find out how long it will remain in effect. When you read a warranty, you should look for answers to the following questions:

1. Exactly what is covered? Are only certain parts covered? Which ones? Are labor charges covered?
2. Who will do any needed repairs?
3. If the product has to be shipped to a factory or service center, who has to pay shipping costs?
4. How might the buyer lose warranty rights?
5. Must the buyer send in a card to register the purchase?
6. Does the warranty cover only the first buyer?

Adam looked in the carton of his popcorn popper for a written warranty, but he did not find one. Still, his purchase is covered by the warranty of merchantability. He has the right to have the popcorn popper repaired or replaced. In order to get what he wants, however, Adam must make an effort to solve his consumer problem.

Used products bought at yard sales or flea markets carry no warranty.

> **One-Year Limited Warranty to Original Owner**
>
> If within one year from the date of original purchase, this HIGH-TONE PORTABLE RADIO fails to function because of defects in material or workmanship, High-Tone North America Company will, at its option, either repair or replace the radio provided the original purchaser:
>
> 1. returns the radio postpaid to High-Tone North America, 100 Main Street, Englewood, Colorado 80110, or one of its authorized service centers listed on the enclosed leaflet.
> 2. submits proof of the date of original purchase.
>
> This warranty does not cover finishes or batteries, not does it cover damage resulting from accident, misuse, abuse, dirt, water, battery leakage, tampering, servicing performed or attempted by unauthorized service agencies, or radios that have been modified or used for commercial purposes.
>
> ALL IMPLIED WARRANTIES INCLUDING ANY IMPLIED WARRANTY OF MERCHANT-ABILITY OR FITNESS FOR ANY PARTICULAR PURPOSE ARE LIMITED IN DURATION TO ONE YEAR FROM DATE OF ORIGINAL PURCHASE. IN NO EVENT WILL HIGH-TONE NORTH AMERICA BE RESPONSIBLE FOR DAMAGES RESULTING FROM THE USE OF THIS PRODUCT.

Figure 16.2 One-Year Limited Warranty to Original Owner

SOLVING CONSUMER PROBLEMS

If a product comes with a written warranty and something goes wrong, you should do what the warranty says to do. If the product does not come with a written warranty, your first step is to go back to the store where you bought the item. Simply talking to a salesperson or manager can often get you an immediate refund or a replacement.

To solve a consumer problem, remember a few points:

1. Try to prevent problems before they occur. Read directions, and take good care of the items you buy.
2. If you did something wrong, be willing to admit it. Did you wash a sweater that should have been dry-cleaned? That kind of problem cannot be blamed on a seller or manufacturer.
3. Do not lose your temper. If you think you should get a refund or replacement, calmly explain what happened and what you think should be done.
4. Be reasonable. Take the time to listen to what the seller or manufacturer says.
5. Be thorough. Provide all the necessary information. Be sure you save your sales slip and your guarantee (if you received one). Return what you bought in the box it came in.
6. Be polite. Politeness can get good results.
7. Do not give up until the problem is solved.

Getting Help

Speaking to a salesperson may not solve your problem. If it does not, ask to speak to the manager. You could also write to the store's owner.

If your problem still is not solved, try writing to the company that made the product. A well-

Explaining your problem calmly and politely will often result in an immediate refund or replacement of a product.

written complaint letter, like a complaint made in person, should be clear and factual. It should also explain what you think should be done.

Lee Davidson's letter, given in Figure 16.3, is a good example of a complaint letter. In this letter, Lee does not waste time losing her temper. Instead, she carefully explains what happened. Rather than criticizing the company, she asks for either a refund or a replacement. In contrast to an angry letter, this kind of letter is much more likely to get results.

However, if a letter of complaint does not work, you can ask the local Better Business Bureau for help. You could also turn to the Chamber of Commerce, which is an organization of local business people. One of these organizations may give you some advice about what to do next. However, neither organization is set up to resolve individual consumer complaints.

Agencies sponsored by the government or by industry may also be able to help you. **Consumer action panels** *have been formed by some manufacturers to handle consumer problems.* Look in the public library for the names and addresses of groups that might be useful to you. One helpful book is the *Consumer's Resource Handbook*. Published by the federal government, it lists the names and addresses of local, state, and federal agencies that help consumers. The book also includes many firms' consumer affairs offices. When all else fails, you might ask a newspaper, radio, or TV consumer action group to help.

Even after trying these sources of help, people sometimes find that their problems have not been solved. If this happens, the next step is to go to court.

Going to Court

The kind of court that is least expensive to use is small claims court. **Small claims court** is *an informal court created to handle legal disputes involving sums of money between $100 and $3,000.* Consumer cases can be presented there without lawyers. There is one drawback to taking a case to small claims court. Even if the judge decides in the consumer's favor, the consumer cannot always be sure that the party that loses will pay what it owes. Because the court is informal and involves small sums, its decisions are sometimes difficult to enforce.

A more complicated way of going to court is to hire a lawyer and sue. You can sue for damages or to force the other party to live up to the terms of the contract. You can find a lawyer through the local bar association. You could also ask a friend or relative if he or she can recommend one. Hiring a lawyer can be expensive, though. And going to court may take months or even years.

People with low incomes may be able to get help from a **legal aid society**. This is *a government-sponsored organization that offers free or low-cost legal help to those who cannot afford to hire their own lawyers.*

A lawyer will be able to tell you whether you have any chance of winning your suit in court. You also have to weigh the cost of legal fees against the cost of the item. If you decide to go ahead with your case, the lawyer can tell you how much the legal costs will be. Sometimes, a lawyer can settle the matter out of court, after a talk with the lawyer for the other side. If the lawyers cannot agree on a solution, the suit must be settled by a judge or jury.

```
                                    6 Redwood Road
                                    Lone Pine, CA  93545
                                    February 26, 1992


Fast Track Shoes
27 Marathon Lane
San Francisco, CA  94107

Dear Fast Track:

Two weeks ago, I purchased a pair of your Fast Track running
shoes, Style 936A, from Howard's Shoe Shop, 33 Main Street,
Lone Pine, California.  After two weeks of normal wear, the
soles started to separate from the uppers on both shoes.  I
am sure that this is a defective pair and would like either
a refund or a replacement.  I have enclosed a copy of my
sales receipt.

Thank you for your attention to this matter.  I look forward
to receiving your reply.

                                    Sincerely,

                                    Lee Davidson
                                    Lee Davidson
```

Figure 16.3 A Sample Complaint Letter

WITH RIGHTS COME RESPONSIBILITIES

Many customers do not want to take the time and trouble to fight for their rights. Adam thinks that he probably should try to return his popcorn popper. He may be too discouraged to do anything to solve his problem. If Adam does not take action, he may be hurting others as well as himself. If no one complains, the salespeople and the manufacturer will continue to believe that the Prince Popcorn Popper works well and that people are satisfied with the product. The popcorn maker will continue to be manufactured in the same way.

You must use your rights as a consumer if you want to keep them. In 1962, President John F. Kennedy stated that consumers have four basic rights:

1. the right to safety—to purchase products that are not harmful
2. the right to choose—to select from a variety of products and services
3. the right to be informed—to receive accurate information
4. the right to be heard—to have ways of communicating problems

In the 1970s, President Gerald Ford added another right:

5. the right to consumer education—to be informed about the marketplace

These important rights go hand-in-hand with **responsibilities**. These are *your obligations to act in your own best interest and in the interest of others*. To keep your rights, you must be sure to use them.

Complaining about faulty products is a consumer responsibility that encourages companies to raise their standards.

Your right to safety makes you responsible for using products safely. This includes using products according to directions. It also means keeping dangerous products away from children. Prompt response to product recalls is another responsibility. A **recall** *occurs when a manufacturer learns about a flaw in a product.* Each person who has bought the product is then asked to return it so it can be fixed or replaced with a safe model. In some cases, the product is withdrawn completely from the marketplace. Purchasers then receive a refund.

Your right to choose makes you responsible for making good choices. This means checking product safety when safety is a concern. You must also avoid dishonest businesses and reject poor-quality products. You are also obliged to pay for your choices.

Your right to be informed makes you responsible for getting information—and using it. You need to learn about credit. You need to be aware of illegal business practices. And you need to understand contracts.

Your right to be heard makes you responsible for speaking up. You can notify businesses or the government when you have a consumer complaint. You can obtain outside help from a consumer group. And you can support your complaints with receipts, warranties, and copies of letters.

Your right to consumer education makes you responsible for using what you have learned. It is also your duty to keep up with changes in laws and business practices that affect consumers.

Responsible consumers also act honestly. **Shoplifting** is *stealing from a store.* It is a crime. A shoplifter risks being caught and punished by fines or a jail sentence. Another dishonest practice is switching price tags in order to buy something for a lower price. Price tag switching, like shoplifting, hurts other consumers. Stores must raise prices to cover the cost of security measures and stolen merchandise.

Other forms of dishonesty also increase costs for everyone. Buying something that you think may have been stolen encourages others to commit crimes. Claiming a refund for something you have used, and breaking an item in a store and not paying for it are both dishonest.

Some people who work for stores also commit crimes. **Worker crime** is *the stealing of supplies or merchandise from an employer.* Claiming to have worked extra hours in order to get more pay is another worker crime. Workers

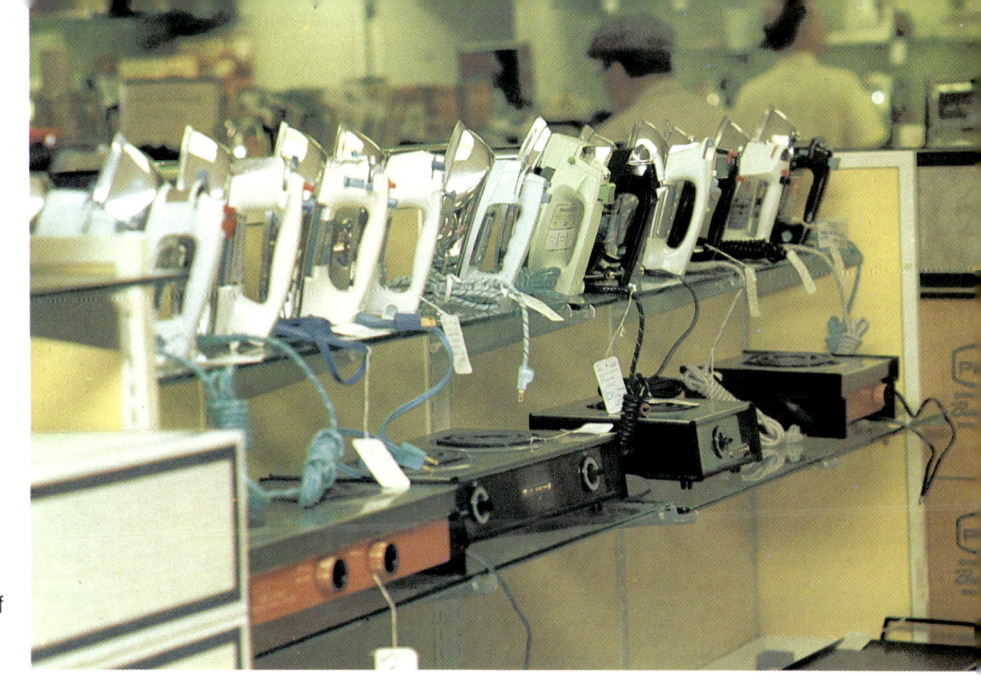

The right to select from competing products is one of the five basic consumer rights.

who steal or cheat drive up the cost of doing business. They force stores to charge more for their products. Those who commit worker crime may be prosecuted and punished. At the very least, they risk losing their jobs.

By acting responsibly, people help the economy run smoothly. Refusing to buy harmful products and complaining about faulty products can encourage companies to raise the standards for the products they make and sell.

Your right to consumer education does not end when you finish school. You need to keep up with continuing changes in laws and business practices throughout your life.

There are many groups today that help protect consumers' rights, but they do not work well unless people are willing to use them. The best protection consumers have is to keep informed, to act responsibly, and to stand up for their rights in the marketplace.

MAIN POINTS

- When someone buys something, he or she is entering into a contract. A contract exists only if both sides agree to the terms, give up something, know what they are doing, and have a legal purpose.
- When someone does not fulfill a contract, the person who has been harmed can cancel the contract, sue for damages, or sue to force the other party to fulfill the contract.
- Sellers guarantee the product will do what it is supposed to do. This is the implied warranty of merchantability. Sellers may also guarantee that the item can be used for a particular purpose. This is the implied warranty of fitness for a particular purpose.
  that it meets certain standards.
- Full warranties guarantee that a faulty product will be repaired or replaced at no cost. Limited warranties provide less protection.
- Consumers may be able to solve problems simply by being calm, thorough, polite, and reasonable.
- Consumers have the right to buy products that work safely, to choose among competing products, to be informed, to be heard if they have complaints, and to be educated about consumer rights. Each right has matching responsibilities.

Terms to Know

Use the following terms to fill in the blanks of the sentences below.

acceptance
breach of contract
competent
consideration
consumer action panel
contract
full warranty
guarantee
legal aid society
limited warranty
minors
offer
puffery
recall
responsibilities
shoplifting
small claims court
sue
warranty
implied warranty of fitness
implied warranty of merchantability
worker crime

1. A guarantee that a store or company will fix or replace a faulty product free in a reasonable amount of time is a(n) _____.
2. Stealing merchandise from a store is called _____.
3. Duties people must carry out are _____.
4. If someone says, "I will sell you this car for $750," he or she is making a(n) _____.
5. A promise made by a business that its merchandise has certain characteristics is known as a(n) _____ or _____.
6. A government-sponsored organization that offers free or low-cost legal help to people who cannot afford to hire lawyers is a(n) _____.
7. A seller's exaggerated claims about a product are known as _____.
8. A warranty that offers the buyer less protection than a full warranty is a(n) _____.
9. A manufacturer asks consumers to return a faulty product by issuing a(n) _____.
10. When both parties to a contract agree to give up something of value, they are offering _____.
11. A guarantee that a product can be used for a specific purpose is known as a(n) _____.
12. The failure of a party to a contract to do as promised is called _____.
13. A guarantee that a product can do what it is supposed to do is known as a(n) _____.
14. Agreeing to an offer and promising to do something in return is known as _____.
15. An agreement that can be enforced by the courts is a(n) _____.
16. An informal court where consumer cases can be presented without lawyers is called _____.
17. People who are not old enough to be treated as adults under the law are known as _____.
18. Stealing supplies or merchandise from an employer is an example of _____.
19. To bring a lawsuit against someone is to _____.
20. A group formed by manufacturers in an industry to handle consumer problems is known as a(n) _____.
21. Someone who is _____ can enter into a contract because she or he is capable of bargaining effectively with others.

Chapter Review

1. What are four requirements of a contract?
2. What kinds of contracts usually have to be written down?
3. What can someone who has been harmed by breach of contract do?
4. Name two kinds of warranties that do not have to be written down.
5. What are three ways a seller can create an express warranty?
6. How does a limited warranty differ from a full warranty?
7. What should you look for when you examine a limited warranty?
8. What steps could you take if something you bought was not satisfactory?
9. Where can a consumer get help if he or she has trouble solving a consumer problem?
10. What five important rights do consumers have?

Activities

1. Imagine that you are Adam, and write a letter to Dubious Electronics, Inc., the manufacturer of Prince Popcorn Poppers. Calmly explain what happened and what you think should be done.
2. Write a response to one of the following questions.
   a. Have you ever returned a purchase that did not satisfy you? What happened?
   b. Have you ever written a letter of complaint about a product that disappointed you? What happened?
   c. Have you ever seen customers or salespeople acting irresponsibly? What did they do?
   d. If you saw a stranger shoplifting, would you report that person? Why or why not?
3. Using the Yellow Pages as a guide, prepare a fact sheet that provides information on places in your area where consumers can get help. Compare your list with those of your classmates. Post the most helpful lists in your classroom.
4. Collect five copies of written warranties. Divide them into full and limited, and rank them in order from the one providing the most coverage to the one providing the least.

Chapter **17**

Purchasing Financial Services

OBJECTIVES

This chapter will enable you to:

- describe the services provided by different financial institutions.
- explain how financial institutions are changing.
- comparison-shop for a financial institution.
- explain how the Federal Reserve assists financial institutions.

Jessie

I've had a savings account at First Savings and Loan since I was seven years old. I still remember walking down there with my grandmother to open the account. I had wanted a game for my birthday, but she said it was time I learned how to save. She told me that when she was a girl, people didn't trust financial institutions as much as they do now. Many of her neighbors used to keep their savings hidden away at home. Nowadays, she explained, the government offers insurance to financial institutions to keep depositors' money safe. She also told me that my money would grow at a financial institution because it pays interest. I didn't understand her then, but I do now.

On every birthday since then, my grandmother has sent me $25 for my savings account. Last year, I started to work part-time, and I began to put some of the money I earned in my account, too. We've just moved across town, and there isn't a nearby branch of First Savings and Loan. It's time for me to find a new place to do my banking.

Besides, I've decided I need more from a financial institution than just a savings account. Every time I want to send for something through the mail, like those records I bought from a store in New York, I have to ask one of my parents to write a check for me. I need a checking account of my own.

When I start to think about what I should do, I feel confused. My old savings and loan looks very safe and official. It has big marble columns and a huge vault. Whenever I go in there, I feel I'm about to do something important. Most of the newer financial institutions aren't nearly so impressive-looking.

Of course, I know that what a financial institution looks like doesn't really matter. It's the kinds of accounts and services it offers that count. The problem is, every place in town seems to offer something different. One financial institution claims to pay higher interest. Another says it charges lower fees. There are many kinds of accounts to choose from. Things just aren't as simple as when my grandmother took me down to the savings and loan on the corner to open my first savings account.

SHOPPING FOR A FINANCIAL INSTITUTION

Comparison shopping is an important aspect of purchasing financial services. Jessie can shop for a financial institution by deciding what financial services she needs and then looking for the bank or other institution that gives her what she wants at the lowest cost. At the same time, she wants her savings to earn the highest possible interest. Jessie may discover that she needs to use more than one institution.

Jessie has a problem because choosing a financial institution is more difficult now than it used to be. At one time, all financial institutions were essentially the same, but in 1980, banking laws were changed to allow financial institutions to compete for your money. Now, they can charge different fees and pay different amounts of interest, so comparison shopping can save you money. The services financial institutions offer are also changing quickly, so you face more choices now than ever before.

Competition for Your Money

Financial institutions need your money to stay in business. Just as stores need merchandise to sell, financial institutions need money in order to invest it, lend it, and earn a profit from those activities. Before 1980, laws controlled many of the things financial institutions could do. Only certain kinds of institutions could offer certain services. The laws were changed, and now there are fewer limits on the services they can provide. As a result, they are free to attract customers in different ways.

Competition among financial institutions can help you. To win your business, financial institutions may provide more *benefits*. An institution's benefits are the interest rates and services it offers. A financial institution can also compete through its *costs*—the fees it charges for its services. Jessie may find that one institution offers higher interest rates than the others. A different institution may charge less than the others for the same services. To find the financial institution that is right for her, Jessie first needs to decide on the services she needs. She then needs to compare fees and benefits for these services.

Financial Institutions

Computers are changing people's lives in many ways. Tasks that people performed only a few years ago can now be done automatically. This is especially true for financial services.

Financial institutions compete for consumers' money through the combination of benefits and costs they offer.

Drive-in windows are a customer convenience offered by many financial institutions.

People used to have to go to a financial institution during certain hours in order to deposit money or withdraw it. Today, many institutions have automated teller machines (ATMs). These machines may be located inside or outside the institutions. They operate 24 hours a day so people can use them anytime. People can also carry out transactions by phone. They can call their institution's computer and tell it to pay their bills or move money from one account to another. Using either the phone or the ATM, customers can also find out how much money they have in their accounts.

Paychecks and other payments can be deposited directly into people's accounts. That way, people do not have to take their checks to the institutions themselves. This is especially helpful for retired people who receive social security checks. People also sometimes arrange to have financial institutions make regular payments from their checking accounts. For example, every month Jessie's mother's institution automatically pays $100 from her checking account into a special fund for Jessie's education after high school. A similar service is available for paying certain types of bills.

Another change is that you do not have to go to a branch of your own institution to obtain or deposit money. If you have an ATM card, you may be able to go to the ATM at another institution in your area or even at an institution in another state. This is convenient for people who work in one state and live in another, and it also helps people who travel a great deal. More changes are coming. It is now possible, for example, for financial institutions to open branches in other states.

More Choices for You

In the past, savings and loan associations were best for savings and home mortgage loans. Commercial banks were best for checking and personal loans, so many people divided their banking business among two or more financial institutions. Today, there are fewer restrictions on the services a financial institution can offer. As a result, financial institutions have become more alike. Many offer a similar range of checking, credit, saving, loan, and investing services.

Because financial institutions are now competing for your business, you can go comparison shopping. Because you can get many financial services in one place, you need to think about *all* the reasons you need a financial institution before you choose one. View your financial needs as a total package rather than as separate items. Then, shop for the institution that best meets the needs of that package.

All your reasons for using a financial institution are related to each other. It is easier to study them separately. In this chapter, you will learn about what financial institutions can do for you and how to decide which institution to choose. Chapter 18 covers credit in more detail.

FINANCIAL SERVICES

Jessie is thinking about choosing an institution where she can cash her paycheck, save some money, and write a few checks of her own. Although she knows that financial institutions offer credit and investment services, she does not need these services yet. Jessie does want an institution that is easy to use. She also wants to be sure her money is safe.

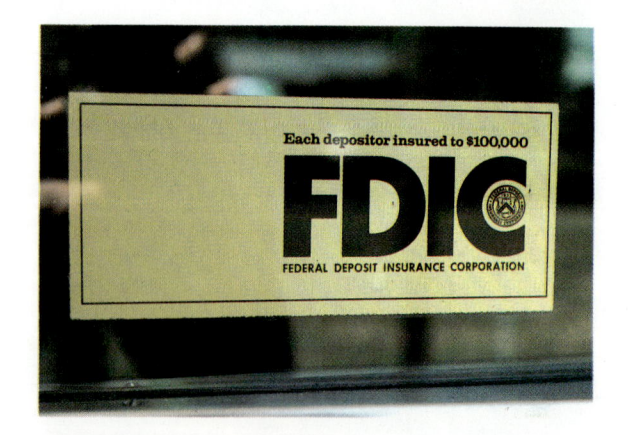

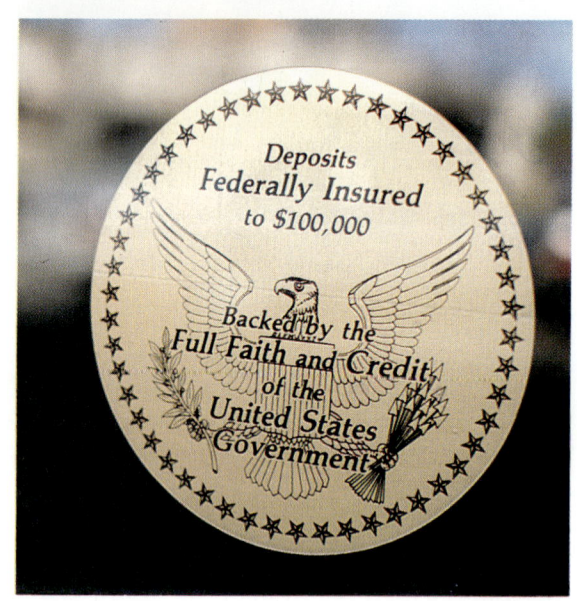

You should check for signs such as these in a financial institution to make sure your money is safe.

Getting Cash and Paying Bills

There are a number of ways to get cash and pay bills. With a regular checking account, you deposit money in an institution. You then write checks to pay bills or get cash when you need it. A **check** is *a written order directing a financial institution to pay money to someone.* Many more payments are made by check than are made in cash.

The kind of check Jessie wants to write is called a personal check. Financial institutions

Chapter 17 Purchasing Financial Services

also offer other kinds of checks, such as certified checks and cashier's checks. One special kind of check is a traveler's check. This kind can be cashed easily at great distances from home. That way, travelers do not have to worry about carrying large amounts of cash. If traveler's checks are lost or stolen, the institution that issued them will replace them. They are easier to use when traveling than personal checks; many businesses will not accept personal checks drawn on out-of-state financial institutions.

Financial institutions also offer some services Jessie does not need right now. If she ever plans a trip abroad, she will need foreign currency. She must exchange American money for the money of the country she is visiting before she can buy anything there. Fortunately, she can go to a financial institution, either in America or in another country. There she can exchange one kind of money for the other. Financial institutions charge a small fee for this service.

Convenience

Some financial institutions are more convenient than others. After you evaluate an institution's service, consider the conveniences it offers:

- Location. Is the institution or one of its branches near your home, school, or job? The location of automated teller machines is also important.
- Hours. Is the institution open when you need it? Some institutions are open later than others, and windows outside the institution are often open later than the institution itself. People can walk or drive to these special windows. Automated teller machines usually can be used many more hours than the regular institution. Most are open 24 hours a day.
- Special services. Are there services that make banking easier? Look for services such as telephone transfer and direct deposit. Your financial institution may also make it easy to move money from one account to another.

Safety

Making sure your money will be safe is another concern when comparing financial institutions. Thirty years ago, an employee em-

Figure 17.1 Deposit Insurance for the Four Main Types of Financial Institutions

Types of Institutions	Source of Insurance	Maximum Amount Insured
Commercial bank	Federal Deposit Insurance Corporation (FDIC)	$100,000
Savings and loan association	Savings Association Insurance Fund (SAIF)	$100,000
Mutual savings bank	FDIC *or* state insurance fund (maximum varies)	$100,000
Credit union	National Credit Union Administration Share Insurance (NCUA)	$100,000

bezzled $2 million from the bank where friends of Jessie's grandmother formerly had their money. So much money was missing that the bank had to close. This kind of thing does not happen very often. Luckily, when it does, most depositors get their money back because it is insured. This type of insurance is called **deposit insurance**. It is *a guarantee that depositors will get back a certain amount of money if a financial institution fails*. At one time, deposit insurance covered only the first $10,000 of a depositor's money. Anyone who had more than that deposited in an institution that failed lost it. Today, the limit on how much is covered by deposit insurance is $100,000 per depositor. People with more money than the limit should open accounts at more than one financial institution, keeping no more than $100,000 in any one institution.

All insured financial institutions post signs stating that they are covered by deposit insurance, which is supplied by federal and state governments. Most of the places where you might want to open accounts are insured. Because this insurance costs depositors nothing, you should be sure you have it. (Figure 17.1 describes the insurance plans for the four main types of institutions.)

Jessie's grandparents have told her about the Great Depression of the 1930s, when many financial institutions failed and there was no deposit insurance. Jessie appreciates the way this insurance protects consumers' money.

Financial institutions offer yet another kind of security—safe deposit boxes. A **safe deposit box** is *a metal container for valuables, such as important papers and jewelry*. Financial institutions keep safe deposit boxes in their vaults. Two keys are needed to open a safe deposit box. The institution has one, and the customer has the other. Only the person who has rented the box, plus others listed on a special form, has access to it. Institutions provide special rooms where renters of safe deposit boxes can have privacy when they put in or remove items from the box. The rental fees for safe deposit boxes vary according to the size of the box.

Credit

Financial institutions lend money in many different ways. As time goes on, Jessie may need a number of these credit services:

- Car, home improvement, appliance, or furniture loans. These help people buy high-priced goods and services. They are usually paid back within two to five years.
- Home mortgage loans. These are loans that allow people to buy homes. People pay back mortgage loans over a long period of time, such as 30 years.
- Personal loans. These are loans people use to meet goals such as going to college or taking a trip. They are paid back in a shorter amount of time than mortgage loans.
- Bank credit cards. These cards can be used to charge purchases. People can also use bank cards to borrow money.
- Overdraft privileges. Usually, an overdraft is a check written for more money than someone has in an account. People can arrange for the financial institution to lend them money if they overdraw their accounts. This kind of loan is similar to a short-term personal loan.
- Passbook loans. These are personal loans in which people borrow against the amount they have in their accounts.

Saving and Investing

When people save money in financial institutions, their money earns interest. Interest is the fee the bank pays depositors for the use of their money. Interest payments make money grow. Another way to make money grow is to invest it. **Investing** is *using money in a way that people hope will be profitable*. Examples of investments are stocks and bonds. Investments usually pay higher returns than savings accounts. Investing, however, is riskier than saving because growth is not guaranteed. In fact, investors run a risk of losing all or part

Chapter 17 Purchasing Financial Services

of the money they have invested.

There are many different ways of saving and investing:

- Savings. One way to save is to open a savings account. You can also buy United States savings bonds. When you buy such a bond, you are letting the government use your money. Either way, your money earns interest payments.
- Stocks and bonds. When you buy stock, you become part owner of a business. When you buy a bond, you lend money to a business or government.
- Mutual funds and investment clubs. By buying a share in a mutual fund, you place your money into an investment pool managed by experts. An investment club is an informal way of pooling your money with other people and investing as a group.
- Real estate and collectibles. You can buy land or buildings and hope that they increase in value. You can do the same with goods that people collect, such as rare coins and antiques.
- Investment counseling. You can pay someone to help you manage your investments or advise you.
- Trust services. You can create a **trust**, which is *property someone manages for the benefit of someone else.* For example,

Home mortgage loans make it possible for people to buy homes. The payback period is often as long as 30 years.

Jessie's grandmother could leave money to Jessie in her will but name Jessie's mother as the person responsible for managing the money until Jessie is no longer a minor.

DECIDING WHERE TO PUT YOUR MONEY

Jessie knows that the first step in deciding what to do with her money is figuring out what services she really needs and wants from a financial institution.

Making a Plan

A checking account would make it easier for Jessie to pay bills and buy things through the mail. She also wants to continue to have a savings account. She knows she may have to pay certain fees for these accounts.

Jessie is making a list of other services she might want from a financial institution. One thing she might do is ask her employer to deposit her paycheck directly to her account. She would also like to find out whether a teenager can use an automated teller machine. When she is older, she would like to apply for a bank credit card so she can charge some of the things she buys. Some of the services she wants are much more important than others. Knowing what she wants most will make it easier for Jessie to choose where to put her money.

Four Main Choices

Today, there are many sources of financial services. Most people use one of the following four:

- commercial banks
- savings and loan associations (S&Ls)
- mutual savings banks
- credit unions

Commercial banks are *profit-making banks authorized by the state or federal government to offer a full range of financial services*. They are also known as *bank and trust companies* or *community banks*. Commercial banks are found in all states. Most of them are corporations, which means that they are owned by the people who own their stock. Someone could own a share in such a bank without having any money in that bank.

Commercial banks offer a variety of savings and checking accounts, direct deposit, bank by mail, various kinds of loans, automated teller machines, investment services, and trust services.

Savings and loan associations (S&Ls) are *savings institutions that once offered only savings accounts and home mortgages but now provide a full range of financial services*. Most S&Ls are owned by their members. When people put money in these institutions, they get shares of ownership. For this reason, S&Ls are sometimes known as *cooperative banks*. Other names for S&Ls are *building and loan associations, savings associations,* and *homestead banks*. Some S&Ls are corporations. S&Ls are authorized by state or federal law and are found in all states. They offer checking accounts and several kinds of investments. They may also offer EFT cards so customers can make direct deposits.

Mutual savings banks are *banks owned by their depositors with the goal of encouraging savings*. They are found in only 18 states and Puerto Rico. Organized under state laws, these banks offer services similar to those of commercial banks. Mutual banks make loans. They also offer checking accounts, bank credit cards, and savings accounts. In some states, they can also sell low-cost life insurance.

Credit unions are *savings and lending cooperatives formed by people with a common bond*. The people may have the same employer or belong to the same labor union. Credit unions make loans to their members at lower interest rates than are offered through other financial institutions. They can also provide savings accounts with slightly higher interest rates than other financial institutions can. Credit unions

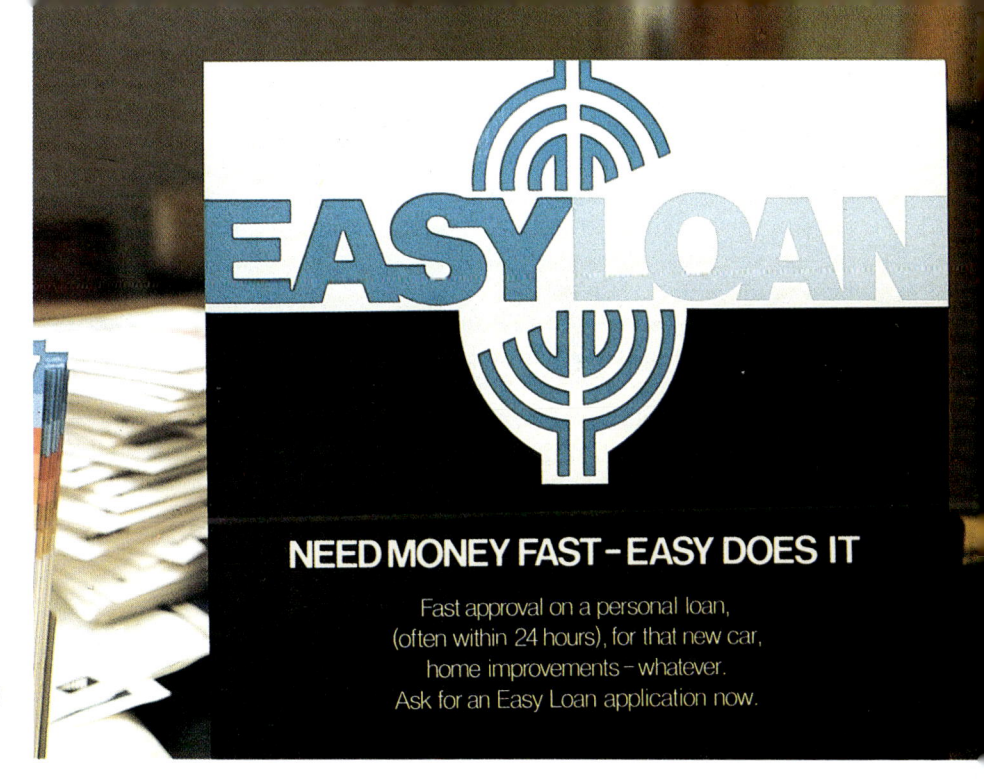

Various signs posted in a financial institution can tell you about the benefits and costs offered by the institution.

NEED MONEY FAST – EASY DOES IT

Fast approval on a personal loan, (often within 24 hours), for that new car, home improvements – whatever. Ask for an Easy Loan application now.

can afford to pay more interest and charge less for loans because they are not intended to make a profit. Many credit unions offer the services involved in electronic funds transfers. Credit unions are found in all states. They can be used only by members.

Other Possibilities

There are other places that offer financial services. People can charge their purchases at many stores and gas stations. People can also borrow money from finance companies. Some automakers and home builders also lend money to people so that they can buy cars and homes. These sources of credit are discussed more fully in Chapter 18.

You can save or invest money in places other than financial institutions. For example, some people invest their money in stocks and mutual funds. People can also invest in real estate or jewelry.

Checking accounts are offered with certain kinds of financial investments. (Usually, these investments must be large ones.) You write checks drawn on the amount you have invested. You can buy traveler's checks from several sources. You can get money orders at different places including the post office. You do not have to have an account in order to buy money orders. Like checks, money orders are safe to send through the mail. You can also get cash at sources other than a financial institution. Some retail stores cash paychecks for their customers. Many supermarkets cash personal checks for customers who have special check-cashing cards issued by the store.

A FINAL DECISION

Jessie first decided which financial services were most important to her. Then, she went to some financial institutions to find out what they could do for her. She also wanted to find out how much their services cost.

Sometimes, she asked people who worked at the institutions to explain their services. She also examined the signs posted in the buildings. Some of the signs listed current interest rates for different kinds of accounts. Others indicated that the institutions had deposit insurance. Jessie also picked up booklets that told her the minimum amounts needed to open certain kinds of accounts and also listed the fees the institutions charged. Now, she must make a decision.

Two institutions close to Jessie's home look promising. One of them is First City Bank, and the other is State Savings Bank. She knows that they both have deposit insurance because she saw the signs that said so in their windows. She also found out that they both accept direct deposit of paychecks. The people who work at both banks seem polite and friendly.

Jessie needs to make a decision based on the services the banks offer and the fees they charge. Both banks have checking accounts that pay interest. However, she needs at least $500 to start one of these accounts, and she does not have that much money. First City Bank will charge a fee of 25 cents for each check she writes. State Savings does not charge for checking unless an account has less than $200 in it. The institution will charge her $5 a month whenever the account has less than the minimum in it. Jessie knows she will not write many checks. She also knows that she will often have less than $200 in her account. That means that a checking account at First City will save her money.

Jessie looked at savings accounts next. She decided to find the answer to three questions: How much interest does each bank pay? How often does each bank compound the interest? When will my money begin to earn interest?

It turned out that both banks paid the same interest rate, but they compounded interest in different ways. **Compounding** means *adding interest to the balance so that the interest also starts to earn interest*. The more often interest is compounded, the more money an account makes. State Savings compounds interest every day. First City compounds every month. This means that a savings account at State Savings will earn more.

Jessie's money would also begin to earn interest at different times in each bank. First City pays interest only on money in the account at the end of each month. State Savings pays interest from the day money is deposited until the day it is withdrawn. Jessie may need to take money out in the middle of the month. At First City, she would lose interest if she did this.

Jessie also considered convenience. Both institutions offer EFT cards. State Savings, however, has more branches, which would make banking easier. Jessie decided to open accounts at State Savings Bank because the advantages it offers outweigh those at First City.

THE FEDERAL RESERVE SYSTEM

The bank Jessie is planning to use is one of many thousands of financial institutions across the country. More than 52 billion checks were written in 1989 by customers of these institutions. Many of these checks are sent from one state to another. How do financial institutions in different states deal with transferring funds and checks to one another? They use the services of the **Federal Reserve System**, *the central banking system of the United States*. The Fed, as it is often called, was established by Congress. The Fed has the job of seeing that funds and checks are processed quickly and efficiently. The Fed processes about 35 percent of the checks written in the United States. Through the Fed's nationwide wire transfer system, institutions can transfer millions of dollars in payments each day. Without the Fed, financial institutions would have to mail checks to each other. This would cost thousands of dollars each year. Fees for financial services would have to go up to pay the extra costs. The Fed, then, saves money for both financial institutions and their depositors.

Chapter 17 Purchasing Financial Services

MAIN POINTS

- You can compare financial institutions to find the one that offers the most for the least money.
- Financial institutions compete for your money by offering different services and different interest rates and by charging different fees.
- Financial institutions offer services such as electronic funds transfer, which includes automated teller machines, telephone transfers, and direct deposits.
- Financial institutions provide convenient and safe ways to get cash and pay bills.
- Federal deposit insurance and safe deposit boxes offered by financial institutions keep your money and valuables safe.
- Financial institutions offer special services for borrowing, saving, and investing.
- The main sources of financial services are commercial banks, savings and loan associations, mutual savings banks, and credit unions.
- Other sources of credit include stores, finance companies, and automakers. You can also invest through stocks, mutual funds, real estate, or collectibles. You can get cash substitutes at retailers or at the post office. Some retail stores will cash personal checks for regular customers.
- The Federal Reserve System saves financial institutions and depositors money by assisting in the transfer of interstate checks and funds.

Terms to Know

Use the following terms to fill in the blanks of the sentences below.

check
commercial bank
compounding
credit union
deposit insurance
Federal Reserve System
investing
mutual savings bank
safe deposit box
savings and loan association
trust

1. The central banking system of the country is called the _____.
2. A written order directing a financial institution to pay money is a(n) _____.
3. The guarantee that depositors will get back a certain amount of money if a financial institution fails is _____.
4. A bank owned by depositors with the purpose of encouraging savings is called a(n) _____.
5. Adding interest to the money already in an account, so that the interest earns interest, is known as _____.
6. A cooperative group that lends money and pays interest on savings without intending to make a profit is known as a(n) _____.
7. If Jessie wants a safe place to keep her valuables, she can rent a(n) _____ at a financial institution.
8. A profit-making bank that offers a full range of financial services and is usually owned by a corporation is called a(n) _____.
9. Property someone manages for the benefit of someone else is a(n) _____.
10. Using money in a way that people hope will be profitable is called _____.
11. A financial institution which is owned by depositors and which once specialized in savings accounts and home mortgages is known as a(n) _____.

Chapter Review

1. How can competition between financial institutions help you?
2. What are two services that financial institutions provide?
3. How have recent laws changed financial services?
4. What are the advantages of using checks instead of cash?
5. What are three ways that one financial institution can be more convenient for you than another?
6. How is a depositor's money protected against the failure of a financial institution?
7. What are some ways a financial institution lends money to people?
8. What is investing? Give some examples of ways to save and invest.
9. What are the four main sources of financial services?
10. What are some places other than financial institutions that offer financial services?
11. What role does the Federal Reserve play in interstate banking?

Activities

1. Write a 30-second radio advertisement for a bank or other financial institution. Choose one feature to emphasize, such as convenience or safety. Make your ad as exciting and memorable as you can.
2. Make a checklist of services to look for in a financial institution. Include topics such as interest rates, EFTs, account minimums, service charges, and the policies affecting compounding. Form search teams to visit local financial institutions to fill in the checklists. Report your findings to the class.
3. Make a list of places other than financial institutions where you could receive financial services in your community. Include places where people can cash personal checks, get credit, invest their money, and get substitutes for cash (such as money orders).

Chapter **18**

Considering Credit

OBJECTIVES

This chapter will enable you to:
- describe how credit affects our economy.
- explain how using credit is paying to use someone else's money.
- plan how to use credit.
- determine how much credit you can afford.
- relate your credit record to the amount of credit you can get.
- compare sources and types of credit.
- explain the rights of borrowers and lenders.
- compare the costs of credit from several sources.
- outline what to do if overborrowing occurs.

Lisa

I worked for my father last summer—he renovates people's homes. By working a lot of overtime, I was able to put over $1,000 in my savings account in just ten weeks. Now, I have a job after school and on weekends lifeguarding at the Y. Most of the money from this job goes to pay for clothes or gifts I charge at the department store in the mall. (My parents let me get a charge plate when they saw how well I handled the money I earned last summer.) I recently opened a checking account—I wanted to be responsible for my own bills when they came in the mail.

I've been taking the bus home from the Y, but it's a drag because the buses are so slow. I asked my parents if they would let me buy a car. They asked why. I told them about the slow buses. I also reminded them I wanted to commute to vocational school next year to learn carpentry. They agreed my reasons were good. Then my father asked, "Where will you get the money?"

The $1,000 I had saved seemed pretty small when I looked at used-car prices. I knew I'd have to get a loan, but who would give a loan to a 17-year-old high school student? Then, my mother pointed out that I already had a good credit record because I always paid my department store bills on time. A good record is the first step to getting a loan.

My department store bills were only $20 or $30 a month, though. A monthly car payment would be about another $90. All of a sudden, my credit record didn't look that impressive. My parents talked it over and said they would cosign a loan with me. I'd be making the payments, but they'd be responsible if I missed any.

I know I won't miss any payments. Each month, I'm going to put enough money aside to cover the payments, my insurance, and gas money. The stereo I've also been thinking about will just have to wait until I save up enough money. One big payment a month is all I can handle right now.

BUY NOW, PAY LATER

Lisa is beginning to learn about **credit**, or *the use of borrowed money to make a purchase*. She has a lot to learn. Borrowing is a complex matter. There are forms to fill out, references to give, and contracts to sign. When used correctly, credit can be a real help. When overused, however, it can be dangerous.

Perhaps more important than learning how to get credit, Lisa is learning a good attitude about its use. She is going to use credit for two types of purchases:

- normal purchases that are well within her budget, for which she will use her department store charge plate
- expensive items that she *needs* (the car), not that she simply *wants* (the stereo)

Lisa is using credit wisely. She has set limits on her credit purchases. She is not using credit to extend her budget, but to make large purchases that fit easily into her budget.

Before World War II, most people used cash for all purchases. If they did not have enough money, they saved until they did.

Every day, consumers like Lisa make decisions about borrowing to buy products and services. One person's decision may not mean much by itself. However, multiply that decision by millions of Americans, and you can see the effect such choices have on the economy.

Buying on credit, or "buying on time," seems to be a way of life in this country. However, until the 1940s, this was not so. Before World War II, most people used cash for all purchases. If they did not have enough cash, they saved until they did.

After the war, stores began to offer their customers "time payments." Customers could take their purchases home and make monthly payments until they paid the cost of the item. These credit plans caught on, and credit buying began to boom.

Now, consumer credit is measured in billions of dollars. (Figure 18.1 shows consumer credit outstanding.) Whole industries depend on credit for their growth. Few people would be able to buy houses, cars, or major appliances without using credit. Borrowing by consumers raises the demand for goods and services. Then, businesses have the desire and means to increase production. The overall effect is economic growth, which creates prosperity.

Dependence on credit can backfire, though. If credit buying slows down, companies make

295

fewer sales. Some companies have to slow down production and may even lay off workers. Whole areas of the economy may suffer.

Paying for Money

The first thing to understand about credit is that you are using someone else's money to make a purchase. Suppose you have a charge account at a store. When you charge a purchase, the store is letting you keep the cash you should have paid. When you receive your bill, however, you must pay it. Otherwise, you will be charged interest, which is the fee you pay for using someone else's money.

When interest rates are high, the cost of using someone else's money is high. For example, interest on many consumer loans in the early 1980s was about 20 percent a year. If you borrowed $1,000 to buy something, at the end of the year you would have spent an extra $200 (20 percent of $1,000) on that item.

You can think of interest as the cost of money. Financial institutions base the interest rates they charge on the amount it costs them to borrow money. These rates go up or down for several reasons. Rates may drop when financial institutions have a lot of money but receive few requests for loans. A lower rate may bring in more loan customers. Rates may rise if many people or companies are looking for loans. Then, financial institutions can charge

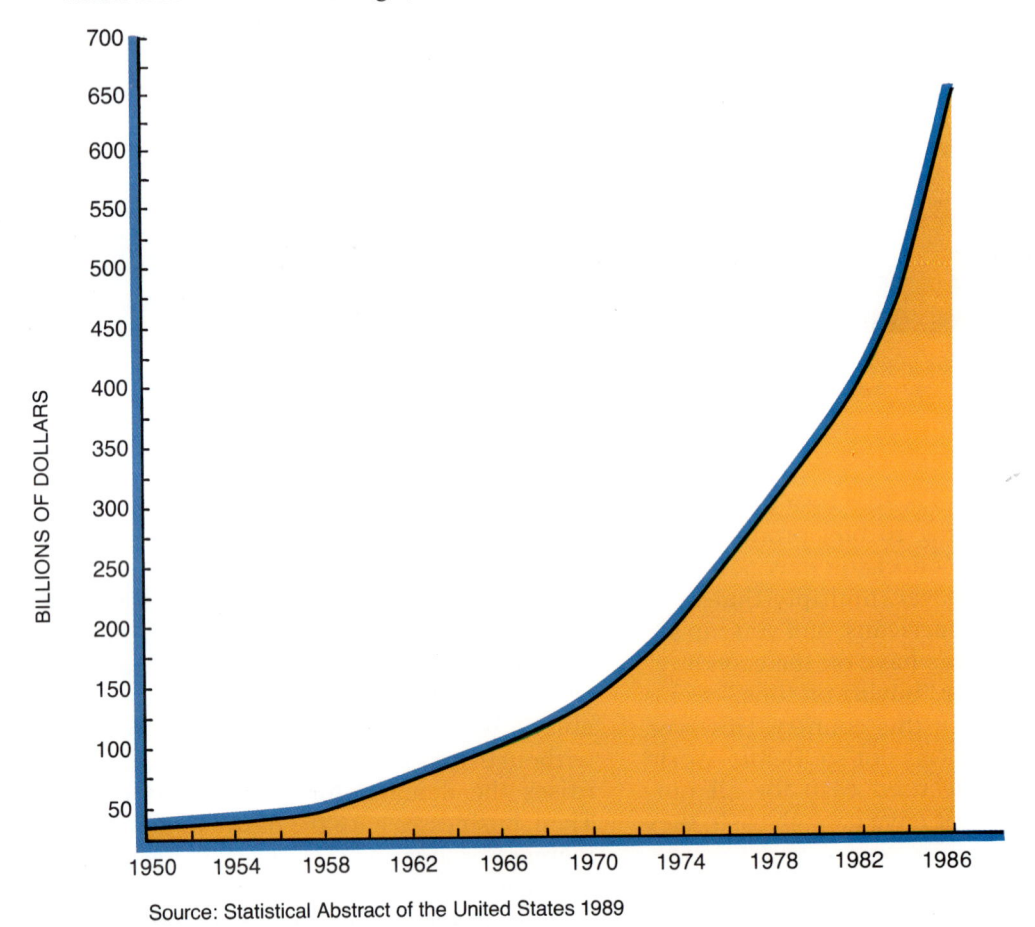

Source: Statistical Abstract of the United States 1989

Figure 18.1 Consumer Credit Outstanding

Chapter 18 Considering Credit

more because demand is greater. Figure 18.2 shows recent changes in interest rates for credit.

Credit is best understood if it is viewed in a neutral way. Thus, consumer credit is neither good nor bad. What counts is how you use credit. Used well and managed well, credit can help you live with more ease and comfort. It can also fuel the growth of the economy. Mismanaged or badly used, credit can get you into financial trouble and perhaps cause problems for the economy.

Reasons for Using Credit

Consumers use credit for four basic reasons:

- To buy a product they need right away but cannot pay cash for. Lisa does not have enough cash to pay for her car, but she does earn enough money to pay off a car loan month by month. She can use the car while paying for it. Cars or expensive appliances are often bought on credit. Most people simply do not have that much cash to pay at one time.

- Convenience. Lisa's father, Mr. Lubarsky, charges lumber and supplies so he will not have to carry large amounts of cash or try to get personal checks accepted.

- Emergencies. If Mr. Lubarsky's truck breaks down on an out-of-town job, he might use a credit card to pay for repairs.

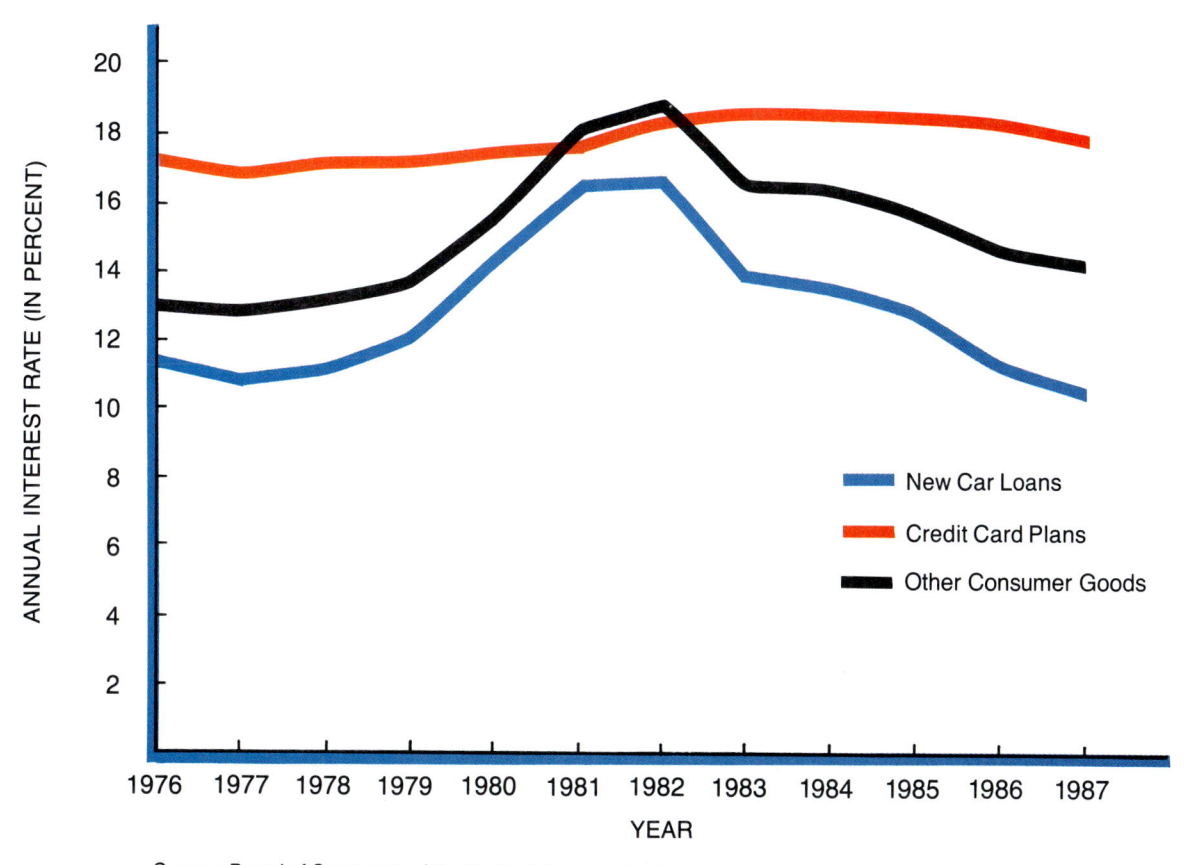

Source: Board of Governors of the Federal Reserve System

Figure 18.2 Interest Rates on Types of Credit for Commercial Banks

- To build a good credit history. A consumer builds a good credit history by repaying debts on time. A lender looks at this record before deciding to lend to the person. Lisa has begun to do this by paying her charge account bills on time. Other credit sources may become available to her if she keeps up her good record.

Using Credit Wisely

Using credit is a decision you can make through the consumer process. First, you need to make a plan. Next, you need to collect information on the types and sources of credit. Then, you need to compare costs and terms. Finally, you can choose whether or not you want credit, where to get the credit, and what terms fit your budget.

A CREDIT PLAN

With a careful credit plan, you can get the most out of your resources. Here are some tips for such a plan.

- Use credit only when necessary. Ask yourself if you really need the item. Do not use credit to buy on impulse. Ask yourself if the purchase is worth the extra cost of

Many people find credit useful for emergencies such as unexpected car breakdowns.

buying on credit. Make sure that the monthly payment will fit comfortably into your budget.

- Compare credit and cash costs. Some stores offer discounts for cash. If a store does offer cash discounts, you may want to postpone your purchase until you can pay with cash. A store might also have a lay-away plan. You can place an item on lay-away with a deposit, then pay a certain amount each week. When you have paid the total cost, you can have the item. There is usually no interest charge for this plan.
- Shop around. Take advantage of the competition among lenders. You may be able to find a better deal by checking with several lenders.
- Reduce credit costs. Be aware of the total cost of the loan. The higher the down payment and the shorter the repayment time, the less money the loan will cost you. Note also that store accounts do not charge interest if you repay before the due date.
- Read credit agreements with care. Ask questions if you do not understand the terms of the credit. Do not sign anything that you have not read or that has spaces to be filled in later. Keep a copy of every contract you sign.
- Do not hurry. Take your time. Do not let a salesperson pressure you.
- Do not take on more debts than you can manage. Buy costly products gradually, not all at once. That way, you can repay debts more easily.

BORROWING ABILITY

Businesses want to give you credit. It is the function of financial institutions to make loans. Other businesses, such as stores and restaurants, find sales improve if they offer credit. So credit is available. How much you can get

Workers at a consumer reporting agency collect information about a buyer's credit history.

depends on how much you can afford and how well you use credit.

How a Creditor Learns About You

A creditor uses information about your past use of credit to decide about your present request. You provide some of these facts when you fill out an application form, which asks you to describe your past and present jobs, income, property, and credit references.

A creditor may get more information from a consumer reporting agency. This firm *collects data about consumers, such as where they live and work and their bill-paying habits, then sells it to other firms.* The collection of data a consumer reporting agency sells is called a **con-**

sumer report. The most common type of consumer reporting agency is the credit bureau. When you apply for credit, the creditor may ask the agency for your credit history. The agency does not decide who will get credit—it only provides information. The creditor makes this choice, based on your application, the information from the agency, and the creditor's own standards.

What Creditors Look For

The main thing a creditor wants to be sure about is that you can repay the debt. The creditor considers the three Cs of credit: character, capacity, and capital.

Character. **Character** refers to *the way a borrower can be expected to act*. A person with good character is honest, responsible, and has good judgment. To assess character, creditors ask the following questions:

- Have you had credit before? Did you repay on time? Were there late charges? Was there repossession or failure to pay?
- Have you promptly paid other obligations, such as rent or phone bills?
- Do you have personal references? Do other people think you are trustworthy?

Capacity. **Capacity** is *a borrower's ability to pay back a loan*. Creditors ask:

- How much money do you earn?
- What is your current job?
- How long have you held your job?
- Do you have other sources of income?
- How much do you already owe?

Capital. **Capital** is *property owned by a borrower*, either cash savings or material possessions. Property can be used to pay back loans, if necessary. Creditors ask:

- How much do you have in savings or checking accounts?
- How long have you had these accounts?
- Do you own a house, a car, or other valuable property?

Based on your answers to these questions, a creditor will assign you a **credit rating.** This is *the category of risk you present as a potential*

Creditors are interested in the property a borrower owns, because property can be used to pay back a loan, if necessary.

borrower. The better your credit rating, the easier it will be to obtain credit.

Creditors sometimes use a point system to create credit ratings. Often, these ratings are made by computer. In such cases, loan customers fill out a form, but they are not interviewed by a loan officer. Points are given based on certain facts about the applicant. Having a phone, keeping a bank account, and living at one address for over two years are given points. Points are also awarded for working for the same employer for two or more years, owning a car, and having paid-up charge accounts. These indicators measure an applicant's stability. The higher the applicant's point total, the better the credit rating.

Sometimes, credit is not granted. Here are some of the reasons why creditors refuse loans.

- No identification. Creditors will not lend to a person without identification. An applicant needs a driver's license, social security card, birth certificate, union card, or employee identification card.
- Floating address. Creditors look for stability. If an applicant's address is a post office box number, a boarding house, or an address in care of a friend, he or she will not be considered a good risk. The creditor wants to feel sure the applicant will be around long enough to repay the loan. An applicant who is new in town may prove stability by providing the creditor with a previous long-term address and some character or employment references.
- Erratic job history. An applicant who has changed jobs often or has only seasonal work will be looked at as a poor risk.
- Age. For an applicant under 18 (or 21 in some states), a creditor may ask that an older person cosign the loan. A **cosigner** is *someone who promises to repay the loan if the borrower fails to do so.*
- Bad credit history. This means the applicant has a record of late payments, unpaid loans, or repossessions.
- No credit history. If an applicant has never had credit, she or he may find it hard to obtain a large loan.

Creditors have different standards. It is possible to be turned down by one creditor and accepted by another. The best way to convince a creditor to give you credit is to have a good credit history. Of course, to have a good credit history, you have to convince a creditor to give you credit. You can do this if you start small. Remember that Lisa charged only $20 or $30 a month at the department store, *but she always paid back on time.* Although her purchases were small, she established that she could be trusted with credit. That was her first step toward greater credit.

You may be able to do what Lisa did. If you can qualify for a charge account at a retail store where you like to shop, you may want to open an account. Use the account to charge small items you would normally buy with cash. Keep in mind that the purpose of the charge account is to establish a good credit history. Do not use the card for expenses that are beyond your budget.

Because you are not handling cash, it may at first seem that you are walking out of the store with items you got for free. The bill will come, however, and it is important to repay promptly. Making yourself aware of the interest charges for late payment can motivate you to make your payments on time.

FINDING OUT ABOUT CREDIT

Before making any decision, a consumer needs to gather facts about the options. A decision about credit is no exception to this rule. A potential user needs to know a lot about the kinds and sources of credit.

Types of Credit

There are two basic types of credit. **Closed-end credit** involves *credit that is extended on a one-time basis, with a specified repayment* *schedule*. This type of credit is also called *installment credit* because the loan is repaid in monthly installments. The rates for installment loans may be fixed or variable. *Fixed-rate loans* have the same interest rate and the same monthly payments over the length of the loan. *Variable-rate loans* have interest rates that can change up or down depending on economic factors. As a result, their monthly payments can go up or down. Car loans, home mortgage loans, and major appliance loans are examples of closed-end credit.

The time for repaying loans can vary greatly. A major appliance loan of $1,000 might take two years to repay. A new car loan of $8,000 might take four years, and a mortgage on a house might take 30 years.

Large loans require **collateral**, which is *something of value that the borrower pledges to ensure repayment*. If the loan is not repaid, the lender can take the collateral. A loan involving collateral is a *secured loan*. *Unsecured loans*, like personal loans, do not require collateral. A person might get a personal loan for college fees or to pay for a trip.

Open-end credit is *credit that is extended on an ongoing basis*. It is also called *noninstallment credit*. Lenders set a **credit limit**, *the maximum amount of credit a borrower is allowed in open-end credit*. The credit limit differs for each borrower. As payments are made, more purchases can be made. On a $500 limit, you can charge up to $500. If you have already charged $350, you can charge just $150 more. When you make your monthly payment, you can repay the whole debt or just a part.

There are several types of open-end credit:

- Service firms. Most doctors, dentists, and utilities give free credit but ask that bills be paid on time, usually within a month.

- Store charge accounts. There are two kinds. An **open charge account** *requires the borrower to pay for the purchase at the end of the billing period, usually a month*. A service charge is added if the account is not paid in full. If the account continues to have a balance due, after several months the service charges might amount to more than the purchases cost. A **revolving charge account** *lets a customer charge up to a set limit and repay in installments of a minimum amount each month*. Interest is charged on the unpaid balance.

- Bank credit cards. These, such as MasterCard and Visa, are issued by banks and used for purchases and for getting cash. Cardholders may have to pay a yearly fee. The cardholder receives a monthly bill. If the entire amount is paid before the bill's due date, no interest is charged. Other-

Bank credit cards can be used to obtain cash as well as to charge purchases.

Chapter 18 Considering Credit

wise, interest is charged on the unpaid balance. The lender sets a limit on how much can be charged.

- Bank debit cards. These cards work more like checks or cash than credit cards. When they are used, money is transferred from the buyer's account to the seller's account. Therefore, a direct transfer of funds takes place. There is no interest charge.

- Travel and entertainment cards. These, which include American Express, Diner's Club, airline cards, and gasoline cards, work like bank credit cards. The user may be able to choose to pay the whole bill with no extra fees or to pay a part each month with added charges. In some cases, the cardholder may have to pay the entire balance. Cardholders must pay a yearly membership fee for some of these cards.

- Overdraft protection. With **overdraft protection**, *a financial institution guarantees a depositor's check up to a fixed sum even if the check is written for more money than is in the account.* The amount of protection is set by the financial institution. Interest may be charged until the overdrawn amount is repaid.

- A single-payment loan. *A loan in which the whole sum plus a finance charge is repaid in one payment* is a **single-payment loan**. This type of loan is not often available, but it carries lower interest rates.

- A passbook loan. A **passbook loan** is *a cash loan from a financial institution using the money in a passbook savings account as collateral.* The interest on a passbook loan is often low because the loan is secured by the person's savings account. The person can be expected to repay because his or her own savings are at risk.

Credit Sources

The four main types of financial institutions offer credit as follows:

- commercial banks (all kinds of credit, including bank credit and debit cards)
- savings and loan associations (mortgages; home improvement, auto, and personal loans; bank credit and debit cards)
- mutual savings banks (all kinds of credit, including bank credit and debit cards)
- credit unions (personal loans, auto loans, and home mortgage and home improvement loans)

Interest rates vary. In the past, credit unions offered the lowest rates and commercial banks the highest. Because the government has eased regulations on banking, rates are now more competitive. As a result, you must shop carefully. Standards for granting credit also vary. Credit unions, however, lend only to their members.

Here are some other sources of loans:

- Finance companies. This is a term used for several different types of institutions. In general, **finance companies** *give credit to merchants and make personal loans.* Some finance companies take care of loans for businesses that want to give their customers credit. Other companies provide second mortgage loans to homeowners. Still others make unsecured personal loans to individuals. Finance companies will lend money to poorer credit risks than a financial institution will. These companies usually charge slightly higher interest than other types of financial institutions do.

- Industrial banks. *Lending institutions that were originally set up to offer loans to industrial workers* are called **industrial banks**. Industrial banks now lend to everyone and function like commercial banks. Their rates are higher than those of other kinds of institutions, but lower than those at finance companies. Industrial banks may require a cosigner for a loan.

- Retail stores and service businesses. Stores, gas stations, and airlines offer credit accounts, usually without interest charges if the debt is repaid within a certain time.

Before 1975, single women were often refused credit even if they had jobs.

However, you may not be able to charge all goods or services this way. A service station may let you charge gas, but not new brakes. Of course, many retailers allow you to use bank credit cards, normally for their full range of products or services.
- Life insurance policy. Interest on these loans is low. However, until an insured person has been paying premiums for several years, the amount available to be borrowed may be low, too. If the loan is not repaid, the debt is deducted from the policy benefits. You do not have to surrender your policy to get at the cash value. You can borrow against it at a rate of interest provided for in the contract.
- Families. Relatives may be the easiest sources of loans—no applications, no references, and little or no interest. Family members may not have enough cash for a large loan, however. Also, what starts out as a friendly agreement can strain a relationship if the loan is not repaid on time. Putting the agreement in writing may prevent trouble.

Here are two credit sources to avoid:
- Pawnbrokers. These are creditors who lend money at a legally specified rate of interest on valuable possessions left as security. The valuables can be redeemed from the pawnbroker within a certain time. Otherwise, the pawnbroker sells the items. It is better to establish credit and apply for loans from more regular sources than to bring your property to a pawnbroker.
- Loan sharks. These are criminal dealers who offer cash loans for extremely high interest rates. Borrowers who miss payments may be threatened with physical harm. Avoid loan sharks at all times.

THE RIGHTS OF BORROWERS AND CREDITORS

There are seven major federal credit laws detailing the rights of creditors and borrowers. One of the laws also involves banking. Here are the main points of each.

1. The Consumer Credit Protection Act of 1969 is also known as the Truth-in-Lending Act. This law protects consumer credit rights. As amended in 1982, the act contains the following main points:
    - For open-end credit, the creditor must

state the annual percentage rate (APR). This is the actual percentage cost of credit on a yearly basis. The creditor must also explain the method used to calculate the finance charge, which is the total dollar amount a borrower must pay to use the credit. In addition, the creditor must state when finance charges start. All credit terms must appear on monthly statements, which must also state the buyer's rights under the Fair Credit Billing Act. Businesses must not mail or issue unrequested credit cards. Finally, cardholders are liable for only $50 if a credit card is lost or stolen. Cardholders are not liable for any unauthorized charges once they report the theft or loss of the card.

- For closed-end credit, the creditor must tell you the finance charge in writing and before you sign any agreement. The creditor must also tell you the APR. Creditors must list the total of principal and interest as the "total sales price." The creditor must also state the amount and conditions of penalties for late payments or early repayment.

2. The Fair Credit Billing Act of 1975 describes how to settle billing disputes with users of open-end credit:
   - Billing dispute. If you feel that a bill is incorrect, write to the creditor. The letter must be received by the creditor within 60 days of the date the creditor mailed the first incorrect statement to you.
   - Disputed charges. Until the dispute is settled, the creditor cannot close the account or give it to a collection agency. You do not have to pay the disputed part of the bill until the matter is settled.
   - Settlement. When the dispute is settled, if you are wrong, you must pay the disputed amount and any finance charges.

3. The Fair Credit Reporting Act of 1971 protects consumers from wrong or outdated credit information in their credit file that is used to deny them credit.
   - Incorrect or outdated information. You have a right to the name and address of the consumer reporting agency that gave information used by a business that denied you credit, insurance, or a job. The same right applies if a business decides to raise the cost of credit or insurance.
   - Credit file. You have the right, with proper identification, to find out what is in your credit file. You can have the agency reinvestigate your credit standing if you feel there is outdated or incorrect material in your file. The agency may decide not to change the information. In that case, you can submit a statement explaining your side to be placed in the file. The agency will send this new information to lenders who refused credit.

4. The Equal Credit Opportunity Act of 1975 forbids a creditor to deny credit for discriminatory reasons. This act was passed primarily to protect women. Before the act, single women were often denied credit even if they had jobs. Married women were not able to build their own credit records, even if they managed the family money. To prevent unfairness, this law originally stopped creditors from denying credit based on sex or marital status. In 1977, the act was broadened. Now, it also forbids refusing credit because of age (as long as the applicant is of legal age), race, religion, or nationality, because you are on welfare or social security, or because you exercise your rights under federal credit laws.

5. The Fair Debt Collection Practices Act of 1977 was enacted to protect consumers against abusive, unfair, or deceptive conduct by collection agencies. A **collection agency** is *a company that collects debts owed to others*. Part of what the agency recovers goes to the creditor. The agency keeps the rest. The act says these agencies cannot use threats, annoyance, or abuse to collect debts. They cannot falsely claim that you have committed a crime and will be arrested. They cannot make other false claims. They cannot, for example, say that your wages or property will be taken away.
6. The Consumer Leasing Act of 1976 is designed to help consumers compare the costs and terms of various leases. These leases are for cars, furniture, and other major products. Because of this act, consumers can compare the cost of leasing an item with the cost of buying it on credit. The act also requires the terms of any lease to be clear.
7. The Electronic Funds Transfer (EFT) Act of 1978 applies to the use of automated teller machines and bank cards. It states that financial institutions do not have to explain why they are denying an application for an EFT card, unless the application is part of a request for credit. In that case, the action comes under the Equal Credit Opportunity Act, and the institution must explain its denial.

COMPARING CREDIT COSTS

Lisa had built a good credit record at a retail store. Her parents advised her to wait to buy a car until summer, when she would be earning more money. In the meantime, Lisa was saving money for the down payment on her car.

When she began to work full-time again the next summer, she started to shop for credit to buy a car. Among her options were a loan from a financial institution and a car dealer's loan. How could Lisa decide which option was best?

Lisa could compare costs by looking at the finance charge and the APR. As you know, the finance charge is the total dollar sum she would pay to use the credit. The APR is the credit cost as a yearly percentage. The federal laws listed earlier do not set interest rates, but they did help Lisa compare credit costs by requiring creditors to give full information.

Lisa also had to consider how long it would take to pay off the loan. The more time it would take, the higher the total cost. Of course, the more payments there were, the less each payment would be. And Lisa had to wonder about the future. What if her capacity to repay changed? She might want to go to school full-time after a year or so of working. How would she meet her car payments then?

Lisa had to weigh these facts and shop with care to find the best terms. She could have decided that the cost of credit right then was too high. She had already put off buying the car for almost a year, and she really did need a car for her future plans. She decided to use credit—with care and after much thought—to get what she needed.

TOO MUCH CREDIT

What happens if, for some reason, you take on too much credit? Perhaps you have lost your job and cannot continue the payments on your car. Maybe you were expecting an increase in pay that did not come through. What should you do?

If you find that your overborrowing has gotten out of hand, the first thing to do is stop buying on credit. This may sound simple, but it is difficult for some people. It requires self-control that they are not used to exercising. You may need to cut up your credit or charge cards in order to stop using them.

If paying your debts on time is impossible, the next step is to contact whoever gave you credit. Do not avoid your creditors. Explain the situation to them. Most creditors will try to

Chapter 18 Considering Credit

help you work out some arrangement to repay what you owe.

Your next step is to find a reputable credit counseling service. Creditors may be able to recommend a good agency. This might be a financial institution, a nonprofit consumer credit counseling service, or a family service agency. All these sources offer advice on how to pay off debts.

Overborrowers can also obtain a **debt consolidation loan**. This is *a high-interest loan for a sum that settles all of a person's short-term debts*. The idea is to boil down many monthly payments to one smaller payment. The consolidation loan payment is less than the total payments for the other debts, but the loan takes longer to pay off. Also, much of the monthly payment goes to pay the interest on the loan. At least the payment itself is manageable.

If this step does not work, cars or appliances may be repossessed from overborrowers who cannot meet their credit payments. **Repossession** means *the creditor takes back the item bought on credit*. The consumer loses the money paid on the loan as well as the item. The consumer also loses his or her good credit rating, which makes it hard to borrow in the future.

Bankruptcy is a last resort for a consumer. If a person declares **bankruptcy**, *a court sells his or her property (except for some items protected by law) and uses the proceeds to pay the borrower's creditors*. Declaring bankruptcy removes all debt, but it makes getting credit nearly impossible for a long time afterward.

As you can see, overborrowing can be cured, but the cure can be a painful one. The best remedy for it is prevention. Follow the steps in this chapter. Plan your credit use. Know how much credit you can handle. Be realistic about your earning power. Get information on the credit available to you. Make sure you know the costs and terms of any credit arrangements you agree to. Ask questions if you need to. And use credit wisely, or do not use it at all.

MAIN POINTS

- Consumers use credit to get things they need immediately but cannot pay cash for. They also use credit for convenience, in an emergency, and to build a good credit history.
- There are two things to watch out for when considering credit. First, credit usually costs money. Second, abusing credit can cause serious problems.
- Decisions about credit should be made through the consumer process. Creating a credit plan promotes wise use of credit.
- Creditors decide whether to grant credit on the basis of information they get from the applicant and from consumer reporting agencies.
- Creditors look for the three Cs of credit when evaluating an applicant: character, capacity, and capital.
- Creditors consider your past borrowing, financial assets, work record, and residence. They want to assess your earning power, stability, and trustworthiness.
- Types of credit include closed-end, or installment, credit and open-end, or noninstallment, credit.
- There are many sources of credit. These include various kinds of financial institutions, finance companies, retail and service businesses, life insurance companies, and family members. Pawnbrokers and loan sharks should be avoided.
- Seven laws govern the rights of borrowers and creditors. The Consumer Credit Protection Act says lenders must state all finance charges and describe the cost of credit in terms of its APR. The Fair Credit Billing Act describes how to settle billing

disputes with open-end credit. The Fair Credit Reporting Act says consumers have the right to find out what information is in their credit file and to ask to have it corrected or updated. The Equal Credit Opportunity Act forbids discrimination in the granting of credit. The Fair Debt Collection Practices Act forbids abuse by debt collection agencies. The Consumer Leasing Act helps consumers compare leases. The Electronic Funds Transfer Act explains banks' responsibilities to their EFT customers.

- Comparing credit costs allows consumers to tell what the true costs of a loan will be and which creditor will give them the best deal.
- Planning how to use credit safeguards against overborrowing. Overborrowing can lead to a consolidation loan, repossession, or bankruptcy.

Terms to Know

Use the following terms to fill in the blanks of the sentences below.

bankruptcy
capacity
capital
character
closed-end credit
collateral
collection agency
consumer report

consumer reporting
   agency
cosigner
credit
credit limit
credit rating
debt consolidation loan
finance company

industrial banks
open charge account
open-end credit
overdraft protection
passbook loan
repossessed
revolving charge account
single-payment loan

1. The maximum amount a person can charge is called the _____.
2. A loan that is repaid in one payment, which is made up of the amount borrowered plus the finance charge, is called a(n) _____.
3. The way a borrower can be expected to act is referred to as _____.
4. The borrower must pay for a product at the end of the billing period, usually one month, with a(n) _____.
5. A loan that uses a savings account as security is called a(n) _____.
6. A company that collects debts owed to others is called a(n) _____.
7. Credit that is extended on an ongoing basis is called _____.
8. A person will have difficulty getting credit again for a long time after declaring _____.
9. If Mr. Lubarsky signs a bank note with his daughter, he will be responsible for any missed payments as _____.
10. If a borrower does not pay for an item bought on credit, the item can be _____.
11. A bank that guarantees a depositor's check up to a certain limit is offering _____.
12. Your ability to repay a loan from current earnings is your _____.
13. An account that lets a borrower charge up to a set limit and repay in installments is called a(n) _____.
14. A company that will lend to a poorer credit risk than a financial institution will, and at higher interest, is called a(n) _____.

15. Credit that is extended on a one-time basis is called _____.
16. Banks that were set up to help workers are called _____.
17. A person who overborrows may seek to repay all of her or his loans with a(n) _____.
18. You have the right to examine the credit information that has been gathered about you by a(n) _____.
19. The category of risk that a creditor assigns to a potential borrower is called a(n) _____.
20. Something of value pledged by the borrower to secure repayment to the creditor is called _____.
21. Property owned by a borrower is known as _____.
22. The use of borrowed money to make a purchase is known as _____.
23. A _____ tells whether or not a person pays bills on time.

Chapter Review

1. How did "buying on time" become so popular in this country?
2. Explain how consumer credit can help and hurt the economy.
3. What are the four reasons that people use credit? Give an example of each.
4. What does a consumer take into consideration when making a credit plan?
5. What are the three Cs of credit? Define each one.
6. What can you do to help your credit rating?
7. Describe the two basic forms of credit.
8. List five sources of credit or loans.
9. Name one law that states the rights of borrowers and creditors. Tell what the law says.
10. What might be the results of overborrowing?

Activities

1. Obtain credit application forms from several stores in your area. Examine and discuss the forms in class. Look for requirements that are the same on all the forms. Discover the special requirements of each store.
2. Conduct a telephone interview with an employee of a consumer reporting agency in your area. Ask questions about the ways in which credit ratings are determined.
3. Suppose you are thinking of buying a car. Gather the facts about credit you could get at a local financial institution and at a used-car dealer. Compare these credit sources using the total finance charge and the APR. Which would you choose? Why?
4. Investigate people's life-styles before credit became so popular. Interview people who grew up before World War II. What changes have they noticed that can be traced to credit buying?

Chapter **19**

Buying Insurance

OBJECTIVES

This chapter will enable you to:

- discuss how insurance works.
- decide what auto insurance you need.
- explain what homeowner's insurance you need.
- name the purposes and kinds of life insurance.
- summarize the types of health care coverage.
- describe how to shop for insurance.
- list some ways to reduce risk.

Jim

Insurance—that's the magic word around our house these days.

My dad has always been big on insurance. I know he has life insurance so that if anything ever happened to him, our family would have enough money. He also has insurance on our house in case there's ever a fire or something like that. Right now, he's looking over our health insurance. Last month, one of our neighbors had a health problem that almost wiped out her savings because her health insurance didn't cover her costs. My dad wants to be sure something like that doesn't happen to one of us. He's thinking about increasing our coverage. He's also looking into the possibility of joining one of those new health maintenance organizations that he's been hearing about.

It all seems very complicated to me. I used to figure I was too young to think about life and health insurance, but Dad says I should understand something about it. That way, if there is an emergency, I'll have a better idea of the kind of protection we have.

One kind of insurance I do have to know about is car insurance. I finally saved enough money to buy a car. That meant I had to save enough money to buy car insurance, too. It's against the law in our state to drive without insurance. I talked it over with Dad, and he explained that there are many different kinds of policies to choose from. There are also many different companies offering car insurance.

Whichever company I choose, I know my insurance is going to cost a lot. It seems I'm in the highest risk group—single males under the age of 30. I get some kind of break because I took driver education in high school, but even with that, I can't believe how much I'm going to have to pay.

I can go to my Dad's insurance agent if I want to, but I think I might get a better deal if I shop around. Anyway, I need someone to explain to me exactly what kind of insurance I need and what my choices are. I have an appointment with one insurance agent today, and two others tomorrow. I also have to check out the companies to see how quickly they settle a claim. Some companies are a lot faster than others, so that's going to affect my decision about insurance, too.

HOW INSURANCE WORKS

Jim is mostly concerned with insuring his car right now, but he is curious about other kinds of insurance, too. He knows that insurance can cover not only cars but also other kinds of property. Insurance can pay for lost income and medical expenses as well. In this chapter, you will learn about how insurance works, what kinds of insurance you can get, and how you can get it.

If nothing ever went wrong, no one would need insurance. Accidents do happen, however, and illness and theft can cost people large amounts of money. People need insurance to protect themselves from these kinds of risks. **Risk** is *the chance of loss.*

Insurance shifts risk from one person to a group. Insurance companies can tell how much risk the whole group faces. One individual may not get sick in a year, but the insurance companies can figure out how many people out of 100 will probably get sick in that time. You can see how this works by tossing coins. If you toss a coin once, you do not know if it will come up heads or tails. If you toss it 100 times, you know that it will come up heads about half the time and tails about half the time.

Insurance companies know that, say, 10 people out of 1,000 will have an accident within a year, but they do not know which ones they will be. The accidents may cost those 10 people a great deal of money—perhaps more than they can afford. Insurance is a way of sharing the risk among the whole group. With insurance, each person pays a little money, and no one runs the risk of losing a large sum of money.

The money that a person pays for insurance is called a **premium.** In exchange for paying premiums, that person gets protection. An **insurance policy** is *a written contract that explains the nature of the protection*. The policy says what is covered, how much the insurance costs, and how long it will last. *The person who buys the policy* is called a **policyholder.**

How much people pay for insurance depends on many things:

- The chance of loss. Young male drivers get into more accidents than older male drivers. Jim may have to pay more for auto insurance than his father does.
- The number of people sharing the risk. The more people who are insured, the lower the cost will be for each of them. That is why group health insurance policies, for

Insuring a home worth $30,000 will cost less than insuring one worth twice that amount.

example, are cheaper than a policy for one person.
- The cost of claims in the past. Insurance companies need to make a profit. The more money they have paid out on a certain kind of policy in the past, the more they will charge for that kind of coverage.
- The characteristics of people. How old people are, where they live, and what they do for a living are some of the things that may affect what they pay for insurance. For instance, an older person may have to pay more for medical insurance than a younger person would. The chances are that the older person will have more medical bills.
- The value of what is insured. The more something is worth, the more it costs to insure it. Buying insurance for a house worth $100,000 will cost more than buying it for a house worth $50,000.
- The deductible. The **deductible** is *the amount of a loss that an insured person agrees to pay*. The insurance company agrees to pay the rest. For example, Jim could buy auto insurance with a $100 deductible. If he had an accident, he would have to pay the first $100 of the repair bill. The insurance company would pay the rest.
- State laws. Some insurance is regulated by the state. Laws cover how much insurance a person must have and how much an insurance company can charge for it. For example, a state might require auto insurance.

DECIDING WHAT YOU NEED

Before Jim chooses an auto insurance policy, he needs to find out how much coverage his state requires. Then, he needs to make some decisions. He could choose a policy that provides the minimum coverage, or he could decide to pay more in return for better coverage.

Homeowner's insurance covers such possibilities as a passerby slipping on an icy walk in front of your house and suing you.

His decisions will be based in part on what kind of coverage he is *likely* to need and what coverage he is willing to risk he will *not* need. You will make the same kinds of decisions when you buy insurance.

People can also buy homeowner's insurance to cover their homes and belongings. (Renters can buy similar insurance.) To do this, homeowners need to know what their homes and property are worth. They should know what it would cost to replace something that is stolen or damaged. They also need to protect themselves in case a person is accidentally hurt on their property. **Liability** is *responsibility for injury to other people or damage to their property*. Someone who falls down on your slippery floor could claim that you were at fault. Liability insurance would help pay the bills if a court agreed.

Life insurance provides income for children when a parent dies. It also provides income for one spouse when the other dies. Someone with a family needs to think about how much money family members would need. In general, a more costly insurance policy would mean

Under no-fault auto insurance, insurance companies pay for financial losses—no matter who caused the accident.

the family receives more money when the insured person dies.

People buying health insurance face many choices. They need to decide which kinds of health insurance they need. They also need to decide how much insurance they can afford. If their employers have a health insurance plan, they need to decide whether to buy more coverage. Jim's parents are facing this decision. People may also decide to get special insurance to cover dental bills or maternity care. Some employer health plans cover dental and maternity care.

PROTECTION ON THE ROAD

Jim knows he has to buy auto insurance for his new car. Each state has its own laws requiring drivers to have a minimum amount of insurance. That way, if someone causes an accident, the insurance will pay at least part of the costs of any injuries or damage.

Jim plans to shop around for car insurance. In his state, companies can set their own rates. Even in states where rates are set by law, people need to decide how much coverage they want to buy, and they can choose the insurance company they think will provide the best service.

Who Pays for Car Accidents? Laws based on assigning blame for an accident require the person who causes an accident to pay for the damage. That person's insurance company would pay all or part of the costs. This kind of law leads to many lawsuits to determine who was at fault. The suits can be costly and lengthy because it is hard to tell who was responsible for many accidents.

Because of these problems, some states passed no-fault auto insurance laws. Under **no-fault auto insurance**, *your insurance company pays for your financial losses no matter whose fault an accident was*. If your insurance company does not cover all your bills, you can still sue the other driver. With no-fault insurance, people usually do not have to sue. One aim of no-fault is to speed the payment of medical bills and lost income. Another aim is to reduce the cost of insurance.

Kinds of Coverage. Liability coverage is one kind of auto insurance. This pays for injury to other people or damage to their property. Many states have laws requiring people to buy at

Chapter 19 Buying Insurance

least a certain amount of this kind of coverage. For example, Jim's state requires him to have at least enough coverage to pay up to $30,000 to one person hurt in an accident he causes. His insurance must pay up to $60,000 if more than one person is hurt. He also needs insurance to pay at least $10,000 for property damage caused by his car.

Jim also has to buy insurance that will pay his medical bills if he is hurt in an accident. This kind of insurance also covers anyone riding with him.

Collision coverage *pays for the insured person's car repairs if there is an accident.* Sometimes, cars are damaged too badly to be fixed. When that happens, the insurance company pays the owner what the car is worth. Collision coverage is the most costly form of auto coverage. It may make up as much as 70 percent of the total premium. Because of the expense, people usually drop collision coverage when a car gets older and its value drops. People often get collision coverage with a deductible. They might agree to pay as little as $50 of the cost of an accident, or they might pay a much higher deductible, such as $2,000.

Despite the laws, a few drivers have no insurance. To take care of the possibility of being

Because motorcycle riders have a higher risk of serious injury than car drivers, their insurance rates are higher.

in an accident with one of these drivers, some people buy **uninsured motorist protection**. This *covers the cost of injuries caused by a driver who has no insurance.*

Comprehensive coverage *protects your car from theft and other kinds of damage.* This kind of coverage is required for cars purchased with loans. Comprehensive coverage pays for damage caused by a flood or fire. Also, if vandals damage your car, comprehensive coverage would pay for repairs. Comprehensive coverage does not include every problem you could have, however. For example, if someone stole a tape deck or CB radio from your car, the loss probably would not be covered by your insurance. You can obtain extra coverage by paying an additional premium.

Wage loss coverage *pays some or all the income people lose if they are hurt in an accident.* It is required in states with no-fault laws. Another kind of insurance is **substitute services coverage**. This *pays other people to do what an injured person can no longer do.* For example, if a parent is hurt, she or he might not be able to care for a child. This kind of insurance would pay the cost of hiring someone else to do it. If you own a motorcycle, you need to buy some of the same kinds of insurance as you would for a car, but your rates will probably be much higher. The reason is that motorcycle accidents are more likely to cause more serious, and thus more costly, injuries.

How Rates Are Set

Jim knows that he will pay high auto insurance premiums. He will have to pay more than people who live in some other states, and he will have to pay more than his father does. Although these differences may not seem fair, they are based mostly on the chances of an accident happening to him and the likelihood that it would be costly if it did happen. Rates are set based on the following factors:

- Your location. Insurance costs more in a city because there are more accidents in urban areas than in rural areas.
- Your age. Younger people pay more than older people. Single males under age 30 and single females under 25 pay the highest rates because they are involved in the most accidents.
- Your sex. Men are involved in more than twice as many accidents as women. This is partly because men drive more than women do, but it does mean that men pay higher premiums.
- Your marital status. Married drivers have fewer accidents than single drivers, so single people pay more.
- Your type of car. You will have to pay more if you have a more expensive car because it will cost more to repair.
- Your driving habits. A salesperson who uses a car for work every day will pay more than someone who uses a car only now and then.
- Your driving record. Good drivers pay lower premiums than people with a record of traffic tickets and accidents.
- Your training. Young drivers who have passed certified driver education courses may pay less than those who have not taken the course.
- Your deductible. The larger the deductible, the lower your premium will be. With a large deductible, however, you will pay more of the bill if you have an accident.
- Theft rate of the car. For example, theft claimed for the 1987 Volkswagen GTI occurred at more than ten times the average rate for all 1987 models.

PROTECTING YOUR PROPERTY

Cars are not the only things people protect with insurance. They also buy insurance for their

Chapter 19 Buying Insurance

homes and other property. **Homeowner's insurance** *pays for damage to people's own property*. It also pays if someone is hurt while on their property.

A homeowner's policy might cover the following:

- Your home. If your home is damaged by a fire or storm, the insurance will help pay for repairs. Even if an airplane crashed into your house, you would be covered. A garage or other outbuilding would also be protected.
- Living expenses. You might need to stay at a motel and eat meals in restaurants while your house is being fixed. The insurance will pay part of the bill.
- Personal property. The things you have in your house or apartment are also covered. Even if you take something out of your home, it could be covered. For example, if your camera is stolen while you are on a trip, the insurance would help you pay for a new one. You can buy extra coverage for something especially valuable such as jewelry and silverware.
- Liability. If someone who comes onto your property is hurt, the insurance will help to pay the bills.
- Damage to other people's property. You might accidentally damage someone else's property. For instance, if your ladder fell onto your neighbor's car, the insurance would pay for the repairs.

Homeowner's policies have two methods of payment. One kind pays the actual cash value of anything you must replace. **Actual cash value** is *what something is really worth*. The other kind of payment is based on the **replacement cost**. This is *what it will cost you to buy something new*. For instance, suppose your clothes are damaged by smoke from a fire next door. If you are paid only what the clothes are worth now, you will not receive enough money to buy similar new clothes. Because the clothes have been worn, their actual cash value is lower than the cost of new clothing. Insurance based on replacement costs would pay you enough money to replace your wardrobe.

Another thing to look for in a policy is exclusions, losses that are not covered. Damage from floods, for example, might not be covered in a particular policy. Do not sign any policy until you know what is—and is not—covered. Also, find out how quickly the company pays if you file a claim.

Keeping a list of your belongings will help you know what was lost if you ever have a robbery or fire. Record the serial numbers and the cost of valuable items such as TV sets. It is also a good idea to take photographs of the things you own. Keep the list and photos in a safe place, preferably not in your home.

LIFE INSURANCE

Many working people support not only themselves but other people as well. Parents support their children. Some children support their parents. One spouse who works may support the other who does not. When a working person dies, the other people he or she supports still need money to live. Life insurance is intended to protect them. It can also pay the debts of the person who died.

A **beneficiary** is *a person named in a life insurance policy to receive payments when the insured person dies*. Before buying a policy, a person needs to estimate how much money will be needed by the people who depend on her or him. This estimate helps determine how much life insurance to buy. A policy that pays more usually costs more. The insured person's age and health also affect the cost of the insurance. Premiums increase with age.

Kinds of Life Insurance

Some life insurance policies are intended only to provide income when someone dies. Others combine this protection with savings plans that the insured may live long enough to use. Often, the savings plans provided with insurance do not make as much money as other kinds of investments would. Some people like the way buying some types of insurance forces them to save money. Others prefer to buy insurance without a savings feature and look for better ways to invest their money. Basically, there are three types of life insurance: term, whole life, and endowment.

Term life insurance is *life insurance payable to a beneficiary only when an insured person dies within a specified period*. It does not include a savings plan. After a certain amount of time (called the term) is up, the insurance ends. The premiums for a term policy will usu-

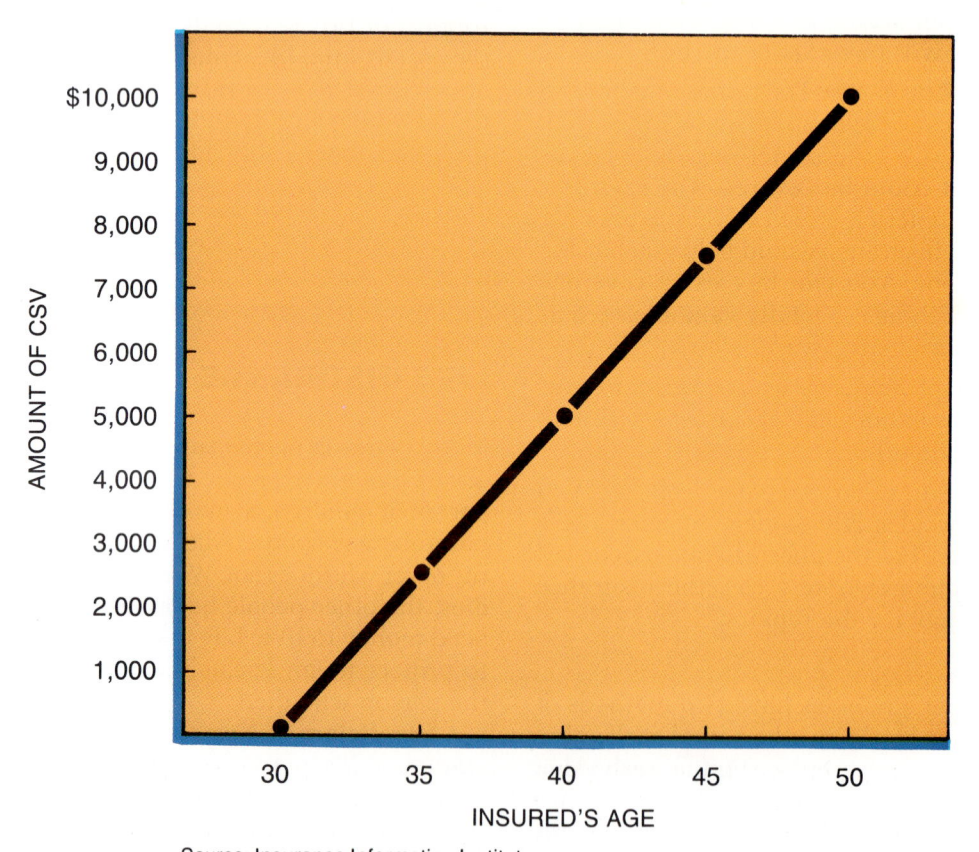

Source: Insurance Information Institute

Figure 19.1 Growth of the Cash Surrender Value for Whole-Life Insurance Bought by a 30-Year-Old Man

Figure 19.2 Comparing Life Insurance Plans

Type of Insurance	Advantages	Disadvantages
Term	Low cost for younger insured; renewable policies can extend period of coverage; convertible policies allow insured to change plans.	Coverage only for limited period; no savings; premiums increased as insured ages.
Whole life (or ordinary life)	Coverage remains throughout insured's life; builds savings; source of loans; premiums stay same during length of policy.	Premiums paid throughout insured's life; higher premiums in early years than term; savings do not earn as much as other investments; benefits lower if savings borrowed and not repaid.
Limited payment	Same as whole life *plus* premiums end at agreed-upon time.	Same as whole life *plus* premiums higher than whole life.
Universal life	Combines term coverage with chance of higher earnings; insured chooses amount going to savings; insured can increase coverage.	Premiums higher than for other types; earnings still not as high as other investments.

ally increase as the insured person grows older. This is especially true if the policy is renewed for another term. People with children may want life insurance only for the years when the children depend on them. Term insurance can be a good choice for them.

Whole life insurance is *life insurance payable to a beneficiary at the time of death of the insured, whenever that occurs*. The premiums for whole life insurance are the same amount each year. There are two forms of whole life insurance: straight life and limited-payment. In **straight life insurance**, *premiums are paid every year until the insured person dies*. The other kind of whole life policy is **limited-payment life insurance**. *Premiums are payable for a specified number of years or until death, if death occurs before the end of that period*. All premiums are paid within maybe 10 or 20 years or by the time the insured reaches age 60.

Some of the cost of whole life insurance goes toward savings. The policy builds up a **cash value**. This is *the money someone gets back if he or she stops paying for a policy*. It is also possible for policyholders to borrow money against the cash value. If they do borrow money this way and do not repay it, the policy is worth less than it was. Figure 19.1 shows the growth of cash value for whole life insurance.

Endowment insurance *combines savings with term life insurance*. After a set time, if the person who has the policy is still alive, she or he

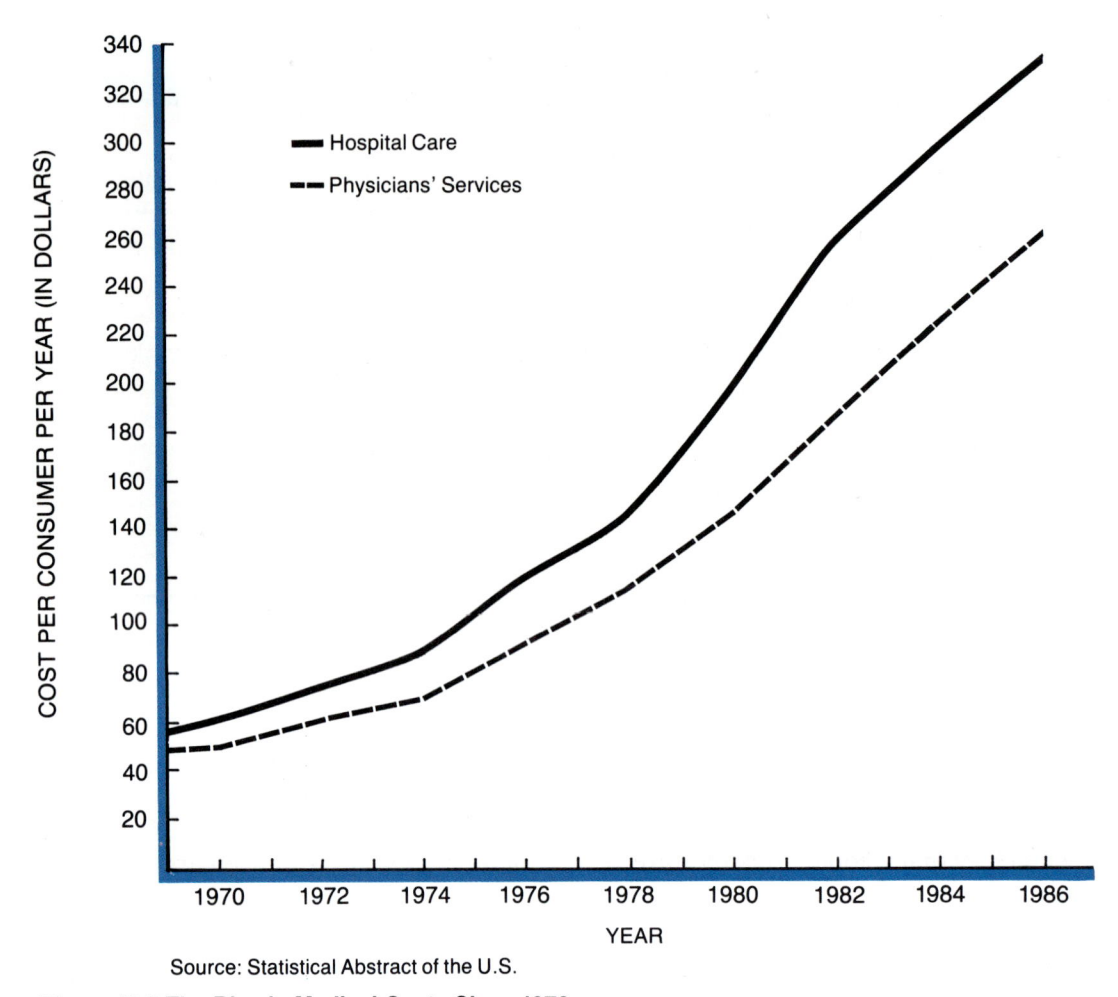

Figure 19.3 The Rise in Medical Costs Since 1970

Source: Statistical Abstract of the U.S.

is paid an agreed amount of money. If the insured person dies before the set time, the amount is paid to the person named as beneficiary in the policy. People could use this kind of insurance to save for a child's education or for retirement.

Universal life insurance *combines term life insurance with a chance to invest.* With this kind of insurance, people can decide how they want their money invested. They can change the amount of money they want to invest. They can also increase their coverage. It is a more flexible way to invest than endowment insur-

ance is. Figure 19.2 compares the different types of life insurance.

If Your Premium Isn't Paid

Not paying your life insurance premium on time does not necessarily mean that you are not covered. Usually, you have a **grace period,** *an extra amount of time during which the insurance is still in effect*. Usually, the grace period is one month long. After the grace period, the policy is no longer in effect.

Chapter 19 Buying Insurance

If you let term life insurance lapse, you might be able to make the back payments and start coverage again. You might also have to have a new medical exam. If you let a whole life policy lapse, you have some choices. You could collect the cash value, or you could change the policy to term insurance. Another possibility is reducing the value of the policy to equal the amount of coverage that can be bought by all the premiums paid up to that time. You can also use part of the cash value to pay premiums until you can resume regular payments.

PAYING HEALTH CARE COSTS

Jim knows that his parents are looking over their health care insurance. They want to be sure that the insurance would pay most of their medical bills if someone in the family has a serious accident or illness. They are also considering adding coverage for more routine health care costs.

Health insurance *covers all or part of the costs of health care.* Doctors' bills and hospital costs can be much higher than people think they are going to be. (Figure 19.3 shows how medical costs have risen since 1970.) Having good health care coverage can make a big difference.

Most health insurance pays only part of people's medical bills. There may be a limit on how much money can be paid in one year or in a person's lifetime. Some policies provide only a certain amount of money in a particular situation. For example, some hospital insurance pays only a certain amount of money per day, regardless of how much the hospital stay costs.

Types of Coverage

Health insurance can help pay for many kinds of health care costs. The amount paid varies from policy to policy. Here are the main types:

- Medical. This kind of coverage pays for visits to a doctor's office. It also covers drugs that a doctor prescribes.
- Dental. This pays for checkups and most dental work.
- Psychological. This covers mental health care.
- Alcohol or drug abuse treatment. This covers care in drug treatment centers and visits to health care professionals.
- Home and nursing home care. This covers the cost of constant nursing care for elderly and disabled persons.

Health insurance also often helps pay for hospital stays. The following types of hospitalization coverage are available. Many have limits on how much they will pay.

- Hospital. This pays for rooms, meals, X-rays, lab fees, and other services.
- Surgical. This kind of coverage pays for operations.
- Maternity. Maternity coverage pays for the costs of having a baby.
- Emergency service. This pays for the use of an ambulance or for emergency medical care.

Sometimes, a long or serious illness can be very expensive. **Major medical insurance** is *intended to cover large medical bills.* Other kinds of insurance are used first, or people may pay smaller bills themselves. Then, a major medical plan takes over to cover the rest of the costs. Another special kind of isurance is **disability insurance.** *It pays some or all of the income people lose if they cannot work because of illness or injury.*

It is possible to get all the health insurance you need in one plan. Buying everything at once could save you money.

Regular health insurance pays your bills after you get them. Another way is to pay in advance. **Health maintenance organizations (HMOs)** work this way. *For a set payment, they provide all the medical care that members need.*

Rather than paying each time they visit a doctor, members of an HMO pay a monthly or yearly fee. When members need to go to a doctor or enter a hospital, the HMO covers the costs. HMOs pay for some services, such as regular checkups, that other plans usually do not cover. HMO policies differ. Many HMOs permit members to use only their own on-site staff. Others allow members to choose their own physicians.

SHOPPING FOR INSURANCE

One decision Jim needs to make is where to buy his insurance. He might buy from the same person his parents buy their insurance from, or he may be able to find a company that offers better rates or better service. Jim plans to compare not just price, but also the kinds of coverage offered in different insurance policies. He knows that shopping for insurance is just like shopping for anything else. He is not going to spend a lot of money on insurance without looking around for the best coverage at the best rates.

Instead of paying for each visit to a doctor, HMO members pay a yearly or monthly fee.

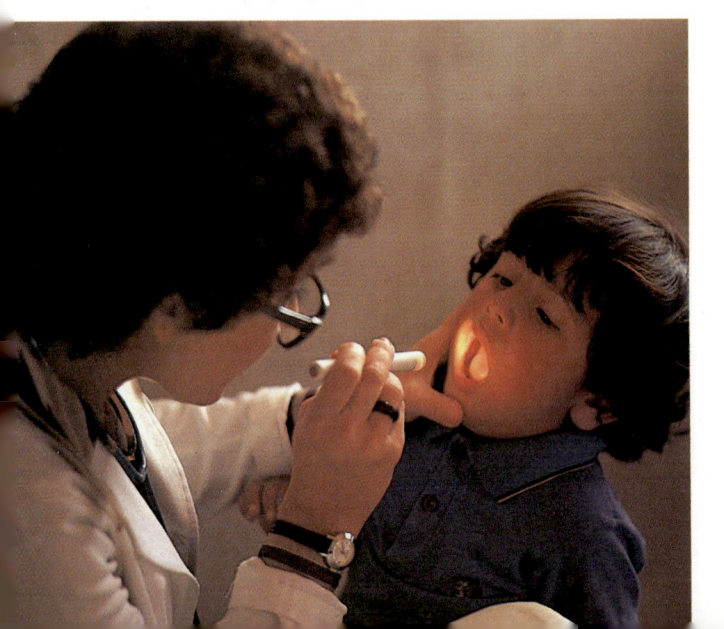

Where to Get Insurance

You can buy insurance for yourself, or you may be able to get insurance through your employer. You may also be able to get insurance through the government.

Many people buy insurance from insurance agents. Some insurance agents work for only one company. Other agents sell the policies of several different companies. Every time insurance agents make a sale, they make a commission. If you buy a more costly policy, your agent makes a larger commission. Be sure, then, to know how much insurance you really want to buy. You could also buy insurance by mail, but if you do, be careful. First, find out about the insurer's reputation. Then, find out exactly what you are getting for your money.

Some jobs offer not only salaries to workers, but also other benefits. One benefit you might get at a job is insurance. The more common kind offered at a job is health insurance, but life insurance may also be provided. You may have to pay part of the cost of the insurance you get, or your company may pay for all of it. In either case, find out if the coverage fits your needs. Also, find out if you can continue the insurance on your own if you leave your job.

The government provides health insurance, too. Medicare helps pay the health care costs of people over 65. Medicaid takes care of costs for people who cannot afford to pay their own bills. These plans help pay for both hospital and doctor bills.

You may also be able to buy health or life insurance through your financial institution or through an organization you belong to. For example, the American Automobile Association (AAA), an automobile club, offers life insurance policies to its members.

Comparing Insurance Policies

Before you buy, look at insurance policies to see how rates and coverages differ. Be sure you understand what everything in a policy means. For example, one disability policy might pro-

Buckling up is a major way to reduce your risk of injury or death in an auto accident.

vide payments only if people cannot work at all. Another might pay people if they cannot go back to their regular jobs, even though they might be able to work at a different kind of job. Another policy might have a long waiting period before payments begin.

You may want to visit a library before you buy insurance. Publications such as *Changing Times* and *Money Magazine* can give you some helpful information about insurance. Do the experts believe the kind of insurance you are thinking about getting is a good buy for a person like you? Does the company you plan to buy from have a good reputation? You should also look to see whether the laws covering insurance have changed. You can also get up-to-date information from insurance agents.

CUTTING YOUR RISKS

Having insurance when an accident or illness strikes can be very important. However, insurance is one product people buy that they would be happy never using. Some accidents or illnesses cannot be avoided, but if you are careful about safety and health, you can cut down on your risks.

You can cut the risk of being injured on the road in several ways:

- Follow speed limits. Driving faster than the speed limit is unsafe, and so is driving faster than road conditions allow. Slow down when the roads are slippery and when you cannot see very well.
- Do not mix drinking and driving. More than half of all fatal car accidents involve a driver who has been drinking. Do not let anyone you know get behind the wheel if he or she has been drinking.
- Use safety belts. Buckle up to protect yourself from serious injuries. Also be sure that small children are buckled up in special car seats. In some states, the law requires the use of safety belts and/or child restraints.
- Wear a helmet when riding a motorcycle. Remember, motorcycles do not offer as much protection as cars. This advice can help you cut your risks of serious head injuries if you are in an accident. In some states, the use of a helmet is mandatory.

You can also cut the risks to your property. One way is to be sure that smoke alarms are installed and working properly. Also, look for hazards that might cause accidents. Check for places where people might trip, and look out for electrical hazards such as overloaded sockets and frayed wires. In addition, protect yourself from burglars by locking doors and windows securely.

Another way to cut risks is to take care of your health. Preventive health care now can reduce medical bills later. Preventive health care means doing what you can to avoid illness. Eating right and staying in shape will help prolong your life. Quitting smoking is another to safeguard your health. Avoiding needless risks is also a good idea. If it is a rainy night and you were planning to drive to the mall to go shopping, postpone your shopping trip until the weather is better.

Protecting yourself from risk means both using good judgment in what you do and buying the insurance that is right for you.

MAIN POINTS

- Insurance is based on sharing risk among the members of a large group.
- How much people pay for insurance depends on the law of averages, the number of people sharing the risk, the cost of claims in the past, the age and location of policyholders, and state laws.
- Types of auto insurance include liability, collision, wage loss, and substitute services.
- Auto insurance rates depend on your location, age, sex, marital status, kind of car, driving habits, driving record, training, and the amount of the deductible.
- A homeowner's insurance policy protects against property damage and personal liability.
- Life insurance can provide both income for the people who depend on the insured person and a savings or investment plan.
- Health insurance pays for many kinds of health care costs such as medical bills, hospitalization, lost income and home nursing care.
- You can buy your own health insurance, or you may be able to get insurance where you work. The government also provides health insurance for the elderly and the poor.
- You can reduce your risks of having an accident or getting ill by driving safely, taking good care of your property, and practicing preventive health care.

Chapter 19 Buying Insurance

Terms to Know

Use the following terms to fill in the blanks of the sentences below.

actual cash value
beneficiary
cash value
collision coverage
comprehensive coverage
deductible
disability insurance
endowment insurance
grace period
health insurance
health maintenance
 organizations
homeowner's insurance
insurance policy
liability
limited-payment life
 insurance
major medical insurance
no-fault auto insurance
policyholder
premium
replacement cost
risk
straight life insurance
substitute services
 coverage
term life insurance
uninsured motorist
 protection
universal life insurance
wage loss coverage
whole life insurance

1. Insurance that pays for damage to a policyholder's own property is _____.
2. Responsibility for injury to other people or damage to their property is called _____.
3. A stay in the hospital would be covered by _____.
4. The money a person pays for insurance is called the _____.
5. Insurance that covers the rest of a large medical bill after someone has paid part of it is _____.
6. The amount it costs to buy an item to take the place of one that was damaged or stolen is the _____.
7. Insurance that pays for an insured person's car repairs if the car is damaged in an accident is called _____.
8. Coverage that pays income to people who cannot work because of illness or injury is _____.
9. If your insurance company pays for your injuries no matter who caused an accident, you have _____.
10. The amount of a loss that an insured person agrees to pay is the _____.
11. Organizations that provide all the medical care members need for a set payment are known as _____.
12. An extra amount of time to pay an insurance premium is known as a(n) _____.
13. Insurance that pays some or all the income people lose if they are hurt in an accident is known as _____.
14. Whole life insurance in which premiums are payable for a specified number of years or until death, if it occurs within that time, is called _____.
15. The money someone gets back if she or he discontinues a whole life insurance policy is the _____.
16. Insurance that pays other people to do tasks that an injured person cannot perform is known as _____.
17. Insurance that protects a car from theft and other kinds of damage is _____.
18. A combination of term life insurance with a savings plan that pays a fixed amount of money after a certain number of years is known as _____.
19. Insurance that covers the cost of injuries caused by an uninsured driver is _____.
20. A written contract that explains

insurance coverage is a(n) _____.
21. Term life insurance combined with a flexible investment plan is called _____.
22. Life insurance payable to a beneficiary at the time of death of the insured, whenever that occurs, is _____.
23. The chance of loss is _____.
24. The amount a stolen or damaged item was really worth is its _____.
25. Life insurance payable to a beneficiary only when an insured dies within a specified period is _____.
26. A person named in an insurance policy to receive payments when the insured person dies is a(n) _____.
27. The person who takes out an insurance policy is called the _____.
28. Whole life insurance in which premiums are paid every year until the insured person dies is called _____.

Chapter Review

1. Why do people need insurance? How does insurance shift risk?
2. What determines how high an insurance premium will be?
3. Why do people need liability coverage?
4. How is no-fault auto insurance different from other kinds of insurance?
5. What are some different kinds of auto insurance coverage? How are auto insurance rates set?
6. What might a homeowner's policy cover?
7. What are some of the reasons that people buy life insurance?
8. How are health maintenance organizations different from other kinds of health insurance?
9. What are three sources of insurance?
10. How can you decrease your risks of having an accident or getting sick?

Activities

1. Imagine that you have been hired to make a five-minute movie for the insurance industry. Choose a type of insurance, such as auto, property, life, or health. Write a paragraph describing the movie you would produce.
2. Conduct an insurance opinion poll to find out what people think about topics such as the difference in premiums paid by men and women, whether single people need life insurance, how well no-fault auto insurance has solved the problems it was meant to solve, and whether price is the most important consideration when shopping for insurance.
3. Find out more about HMOs by visiting one in your area. Obtain brochures that describe the services an HMO offers. Discuss the advantages and disadvantages of HMO membership in class.

Chapter **20**

It Is Your Decision

OBJECTIVES

This chapter will enable you to:

- explain recent trends in the job market.
- relate your values, goals, and skills to your roles as a worker, citizen, and consumer.
- list the steps in the decision-making process.
- describe how planning helps you use and develop your resources.
- determine the financial services, sources of credit, and kinds of insurance you may need.
- summarize the ways your decisions affect your family, your school, your community, and society as a whole.
- identify the ways your job performance affects your employer, consumers, and the economy.

Try to picture your future. Suppose someone were to make a movie about your life as it will be five years from now. What would you be doing? Would you have moved up your career ladder? Would you have changed careers? Would you be continuing your education? Would you be doing the kind of job that suits you best? How would you be filling your roles as worker, citizen, and consumer?

Suppose the movie showed you at a job interview. What kind of job would you be applying for? How would you answer the interviewer's questions about your skills and aptitudes? If you were asked whether you were good at working with other people, how would you answer? If you were asked how well you organize your time, what would you say?

Right now, are your dreams and plans for the future realistic? Perhaps you wonder whether you will be ready to make the numerous decisions that confront a responsible adult every day. Making careful decisions today—about working, about using your resources, and about cooperating with others—will help you become the kind of person you would like to be.

How well do you understand yourself today? Do you know what is really important to you and what you believe in? Have you set goals for yourself for the future as well as for this month and this year? Do you understand yourself?

Are you good at making decisions and planning to meet the goals you've set for yourself? Do you know enough about the job market and the economy to make good financial decisions? Are you willing to think about the impact your choices will have on other people at home, at school, at work, and in the economy as a whole?

Finding the answers to these questions will help you find a direction for your life. It is up to you.

DECISIONS ABOUT WORKING

Throughout this book, you have been asked to think about who you are and how you will fit into the adult world. You may have thought about what jobs you might choose, what your strengths and weaknesses are, and how to make the right decisions about the many choices you face in your future as a worker, citizen, and consumer.

Learning About the Workplace

We live in exciting times. Our way of living has changed more rapidly in the past 100 years than in all of history, and the rate of change is growing. The world will be a very different place 20 years from now in ways we can only begin to imagine.

Many of these changes will take place in the ways people work. Already, many new kinds of jobs have come into being. Other jobs have changed a great deal. Secretaries who used to type on electric typewriters now work with electronic word processors. Auto mechanics

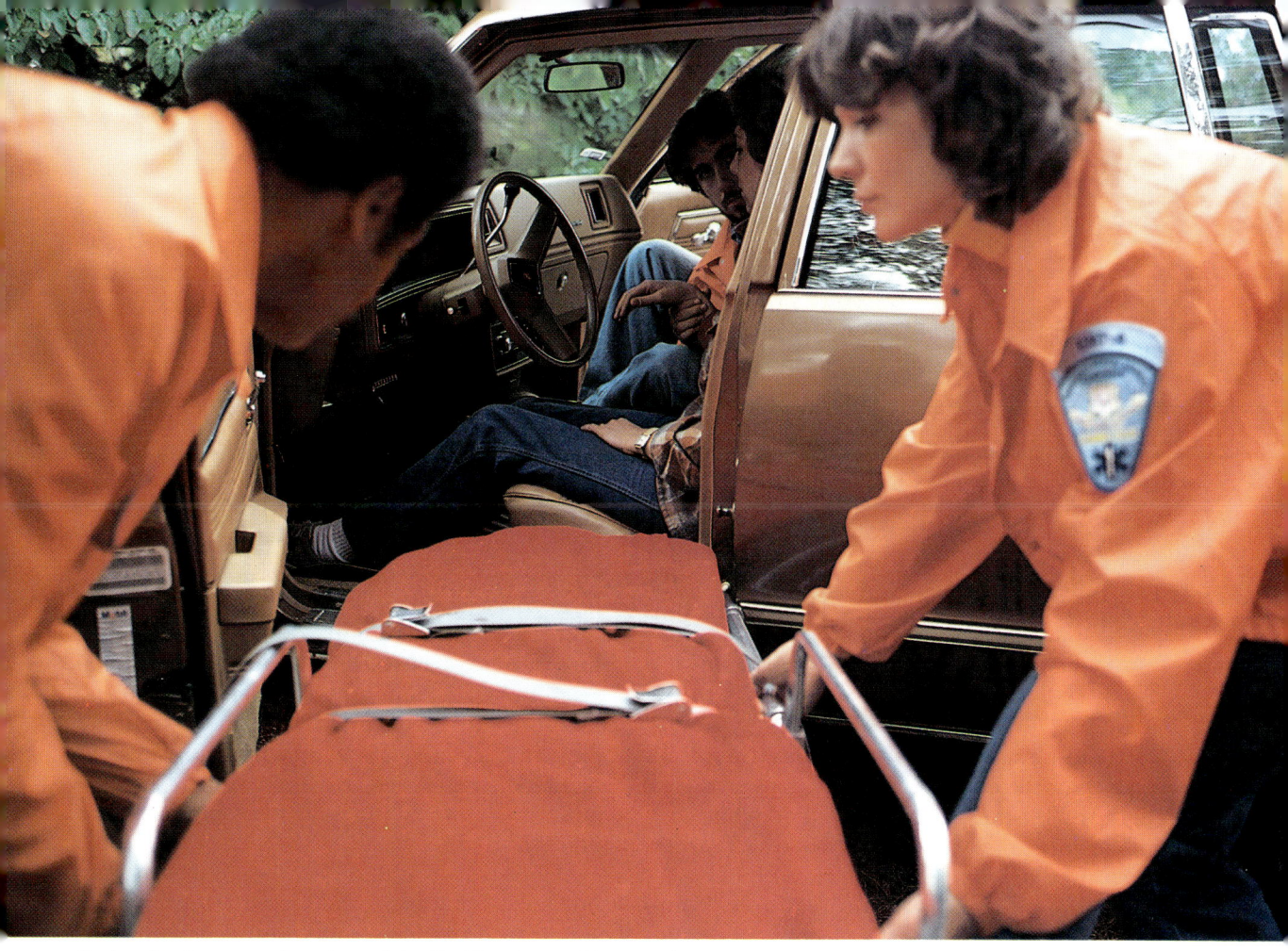

Today, far fewer workers have jobs that involve making products, whereas many more workers provide services such as health care.

now must know about computer diagnosis machines as well as about brakes and ignitions. Some jobs have disappeared. Just as ice carriers were no longer needed after the electric refrigerator was invented, some people nowadays find themselves replaced by computers or robots.

Entire fields of business are also changing rapidly. In the past, most jobs were concerned with making products. Today, most jobs provide services. Fewer people are needed to assemble cars because so much of the work is now done by machine. However, many more people are needed to provide health care services because people are living longer and growing more aware of the value of medical and dental care.

Despite these changes in the workplace, the nature of business remains the same. Whether it is a small grocery store or a large corporation, a business must still make a profit to survive. Workers must be constantly aware of what customers want and will pay for.

Keeping up with the constant changes in what people need and want is a task that is both difficult and challenging. People who can devise new products and services, such as a new kind of frozen food or a quicker way to ship packages across the country, can start new businesses. Investors who provide the money

If you are good at organizing club activities, keep that skill in mind when you explore job possibilities.

for these new businesses also play their part in helping the economy.

Just as businesses must predict what they will be able to sell, so you, in choosing a career, must predict what job fields will be most promising for you in the future. Career counselors or such books as the *Occupational Outlook Handbook* can help. You can also stay aware of trends by reading the newspapers and watching the news on TV.

After you choose an occupational field that interests you, you can begin to look at the kinds of jobs available within that field. Each field offers a wide variety of related jobs (called career clusters) from which to choose. Each of these jobs requires different skills and aptitudes. In the health care field, for example, those who like to work with people can become nurse's aides or dental hygienists. Those who enjoy problem solving might like working in a laboratory. Those who are good organizers might go into hospital management. Finding the job that is right for you means matching your own skills and interests to the ones needed on that job. Figure 20.1 shows the many kinds of jobs available in the health care field.

LEARNING ABOUT YOURSELF

To find out where you belong in the world of work, you need to understand yourself. Knowing your values, goals, skills, and aptitudes can help you choose the right kind of work rather than drifting from one job to another. Understanding and ranking your values are important steps in matching yourself to a career that will not conflict with your values. For example, if independence is something you value, you can choose work that allows you to make your own decisions. If spending time with family members and friends is important to you, you can look for a job that does not require long hours of overtime.

Once you understand your values, you can do a better job of setting your goals. When you set your goals, remember that short-range and medium-range goals are the stepping-stones to long-range goals. Knowing what you want out of life in five years will help you decide the actions to start taking now in order to get what you want.

Maybe you want to become an electrician, but you also want to own your own business someday. These two goals would mean learning about more than electricity. You might set a short-range goal of starting to learn now about how businesses operate. For example, if you are in a cooperative education program, you could start to ask the employer at your training station questions about what is involved in running a business. A medium-range goal might be to take courses in business management at a community college after you finish high school. Good advance planning can help you reach your long-term goals step by step.

Understanding your skills can also point you toward the kind of job that is right for you. If you are good at math in school, you may have already considered finding jobs that use your special skills. You may also have other kinds of skills that could help you in a future job. To find out what they are, you need to look at all areas of your life, not just your courses in school. For example, suppose that you are the person

Chapter 20 It Is Your Decision

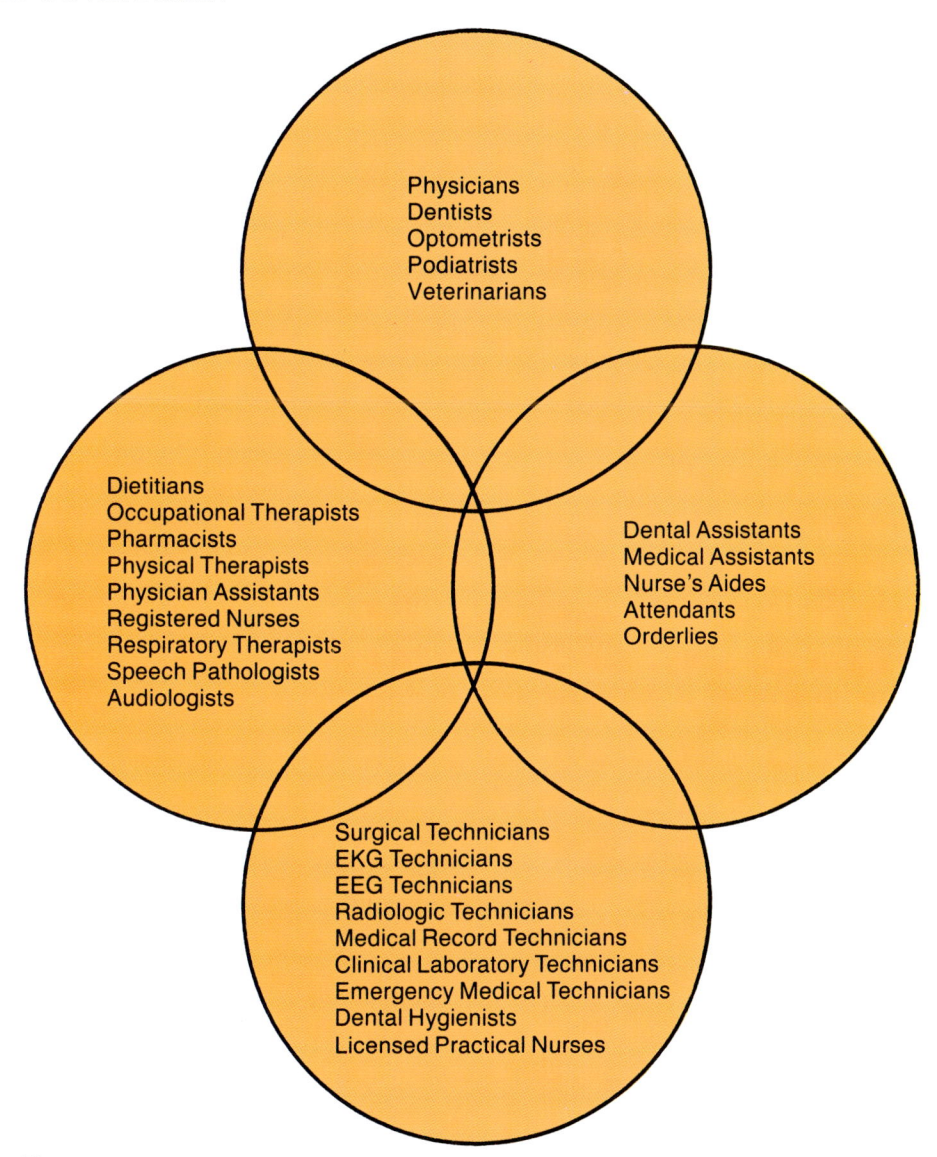

Physicians
Dentists
Optometrists
Podiatrists
Veterinarians

Dietitians
Occupational Therapists
Pharmacists
Physical Therapists
Physician Assistants
Registered Nurses
Respiratory Therapists
Speech Pathologists
Audiologists

Dental Assistants
Medical Assistants
Nurse's Aides
Attendants
Orderlies

Surgical Technicians
EKG Technicians
EEG Technicians
Radiologic Technicians
Medical Record Technicians
Clinical Laboratory Technicians
Emergency Medical Technicians
Dental Hygienists
Licensed Practical Nurses

Figure 20.1 Jobs in the Health Field

the baseball team depends on in a tight spot. Your ability to stay calm under pressure could help you in many kinds of jobs. Are you a leader in a club such as FHA or FBLA? Are you good at organizing club activities? Such skills could also open job opportunities for you.

You need to be realistic about your limitations, but you should also think about your strengths. You probably have more aptitudes than you realize. School guidance counselors can help you identify them. Family members and friends can help you recognize talents that you have not yet developed.

As you use your skills to reach your goals, you play three roles, as a worker, as a citizen, and as a consumer. One way to learn more about your role as a worker is to try a part-time job or to volunteer your time to help others. Volunteer work could help you find out about the kinds of work you like and give you a chance to do something worthwhile at the same time. Another way to make a contribution to the public good is to become informed about the issues so that you can vote in an intelligent manner. Being informed will also help you make choices in your third role, as a consumer. Informed consumers have a better chance of using their resources wisely.

In each of these roles, you have both rights and responsibilities. You are free to make many choices, but you also have some obligations. As a worker, you have the obligation to do your best. As a citizen and a consumer, you have the responsibility of speaking up.

LEARNING HOW TO MAKE DECISIONS

We all need to make hundreds of decisions every day. Most of them, such as what shirt to wear or which movie to see, are not very important. A few, however, can change our whole lives.

When faced with an important decision, many people try to put off making up their minds as long as possible. They may ask friends, or even strangers, for their opinions, stay awake nights worrying, and at last come to feel completely confused. Finally, when they cannot put off a decision any longer, they choose one alternative or the other based on how they feel at that moment. Because they are under pressure, they may make a poor choice.

If you have a system to help you make important decisions, life gets easier. You will not always make the right choice, but at least you will have a much clearer idea of what your alternatives are and why you are choosing the one you are.

You could be making several decisions at the same time. As a worker, you might be deciding whether to change jobs. As a citizen, you could be wondering if you should give your time and energy to support a political candidate. As a consumer, you might be trying to choose which car to buy.

Systematic decision making involves seven steps. First, you define your problem. For example, suppose you have a job you like that does not pay very much. Should you leave it to take a higher-paying job you may not like as well? Suppose that Jane Smith is running for mayor. She has asked you to work in her campaign. Do you have the time to devote to campaigning? Do you understand the tasks you might be asked to perform? Should you buy a new car and go into debt, or should you buy your brother's used car at a much lower cost?

Next, you identify your goals, and rank them in order so that you know which ones are most important to you. For example, do you value job satisfaction more than money? Do you think electing the best person as mayor is so important that you are willing to give up many hours of your leisure time? Would you rather have a new car or an inexpensive one?

Third, you determine your options. This means that you list all the possible solutions to your problem so that you know where your choices lie. Do you really have to choose between only two jobs, or can you find a third that is even better? Must you give up every weekend to Smith's campaign, or will one weekend a month be enough? Is there an inexpensive car you can buy that is in better shape than your brother's?

The fourth step is to figure out what would happen if you chose each of the possible solutions. You will find that each option has advantages and disadvantages. You know what the job you have is like. How will it feel to work at a new one? If the current mayor is reelected, what will life be like in your community for the next four years? Finally, if you buy the new car, how much overtime will you need to work to meet the payments?

The fifth step is to decide which choice brings the most benefits and the fewest disadvantages. Then comes the sixth step: Once you determine the best choice, it is time to put your decision into action. The new job may go to someone else if you do not take it now. The election will take place on November 5. If you do not help Smith now, she will have to take her chances without you. Your brother will sell his car to his friend Claude if you do not make up your mind by Saturday.

In the seventh and last step, you evaluate your decision to make sure you were right about its advantages and disadvantages. If your decision does not work out the way you had expected, you may be able to try another option. It is important to remain flexible and to remember that few decisions are permanent. (Figure 20.2 shows you the decision-making process at a glance.)

Figure 20.2 The Decision-Making Process

Step 1: Define your problem.
Step 2: Identify your goals, and rank them in order of importance.
Step 3: Determine your options.
Step 4: Analyze the advantages and disadvantages of each option.
Step 5: Decide which option has the most advantages and the fewest disadvantages.
Step 6: Put your decision into action.
Step 7: Evaluate your decision.

Decisions About Your Resources

You have great potential to accomplish your goals because of the resources available to you. Realizing what resources you have and appreciating the value of planning can be important steps in achieving your goals. Time is one of your most important resources. Everyone has the same amount of time, but have you noticed how some people get much more done than other people? The people who are good time managers have not given up their free time. If anything, their careful management may reward them with more free time. Getting organized will help you meet your goals, such as getting a homework assignment fin-

Playing a musical instrument is one of many skills that require practice on a regular basis.

ished or remembering an appointment. You will do a better job of finding time for some other important things, such as exercising and getting enough sleep.

Using your time more effectively will mean that you have a better chance to develop your other resources, such as your skills. It takes time to develop skills. Training a dog or designing your own clothes cannot be done very well in odd moments. If there is a skill you would like to master, such as swimming or speaking a foreign language, invest some time in finding out what is involved. Then, see if you can rearrange your schedule so that you have time to master the new skill.

Another resource you have is your energy. Have you ever noticed that the more you do, the more you feel like doing? On the other hand, doing nothing for a long period of time can make you feel tired rather than rested. If you stay active, you will have more energy. Keeping in shape and eating right will also increase your energy level.

As you can see, your resources interact with each other. Good use of your time can increase two resources—skills and energy. You can also increase another resource, your money, as you become a better manager. For example, could you turn one of your talents, such as speaking a second language or drawing, into a skill someone might pay you for? One of your neighbors might be willing to pay you to tutor him in Spanish or to draw a design on a T-shirt.

You can trade one resource for another, too. If you want more money, you can find ways to devote time and energy to earning it. If you are working, you might find that you are too busy or too tired to do some of the other things you enjoy. Suppose you get a job working part-time as a lifeguard at a health club. You may discover that cleaning the pool and taking care of equipment are much more tiring than you expected. You will be making extra money, but you may find you are too tired to go to a movie at night.

The job you choose affects your resources in other ways, too. Almost any job you get will mean mastering new skills. You may already be a good cook, but working at a restaurant would mean learning how to prepare large amounts of food quickly and efficiently. If you are excited about the work, you may find that you have more energy than you did before you started.

You might have to devote large amounts of your resources to preparing yourself for the job you want. Suppose you would like to become an aircraft mechanic. The training required would obligate you to spend a significant amount of time, energy, and money to reach the goal you have set for yourself.

Even after you have begun full-time work, your education is not over. You can and should continue to add to your skills. Continuing education is just what its name suggests: education that goes on rather than ends when you finish high school, technical school, or college. Many working people improve their skills by taking courses, attending workshops, and studying on their own. They get extra training because the skills that they need on the job change so quickly. Nurses must keep pace with new treatments. Managers need to learn better ways to run companies. Office workers must learn to use new equipment.

THE VALUE OF PLANNING

Careful planning has many advantages for you. If you become a better planner, you will reach more of the goals you have set for yourself because you will use your resources more efficiently. Because part of good planning is determining which of the things you want are most important to you, you will find yourself working to meet your most important goals first. Once you start planning carefully, making decisions will become easier. You will be able to measure your progress toward your goals, and you will do a better job of predicting your future needs and wants.

An important step in planning more effectively is identifying what you really want. If you are thinking about buying something, deciding what you want is partly a matter of gathering and judging information. Suppose you decide to buy your own telephone. Some of the information you will need might come from advertisements and salespeople. You could examine a variety of competing telephones to compare features and prices. Sales brochures and warranties could provide more information that would help you plan your purchase. In addition, magazine and newspaper articles might contain facts about competing companies and kinds of phones. You could also look into different kinds of services provided by the stores and companies you might buy from.

After you have gathered and analyzed information and done your comparison shopping, you would be likely to make a satisfactory choice, but your planning would not be over. You might still have to decide whether to take money from your savings, spend the cash you have on hand, or try to borrow money to pay for the phone. You could decide to wait until you have earned more money rather than buying right away. Even after you bought your phone, you would still need to evaluate your choice to see whether you had made a good decision. This final stage in the planning process would help you do an even better job of planning your next purchase.

There are also important advantages to planning at work. You can, for example, budget your time at work. A time budget is much like a budget you might make for your money. To plan your time more efficiently, first identify your goals as precisely as you can. Then, figure out how you can measure your progress. For example, try setting some specific goals for yourself, such as stocking ten shelves in an hour. Knowing what you can accomplish in a given amount of time will make you more efficient. The result of your time budget should be that you meet your goals more quickly and easily. You will probably enjoy your job more. Your employer will appreciate your improved work, which can lead to a raise. In addition, becoming a good planner on the job can help you gain the kinds of management skills that can lead to advancement.

Budgeting your time at work can help you set goals—and meet them.

YOUR FINANCES

When most people think of their resources, they tend to think of their money first. Money seems most real to them. Besides, it is easier to keep track of money than of time or energy. You should use all your resources wisely, but financial decisions are among the most important you make.

You need to shop carefully for financial services because financial institutions are changing rapidly. New laws permit both commercial banks and savings and loan associations to offer savings accounts, checking accounts, investment planning, and many other services. In addition, some services are being offered by other institutions as well.

When choosing a financial institution, you should consider what services you want and which institution you can use most conveniently. Different financial institutions charge different amounts for the same services, so you will need to find the one that offers you the most for your money. You will also need other financial services someday. You might want to buy traveler's checks from an automobile club, for example, or get advice from a broker about buying stocks or bonds.

At some time in your life, you may decide to borrow money, perhaps to pay school tuition or to buy a car. You may also want to buy other things on credit. If you do, you could apply for a major credit card as well as charge accounts in department stores.

How much you can borrow depends on how much you earn and on your credit record. Creditors need to know whether the people who want to borrow money can be depended on to pay it back. In general the more dependably you pay back money you have already borrowed, the better your credit rating becomes.

Another kind of financial decision you will need to make concerns the kinds and amounts of insurance to buy. Insurance is based on the idea of sharing risk. Thousands of people pay small amounts to an insurance company to buy protection against losing a great deal of money if disaster strikes.

You can buy life insurance to make sure that when you die, the people who depend on you for support will have enough money to live. You can also protect yourself against damage to your property and against financial loss due to an illness or a car accident. Deciding which kinds of insurance you need and where to get it requires careful thought. As with other financial decisions, planning ahead can prevent many problems later on.

Because the financial decisions you make are so important, you should invest time in selecting a financial institution.

HOW YOUR DECISIONS AFFECT OTHERS

Did you ever hear anyone say, "I don't have any obligations to anybody. I'm responsible only to myself"? A person who says that is wrong. One person's decisions influence many other people. Have you thought about the way your actions affect people at home, at school, and in your community as a whole? All the groups you belong to are affected by your actions.

At home, think about the ways in which your contributions of time, energy, and skills help the other members of your family. Washing the dishes after a meal can give your parents some much-needed time to relax. Helping your sister study for a test on multiplication can help her increase her math skills. Your actions can help other members of your family reach their own goals.

At school, too, what you do can make things better for other people, often without your realizing it. If you participate in class discussions, for example, your ideas and opinions can enrich the classroom experience of other students. If you are involved in activities at school, such as the baseball team or the DECA club, your involvement helps the team or the club and sets an example for other people.

What you do in your community makes a difference, too. Every time you throw trash in a trash can, for example, you are helping to keep your community clean and attractive. If you become interested in turning your time, energy, and skills to community service, you can probably find a number of projects to work on. Is there a vacant lot you could help clean up and turn into a neighborhood park? Are there members of your community who cannot do some everyday tasks such as buying groceries or writing letters? Lending a helping hand would give you a chance to contribute. You may gain a sense of satisfaction as well.

You also need to remember that your decisions affect society as a whole. Every time you

The way you do your job can help determine the success of the company you work for.

buy something, for example, you set in motion a chain reaction that affects many people. Suppose you decide to buy a certain brand of shoes. Making that decision is like voting with your money. Your choice means that the store you buy from benefits. Your money may contribute toward paying the expenses of the business, such as the salary of the person who sold you the shoes or the cost of heating and air conditioning the store. The company that made the shoes also benefits. In this way, all economic decisions are related to each other. People's jobs are affected, even perhaps the job you have now or the job you would like to have someday.

Your political involvement also makes a difference. Deciding to get involved in politics now, as a teenager, could give you a chance to affect many other people's lives. Passing out leaflets for Jane Smith's campaign, for example, may help convince voters to elect her to office. The decisions she makes as mayor may then affect the whole community.

When you start working at your first job, whether it is selling clothes in a department store or assembling computers, you will become a member of the work force. No matter what your job is, you can help determine whether the company you work for succeeds or fails. A job well done, even a small one, can help the business earn the profit it needs to stay open. A poor job will have the opposite effect. Customers may decide to go elsewhere and profits will go down. If enough workers do poor jobs, the business may fail.

Consumers depend on workers to make good products and to provide good services. Doing so can go beyond providing consumer satisfaction. Well-made products and carefully performed services can help protect the health and safety of consumers. Consumers also depend on people in the work force to help them make intelligent decisions. If salespeople are helpful and can provide correct information about the products they are selling, then consumers know what choices are open to them before they buy.

Everyone who lives and works in America plays a vital role in the economy. When you earn money at a job, you become a consumer, because you use your earnings to buy the goods and services you need and want. Your consumer decisions enable a variety of businesses to earn profits. These profits benefit other workers throughout the country. You will also pay taxes on your earnings so that the government can continue to provide essential services. The economic activity of millions of American workers helps the economy grow and prosper. A healthy economy in the United States is important not only for this country but also for the entire world.

Consumers depend on workers for products that are well made and safe.

Chapter 20 It Is Your Decision

MAIN POINTS

- The world is changing rapidly, especially in the ways people work. Both businesses and workers must adapt to these changes. To find a job that is right for you, you must keep alert to trends in society and to the ways in which businesses respond to these trends.
- Your first step toward finding the right job is to learn about yourself. If you understand your values, goals, skills, and aptitudes, you can meet the challenges of your three roles as worker, citizen, and consumer.
- A seven-step method of systematic decision making can help you make satisfying choices. You define the problem, rank your goals, determine your choices, and analyze the consequences of each choice. You then choose the best course, put your decision into action, and evaluate the outcome.
- If you make wise use of your resources such as time, energy, and money, your chances of reaching your goals greatly increase. By continuing your education, you can learn new skills that you can use to keep up with changes on your job.
- Planning carefully can also help you reach your goals. Both at home and at work, a good plan can be valuable in allowing you to make the best possible use of your resources.
- Using your financial resources wisely can be much easier if you plan. A plan can enable you to choose the right financial services, sources of credit, and insurance.
- When you make a decision, you affect not only yourself but others as well. Your family, school, community, and country all have a stake in your decisions. Many people can benefit from your decisions.
- Every worker counts. Whatever your job, if you do it well, you can be an asset to your employer, to consumers, and to the entire economy. A healthy economy depends on each worker doing his or her best.

Chapter Review

1. What are some of the changes that have taken place in the job market in the last few years?
2. What goals must businesses reach in order to stay in business?
3. What are career clusters?
4. How do people's values affect their work?
5. What can people do to increase the chances that they will reach their goals?
6. What are some rights and responsibilities people have as workers, citizens, and consumers?
7. What are the seven steps in the decision-making process?
8. What are some of the resources people have? Which of them do you consider most important?
9. How do people's resources interact with each other?
10. What is continuing education?
11. What advantages does a consumer gain by planning carefully?
12. What are some of the ways the decisions you make affect other people?
13. How do the choices an individual worker makes affect other people?

Activities

1. Write an imaginary diary entry from the point of view of yourself ten years in the future. Include references to your interests and skills, your job, and the financial decisions you have made.
2. Select a career cluster that you are considering entering. Look at some recent books and magazine articles that predict changes in the nature of jobs in that cluster. Write a report summarizing the predictions.
3. Write character sketches of people who illustrate ideas in the chapter, such as Jobless Joe, who did not get the training he needed to update his job skills; Aimless Annie, who has no idea of her goals and aptitudes; Organized Otto, who follows step-by-step procedures for planning and decision making; and Careless Carrie, who never considers the impact her decisions have on other people.
4. Imagine that you have a chance at a job that pays well and gives you a chance to do some of the things you would like to do. Write a letter in which you explain your qualifications for the job. Emphasize the skills and attitudes that would make you a good worker.

UNITED STATES OFFICE OF EDUCATION
15 OCCUPATIONAL CLUSTER CLASSIFICATIONS

Agribusiness and Natural Resources ②	Hospitality and Recreation ⑯
Business and Office ① ⑩ ⑱	Manufacturing ④ ⑩ ⑫ ⑭
Communications and Media ⑱ ⑳	Marine Science ② ⑬ ⑱
Construction ③ ⑤	Marketing and Distribution ⑪
Consumer and Homemaking ⑮ ⑯	Personal Services ⑯
Environment ② ⑬ ⑱	Public Services ⑧ ⑨ ⑰
Fine Arts and Humanities ⑨ ⑳	Transportation ⑲
Health ⑥ ⑦	

UNITED STATES DEPARTMENT OF LABOR
20 OCCUPATIONAL CLUSTER CLASSIFICATIONS

① Administrative Support Occupations, Including Clerical	⑪ Marketing and Sales Occupations
② Agriculture, Forestry, Fishing, and Related Occupations	⑫ Mechanics, Installers, and Repairers
③ Construction Trades and Extractive Occupations	⑬ Natural, Computer, and Mathematical Scientists
④ Engineers, Surveyors, and Architects	⑭ Production Occupations
⑤ Handlers, Equipment Cleaners, Helpers, and Laborers	⑮ Registered Nurses, Pharmacists, Dietitians, Therapists, and Physical Assistants
⑥ Health Diagnosing and Treating Practitioners	⑯ Service Occupations
⑦ Health Technologists and Technicians	⑰ Teachers, Librarians, and Counselors
⑧ Armed Forces	⑱ Technologists and Technicians, Except Health
⑨ Lawyers, Social Scientists, Social Workers, and Religious Workers	⑲ Transportation and Material Moving Occupations
⑩ Managerial and Management-Related Occupations	⑳ Writers, Artists, and Entertainers

Career clusters are designed to group occupations of a similar nature. Several cluster systems have been developed, but two of the more popular and useful ones are those developed by the United States Office of Education and the United States Department of Labor. The Office of Education uses a 15-cluster classification. The Department of Labor uses a 20-cluster classification. The following charts show how the two compare. The numbers after each of the 15 clusters in the top chart are correlated to the 20 clusters listed in the bottom chart.

Appendix: A Guide to Career Clusters

The purpose of this appendix is to help you get started on your career search. To this end, the appendix contains brief overviews of the 20 job clusters described in the *Occupational Outlook Handbook (OOH)*. Each overview explains the general nature of the jobs in that cluster and highlights a number of specific jobs as well. There is also a description of the kinds of training, skills, and aptitudes required for entry into the cluster. The overviews conclude with a list of the specific jobs in the field. Once you find the clusters and jobs that interest you, you can turn to the *OOH* itself for more detailed information.

Appendix

Managerial and Management-Related Occupations

Managers usually have to juggle many different activities. To accomplish that, they must be good organizers. It is the manager's job to direct the work of others and make decisions about what direction a business or group should take. Almost every field mentioned in this appendix needs managers.

In a single day, a manager may work on a plan for the next year's business activities and meet with a worker whose business project has gone over the budget. He or she may also interview someone for a secretarial job and listen to a report from another worker who wants the company to buy two new computers.

Managers must be able to make decisions, accept responsibility, and get along with people. They must be able to communicate well. A good manager can make workers want to do their best and can be firm but tactful in difficult situations. In many positions, managers must be able to handle the financial details of their group. Many managers use computers to send memos and correspondence and to plan budgets.

In a small business, the owner may be the manager and do some of the hands-on work as well. The owner of an auto-body shop may meet with customers and give them written estimates of repair costs. He or she is the one who must decide the budget—how much to charge for each type of service and how much to pay employees. The owner also supervises a bookkeeper and trains new repair people. If someone is doing sloppy work or if two workers are not getting along, the owner is the one to step in. He or she also does some of the actual repair work.

The training and education required for a management job vary. Some people enter a certain career field and become managers when they become more experienced. They do not receive formal training in managing. Retail store managers, for example, often get their start as salespeople. They gain experience on the job or through store training courses. A college degree is becoming a more common requirement for a management position. However, it is still possible in some stores to become a manager without one.

College educations are required for many management positions. Not all call for specific management courses. A college degree, plus a few years' work in the field, is often enough. An engineer, for example, often moves into management after several years of engineering experience. Classes in economics, computers, and management will be useful to any manager.

Some management jobs call for college study beyond the four-year B.A. or B.S. degree. Hospital administrators, for example, must also earn a master's degree in health or hospital administration. People aiming for a top job with a large company often earn a master's degree in business administration. Such a degree usually requires two years of graduate study.

Administrative and managerial occupations include the following:

- accountants and auditors
- construction and building inspectors
- cost estimators
- education administrators
- employment interviewers
- financial managers
- general managers and top executives
- health services managers
- hotel managers and assistants
- loan officers
- occupational safety and health workers
- personnel and labor relations specialists
- purchasing agents and managers
- retail buyers
- retail store managers
- underwriters

Engineers, Surveyors, and Architects

Engineers, surveyors, and architects use their technical skills to design things and solve problems.

Engineers design, develop, and test technical products. They may also work in the operation and upkeep of these products. They may be involved in research, management, sales, or teaching. There are many kinds of engineering. The most common are civil engineering, electrical engineering, mechanical engineering, aerospace engineering, and chemical engineering.

Civil engineers plan and supervise the building of roads, bridges, water supply systems, airports, and buildings.

Electrical engineers plan, test, and supervise the making of electronic and electrical equipment. They may design stereos, computers, electronic controls for aircraft, or electric motors.

Mechanical engineers design machines that produce power, such as gas turbines or jet engines. They also design machines that use power, such as heating systems or automated machines for factories. A growing specialty for mechanical engineers is called robotics, which is the planning and building of robots.

Aerospace engineers design and supervise the building of aircraft and space vehicles. They may work on military aircraft and other defense projects, or they may take part in space exploration projects.

Chemical engineers work on many aspects of the production of chemicals and chemical products. These chemical products include plastics, synthetic fibers, fuels, and fertilizers. Chemical engineers may design the machinery to produce new chemical products or plan the processes for their production.

Engineering calls for science and math ability. Good engineers are creative problem solvers who pay attention to detail.

Engineers must usually have a bachelor's

Appendix

degree in engineering. Many go to graduate school for further training in a specialty such as biomedical engineering. A master's degree or doctorate is often required for supervisory or advanced technical jobs.

Surveyors work with engineers to measure land boundaries and construction sites and to collect information for maps. Some enter the field as surveyor helpers right after high school graduation. They must work their way up to the position of instrument assistant and then to licensed surveyor. A community college or bachelor's degree in surveying or civil engineering leads to faster promotion to surveyor. Every state requires surveyors to take a state licensing exam.

An architect designs a building's layout, appearance, and structure. The architect must keep in mind costs, the needs of the building's users, engineering principles, and the building's looks.

Becoming an architect calls for a five- or six-year college program, three years' work experience, and a licensing exam. Architects should be creative and good with details. They also need to be good at solving technical problems. The ability to communicate well is also valuable.

The various jobs in this career cluster include the following:

- aerospace engineers
- agricultural engineers
- architects
- biomedical engineers
- chemical engineers
- civil engineers
- electrical engineers
- industrial engineers
- landscape architects
- materials engineers
- mechanical engineers
- mining engineers
- packaging engineers
- structural engineers
- surveyors and surveying technicians

Job Opportunities in the Armed Forces

The job of the armed forces is to prepare for our country's defense. If you are considering a career in the armed forces, this means learning how to fight, take orders, and work as a team member. The armed forces is the country's largest employer. They offer training opportunities and work experience in more than 2,000 basic and advanced occupational specialties for enlisted personnel and 1,600 for officers.

Through the year 2000 job opportunities should be excellent in the armed forces. Better educated applicants will be in high demand as military jobs become more technical. Women are actively recruited. By 2000 women are expected to make up 12 percent of all military personnel. Military personnel enjoy a greater degree of job security than their job peers in the civilian world. In general, good on-the-job performance assures a member of the armed forces steady employment and earnings.

If you are interested in additional information, write to:

U.S. Army Recruiting Command, Fort Sheridan, IL 60037.

USAF Recruiting Service, Directorate of Advertising and Publicity, Randolph Air Force Base, TX 78150.

Director, Personnel Procurement Division, Headquarters, U.S. Marine Corps, Washington DC 20380.

Navy Opportunity Information Center, P.O. Box 5000, Clifton, NJ 07015.

Commandant, (G-PMR), U.S. Coast Guard, Washington, DC 20593.

Natural, Computer, and Mathematical Scientists

Many natural scientists and mathematicians are led to their careers by a strong curiosity about how things work. Through study and research, they seek answers to basic questions about the universe and life on our planet. What they learn about science and mathematics increases our knowledge about the world around us. Their work has practical results as well. Scientific research leads to new products and medical advances.

Some mathematicians study the subject as a pure science. They look for new mathematical principles. Usually, such mathematicians teach in universities and colleges.

Other people with a math background use their knowledge as a tool. They may be actuaries who study accident information to set insurance rates. They may be statisticians who analyze survey results to predict the outcome of an election. Or they may be systems analysts who solve business problems by streamlining ways to handle data.

Physical scientists study the structure of the earth—from molecules to mountain ranges. Some physical scientists—astronomers—look beyond the earth to study the solar system and the stars. Still others—chemists—study the properties of substances to create new products.

A career in a physical science calls for a strong math and science aptitude. A bachelor's degree is the minimum requirement. There are jobs for people with a bachelor's degree in chemistry. But most other physical science careers call for a Ph.D.

Another large group of scientists are the life scientists. They are concerned with the study of living things, both plants and animals. They usually specialize in the study of a particular form of life. Botanists study plants. Zoologists study animals. Microbiologists study microscopic life forms such as

Appendix

bacteria and viruses. Some life scientists work in agriculture and food technology. They develop better strains of plants. They also work to increase crop yields by reducing pests and improving the soil.

Foresters and range managers are life scientists with a knowledge of how best to use and protect forests and grasslands.

Life scientists involved in research and college teaching usually have Ph.D. degrees. A master's degree is enough for some work in applied research. A bachelor's degree is sufficient for some entry-level jobs. But the chance for promotion from these jobs is low. Some life science fields, such as food technology and forestry, offer more opportunities for someone who doesn't have an advanced degree.

People with careers in the fields of natural science and mathematics include the following kinds of workers:

- actuaries
- astronomers
- biologists and agricultural scientists
- chemists
- computer systems analysts
- food technologists
- foresters and conservation scientists
- geologists
- life scientists
- mathematicians
- meteorologists
- oceanographers
- operations research analysts
- physical scientists
- physicists
- statisticians

Lawyers, Social Scientists, Social Workers, and Religious Workers

You may be concerned with the problems of poverty, alcoholism, poor health care, or drug abuse. If you have a strong desire to help others, you may choose a career from this cluster. Some workers in the cluster, such as social workers and recreation workers, work directly with people. Others—social scientists—study how people act in different groups and societies.

Social workers help people and groups to deal with their problems. Some work with individual families who are troubled by alcoholism or drug abuse. If a family is in need, social workers may help the family obtain food and medical care. Social workers may arrange foster care and counseling for victims of child abuse.

Other social workers are employed by hospitals, senior citizen centers, youth clubs, or nursing homes. They help people adjust to changes in their lives, such as the onset of a long-term illness.

Recreation workers plan and supervise activities for people's leisure time. They may work with school-age students or the elderly They may find work at an inner-city playground or a camp in the mountains. Many teach sports such as swimming, or arts and crafts. Some recreation workers help the sick or physically disabled.

Social and recreation workers must truly

Appendix

enjoy working with people. They must be patient, deeply sympathetic, and sensitive to people's needs. They must also be able to take responsibility and work independently.

Depending on the position, social work may require a bachelor's degree. A master's degree may be needed for advancement. Some recreation jobs are available to high school graduates. An associate's or bachelor's degree may open more job opportunities for certain workers.

Social scientists study people's behavior. Anthropologists study archaeology, the development of humans through the ages, and different cultures. Economists study how people use money and goods and how these resources flow through society. Political scientists study how people act in political activities such as elections and government. Market research analysts survey consumers' likes and dislikes to help companies decide on new products.

Social scientists must be creative and curious. They also need to be thorough and methodical. Today, most must be able to use computers to store and analyze data. A college degree is necessary for jobs in this field. Graduate study may also be required.

Most religious workers are members of the clergy of their faith. Their work includes spiritual and personal counseling, conducting religious services, teaching, and administration. Most clergy have a college background plus training in a theological school.

Lawyers study and interpret the law and counsel people on how the laws affect them. To become a lawyer, you must have a college degree plus three years of law school. You must also pass a licensing, or bar, exam.

Careers in this people-oriented cluster include the following:
- economists
- judges, magistrates, and judicial workers
- lawyers
- market research analysts
- ministers
- political scientists
- priests
- psychologists
- rabbis
- recreation workers
- social service aides
- social workers
- sociologists
- urban and regional planners

Teachers, Librarians, and Counselors

By this point in your life, you have probably had more contact with people in these professions than with people working in any other field. You have had daily contact with teachers, as well as contact with school counselors and librarians. You know quite a bit about their day-to-day responsibilities, but there are aspects to these jobs that a student does not see. There are many other opportunities in the teaching field. There are nursery school teachers, dance teachers, and adult education teachers. There are employment counselors in private firms. There are also librarians who work for universities and large companies.

Elementary school teachers have a great effect on children's later schooling. It is their responsibility to provide a solid basis in reading and math. They also help teach children how to get along with others. They try to teach such values as consideration for others. Teachers must spend time after school preparing lessons, correcting papers, and attending meetings.

Secondary school teachers often choose the profession because they want to share a particular subject area with young people. They usually teach several different courses within that subject area each day. For example, a science teacher may teach introductory science, biology, and physiology. As with elementary teachers, a high school teacher's workday extends well beyond classroom hours.

Teachers must be well organized, patient, and sensitive to student needs. They must be able to handle behavior problems calmly and effectively. Becoming a teacher calls for a bachelor's degree and, in many states, a graduate degree.

College and university professors teach

Appendix

more advanced and specialized subjects. They may teach anything from specific job skills to advanced topics that have little practical use. Professors who teach at universities are often involved in both research and teaching. They explore new avenues in their field and publish books and articles on their findings.

A Ph.D. is usually required for college teaching, although it may be possible to find a teaching position with a master's degree.

As you have learned in this book, lifetime learning is becoming much more important. People take additional classes in order to change careers, advance on the job, or enrich their lives. For all these classes, teachers are needed. These teachers include cooperative extension agents who lead programs in agriculture and home economics. There are also teachers who work in continuing education centers and private vocational schools.

Counselors help people make educational and career decisions. They may work in high schools, colleges, or public employment offices. Still others have jobs in private career counseling or employment offices.

Librarians plan library purchases and help library users find the information they need. Librarians are now responsible for more than books. They help people use computers to gain information from other libraries and information sources. To become a librarian, a master's degree in library science is required.

Careers in this well-known cluster include the following:
- career planning and placement counselors
- college and university faculty
- computer camp teachers
- employment counselors
- kindergarten and elementary school teachers
- librarians
- recreational teachers
- school guidance counselors
- secondary school teachers

Health Diagnosing and Treating Practitioners

You wake up one morning with a fever, a sore throat, and a rash over most of your body. You need a health practitioner to diagnose and treat your illness. People with careers in this cluster can do just that.

Most of those employed in this group are physicians—medical doctors. They perform medical examinations, diagnose illnesses, and treat people who are sick or injured. Seven out of ten physicians are specialists in a particular area. The following are the most common specialties:

- anesthesiology
- general surgery
- internal medicine
- obstetrics and gynecology
- ophthalmology
- orthopedic surgery
- pathology
- pediatrics
- psychiatry
- radiology

A career as a physician calls for a great deal of training. In addition to three or four years of college, a doctor must complete a three- or four-year medical school program. Following that, almost all doctors complete additional training, called residency, in a specialized field. The residency period lasts at least three years.

If you wish to become a doctor, you should have a strong desire to help the sick and injured. Medical training is a competitive and difficult process. This means you should be a good student who is willing to put in the required years of study. Good doctors are able to make decisions in emergencies and are sensitive to the needs of their patients.

Osteopathic physicians differ somewhat from physicians in their training and outlook. In treatment, osteopathic physicians place more emphasis than physicians on manipulating the bones, muscles, and ligaments. Like physicians, they also use surgery and drugs in medical care. Becoming an osteopathic physician calls for a bachelor's degree plus three or four years' study at a col-

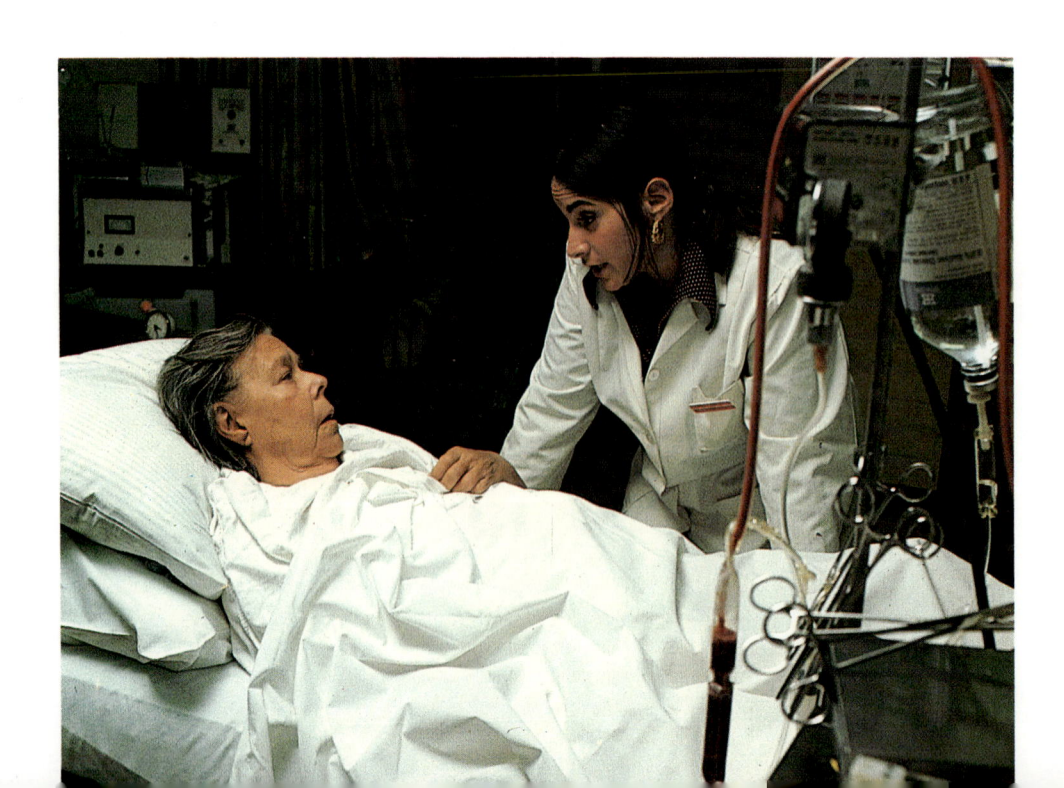

Appendix

lege of osteopathic medicine. Additional training consisting of internship and residency lasts from one to five years more.

Podiatrists treat foot disorders. Most earn a bachelor's degree before entering the four-year program in podiatry school.

Dentists provide preventive care of the teeth and treat diseased teeth and gums. They take X-rays, fill cavities, measure and fit artificial teeth, and do surgery on the mouth and gums. Some specialize in such areas as straightening teeth or surgery.

A dentist's job calls for the ability to analyze problems and the skill to do careful, exacting work with the hands. The ability to put patients at ease is also useful. Dentists usually complete a bachelor's degree before spending four years in dental school.

Optometrists examine people's eyes and prescribe glasses if needed. If they detect eye disease, they refer the patient to a physician. Becoming an optometrist calls for two or three years of college plus four years of optometry school.

Veterinarians are animal doctors. Some treat only small animals and pets. Others work with farm, circus, or zoo animals. Still others work in medical research or in government meat inspection. Becoming a veterinarian requires two to four years of college plus four years in veterinary school.

Careers in the health diagnosing and treating cluster include the following:

- dentists
- optometrists
- orthodontists
- physicians
- podiatrists
- veterinarians

Registered Nurses, Pharmacists, Dietitians, Therapists, and Physician Assistants

There are many careers available in the health field. Some require more schooling than others, and each has different responsibilities. People in the health careers described here are professionals. Many have gone through four or more years of schooling after high school. Most work directly with the sick or disabled. (If you are interested in a career that would require somewhat less schooling or one in which you would operate medical equipment, check the careers described in the next section. For health careers that require little training beyond high school, see the health careers listed in the service occupations cluster.)

Dietitians study the science of nutrition and plan diets and menus to ensure healthful eating. Some plan and supervise meals for large facilities such as schools, prisons, and cafeterias. Others work in hospitals to plan meals for the individual needs of patients. Dietitians may hire and supervise kitchen workers. A good dietitian has both scientific knowledge and administrative ability. Becoming a dietitian requires a bachelor's degree with a major in foods and nutrition or institution management.

Occupational therapists teach vocational skills and the skills of everyday living to those recovering from illness or injury. They plan activities that will help the patient become as independent as possible. Occupational therapists should be friendly and patient. The career calls for a bachelor's degree in an occupational therapy program.

Pharmacists dispense the prescription drugs ordered by doctors and dentists. In the past, this meant mixing the drug itself,

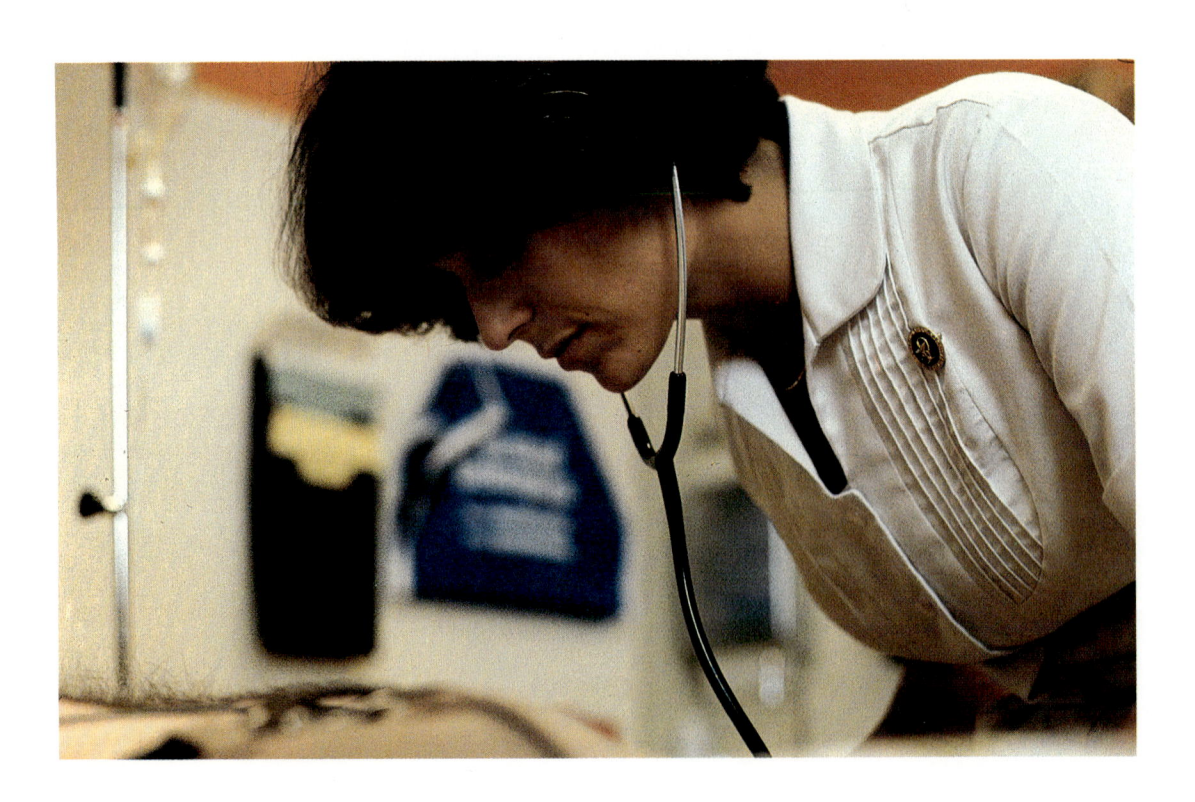

Appendix

but now most drugs come ready to use from the drug manufacturer. Pharmacists must know enough about drugs to advise doctors and patients on their effects and proper dosage. They also advise customers on drugs available without a prescription. Many pharmacists manage or own a pharmacy. Both scientific and business aptitude are valuable characteristics for someone entering the field. Becoming a pharmacist requires five years of study beyond high school to earn a bachelor of science degree.

Physical therapists work with patients such as disabled children and accident victims to help them restore their muscle functions. Their work may also help relieve pain and prevent further injury. They plan and carry out patient exercise programs. They also provide therapy involving massage, water, heat, and cold. Like others in the health care field, physical therapists must be patient, tactful, and emotionally mature when dealing with people. Becoming a physical therapist requires completing a bachelor's or master's degree program.

The career of physician assistant is a relatively new one. Physician assistants are trained to perform many of the routine jobs usually done by a physician. This includes taking medical histories and performing medical examinations. Because this is a new field, physician assistants in some areas do not have a clear place in the network of health care providers. Currently, most people who enter the field already have experience in health care. Requirements for entering a physician assistant program vary from a high school diploma to a B.A. degree. The training itself usually lasts two years.

Registered nurses can work in hospitals, offices, private homes, schools, or industries. They give medications and observe and record the symptoms and progress of patients. They may teach patients and family members how to treat an illness or injury. In a hospital, registered nurses may assist physicians in surgery or emergency care. In many situations, registered nurses supervise the work of licensed practical nurses and nurse's aides.

You can become a nurse in a two-, three-, or four-year program. The four-year program leads to a bachelor's degree in nursing and is usually required for supervisory and research jobs.

Respiratory therapy workers use special equipment to treat patients with breathing problems. Depending on the program, training can last from one to four years.

Speech pathologists give therapy to improve the speech of children and adults. Audiologists test people's hearing and treat hearing problems. A master's degree is often necessary for work in these fields.

Careers in this health-related cluster include the following:

- dietitians
- occupational therapists
- pharmacists
- physical therapists
- physician assistants
- registered nurses

Health Technologists and Technicians

Health technologists and technicians act as a support team for physicians and other health diagnosing and treating practitioners. One group of workers in this cluster performs a variety of testing and treatment procedures. To do so, these workers often use sophisticated machines or laboratory procedures. Another group of workers provides medical or nursing attention to patients.

The largest career group in this cluster is practical nursing. Licensed practical nurses provide many forms of bedside care, from bathing patients to taking their blood pressure and temperature. Their work requires nursing knowledge. They do not perform the more advanced tasks of registered nurses. A licensed practical nurse must be patient and understanding in difficult situations. Training involves one year of classroom and on-the-job instruction. Most, but not all, programs require applicants to have a high school diploma.

Dental hygienists clean patients' teeth and expose and develop X-rays. The do some of the routine work formerly done by dentists. Dental hygiene school is a two-year program. Many community colleges offer this training.

Emergency medical technicians drive emergency vehicles and perform emergency care at the scene of an accident or emergency situation. They may need to restore breathing or heartbeat, open a blocked air passage, or stop bleeding. Their job requires a calm disposition and the ability to make difficult decisions quickly. A 100-hour course is required for becoming an EMT. An EMT

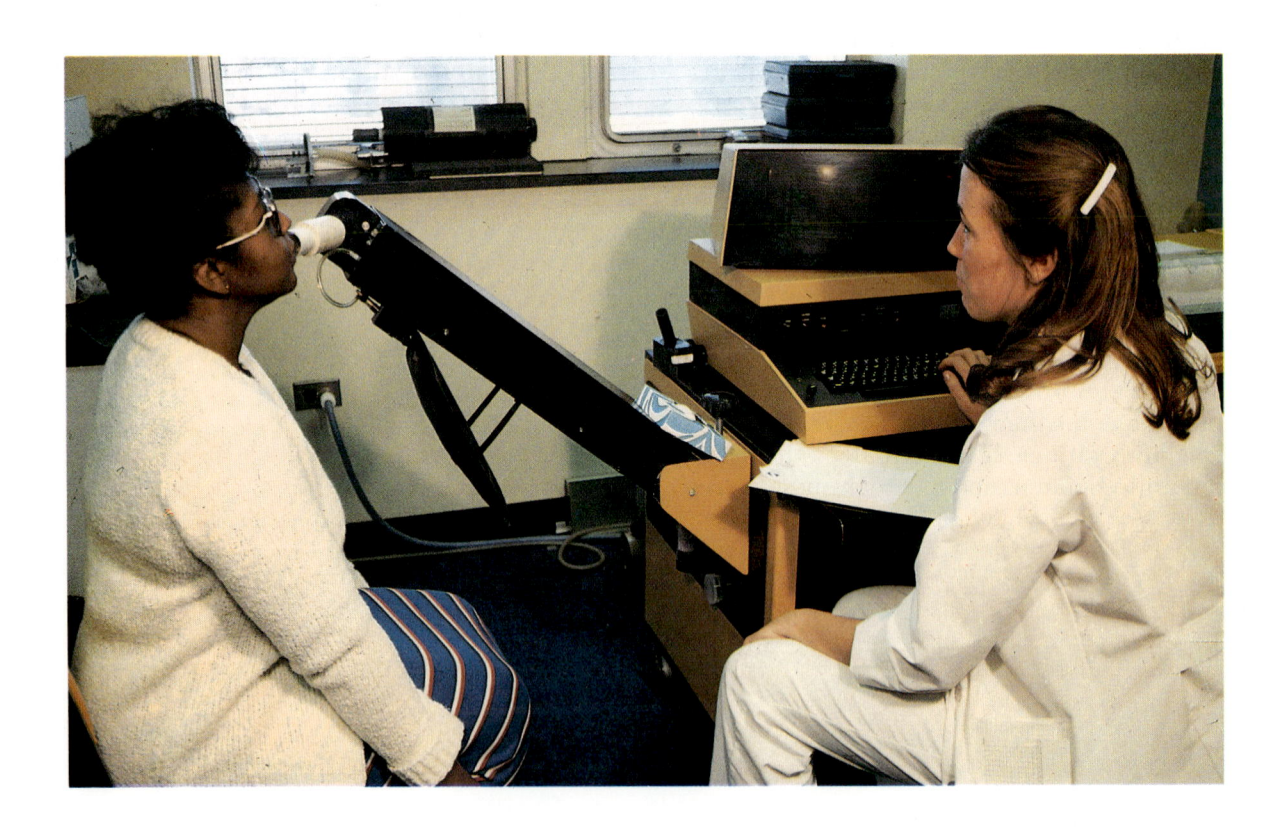

Appendix

can become an EMT-paramedic with an additional three- to five-month course.

Medical laboratory workers do laboratory tests on blood, tissue, and other specimens. Their work enables doctors to diagnose many kinds of diseases and other medical problems. Medical laboratory technologists perform the most complicated tests. Their tasks require four years of college training. Technicians with two years of training can perform many but not all of these tests. Technical assistants are trained in a one-year program to perform routine work.

Medical record technicians and clerks develop and maintain the individual medical records for hospital patients. They do detailed work in organizing these records and coding information for patients' files. A technician's work calls for a two-year associate's degree.

As their name suggests, surgical technicians assist surgeons and anesthesiologists in the operating room. They set up equipment and hand tools to the surgeons during operations. They also assist nurses in preparing the operating room before operations. Although some surgical technicians learn on the job, most learn their skills in community college programs.

Several of the careers in this cluster involve the use of complicated medical equipment. Electrocardiograph (EKG) technicians use EKG machines to check a patient's heartbeat. They attach electrodes to the patient's chest, arms, and legs and then send small electrical impulses through them. The reading appears on graph paper and is then interpreted by a doctor. EKG technicians sometimes use other machines to give tests. EKG technicians usually learn their work on the job. Training programs lasting one or two years are also available at community colleges and vocational schools.

An electroencephalogram (EEG) shows the electrical activity of the brain. Looking at an EEG helps doctors diagnose brain tumors, strokes, and epilepsy. EEG technicians apply electrodes to various spots on a patient's head and run the EEG machine to measure brain activity. EEG technologists do this job in addition to using other equipment and supervising technicians. Most technicians learn their skills on the job. Some take one to two years of formal training at a college or vocational school. Training and experience allows advancement to technologist.

Radiologic (X-ray) technologists operate yet another type of medical equipment. Guided by written instructions from a doctor, X-ray technologists position the patient and the machine for X-rays. They protect with lead or other shields parts of the body not to be X-rayed. They then operate the machine to take the X-rays and develop the film. Training programs for X-ray technologists range from two to four years. The longer programs give technologists a greater chance for advancement.

Other technologists operate CAT-scanning machines, dialysis machines, and nuclear magnetic resonance machines.

Careers in the health technologists and technicians cluster include the following:

- dental hygienists
- electrocardiograph technicians
- electroencephalograph technologists and technicians
- emergency medical technicians
- licensed practical nurses
- medical laboratory workers
- medical record technicians and clerks
- radiologic (X-ray) technicians
- surgical technicians

Writers, Artists, and Entertainers

Jobs in this cluster are considered by many to be glamour occupations. Successful people in this field are often highly visible, and their work and life-style often seem attractive. A creative career requires talent and hard work. For many of these careers there are far more people seeking work than there are jobs available.

People in communications work with the written and spoken word. They may use their skills to inform, persuade, or entertain. Communications careers require writing ability and generally a college background.

Reporters and correspondents find the news events, interview the people involved, and write news articles. Most work for newspapers, although others work for TV stations and magazines. Correspondents are stationed by their employers in out-of-town locations and are responsible for writing stories about that city or country. Reporters must be outgoing and persistent in tracking down stories. They must be able to express themselves quickly and clearly. A college degree in journalism is the surest path to a journalism career, although another liberal arts major may be sufficient.

Radio and television announcers and newscasters are the voices of the stations they work for. Radio announcers are usually disc jockeys or newscasters. TV announcers are usually part of a station's newscast. They present the news by reading a script written by them or by another worker. Competition is stiff for these jobs. Appearance, personality, and a good speaking voice often count more than journalistic ability in getting a job.

Public relations workers write news articles, speeches, and other forms of communication for companies. It is their job to help a company or organization present a good image to the public. They may also answer consumer questions and explain the public's viewpoint to company management. Many people move from news reporting into public relations.

Writers and editors may work on textbooks or other books, advertising brochures, or company publications. Writers work from a topic they have chosen or one assigned by an editor. They research the topic and write the material. Editors supervise and hire writers. They also rewrite and polish writers' work and supervise the planning and publication of the material. Writing experience is essential for work as a writer or editor. A degree with a major in English, journalism, or another one of the liberal arts is recommended.

The book you are currently holding was designed by a graphic designer to be both

Appendix

attractive and readable. Graphic designers are responsible for the visual look of books, magazines, ads, and record jackets. A two- to four-year program in a commercial art school is usually required for a graphic arts position.

Display workers plan and execute window and store displays. They try to catch the shopper's eye and entice her or him to buy. Although a flair for design is useful, many display workers learn on the job. Display work is often included in high school and community college cooperative education courses.

Floral designers arrange flowers in floral shops. Traditionally, they have learned their tasks through on-the-job training. However, formal training is now offered by community colleges and vocational schools.

Industrial designers plan the look of everything from toasters to automobiles. They must use artistic sense plus a knowledge of materials, costs, and production methods. When hiring, companies usually look for someone with at least a bachelor's degree in industrial design.

Interior designers plan the layout, furnishing, and decorating of homes, offices, and public buildings. Their job calls for a two- to four-year college program in interior design.

Photographers generally work on assignment to make still photos, films, or videotapes. They may specialize in one of many areas, such as wedding photos, scientific photography, or feature films. Photographic skills can be learned independently, on the job, or through formal training.

Performing artists such as actors, dancers, and musicians must usually put in years of effort in order to gain recognition or even a regular job. Many musicians and dancers begin their training in childhood. Many performing artists gain experience locally and then move to major cultural centers such as New York or Los Angeles.

Careers in this highly competitive cluster include the following:

- actors
- graphic designers designers
- display workers
- floral designers
- industrial designers
- interior designers
- musicians
- photographers
- public relations specialists
- radio and television announcers and newscasters
- reporters and correspondents
- singers
- writers and editors

Technologists and Technicians, Except Health

Technologists and technicians are the support system for professionals in a number of fields. Most use specialized equipment or technical books in their work. Workers in this field must be able to do precise, detailed work. Their work requires less training than is necessary for professional careers in the field.

Air traffic controllers guide aircraft in and out of airports and keep track of them in the air. They must make sure that a safe distance is kept between aircraft at all times. People interested in becoming air traffic controllers must have three years of general work experience or four years of college. They must also pass a civil service test and receive 12 to 16 weeks of schooling and on-the-job training.

Broadcast technicians do the technical work at a TV or radio station. They handle audio and video equipment such as microphones and television cameras. Some specialize in areas such as sound recording or special effects. Competition is keen for the few openings available. Technical school or community college training is good preparation for a job as a broadcast technician.

Drafters prepare detailed engineering and architectural drawings that show exactly how something should be built. In the past, these drawings were done completely by hand. More and more are now being done with the aid of computers. Technical schools, community colleges, and the armed

Appendix

services offer training in this field.

Engineering and science technicians can work in a great many fields. They often assist engineers and scientists by building, operating, and maintaining scientific equipment. They work in all fields of engineering and science, from geology and chemistry to aerospace engineering. They may operate radar equipment, build electronic equipment, or estimate the cost of a highway overpass. Technical education at a community college or technical school is generally required for a job in the field. On-the-job training is occasionally possible.

Legal assistants, also known as paralegals, help lawyers by doing legal research and preparing reports. They may help prepare contracts and other documents. The career of legal assistant is a relatively new one. Career paths for entering the field vary. Some legal assistants work their way up from the job of legal secretary. Others take two- to four-year programs at colleges or business schools.

When you visit the public library, the person you see at the checkout desk is probably a library assistant. Library assistants may also shelve books, do clerical work, and help library users operate equipment. Many library assistants are high school graduates who learned their skills on the job. Others enter the field through a two-year college program.

Computer programmers prepare the detailed coded instructions that teach a computer to handle a certain task. They may teach a computer to prepare a company's bills or to manipulate a robot. Most programmers are college graduates with degrees in such areas as computer science, accounting, or engineering.

The varied careers in this cluster include the following:

- air traffic controllers
- broadcast technicians
- computer programmers
- drafters
- engineering and science technicians
- legal assistants
- library technicians and assistants

Marketing and Sales Occupations

Convincing consumers to buy is the main goal of workers in marketing and sales occupations.

The planning and writing of advertisements is often done in advertising agencies by advertising workers. Some workers decide what kind of ad will be best for a product. Others write the ad or do the artwork. Ad workers must be creative and able to work under time pressure. A college degree is usually required for the job.

Advertising often includes photos of attractive models. People interested in a modeling career sometimes forget that a model's real goal is to help sell a product. Some models appear in photographs. Others are runway models who model clothing for garment makers and designers. An attractive appearance is the most important qualification for modeling. There are no special training requirements. Modeling classes may be helpful.

Retail sales associates sell thousands of different products. Salespeople who sell expensive items such as cars usually receive a commission for each item they sell. Those who sell less expensive items usually work for a straight salary. A high school diploma is preferred for sales work.

Manufacturer's sales associates sell to stores and other businesses. Some try to interest clothing stores in carrying a particular designer's line. Others visit hospitals to sell them equipment and supplies. Such a job requires a good deal of travel, because they spend most of their time visiting customers. Their income is usually based on how much they sell. Persistence and a

Appendix

pleasant personality are needed for a sales job. Although some jobs do not require a college degree, others call for a college background in a specific field such as chemistry or engineering.

Automobile parts counter workers sell to both wholesale and retail customers. They must store and keep track of thousands of auto parts. They use parts catalogs to locate and order parts. An understanding of auto mechanics is useful for the job because counter workers must advise people. They need to be knowledgeable about what they sell.

Cashiers operate cash registers in stores, restaurants, and other businesses. They must be patient in dealing with the public all day long. They must also have good manual dexterity. Most employers look for a high school diploma when hiring cashiers.

Insurance agents and brokers sell life, property, and health insurance. Most insurance employers hire high school graduates who have shown sales ability. Various insurance organizations offer training programs.

Real estate agents and brokers work on commission to sell homes and other kinds of property. They also help property owners sell their property and assist renters in finding suitable homes and offices. In addition, brokers manage office buildings and arrange the financing for real estate deals. Real estate agents must take classes and pass a test to become licensed. Brokers must take additional classwork and have several years of real estate experience.

Other people in sales are securities sales workers. They sell stocks, bonds, and mutual funds. Still other sales workers are travel agents. Their job is to help people plan trips and make reservations for plane tickets, hotel reservations, and tours.

Careers in the marketing and sales cluster include the following:

- advertising workers
- automobile parts counter workers
- automobile sales workers
- cashiers
- insurance agents and brokers
- manufacturer's sales workers
- models
- real estate agents and brokers
- sales associates and clerks
- securities sales workers
- travel agents
- wholesale trade sales workers

Administrative Support Occupations, Including Clerical

Workers in this cluster keep offices and businesses running smoothly. They send the letters, balance the books, and make the phone calls. Administrative support workers can be found in almost every type of business. The range of jobs is so wide that there is not space here to describe all the jobs listed.

Airline reservation and ticket agents work for airlines to book reservations and write out tickets. They use computers to determine the availability of tickets. A high school education is required for the job, and some college is preferred. Airlines offer formal training for each position.

Checks, deposit slips, bank statements—the flow of paper and paperwork through a bank seems endless. Tellers begin the process when they receive checks and deposits from the public. They must check every transaction they handle for accuracy. All checks and other records must be sorted and tallied. Tellers may use computers to keep track of customer accounts and other financial records. A high school diploma is preferred for an entry-level bank job.

Bookkeepers and accounting clerks keep financial records of money a company has received and paid out. They use calculating machines and computers to do their work. Bookkeeping classes are offered in high schools and community colleges.

Insurance companies hire claim representatives to investigate and settle the insurance claims filed by policyholders. For example, in an auto claim, a worker checks to make sure that the damage claimed was really caused at the time of the accident. He or she then decides fair payment for repair work. College graduates are sometimes preferred for jobs in the field. High school graduates are often hired as well.

Computer operators enter information into a computer. In the past, much of this was done by keypunch operators. Now, with computer advances, many computer operators enter information directly into the computer from a typewriter keyboard. They use a TV-like monitor to see information that is being entered or retrieved. Eventually, there will be little demand for keypunch operators. Many high schools and two-year colleges offer courses in computer operation. The armed services offer training as well.

Hotel desk clerks take room reservations and assign rooms. They also figure and accept room payments and answer questions about hotel services. In a small hotel, they may perform many services. In larger hotels, their duties may be more specialized. Courtesy is extremely important in this job because the public forms its opinion of a hotel from its desk clerks. A high school diploma is required for the job.

Appendix

Mail carriers and postal clerks are the backbone of the postal service. Carriers begin their day at the post office. There they sort the mail for their assigned routes. They then deliver the mail on foot or in a vehicle. Most postal clerks sort mail at central distribution centers across the country. As the mail passes by in an electronic mail sorter, workers enter the zip code for each letter into the machine. The machine then sorts the letters according to their destination. Those interested in a postal job must take a written test and wait for vacancies to occur.

Receptionists greet office visitors and direct them to the person who can help them. No special skills are needed for the job, but a high school diploma and a pleasant personality are required.

Secretaries take care of many administrative details for their employers. They take dictation, type, and handle correspondence. They also set up appointments and do filing. They may take care of office expense accounts and answer the questions of telephone callers. Typing and shorthand skills are usually required for a secretarial job. More and more secretarial jobs now call for the ability to use a word processor. These skills can be learned in high school or in community colleges and business schools.

Teacher aides assist teachers in the classroom. They also have clerical duties such as correcting papers and preparing worksheets. Requirements for the job vary from school to school. Some workers have associate's degrees. Others find work without a high school diploma.

Careers in this wide-ranging cluster include the following:
- airline reservation and ticket agents
- bank clerks
- bank tellers
- bookkeepers and accounting clerks
- claim representatives
- collection workers
- computer operators
- hotel desk clerks
- mail carriers
- postal clerks
- receptionists
- secretaries
- teacher aides
- telephone operators
- typists

Service Occupations

There is good news about this job cluster. There are already more than 20 million people employed in service occupations. Still, the service industry is expected to be the fastest-growing job group in the next ten years.

Being in a service occupation can mean you are protecting the public. You may work as a correction officer in a prison or as an FBI special agent. More common protective jobs are those of fire fighter, police officer, and guard. Fire fighters have a dangerous and complicated job. Those interested in the field must pass written and medical exams as well as tests of strength and endurance. When accepted as fire fighters, these workers go through classroom and on-the-job training.

The responsibilities of police officers range from traffic control to crime investigation. Applicants must pass exams and interviews that assess their educational, emotional, and physical qualifications.

Guards work in public or private buildings, at ports and railroads, and at large public gatherings. Their job is to protect property from vandalism and theft. Most employers prefer to hire high school graduates. Many guards have prior experience in the military.

More people are eating more meals away from home. That means a great deal of growth in the food service industry. The most highly skilled worker in this group is the cook or chef. A fry cook in a coffee shop may learn on the job, but a chef in an elegant restaurant may have had years of for-

Appendix

mal training. Servers and other food service workers usually learn their work on the job.

Health service assistants work with health professionals such as doctors, dentists, and nurses. Medical assistants may help doctors with physical exams. They also perform clerical duties. Occupational therapy assistants work with therapists to teach activities and self-care skills to patients. Dentists and physical therapists also use trained assistants to help them care for patients. Training for these careers calls for one or two years of study beyond high school.

People in the personal services occupations perform tasks for others. Their careers range from barber to flight attendant. Barbers and cosmetologists cut and style hair. They receive their training largely through private vocational schools. Flight attendants are trained by airlines in four- to six-week training courses. They are trained to see that supplies are in order, to brief passengers on emergency instructions, and to serve food and beverages. Most important, they must be ready and able to help passengers in an emergency.

The many kinds of careers in this cluster include the following:

- barbers
- bartenders
- bellhops and bell captains
- cooks and chefs
- correction officers
- cosmetologists
- dental assistants
- FBI agents
- fire fighters
- flight attendants
- food and counter workers
- guards
- hotel housekeepers and assistants
- meatcutters
- medical assistants
- occupational therapy assistants
- optometric assistants
- physical therapy assistants
- police officers
- servers
- state police officers
- waiter's assistants and kitchen helpers

Agriculture, Forestry, Fishing, and Related Occupations

Farm owners and managers are responsible for tilling the soil and for planting, fertilizing, cultivating, and harvesting crops. In addition to the physical work, there is a great deal of planning involved in deciding which crops to plant and how to manage farm fi-

Appendix

nances. Most farmers borrow money to purchase fertilizer, machinery, and other materials. They take risks in getting loans, deciding on crops, and holding their farm products to get a better price at a later time.

Traditionally, the farmer has enjoyed job independence. Farming is a hard life that depends on the weather. Most farmers get satisfaction in watching things grow. Now, however, many farmers face the financial problems of rising costs and mounting debts. Many still would not trade their job for any other. However, their job is increasingly complex. Because of the costs of starting up, it has become very difficult for someone not from a farm family to begin farming.

Farm laborers work on many farms. Depending on the type of farm, they may care for livestock or run farm machinery. They may operate irrigation equipment or pick fruit and vegetables.

There are also agricultural occupations off the farm. There are researchers who work to improve crop and animal production. Agricultural technicians assist researchers in their work. Teachers and other educators teach agriculture at high schools and colleges and through cooperative extension services.

Growing up on a farm provides an excellent background for entering the field. More and more farm owners and operators are finding that a two- or four-year college course gives them essential technical and administrative information. Those entering agricultural research or engineering must have a college degree in the field.

Some forestry workers plan the best use of forest lands and manage logging and replanting. Forestry workers may also prevent and control fires. Many supervise the recreational use of forest lands. Other forestry workers harvest trees.

Careers in this cluster include the following:

- agricultural researchers
- farm laborers
- farm operators and managers
- forestry technicians
- timber-cutting and logging workers

Mechanics, Installers, and Repairers

Your car will not shift out of first gear. A plane is delayed due to a faulty electrical device. These problems call for the skills of trained motor vehicle mechanics.

Aircraft mechanics must take better care of an aircraft than an average person does of his or her car. Different parts of the aircraft must be checked or replaced after the aircraft has been flown a certain number of hours. Mechanics take the engine apart and use X-ray equipment and other special tools to check for cracks and wear. In addition to scheduled maintenance, aircraft mechanics repair any problems noticed by the pilot. Some mechanics are licensed by the Federal Aviation Administration as airframe mechanics. They are trained to work on the body of the plane. Others are powerplant mechanics who work on the engine. Aircraft inspectors check the work of other mechanics. Most mechanics get their training from the military or from vocational schools. The training program lasts from 18 months to two years.

After a fender bender or a major collision, automotive body repairers undo the damage done to the body of the car. Their tasks depend on the amount of damage. They may pound out a bent fender, fill a dent with plastic or solder, or replace a section of the car. This work requires manual skill and the judgment to decide which technique is best for each job. Auto-body repairers learn their skills in high school, on the job, or through trade schools.

Someone newly arrived in town might ask a new acquaintance for a few recommendations—where to find a good doctor and where to find a good auto mechanic. Having a skilled mechanic to turn to is important to every car owner. An auto mechanic must be able to diagnose what is wrong with a car and to repair or replace the faulty part. Experience in working on cars is a plus for would-be mechanics. Skills can be learned on the job, in high school, or through trade school and community college programs.

Another group of repair people fix electrical and electronic equipment. Appliance repairers service large and small home appliances. Workers at central offices of telephone companies install and repair equipment. Line installers do the outside wiring that brings telephone service to your home. Computer service technicians work in a rapidly growing field. They often work directly for a computer company to serve clients who use computers made by the company. They do routine maintenance as well as repairs. Television and radio service technicians work on TVs, stereos, VCRs, and other sound and video equipment. All the jobs in this area require a knowledge of

Appendix

electronics or electrical work. Telephone company workers usually learn their skills on the job. Other electronics workers have studied electronics in high school or community college. Some careers have a formal apprenticeship program.

Other mechanics and repairers have jobs working on air conditioning or heating systems. Still others service office business machines. Millwrights work in factories to set up and assemble machinery. The training required for these and other repair worker jobs varies.

Careers in this problem-solving cluster include the following:

- air conditioning, refrigeration, and heating mechanics
- aircraft mechanics and engine specialists
- appliance repairers
- automotive mechanics
- automotive body repairers
- business machine repairers
- central office craft occupations
- central office equipment installers
- computer service technicians
- electric sign repairers
- elevator installers and repairers
- farm equipment mechanics
- industrial machinery repairers
- line installers and cable splicers
- maintenance electricians
- millwrights
- musical instrument repairers and tuners
- pinsetter mechanics
- telephone installers and repairers
- television and radio service technicians
- truck mechanics and bus mechanics
- vending machine servicers and repairers
- watch repairers

Construction Trades and Extractive Occupations

Perhaps you would not mind spending several years training for an interesting career, but you know that college is not for you. You would like a skill you could be proud of, and you would like to earn a very good hourly wage. Maybe you would also like to work outdoors. If so, a job as a construction craft worker might be right for you.

Construction workers build and repair every kind of building and structure imaginable. Their jobs fall into three groups. The first on the work site are the structural workers. Concrete masons and bricklayers are among these workers. They may build a concrete block foundation or pour the foundation in forms built by carpenters. On some buildings, stonemasons and bricklayers build ornamental walls. In structures such as large buildings or bridges, reinforcing metal workers lay steel bars in the foundation forms before the concrete is poured. Large structures also call for the work of structural steelworkers to put up the steel beams. These workers often work high above the ground. Carpenters work during many parts of the construction process. Those that work during the early structural phase to build concrete forms or the framework are called rough carpenters.

The second group of construction workers are the mechanical workers. Among them are the construction electricians. They do the electrical wiring in a building and hook up lighting, air conditioning, and other electrical systems. Early in the building process,

Appendix

plumbers arrive to build the complex network of pipes for the water system. They return later to connect these pipes with bathroom fixtures and appliances. Other mechanical workers include sheet metal workers.

Once the initial work on a building is done, finishing workers arrive. Drywall installers and finishers put up drywall panels over the building's frame. Drywall finishers apply a special paste and tape to the seams between each panel. These drywall panels have largely replaced plaster walls. Plasterers, however, still find work in the Sunbelt states, where the use of outside plaster—stucco—is common. Plasterers also help restore old buildings and homes.

Finish carpenters put in paneling and molding. Some specialize in putting in hardwood floors or building cabinetry. Glaziers install glass windows and doors. Working on scaffolding, they may even cover the entire surface of a skyscraper with glass. Roofers can apply many kinds of roofs, from tar and gravel to tile and wooden shingle. Among the last workers are the painters and paperhangers. They put the finishing touches on a building.

Most construction workers learn their trades through formal apprenticeship programs. These programs are often sponsored by the particular craft union. Most programs last three to four years. During that time, apprentices take some classroom training. On the job, they work under the supervision of an experienced craft worker.

More than most careers, construction work is influenced by the economy. When the economy is slow, there is less new construction. Construction workers may be out of work during those times.

Most construction workers—especially those in the structural and mechanical trades—must be able to read and follow blueprints. Blueprints are detailed scale drawings that show how the structure is to be built. Workers must also be good with their hands. Good business ability is needed for those who want to go into business for themselves.

Workers in mining and oil-drilling jobs provide the coal and oil for our country's energy needs. Mine workers in surface coal mines may operate heavy machinery such as bulldozers and ore-stripping shovels. Others use explosives to strip away rock. Workers in underground mining use other kinds of machinery to cut coal from the walls of the mine. In an oil field, workers use huge drilling machines to reach the oil. Roustabouts do the manual labor in an oil field. Miners and oil field workers usually learn their trades on the job.

Careers in the constructive and extractive cluster include the following:

- bricklayers and stonemasons
- carpenters
- concrete masons and terrazzo workers
- drywall installers and finishers
- electricians
- floor covering installers
- glaziers
- insulation workers
- ironworkers
- oil drillers (roustabouts)
- painters and paperhangers
- plasterers
- plumbers and pipe fitters
- roofers
- sheet-metal workers
- tilesetters

Production Occupations

Production workers produce everything from false teeth and books to automobiles and computers. They may be highly skilled workers with years of training who work on a product from start to finish. They may be assembly workers—people who repeat a single step of a production process on the job. There are thousands of production occupations.

Some production workers do very precise, detailed work. They may be machinists who do exacting metal work to make machinery parts.

Boilermakers make the vats and large vessels used in many industries. They cut the metal, shape it, and weld the pieces to form the shape called for in a detailed drawing. Bookbinders operate the machinery that assembles books. Dispensing opticians help people select glasses and assure their proper fit. Using a doctor's prescription, opticians prepare the work order for the technician who grinds the lenses.

Another group of production workers consists of plant and systems operators. They operate and maintain power plants and sewage treatment systems. Stationary engineers monitor control panels to increase and decrease the supply of power for an area. They maintain equipment and make repairs. Wastewater treatment plant operators oper-

Appendix

ate and maintain pumps and water processing equipment. They may also test wastewater samples. Most stationary engineers get their training in the armed forces or the merchant marine or through formal apprenticeship. Wasterwater treatment plant operators begin as assistants and are trained on the job.

The next group of production workers are machine operators, tenders, and setup workers. They operate machines ranging from a drill press or a printing press to an industrial sewing machine or a spray-painting gun. Most machine operators work in factories. Their jobs can be tiring because they may stand for long periods of time. There are many kinds of machine tenders and operators. Forge shop workers operate the furnaces that heat metal until it is workable. They then use power hammers and presses to shape the metal. Printing press operators set up presses and control the amount of ink used. Machine tool operators operate machines such as drill presses and lathes. Their jobs differ from those of machinists because most do not set up the machines themselves. Many repeat the same machining process again and again. Some skilled machine tool operators have more complex jobs.

The final group of production workers consists of those who put together products or do handwork on them. Those who put together products are called assemblers. They often do just one part of the assembly—lowering a car's engine onto its chassis, for example. Bench assemblers put together many more parts of a unit, and sometimes the entire product. No special training is needed for most assembly jobs. A high school diploma is not always required.

Careers in the production cluster include the following:

- assemblers
- automobile repair service estimators
- automotive painters
- blue-collar worker supervisors
- boilermakers
- boiler tenders
- bookbinders and bindery workers
- compositors and typesetters
- coremakers (foundry)
- dental laboratory technicians
- dispensing opticians
- electrotypers and stereotypers
- forge shop occupations
- furniture upholsterers
- instrument makers (mechanical)
- jewelers
- lithographers
- machine tool operators
- machine tool setup workers
- machinists
- molders (foundry)
- ophthalmic laboratory technicians
- patternmakers (foundry)
- photoengravers
- photographic process workers
- printing press operators and assistants
- production painters
- shoe and leather workers and repairers
- stationary engineers
- tool-and-die makers
- water and wastewater treatment plant operators
- welders and flamecutters

Transportation and Material Moving Occupations

This cluster is made up of workers who carry people or goods from one place to another. Among them are the nation's bus drivers, truck drivers, and airplane pilots.

Intercity bus drivers carry passengers from one city to another. Before starting a trip, they are responsible for inspecting the mechanical condition of the buses. They are also responsible for the safety of their passengers. They must be safety-conscious drivers. The federal government requires that bus drivers be at least 21 years old and have good eyesight. They often receive their training in courses given by the bus company. Drivers must be good at dealing with the public.

Local transit bus drivers follow routes within a city area. They pick up and drop off passengers at bus stops. They also accept fares and give out transfers. They must work to keep a tight schedule in city traffic. Their training and qualifications are similar to those of intercity bus drivers.

Local truck drivers carry goods between local warehouses and stores or offices. Although they are not usually the ones to load the trucks, they do unload products at each store on their route. They also make sure that customers sign receipts for the goods they receive. Truck drivers sometimes get their start as truck driver's helpers or dockworkers. Others gain experience in the armed forces. Most states require truck drivers to have a special commercial driver's license.

Long-distance truck drivers travel the highways, often at night, to carry products from one end of the country to the other. Some drivers can make a round trip in one day. Others drive their rigs to one city, pick up another loaded rig, and go on to yet another city. They may not return home for several days. Drivers must learn to drive their rigs safely. Tractor trailers take longer to stop than other vehicles and do not accelerate quickly. Truck drivers must pass a physical exam and meet certain physical requirements. Many truckers begin work as dockworkers or local truck drivers. A few vocational schools offer truck-driving courses.

Flying a plane is a complex task. In the cockpit of most planes, two or three pilots are at work. The head pilot, or captain, is in charge. He or she works with the copilot to monitor the controls, talk to flight controllers, and fly the plane. The third pilot is the flight engineer. He or she operates many instruments, makes small repairs, and watches for other planes. The most difficult parts of the job are takeoff and landing. Flying by instruments alone during bad weather is another difficult task. Pilots can learn to fly either in private flying schools or in the military. Pilots must pass a series of Federal Aviation Administration flying and written tests to become commercial pilots. As they gain experience, they move up the ranks from flight engineer to copilot to captain.

Merchant marine officers run the nonmilitary ships that carry cargo and passengers. Deck officers supervise deck maintenance and navigation. Marine engineers supervise engine operation. It is possible to rise through the ranks to become an officer. Most officers, however, attend a four-year college program at either the United States Merchant Marine Academy or one of the six state-run merchant marine academies.

Merchant marine sailors work under the supervision of officers. Those in the deck department clean and maintain the deck area and operate cargo-handling equipment. Workers in the engine department clean and service the engines. In the steward's department, workers prepare meals for the ship's crew. Experience in the armed forces is useful for getting a job in the merchant marine. Those without such experience may have difficulty finding work.

Workers who operate construction machinery are called operating engineers. It takes training and skill to handle the controls of bulldozers, cranes, paving machines, and other pieces of heavy equipment. A high school diploma is recommended for those who want to enter the field. A number of vocational schools offer training in the field. Many people who want to enter the field begin as helpers or truck drivers. Some go through a three-year formal apprenticeship.

Careers in the transportation and material moving cluster include the following:

- aircraft pilots
- bus drivers
- material moving equipment operators
- merchant marine sailors
- operating engineers (construction)
- taxi drivers
- truck drivers

Handlers, Equipment Cleaners, Helpers, and Laborers

Many industries need helpers to assist other workers or to load and move materials. There are jobs for helpers, handlers, equipment cleaners, and laborers in a great many fields—as construction helpers, as stevedores who load and unload ships, as garbage collectors, as gas station attendants, and so on. Most workers learn their tasks in a short time on the job.

The largest number of laborers work in construction. They work on buildings, roads, bridges, and water projects. Laborers assist craft workers such as carpenters and bricklayers by setting up scaffolding, carrying materials, and mixing concrete. Their work is very strenuous and involves a lot of bending and heavy lifting. Laborers must be in good physical condition. There are no educational requirements for the job. Workers learn their skills on the job.

The varied jobs in this career cluster include the following:

- construction trades helpers
- garbage collectors
- gas station attendants
- grocery baggers
- machine feeders
- parking lot attendants
- production packagers
- rotary drill operator helpers
- shipping packers
- surveyor helpers
- vehicle cleaners

Glossary

acceptance (16) the agreement a person makes to an offer and the promise that person makes to do something in return

accreditation (6) certification that a school meets certain educational standards

actual cash value (19) the amount a stolen or damaged item was really worth

adjusted balance method (15) a way of figuring interest in which the creditor subtracts payments made during a billing period

adult education program (6) a program designed for post–high school adults who want to learn a new skill or refresh an old one

advertisement (13) a message meant to persuade consumers to buy certain products or services

alternatives (12) choices between two or more things

amend (10) to change an original motion during a meeting conducted by parliamentary procedure

annual percentage rate (APR) (15) the yearly cost of a loan, expressed as a percentage of the principal

antidiscrimination laws (8) laws that forbid employers from discriminating against an individual on the basis of race, color, national origin, age, sex, religion, or other traits

application form (7) a standard questionnaire that all potential employees must complete

apprenticeship (6) a formal system for teaching people technical and/or manual skills

aptitudes (2) those mental and physical talents that are most natural to a person

arbitrator (8) a neutral person who looks at the proposals of the negotiating parties in a labor dispute and decides what they must accept

assertiveness (10) a person's ability to stand up for himself or herself and to let others know how he or she feels

attitude (10) a person's outlook on something or feeling about a situation

auction (14) a public sale where products are sold to the highest bidders

automated teller machine (ATM) (15) a computer-run unit that takes deposits, gives cash, transfers funds, and tells a depositor his or her account balance

average daily balance method (15) a method of figuring interest in which the creditor adds the balances for each day in the billing period and divides the total by the number of days in the billing period

bait-and-switch advertising (13) an illegal practice by which a store owner advertises a low price on one product to lure shoppers into the store and then tries to persuade them to switch to a higher-priced product

bankruptcy (18) a situation in which a court sells a borrower's property (except for items protected by law) and pays the proceeds to her or his creditors

barter (12) to trade goods or services with someone else
beneficiary (19) a person named in a life insurance policy to receive payments when the insured person dies
Better Business Bureau (BBB) (13) a group set up by businesses to regulate themselves
body language (7) the message a person communicates about her or his attitude by means of posture and movements
bonus (9) an extra payment that an employer gives to a worker for excellent work or as a share in the profits
boycott (8) refusal to do business with an organization or to buy its products or services
brand (14) the name or trademark that identifies a product
breach of contract (16) the failure of a person to do as he or she promised in a contract
budget (12) a plan for spending, saving, and investing income
business (5) a person or group that produces goods and services for profit
buying cooperative (5) a group of businesses or consumers whose purpose is to save money for its members by buying products in large quantities
buying power (12) the amount of goods and services a dollar can purchase

cafeteria plan (9) a plan set up by a company, allowing employees to select a benefit menu that suits their individual needs
capacity (18) a borrower's ability to pay back a loan
capital (5, 18) 1. the money used in trade, manufacture, or business; 2. property owned by a borrower, either cash savings or material possessions
capital resources (5) the tools, machines, and buildings of a business
carcinogenic (11) cancer-causing

cardiopulmonary resuscitation (CPR) (11) a procedure to restore a person's heartbeat by applying rhythmic external pressure
career (3) an occupation that a person plans for, trains for, and intends to keep for a long time
career cluster (1, 3) a group of jobs that require similar abilities and skills
career counselor (2) a person whose job it is to provide information about careers
career ladder (3) a sequence of jobs in which each job builds on the experience of the preceding ones
cashier's check (15) a check drawn on a financial institution's funds
cash value (19) the money returned to someone by an insurance company if he or she stops paying for a policy
catalog selling (14) a method of selling by which products are offered for sale through the mail
certified check (15) a personal check that a financial institution guarantees an account has enough money to cover
character (18) the way a borrower can be expected to act with regard to honesty, responsibility, and judgment
charter (5) a legal document that states a corporation's name, business, and procedures
check (17) a written order directing a financial institution to pay money to someone
check register (15) the record for a checking account
citizen role (4) the role a person takes on when deciding how to use and contribute to public resources
clearance sale (14) a sale during which stores offer lower prices to get rid of unwanted supply
closed-end credit (15, 18) a type of one-time credit in which a fixed amount is borrowed at a fixed charge for a fixed period and repaid in fixed sums
collateral (18) something of value that a

Glossary

borrower pledges to ensure repayment of a loan

collection agency (18) a company that collects debts owed to others

collective bargaining (8) negotiation over the terms of employment between officals of a union and representatives of an employer

collision coverage (19) motor vehicle insurance coverage that pays for the insured person's vehicle repairs if there is an accident

commercial bank (17) a profit-making bank authorized by the state or federal government to offer a full range of financial services

commission (9) a form of payment to a worker made up of a percentage of sales made

community college (6) a school that offers students one- and two-year courses of study in many fields

comparison shopping (14) comparing the prices and quality of goods and services to find the best value for one's money

competent (16) capable of bargaining effectively with others

compounding (17) adding interest to the balance in a savings account so that the interest also starts to earn interest

compound interest (15) interest that is added to the principal as it is earned

comprehensive coverage (19) motor vehicle insurance coverage that protects a policyholder's vehicle from theft and other kinds of damage

compromise (2, 10) 1. to give up some goals in order to reach others; 2. a situation in which each person in a conflict gives up something in order to reach an agreement

conflict (10) a sharp disagreement about an idea or a procedure

consideration (16) something of value that a person must give up in order to get what she or he wants in return

consistent (10) acting in the same way each time a certain thing happens

consumer action panel (16) a group formed by manufacturers in an industry to handle consumer problems

consumer cooperative (14) an organization formed by consumers to save money by buying goods in bulk directly from producers

consumer process (12) a step-by-step method for making decisions about how one should use his or her time, energy, skills, and money

consumer reporting agency (18) a business that collects data about consumers and sells it to firms

consumer role (4) the role a person takes on when deciding how to use his or her resources to obtain and use goods and services

contract (16) an agreement that can be enforced by the courts

controlling (5) examining a business's product or service to be sure goals have been met

convenience store (14) a small neighborhood food store which stays open all day and most of the night and which sells the foods people need most often

cooperative (5) an enterprise, owned by more than one person or business, that acts for the benefit of its members

cooperative education (6) a program in which students go to school part of each day and work at a business part of each day

corporation (5) a business owned by stockholders

correspondence course (6) a course of study in which the student receives lessons through the mail

cosigner (18) someone who promises to repay a loan if the borrower fails to do so

credit (18) the use of borrowed money to make a purchase

credit limit (18) the maximum amount of credit a borrower is allowed in open-end credit

credit rating (18) the category of risk a person presents as a potential borrower

credit union (17) a savings and lending cooperative formed by people with a common bond

debit card (15) a plastic card that lets the holder get instant cash or pay instantly for purchases

debt consolidation loan (18) a high-interest loan for a sum that settles all of a person's short-term debts

deductible (19) the amount of a loss that an insured person agrees to pay

deflation (12) a general decrease in the level of prices

delegate (10) to assign work to others

department store (14) a large retail business that sells a wide variety of products

deposit insurance (17) a guarantee that depositors will get back a certain amount of money if a financial institution fails

direct deposit (9) a method of payment by which funds are transferred electronically from an employer's bank account to that of a worker

directing (5) coordinating how different resources are used in a business

direct selling (14) a method of selling to consumers in their homes

disability (2) a mental or physical handicap

disability insurance (19) health insurance that pays some or all of the income people lose if they can't work because of illness or injury

discount department store (14) a retail store that sells a variety of products at lower prices than department stores do

discount supermarket (14) a large self-service food store which charges lower prices than a regular supermarket does but which offers fewer services

disposable income (9) the money a person has left after paying his or her income taxes

distributor (5) a business that helps get goods to producers and consumers

dividend (5) the part of the profits of a corporation that its directors decide to pay the stockholders

dual-career family (1) a family in which both the wife and the husband hold jobs

earned income (9) the money a worker is paid for her or his labor

economics (4) the study of the way people and governments use their resources to reach their goals

economy (4) a system of producing, distributing, and consuming goods and services

effective annual yield (15) the actual yearly interest rate for savings

electronic funds transfer (EFT) (15) a method of handling money by which people can pay bills and make deposits electronically

empathy (10) the ability of one person to share another person's emotions or feelings

employment agency (7) an agency that matches suitable people to available jobs

endorsement (13, 15) 1. a type of advertisement in which a famous person proclaims satisfaction with a product; 2. the signature of the recipient of a check on the back of the check

endowment insurance (19) insurance that combines savings with term life insurance

energy (12) the body's capacity to do work

entrepreneur (5) a person who has an idea, takes risks, and combines resources to produce goods or services for profit

evaluate (4) to judge the worth of something

exemption (9) a reduction in taxable income given to a taxpayer for himself or herself and for each dependent

extractor (5) a business that takes raw materials from the earth, air, or water

factory outlet (14) a store that sells specialized products at discount prices

fatigue (11) extreme tiredness

Glossary

Federal Reserve System (17) the central banking system of the United States

finance charge (15) the amount of interest plus any other fees charged for a loan

finance company (18) a company that gives credit to merchants and makes personal loans

firing (8) the permanent dismissal of a worker

first aid (11) emergency medical care that can be given before a doctor or other trained medical person arrives

first draft (7) a rough copy that can be corrected and changed

fixed expenses (12) expenses that stay the same and that must be met, often by a certain time

fixed income (12) an income that is usually the same from week to week and month to month

flea market (14) a gathering place where new and used goods are sold

flextime (1) a system that allows workers leeway in the times they begin and end their workdays

four-year college (6) a school of higher education that offers courses of study in many fields resulting in a bachelor of arts (B.A.) or a bachelor of science (B.S.) degree upon graduation

franchise (5) a business that sells another business the right to use its name and sell its products in a certain area

franchisee (5) a person or business that buys a franchise

franchisor (5) a person or business that sells a franchise

fringe benefits (9) forms of payment for labor other than earned income, such as insurance coverage, vacation time, sick days, and pensions

full warranty (16) a guarantee that a store or company will fix or replace a faulty product free of charge

generic product (14) a product not labeled with a store or company name

goals (4) aims, or the ends that people try to reach

grace period (19) an extra amount of time given by an insurance company to a policyholder during which the insurance is still in effect even if a premium payment has not been made

grievance procedures (8) steps workers can take to protest and appeal any employer decision they think breaks the union contract

gross pay (9) the total amount of income an employer owes a worker for a given period

guarantee (16) a warranty

hazard (11) a workplace condition that threatens workers' safety or health

health insurance (19) insurance that covers all or part of the costs of health care

health maintenance organization (HMO) (19) a medical organization that provides its members with all the medical care they need for a set payment

high technology (1) the advanced scientific research that has led to new products in electronics, telecommunications, health care, and other fields

homeowner's insurance (19) insurance that pays for damage to people's own property

human resources (4, 5) workers who use their time, skills, and energy to produce goods and services

impartiality (10) the ability of a person to be fair by refusing to take sides in someone else's argument

implied warranty of fitness for a particular purpose (16) a guarantee that a product can be used for a certain task

implied warranty of merchantability (16) a guarantee that a product being sold can do what it is supposed to do

impulse (4) a sudden desire to act

impulse purchase (12) an unplanned purchase made on the spur of the moment

income (3) the amount of money a person makes

income tax return (9) the form people use to state their income and figure the tax they owe

industrial bank (18) a lending institution which was originally set up to offer loans to industrial workers but which now functions as a commercial bank

inflation (12) a general increase in the level of prices

influences (13) forces that appeal to the emotions as well as the mind

initiative (10) the ability of a person to begin work on a project without a specific order or instruction from someone else

injunction (8) a judge's order that a person or organization stop an illegal action

insurance policy (19) a written contract that explains the nature of insurance protection

interest (15) a fee for the use of money

interest-bearing checking account (15) a checking account in which a financial institution pays interest on the balance of the account

investing (17) using money in a way that people hope will be profitable

job (3) a position at which a person works to earn a living

job lead (7) information about a possible job opening

job sharing (1) a practice in which two people are hired part-time to do one full-time job

journeyworker (6) a skilled craftsperson

labor unions (8) groups of workers who have joined together to achieve better bargaining power with their employers

layoff (8) a temporary or permanent end to a worker's employment at a company because of poor business

legal aid society (16) a government-sponsored organization that offers free or low-cost legal help to those who can't afford to hire their own lawyers

letter of application (7) a letter written by a person to a potential employer in which the person asks to be considered for a job

liability (19) responsibility for injury to other people or damage to their property

life-style (3) the way a person chooses to live and spend his or her time

limited partnership (5) a business arrangement in which the liability of some partners is limited to the amount of money they invested in the business

limited-payment life insurance (19) life insurance in which premiums are payable for a specified number of years or until death, if death occurs before the end of that period

limited warranty (16) a limited promise made by a manufacturer or seller to fix or replace a product, which offers the consumer less protection than a full warranty

long-range goals (12) goals that may take three years or longer to achieve

loss (5) the amount by which a business's expenses exceed its income

loss lender (14) a product that is sold at or below cost to attract customers into a store

mail-order club (14) a method of selling by which purchasers, or members, are offered one kind of product through the mail

major medical insurance (19) health insurance that covers the rest of a large medical bill after someone has paid part of it

manager (5, 8) a person who turns the goals of a business into directions for the workers to follow

manufacturer (5) a business that uses raw materials and processed goods to make finished products

mediation (10) a process by which a neutral third person steps in to help conflicting

Glossary

people work out a satisfactory solution to their problem

mediator (8) a neutral person who joins labor negotiations to help bring about an agreement between an employer and a union

medium-range goals (12) goals that may take six months to three years to achieve

minor (16) a person who is not old enough to be treated as an adult under the law

minutes (10) the official notes taken at a meeting of an organized group

money order (15) a cash substitute bought from a financial institution or the post office

motion (10) at a meeting conducted by parliamentary procedure, a suggestion that the group do a particular thing

motivate (10) to give workers the desire to do their jobs to the best of their abilities

mutual savings bank (17) a bank owned by its depositors with the goal of encouraging savings

National Institute for Occupational Safety and Health (NIOSH) (11) an institute that collects data about workplace accidents and illnesses, does research on the effects of workplace substances, and recommends new standards

natural resources (5) the raw materials that can be taken from the earth, air, or water

needs (2) those things required to sustain human life, such as food, clothing, and shelter

net pay (9) the amount left after subtracting various deductions from a worker's gross pay

no-fault auto insurance (19) motor vehicle insurance coverage that pays for the insured person's financial losses no matter whose fault an accident was

nonprofit organization (5) an organization that aims to perform a public service rather than to make a profit

Occupational Safety and Health Administration (OSHA) (11) an administrative board set up by the federal government to create national health and safety standards for business and industry

offer (16) a promise to do something, which is made by a person in exchange for something that another person agrees to do

open charge account (18) the type of open-end credit that requires the borrower to pay for a purchase at the end of the billing period, usually a month

open-end credit (15, 18) a type of ongoing credit in which the amount owed goes up with each purchase and goes down with each payment

open shop (8) a business that does not require employees to join the union that may have a contract with the employer

option (4) a choice

organization (8) a group of people working toward the same goal

organizing (5) arranging resources in order to carry out the plans of a business

overdraft (15) a check written for more money than an account contains

overdraft protection (18) the guarantee of a financial institution that a depositor's check will be covered up to a fixed sum even if the check is written for more money than is in the account

overtime (8) any time worked beyond the regular number of hours, for which an employee may be paid extra

owner (5) a person who invests money in a business

parliamentary procedure (10) a system of rules for organizing and conducting the formal business of groups

partnership (5) a business owned by two or more persons

passbook loan (18) a cash loan from a financial institution using the money in a passbook savings account as collateral

payroll deductions (9) amounts subtracted from a worker's gross pay to cover certain kinds of regular payments

peer pressure (13) a force that makes a person want to act the same way as his or her friends in order to gain acceptance

pension plan (9) a retirement fund for workers

performance review (10) an official evaluation that an employer makes about an employee's work

personal check (15) a written order drawn on a checking account to pay cash on demand

personal liability (5) the responsibility of an owner for all business debts

personal resources (4, 12) a person's time, energy, skills, and money

personnel department (7) the section of a company concerned with filling jobs within the company

personnel officer (3) an employee at a company who handles the first phase of hiring new workers

piecework rate (9) a set rate of pay for each unit of work produced

planning (5) finding the best way to meet the goals of a business

policyholder (19) a person who buys an insurance policy

premium (19) the money a person pays for insurance

previous balance method (15) a method of figuring interest in which the lender does not subtract payments made during a billing period

principal (15) the sum of money saved or borrowed

private corporation (5) a corporation whose stock is held by only a few people, often by members of the same family

private employment agency (7) a profit-making business that helps people find jobs and helps companies fill jobs

private vocational school (6) a school that offers practical, intensive training in specific career fields

processor (5) a business that changes raw materials into a usable form

producer (5) a business that makes goods

productivity (1, 8) 1. the amount a person can produce per hour of work; 2. a measure of how many goods or services can be produced with a given amount of resources

profit (5) the amount by which a business's income exceeds its expenses

profit-sharing plan (9) a plan set up by a company to share part of its profits with the workers

promotion (8) an advancement to a higher position in a company

promotional sale (14) a sale during which stores offer lower prices to increase the demand for products

public corporation (5) a corporation that trades stock on the open market

public employment agency (7) a nonprofit employment agency operated by state governments

public resources (4) the services provided by local, state, and federal governments

puffery (16) exaggerated claims about a product

qualifications (3) the skills, knowledge, and experience that fit people for a job

quorum (10) a majority of members of an organized group, which must be present in order for a meeting to be conducted by the rules of parliamentary procedure

raise (8) an increase in a worker's pay

rebate (14) the refund of part of the purchase price of a product

recall (16) a situation in which a manufacturer that learns about a flaw in a product asks owners to return it to be fixed or replaced

reconcile an account (15) to match one's own checking account figures with those from the financial institution

Glossary

references (7) statements that people give to employers about a job applicant's abilities and character

regular checking account (15) a demand deposit account offered by a financial institution

rent (12) to pay a fee for using something temporarily

replacement cost (19) the amount it costs to buy an item to take the place of one that was damaged or stolen

repossession (18) the action of a lender who takes back from a consumer an item bought on credit because the buyer cannot meet the payments

resign (8) to give up one's position at a company

responsibility (16) an obligation a person has to act in her or his own best interest and in the interest of others

resume (2, 7) a written summary of a person's education, work experience, skills, and accomplishments

retailer (5) a business that sells products directly to consumers

retirement (8) withdrawal from work at the end of one's career

revolving charge account (18) the type of open-end credit that allows a customer to charge up to a set limit and repay in installments of a minimum amount each month

risk (19) the chance of loss

risk factor (4) the chance that a choice will have more disadvantages and fewer advantages than expected

safe deposit box (17) a metal container for valuables, such as important papers and jewelry

salary (9) a rate of pay for work that is figured by the week, month, or year

sales pressure (13) the use of certain tactics by salespeople to convince consumers to buy

savings (12) money put aside for use in the future

savings and loan association (S&L) (17) a savings institution which once offered only savings accounts and home mortgages but which now provides a full range of financial services

scholarship (6) a grant of money that does not have to be paid back

second (10) to show a desire for the group to consider a motion during a meeting conducted by parliamentary procedure

self-analysis (2) an attempt by a person to think hard and realistically about who he or she is and what matters to that person

self-esteem (3) an individual's sense of personal worth

selling cooperative (5) a group of small businesses organized to help members sell their goods

services (5) businesses that perform actions of value for consumers or other businesses

sex discrimination (1) a form of prejudice directed against members of one sex

shoplifting (16) a crime that involves stealing from a store

short-range goals (12) goals that a person can reach in one day to six months

simple interest (15) interest that is compounded once a year

single-payment loan (18) a loan in which the whole sum plus a finance charge is repaid in one payment

skill (12) the ability to do something well

small business (5) a firm that employs fewer than 500 people

small claims court (16) an informal court created to handle legal disputes involving sums of money between $100 and $3,000

social insurance plan (9) a federal plan for workers that provides retirement, disability, survivors', and health insurance

sole proprietorship (5) a business owned by just one person

specialty store (14) a store that carries only one kind of merchandise

statement (15) a financial institution's record of a depositor's monthly deposits and withdrawals, as well as the balance at the end of the statement period

stereotypes (1) fixed ideas about groups of people that are either too simple or completely false

stock (5) a share or shares of ownership in a corporation that can be transferred from one person to another

stockholder (5) a person who owns stock in a corporation

stop-payment order (15) an instruction to a financial institution to refuse to make payment on a check

straight life insurance (19) life insurance in which premiums are paid every year until the insured person dies

stress (1, 10) the body's response to mental or physical change

stressor (10) external or internal factors that cause a person stress

strike (8) an organized refusal by workers to continue working

substitute services coverage (19) insurance coverage that pays other people to do what an injured person can no longer do

sue (16) to bring a lawsuit against someone

suggested list price (14) the price a manufacturer suggests for a product

supermarket (14) a large self-service food store that also sells a wide variety of other products

tax deduction (9) an expense that reduces the income on which taxes must be paid

teacher-coordinator (6) the person who acts as the bridge between school and work for the cooperative education student

term life insurance (19) life insurance payable to a beneficiary only when an insured person dies within a specified period

testimonial (13) a type of advertisement in which a person or group proclaims satisfaction with a product

tips (9) small sums of money given to workers by satisfied customers

toxic (11) poisonous

trade and professional associations (13) groups of people or businesses that join together to promote their common interests

trade-off (4) the giving up of one desirable thing in order to get something more desirable

trade publication (7) a regularly published magazine or newspaper for members of a certain trade or occupation

training agreement (6) a contract for a cooperative education program in which the duties and responsibilities of student, employer, school, and parents or guardians are listed

training plan (6) a plan that outlines the knowledge, skills, and attitudes a cooperative education student should develop at his or her training station

training station (6) a cooperative education student's job assignment

transfer (8) an assignment to a job in a different place

transferable skills (1) abilities that can be used in many different jobs

traveler's checks (15) checks for fixed sums protected by the issuer against loss or theft

trust (17) property someone manages for the benefit of someone else

uninsured motorist protection (19) insurance coverage that covers the cost of injuries caused by a driver who has no insurance

union shop (8) a business that requires every employee to become a member of the union within 30 days of being hired

universal life insurance (19) life insurance that combines term life insurance with a chance to invest

university (6) a school that combines an undergraduate college with several graduate colleges

Glossary

upward mobility (3) chances for advancement

values (2) the standards by which people want to live their lives and the things they consider important in their lives

variable expenses (12) expenses that change from week to week and month to month

variable income (12) an income that changes from week to week and month to month

W-2 form (9) a form sent each year by an employer to all employees, which lists gross pay and payroll deductions for the previous year

W-4 form (9) the form a worker uses to tell an employer how much money to withhold for income tax

wage (9) an hourly rate of pay for work

wage loss coverage (19) insurance coverage that pays some or all the income people lose if they are hurt in an accident

wants (2) things people desire that they believe will make their lives more enjoyable or fulfilling

warranty (13, 16) a promise made to a consumer by a maker or seller of a product that the product meets certain standards

warranty of fitness (16) a guarantee that a product can be used for a certain purpose

warranty of merchantability (16) a guarantee that a product being sold can do what it is supposed to do

whole life insurance (19) life insurance payable to a beneficiary at the time of death of the insured, whenever that occurs

wholesaler (5) a business that buys goods from producers to sell to other producers and retailers

work environment (3) the actual surroundings in which a person works

worker (5) a person who makes a product or provides a service that a business sells

worker crime (16) a crime that involves stealing supplies or merchandise from an employer or lying about extra time worked

worker role (4) the role a person takes on when he or she decides how to use, or uses, his or her time, energy, and skills to earn money

work permit (8) a document that allows a person under the minimum working age in a state to be legally employed

yield (15) the net amount earned when interest is added to an account in a financial institution

Index

acceptance, 268
accidents
  auto, 314–316
  causes of, 180–187
  costs of, 187–188
  prevention of, 188–192
  types of, 187
  at work, 180–187
accreditation, 101
accuracy, in résumés, 112–113
actual cash value, 317
adaptability, 18, 129
adjournment of meetings, 175
adjusted balance payment method, 252
adult education, 100
advancement, 43, 168–171
advertisements, 220
advertising
  criticism of, 226–228
  regulation of, 225–226
  techniques, 223–228
  of top five product types, 223
  words to look for in, 225
advisors, 43–47
  see also counselors
age groups
  credit and, 301
  influence on job trends, 10
agriculture, and higher education, 98
  see also farming
alcohol
  abuse treatment
  accidents and, 184–185
alternatives, 201
amendments at meetings, 174
American Advertising Federation, 226
American Association of Advertising, 226
American Automobile Association, 322

American Cancer Society, 82
American Industrial Arts Student Association (AIASA), 172
announcements, at meetings, 175
annual percentage rate, 251, 305
antidiscrimination laws, 127–128
Apple Computer, Inc., 82
applications
  forms, 116–118
  for jobs, 114–118
  telephone, 114
apprenticeship programs, 94–95
aptitudes, 26–27
aptitude tests, 29–31
arbitrator, 131
armed services, career training in, 95–96
  see also military careers
Armed Services Vocational Aptitude Battery (ASVAB), 31–32, 95–96
asbestos, 186
assertiveness, 167–168
attitudes
  changing, 168
  workers', 162–165
  unsafe, 183–184
auctions, 239–240
auto insurance, 314–316
automated teller machines (ATM), 257, 259–260, 283–284
average daily balance method, 252

bait-and-switch advertising, 226
bandwagon ads, 225
bank credit cards, 286, 302–303
bank debit cards, 303
bank statements, sample, 258–259
bankruptcy, 307
bargaining, 129–131

391

bartering, 201
beneficiary, 318
benefits of financial services, 282
Better Business Bureau, 29, 220, 226, 274
blank endorsement, 255
body language, 121
Boise Cascade, 193
bonus, 146
borrowers, rights of, 304–306
borrowing
   ability, 299–301
   interest on, 249–251
boycott, 132–133
brand names, 242
breach of contracts, 270–271
budgets, 205–212
   adjustments to, 209
   balancing, 209
   beginning, 207–208
   economy and, 210–212
   preparation of, 207–208
bulletin boards, 108
Bureau of Labor Statistics
   job trends recorded by, 6–7
   Occupational Outlook Handbook, 12–13
   predictions by, 10
business
   consumer choices and, 243–244
   defined, 72–73
   higher education and, 98
   information from, 220–221
   organization of, 78–82
   profits, 73–74
   resources of, 75–78
   working parents and, 15
business administration degree, 99
buying cooperatives, 80
Buying Guide, 221
buying power, 211

cafeteria plans, 147
capacity, borrowing, 300
capital, 75
   credit and, 300
carcinogens, 186
cardiopulmonary resuscitation (CPR), 192

care of products, 234
careers
   changing, 6, 8
   defined, 39
   jobs and, 39
   life-style and, 38–41
career choices, 8–13
career clusters, 13, 47–49
career counseling, 29–31
career decision-making
   process of, 54–60
   responsibility for, 49–50
   see also decision-making
career ladder, 39
career training, military, 95–96
cash substitutes, 252–257
cash surrender value, life insurance, 304, 318
cash value of life insurance, 319
cashier's checks, 253–254
cash, 252–257
catalog selling, 238
certified checks, 253
Chamber of Commerce, 274
change
   anticipating, 10–13
   preparing for, 15–18
   social, 13–15
   stress and, 15–16
character, borrowing ability and, 300
charter, corporate, 79
checks
   defined, 284
   payment by, 148
   register, 255
   types of, 253–254
   See also specific types of checks
checking accounts, 254–257
child labor laws, 155–157
citizen role, 61–62
Civil Rights Act of 1964, 127
civil service announcements, 108, 110
civil service tests, 118
classified ad abbreviations, 109
clearance sales, 242
closed-end credit, 251, 301–302
   annual percentage rate of, 305
club activities, 173

Index

collateral, 302
collectibles, 287, 289
collection agency, 305–306
collective bargaining, 130–131
colleges. *See* community colleges; four-year colleges
collision coverage, 315
commercial banks, 284, 288, 303
commercial loans, 286
commission, 144–145
communication skills, 18, 127, 163–164
community activities, 336–338
community colleges, 97–98
comparison shopping, 200, 232–236
    for financial institutions, 282–284
    for insurance, 322–323
competence, in contracts, 269
competition, 119, 241
complaint letter, 274–275
compound interest, 250, 290
comprehensive coverage, 316
compromise, 34, 168–169
    see also trade-off
computer shopping, 238–239
conflict, 165–168
consideration, in contracts, 269
consistency, 171
consumer action panels, 274
consumer choices, decision-making and, 63
consumer cooperatives, 241
consumer credit, 295–296
Consumer Credit Protection Act of 1969. *See* Truth-in-Lending Act
Consumer Leasing Act of 1976, 305–306
consumer organizations, 221–223
consumer planning, 200–202
consumer problems, 273–275
consumer process, 200–201
consumer protection, 234–235
consumer reporting agency, 299–300
Consumer Reports, 221, 323
Consumer's Research, 221
Consumer's Resource Handbook, 274
consumer role, 62
contracts, 29, 268–271
controlling a business, 77

convenience, of financial institutions, 285
convenience stores, 237–238
cooperation, 127, 129, 163–165
cooperative education, 88–94
Cooperative for American Relief (CARE), 82
cooperatives, 80
    see also consumer cooperatives
corporations, 79–80
correspondence courses, 99–100
cosigner, 301
counselors, 43–47
    see also advisors
counteroffer, 269
courtesy, 164
credit, 251–252
    alternate sources of, 289
    cost comparisons of, 306
    defined, 294–296
    financial institutions and, 286
    overborrowing and, 306–307
    planning for, 298–299
    reasons for using, 297–298
    refusal of, 301
    sources, 303–304
    types of, 301–303
credit counseling service, 306–307
credit limit, 302
credit rating, 300–301
credit unions, 288–289, 303
currency, foreign, 285

day-care centers, 15
death, causes of job-related, 187
death rates, job-related
    by major industries, 181
    changes in, 186
debit cards, 257–258
debt consolidation loan, 307
decision-making, 18, 332–334
    acting on, 58
    benefits of, 60
    as citizen, 62
    as consumer, 62
    economy and, 64–65
    effects on other people, 62–63
    evaluating, 58–59
    importance of, 54–55

decision-making, cont.
   process, 56–60
   roles, 60–62
   shortcuts, 54
deductibility, 313
deflation, 212
delegating skills, 171–172
demand, supply and, 241
demonstration ads, 224
dental coverage, 321
department stores, 237
deposit insurance, 285–286
Dictionary of Occupational Titles, 30, 49
diet, health and, 189–190
diploma, value of, 88
direct deposit, 148, 258
Direct Mail Advertising Association, 226
direct selling, 239
directing a business, 77
disability, 28
   benefits, 154
discount department stores, 237
discount supermarkets, 237
dislikes and career planning, 27
disposable income, 151–152
Distributive Education Clubs of America
   (DECA), 172
distributors, 72–73
dividends, 79–80
drugs
   accidents and, 184–185
   treatment for abuse of, 321
dual-career families, 14–15
Dun & Bradstreet Reference Book, 119

earned income, 144–146
economics, 64
economy
   budgets and the, 210–212
   decision-making and the, 64–65
   effect of productivity on the, 135–136
   job outlook and the, 11
education
   choices in, 101–102
   cooperative, 88–94
   costs and financial aid, 100–102

   transferable skills and, 17
   value of, 23, 88
   see also higher education
efficiency, 129
EFT cards, 290
electronic banking, 257–260
Electronic Funds Transfer (EFT) Act of 1978,
   257, 260, 306
emotional appeal technique, 224
empathy, 164
employers
   part-time work and, 93
   training agreements and, 89–90
employment agencies, 107–108
endorsement, 224, 255
endowment insurance, 319–320
energy, 205
entertainment cards, 303
entrepreneurs, 75–77
Equal Credit Opportunity Act of 1975, 305
evaluation
   of career decisions, 58–59
   of purchases, 201
exemptions, tax, 150
exercise, health and, 190
expenses, estimating, 207
extra purchases, 233–234
extractors, 72

factory outlets, 238
Fair Credit Billing Act of 1975, 305
Fair Credit Reporting Act of 1971, 305
Fair Debt Collection Practices Act of 1977,
   305–306
Fair Labor Standards Act (FLSA), 156–157
families
   as advisors, 43–44
   budgets for, 209–210
   changes in and careers, 14–15
   credit from, 304
   as information sources, 219
   job leads from, 107
   value of, 23
farming, changes in, 7
fatigue, accidents and, 185
fear appeal, 224

Index

federal government
   consumer information from, 222–223
   as nonprofit organization, 82
Federal Reserve System, 290
Federal Trade Commission (FTC), 226
finance charge, 251
finance companies, 303
financial aid, education and, 100–102
financial institutions, 282–284
financial management, 335–336
financial planning, 288–289
firing, from job, 134
first aid, 191–192
fixed expenses, 207
fixed income, 207
fixed-rate loans, 302
flea markets, 239
flexible benefits, 147
flextime, 15
follow-up letter, 121
Food and Drug Administration, 226
food service industries, job growth in, 7
4-H Clubs, 172
four-year colleges, 98–99
franchisee, 80
franchises, 80
franchisor, 80
friends
   as advisors, 43–44
   job leads from, 107
   value of, 23
fringe benefits, 144, 146–147
full warranty, 272
Future Business Leaders of America (FBLA), 62, 172
Future Farmers of America (FFA), 172
Future Homemakers of America-Home Economics Related Occupations (FHA-HERO), 172

Galbraith, John Kenneth, 226
garage sales, 239
General Aptitude Test Battery (GATB), 31
generic products, 242
geographic area, influence on job selection, 11

goals, 23–24, 202–203
   identification and ranking of, 56–57
   long-range, 24
   medium-range, 24
   short-range, 24
grace period, 320
grievance procedures, 132
gross pay, 148
guarantee, 271–273
guidance counselors, 44–45
   job leads from, 107
Guide for Occupational Exploration, 48

hazards
   correction of, 192–193
   at work, 180, 186
health care
   costs, 321–322
   higher education in, 98
   jobs in, 330–331
health inspections, workplace, 192
health maintenance organizations (HMOs), 321–322
Health Occupations Student Association (HOSA), 173
health standards, benefits of, 193–194
high technology, 7
higher education, 96–100
hobbies, career planning and, 25–26
home computer banking, 258–259
home mortgage loans, 286
home and nursing home care, 321
homeowner's insurance, 316–317
honesty, 129
hotel business, jobs in, 11
human resources, 64–65, 75–78
humor
   in ads, 224
   on the job, 164

IBM, 80
ignorance, accidents and, 180–181
illness
   accidents and, 185
   costs of, 187–188
   prevention of, 188–192
impartiality, 164

implied warranty, 220, 271-273
    of fitness, 271
    of merchantability, 271
impressing prospective employers, 120–121
impulse, defined, 54
impulse purchases, 202

income, 38
    estimating, 207
income tax return, 148–151
income taxes, 148–151
independence, value of, 23
industrial banks, 303
inflation, 210–212
influences, 217–219
information
    advertisements as, 223–224
    evaluating, 217
    sources of, 219–223
    value of, 216–218
initiative, 129, 169
injunction, 133
injuries, common on-the-job, 187
injury patterns, work-related, 188
installment buying, 251–252
installment credit, 302
insurance
    comparison shopping for, 322–323
    defined, 312–313
    needs, 313–314
    rates, 316
insurance policy, 312
intended use of products, 233
interest, 249–252
    credit and, 296–297
interest-bearing checking accounts, 254
interests, career planning and, 25–26
internal influences, 218
Internal Revenue Service (IRS), 151
International Ladies' Garment Workers' Union (ILGWU), 129
interpersonal skills, 169
interviews, 118–121
    practicing for, 119–120
investing, 286–289
investment clubs, 287, 289
investment counseling, 287

job counseling services, 29–30
job leads, 106–110
job list, 34
job market
    anticipating changes in, 10–13
    changes in, 6–13
    preparing for changes in, 15–18
job performance, 127
job search, 110
job shadows, 46
job sharing, 15
job versus career, 39
jobs
    availability of, 43
    characteristics of, 41–42
    decrease in selected, 9
    defined, 39
    increase in selected, 9
    matching personalities with, 33–34
journeyworkers, 94–95

labels, 220
labor unions, 129–131
    membership in, 130
    ten largest in U.S., 131
lawsuit, 271
layoff, 134
leadership qualities, 171–175
leadership satisfaction, 175
legal aid society, 274
legality of contracts, 270
leisure time, job outlook and, 11
lenders, rights of, 304–306
letter of application, 114–115
liability, 313–315
librarians, 46
lie detector tests, 118
life insurance, 304, 317–318
    types of, 317–320
life span of services, 235
life-style, 38–41
    in ads, 224–225
limited partnerships, 78–79
limited warranty, 272
limited-payment life insurance, 319
loan sharks, 304
loans. See credit; *specific types of loans*

Index

local taxes, 151
long form, 150
long-range goals, 203
long-range job outlook, 43
loss leader, 242
losses, 73

magazines, trade and professional, 46
    want ads in, 108
mail-order clubs, 239
major medical insurance, 321
management's rights, 129
managers, 77
    defined, 126–127
manufacturing, 72
    changes in, 7
Mars, Inc., 80
mass media, 220–221
mathematics skills, 18
McDonald's Corporation, 80
mediation, 168
mediator, 131
Medicaid, 322
medical costs, increases in, 320–321
medical tests, 118
Medicare, 155, 322
medium-range goals, 203
mental illness coverage, 321
military career training, 95–96
    financial benefits, 96
military recruiters as job counselors, 47
minimum wage, 128
minors, contracts involving, 269
minutes of meeting, 173
Mobil, 80
money orders, 254, 289
money, 205–212
Moody's Industrial Manual, 119
motions at meetings, 174
motivation, 171
mutual funds, 287, 289
mutual savings banks, 288, 303

National Advertisers Division (NAD), 226
National Advertising Review Board (NARB), 226
National Association of Broadcasters, 226

National Association of Trade and Technical Schools (NATTS), 101–102
National Home Study Council, 102
National Institute for Occupational Safety and Health (NIOSH), 193
natural resources, 75
neatness, in résumés, 112–113
needs, 22
negative appeal, 224
negative thinking, 162–163
neighbors, as job leads, 107
net pay, 148
new business at meetings, 174
newspapers, 108
Nidetch, Jean, 75
no-fault auto insurance, 314
no-plan trap, 39
nonprofit organization, 82
NOW accounts, 254

Occupational Outlook Handbook, 12, 30, 330
    career clusters in, 47–48
    educational requirements and, 98–99
    job availability and, 43
    job characteristics and, 41
    key terms in, 44
Occupational Safety and Health Administration (OSHA), 128–129, 192–193
offer, in contract, 268
Office Education Association (OEA), 173
officers' reports, 173
on-the-job training, 94–95
open charge account, 302
open shops, 132
open-end credit, 252, 302
    annual percentage rate of, 304–305
options
    analysis of, 58
    narrowing of, 47–49
    selection, 57–58
organization
    of businesses, 78–82
    defined, 126
Outdoor Advertising Association, 226
outside influences, 218–219
outstanding checks, 257
overborrowing, 306

overdraft privileges, 255, 286, 303
overtime, 128, 144
owners, 77

pamphlets, 220
parents, signing training agreements, 91
parliamentary procedure, 173–175
part-time work, 91–94
partnerships, 78–79
passbook loans, 286, 303
pawnbrokers, 304
pay stub, 148–149
payment methods, 147–148, 200, 248–252
payroll deductions, 148
peer pressure, 218
pension plans, 147
performance reviews, 169–170
personal checks, 253
personal identification, 257, 259
personal liability, 78
personal loans, 286
personal resources, 54
   consumer process and, 200–201
personality profiles, 28
   job matching and, 33–34
   opinions of others and, 28–29
   part-time work and, 93
personnel officers, 47
   as job leads, 107
persuasion, ads as, 224
physical limitations and jobs, 182–183
piecework rate, 144
planning
   business, 77
   career, 334–335
policyholder, 312
political participation, 23
polygraph tests, 118
Poor's Register of Corporations, Directors and Executives, 119
positive appeals in ads, 224
positive thinking, 162–163
preemployment tests, 118
premiums, 312
   unpaid, 320–321
previous balance payment method, 252
prices, 211–212

   changes in, 241–243
   comparing, 233
   controls on, 242
   of services, 234

principal, 250
private corporation, 80
private employment agencies, 107–108
private vocational schools, 96–97
problem, defining the, 56
problem-solving ads, 224
processors, 72
producers, 72
product comparison, 233–235
productivity, 7, 129
   business, 135
   economic growth and, 135–136
   flextime and, 15
profit-sharing plans, 147
profits, 73–74
   social benefits of, 73–74
programs, at meetings, 174
promotional sales, 242
promotion, job, 133
   see also advancement
psychological tests, 118
public corporation, 80
public employment agencies, 107–108
public resources, 61
puffery, 272
purchases
   timing of, 211
   where to buy, 236–241

qualifications for jobs, 41–42
quality
   of products, 233
   of services, 235
   of work, 129
quantity purchases, 211
quorum, 173

raise in salary, 133
rational appeal technique, in ads, 224
real estate, 287, 289
rebate, 242
recall of products, 276

Index

reconciliation, of checking accounts, 257
references for jobs, 112
regular checking accounts, 254
reliability, 129
religion, 23
rent, 201
replacement cost, 317
repossession, 307
resignation, 134
resources, 333–334
    see also specific types of resources
responsibilities
    consumer, 275–276
    social, 336–338
restaurant business
    jobs in, 11
    part-time work in, 93
restrictive endorsement, 255
resume, 31
    first draft of, 112
    preparation of, 110–113
retail stores, 73, 303–304
retirement, 134
    benefits, 152–153
revolving charge account, 302
rights, responsibilities and, 275–277
risk, 59–60, 312
    reducing, 323–324
Robert's Rules of Order, 173
roles, careers and, 60–62

safe deposit box, 286
safety, 129
    clothing and equipment, 190
    of financial institutions, 285–286
    habits, 191
    inspections, 192
    of products, 234
    standards for, 193–194
    three-way partnership for, 192–194
salary, 42, 144
sales pressure, 218–219
salespeople, 220
sales, 242–243
savings, 286–288
    defined, 208
    interest on, 249–250

savings and loan associations (S&Ls), 284, 288, 303
scholarships, 101
school guidance counselors, 29
scientific ads, 224
Screen Cartoonists Guild, 129
seconding motions, 174
security, value of, 23
self-analysis, 22–29, 168–169, 330–332
self-esteem, 38–39
sellers
    advantages and disadvantages of, 240
    types of, 237–241
selling cooperatives, 80
service on products, 234
    comparison of, 234–236
    nature of, 234–235
service industries, 303–304
    defined, 72
    job growth in, 7
sex appeal, in ads, 224
sex discrimination, 13–14
Sheet Metal Workers' International Association, 129
shoplifting, 276
short form, 150
short-range goals, 203
simple interest, 250
single-payment loan, 303
skills
    accidents and, 181–182
    as resource, 204
    improving, 204
    tests of, 118
sleep, health and, 190
small business, importance of, 80–82
Small Business Administration (SBA), 81–82
small claims court, 274
social changes, job outlook and, 13–15
social insurance plan, 152–155
social role, 336–338
social security, 152–155
Social Security Administration, 152–153
social security number, 153–154
sole proprietorships, 78
special committee reports, 174
special endorsement, 255

specialty stores, 238
spending patterns, 205–206
sports and recreation, jobs in, 11–12
stability, credit and, 301–302
standards of comparison
   for products, 235
   for services, 236
standing committee reports, 174
state government and social insurance plans, 155
state taxes, 151–152
statements for checking accounts, 257
stereotypes, 13–14
stockholders, 79
stocks and bonds, 287, 289
   in corporations, 79
stop-payment order, 255
straight life insurance, 319
stress
   change and, 15–16
   conflict and, 165–168
   job, 165
   management of, 165
stressor, 165
strike, 132
student and training agreement, 90
substitute services coverage, 316
suggested list price, 242
suing, in contracts, 271
supermarkets, 237
SuperNOW accounts, 254
supplier reputation, 236
supply and demand, 241
survivors' benefits, 154–155

tax deduction, 150
tax forms
   Form 1040, 150
   Form 1040 A, 150
   Form 1040 EZ, 150
taxes, state and local, 151
teacher-coordinator, 88
   training agreement and, 91
teachers
   as advisors, 44–45
   job leads from, 107

telephone applications, 114
telephone transfers, 258
term life insurance, 318–319
testimonial, 224
time
   budgeting, 203
   use of, 202–204
time payments, 295
tips, 145–146
toxicity, 187
trade and professional associations, 46–47
   as information sources, 220
trade publications, want ads in, 108
trade-off, 58
trades and higher education, 98
training, job, 42
training agreement, 89–91
training plan, 91–92
training stations, 88
transferable skills, 17
transfer, 133
travel cards, 303
traveler's checks, 254, 284–285, 289
trusts, 287–288
Truth-in-Lending Act, 251, 304–305

Underwriters' Laboratories (UL), 220
unemployment compensation, 155
unfinished business at meetings, 174
uninsured motorist protection, 315–316
union contracts, 131–133
union shop, 132
U.S. Government Manual, 223
universal life insurance, 320
universities, 98–99
unsafe behavior, 183–184
upward mobility, 43
use-and-care manuals, 220

values, social, 23
variable expenses, 207
variable income, 207
variable-rate loans, 302
Vocational Industrial Clubs of America (VICA), 173

Index

vocational schools
   private, 96–97
   transferable skills and, 17–18
volunteer work, 40–41

W-2 form, 148–149
W-4 form, 150
wage loss coverage, 316
wage, 144
Wagner Act, 127
want ads, 108–110
wants, 22
warranty, 220, 271–273
   of fitness, 271
   of merchantability, 271
weaknesses, 27–28
Weight Watchers, 75
whole life insurance, 318–319
wholesaler, 72–73
willingness to learn, on the job, 164
women in job force, 13–15
work, nature of, 41
work environment, 42–43
   safety and, 185–187
work experience, 39–41

work habits, 18, 169
work permit, 128
work skills, 169
workers, 77–78
   as advisors, 45–46
   attitude of, 129
   crime by, 276–277
   rights, 127–129
   role, 60–62
   status, 133–135
workers' compensation, 155
working conditions, 42–43
workplace
   changes in, 328–330
   learning about, 191
   rights and duties of, 127–129
   see also work environment
writing skills, 18
written contracts, 270
written warranties, 272

yard sales, 239
yield, 250–251
   effective annual, 251

Photo Credits

Page 1 (top left) Mark Gibson; (top right) Carlye Calvin; (bottom left) Robert Fried; (bottom right) Richard Hutchings

Page 2 (Part One opener): Tom Tracy/FPG.

Page 4 (Chapter 1 opener): Jim Balog/Black Star; page 6: staff photographer; page 7: staff photographer; page 8: Jim Howard/FPG; page 11: John Neubauer/PhotoEdit; page 13: J. M. Jejuto/FPG; page 16: Yada Claassen/Stock, Boston.

Page 21 (Chapter 2 opener): Peter Menzel/Stock, Boston; page 23: Wendy Rosin Malecki/PhotoEdit; page 25: Erik Calonius/EPA-Documerica; page 26: staff photographer; page 27: Tony Freeman/PhotoEdit; page 28: Jim Pickerell/FPG; page 30: staff photographer; page 33: staff photographer.

Page 37 (Chapter 3 opener): Lee Balterman/FPG; page 39: Billy E. Barnes/FPG; page 40: staff photographer; page 41: Wayne Miller/Magnum; page 42: Tony Freeman/PhotoEdit; page 44: staff photographer; page 45: Terry Qing/FPG; page 48: staff photographer.

Page 52 (Chapter 4 opener): staff photographer; page 55: Billy E. Barnes/FPG; page 56: The New York Public Library Picture Collection; page 57: staff photographer; page 59: staff photographer; page 61: Carlye Calvin; page 64: staff photographer; page 65: staff photographer.

Page 69 (Part Two opener): Gary Gladstone/Image Bank.

Page 70 (Chapter 5 opener): Icon Communications/FPG; page 72 (top): IBM; page 72 (middle): Stephen McBrady/PhotoEdit; page 72 (bottom): Mary Kate Denny/PhotoEdit; page 75: Bernard G. Silberstein/FPG; page 76: staff photographer; page 77: Honeywell Inc.; page 81: staff photographer.

Page 86 (Chapter 6 opener): Unicorn Stock Photos/Martin R. Jones; page 89: staff photographer; page 93: courtesy of VISTA, a part of ACTION, the national volunteer agency; page 94: staff photographer; page 95: Alpha/FPG; page 96: U.S. Army Recruiting Command; page 97: FPG; page 101: staff photographer.

Page 105 (Chapter 7): Billy E. Barnes/FPG· page 107: Mary Kate Denny/PhotoEdit; page 110: staff photographer; page 113: Minnesota Educational Computing Corp.; page 114: staff photographer; page 118: staff photographer; page 119: staff photographer.

Page 124 (Chapter 8): staff photographer; page 126: staff photographer; page 128: staff photographer; page 132: Paul O. Boisvert/FPG; page 133: IBM; page 134: staff photographer; page 136: Tony Freeman/PhotoEdit.

Page 141 (Part Three opener): Campbell & Boulanger/FPG.

Page 142 (Chapter 9 opener): K. Ober/FPG; page 144: staff photographer; page 145: staff photographer; page 146: Jeffry W. Myers/FPG; page 147: Bernard Botfryd/Woodfin Camp & Associates; page 151: Carlye Calvin; page 153: staff photographer; page 155: The New York Public Library Picture Collection; page 156: K. Krueger/Alpha.

Page 160 (Chapter 10 opener): staff photographer; page 163: Bob Daemmrich; page 166: staff photographer; page 167: staff photographer; page 169: Cary Wolinsky/Stock, Boston; page 171: staff photographer; page 172: Myrleen Ferguson/PhotoEdit; page 173: Farrell Grehan/Alpha; page 174: Ellis Herwig/Stock, Boston.

Page 178 (Chapter 11 opener): staff photographer; page 182: Gary Bublitz/M.L. Dembinsky, Jr. Photography Associates; page 183: Cezus/FPG; page 184: Joe Baker/FPG; page 189: Fairview Ridges Hospital; page 190: staff photographer; page 191: Billy E. Barnes/FPG; page 193: Jon Brenneis/Alpha.

Page 197 (Part Four opener): Leonard Freed/Magnum Photos, Inc.

Page 198 (Chapter 12 opener): staff photographer; page 200: staff photographer; page 202: Clyde H. Smith/Alpha; page 204: staff photographer; page 205: EPA-Documerica; page 207: staff photographer; page 210: Karelle Scharff.

Page 215 (Chapter 13 opener): Stephen McBrady/PhotoEdit; page 217: staff photographer; page 218: staff photographer; page 219: staff photographer; page 221: Tony Freeman/PhotoEdit; page 227: The New York Public Library Picture Collection.

Page 231 (Chapter 14 opener): Richard Hutchings; page 233: staff photographer; page 234: National Highway Traffic Safety Administration; page 238: staff photographer; page 239: staff photographer; page 241: J. McClung/FPG.

Page 247 (Chapter 15 opener): FPG; page 249: Richard Hutchings; page 251: FPG; page 253: staff photographer; page 254: Bruce Byers/FPG; page 259: Terry Qing/FPG.

Page 265 (Part 5 opener): Barbara Adams/FPG.

Page 266 (Chapter 16 opener): Robert Brenner/PhotoEdit; page 268: staff photographer; page 269: staff photographer; page 272: P. Gridley/FPG; page 274: staff photographer; page 276: staff photographer; page 277: staff photographer.

Page 280 (Chapter 17 opener): staff photographer; page 282: Karelle Scharff; page 283: staff photographer; page 284: Karelle Scharff; page 287: J. Sylvester/FPG; page 289: staff photographer.

Page 293 (Chapter 18 opener): Tom Tracy/Alpha; page 295: staff photographer; page 298: Chris Minerva/FPG; page 299: Dick Luria/FPG; page 300: staff photographer; page 302: Tom Tracy/Alpha; page 304: staff photographer.

Page 310 (Chapter 19 opener): Riley Caton/Alpha; page 312: staff photographer; page 313: Chris Minerva/Alpha; page 314: staff photographer; page 315: Thomas Zimmermann/FPG; page 322: Stephen McCarroll/Alpha; page 323: staff photographer.

Page 327 (Chapter 20 opener): Mike Valeri/FPG; page 329: Education Director/FPG; page 330: J.M. Mejuto/FPG; page 333: J. Sylvester/Alpha; page 335: Tony Freeman/PhotoEdit; page 336: Phil McCarten/PhotoEdit; page 337: staff photographer; page 338: Terry Qing/Alpha.

Page 342 (Appendix): Mary Kate Denny/PhotoEdit; page 344: U.S. Army Recruiting Command; page 346: Paul Fusco/Magnum

Photo Credits

Photos, Inc.; page 348: Momatiuk/Eastcott/Woodin Camp & Associates; page 350: Michal Heron/Woodfin Camp & Associates; page 352: staff photographer; page 354: Bob Peterson/FPG; page 356: J. M. Mejuto/FPG; page 358: Tom Tracy/FPG; page 360: Robert Rathe/Alpha; page 362: Michal Heron/Woodfin Camp & Associates; page 364: Tom Tracy/FPG; page 366: Mary Kate Denny/PhotoEdit; page 368: Bill Weems/Woodfin Camp & Associates; page 370: Edward J. Edahl/FPG; page 372: John Blaustein/Woodfin Camp & Associates; page 374: Karelle Scharff; page 376: Jeff Lowenthal/Woodfin Camp & Associates; page 378: Craig Aurness/Woodfin Camp & Associates.